THE DEFINITIVE GUIDE TO POLITICAL IDEOLOGIES

KEVIN BLOOR

authorHOUSE®

AuthorHouse™ UK Ltd.
500 Avebury Boulevard
Central Milton Keynes, MK9 2BE
www.authorhouse.co.uk
Phone: 08001974150

First published by AuthorHouse 2/4/2010

ISBN: 978-1-4490-6761-8 (sc)

This book is printed on acid-free paper.

Contents

"To all my former students at Freemen's, this book is for you."

Introduction
What is ideology?

Why does political ideology matter?

Try as you might, you *cannot* escape politics. It has you in its grip from the minute you are conceived to the moment you shuffle off this mortal coil. Virtually all aspects of our behaviour are influenced – even governed – by the parameters of politics. There is surely nothing within the realm of human understanding more all-pervasive than politics. Therefore, it must logically follow that the inquisitive amongst us should cultivate our understanding of politics in order to better understand ourselves and the world that surrounds us.

Political ideas determine the course of human history. They reflect the very best of human nature and the very worst that humanity is capable of. Political ideas can be an overwhelming force for good, or the basis for almost unimaginable destruction. Hope and fear are always present at the table of political ideas - very often in the *same* ideology. Take the concept of freedom as an example. Virtually all of us lead more hopeful and fulfilling lives due to the march of freedom. However, the concept of 'freedom' has been used to justify terrible atrocities throughout the ages. In the immortal words of one of the many nameless victims of the Robespierre-led terror following the French Revolution; *"Freedom – how many crimes have been committed in your name!"* A similar observation could be made about a myriad of other political concepts and ideas ranging from equality to national unity.

The origins and importance of the term 'ideology'

The term 'ideology' derives from the French theorist Antoine Destutt de Tracy (1754-1836) around the time of the aforementioned revolution of 1789. He saw the need for a scientific approach to the human understanding of ideas in a manner akin to the methods employed in the natural sciences. He believed that such an approach would form the basis for a rational society. It seems particularly appropriate to begin with a scholar from the Enlightenment because political ideology itself owes so much to that important historical epoch, and that the French revolution was driven by radical political ideas.

Ideology has an impact in a multiplicity of ways. At its most direct, ideology provides the basis for a conflict that impacts upon millions of lives. On a more everyday level, ideology can offer a sense of identity and a connection to others. Political ideology can therefore help to identify and define us, but it can also restrict us too. The attitude of others towards a particular ideology can sometimes be hostile. In the context of the various agents of the state, a person's ideological beliefs can quite literally carry a prison sentence (even a death sentence in some cases). For others, an adherence to an ideology is merely a passing affectation – particularly during their student years. During the life course our commitment to an ideology may fluctuate and even dissipate altogether. Nonetheless, the ideologies you will discover more about in this book have shaped the course of history and continue to influence events within the world we inhabit today. Political ideas and ideologies have shaped our past and will doubtless influence our very futures. They have been deemed worth fighting for and worth dying for; and that is what I hope makes them so interesting …

The ideological spectrum

When learning about political ideologies it is often beneficial to begin with an understanding of the ideological spectrum and the notion of Weltanschauung. In the case of the former, the ideological spectrum has been portrayed in both a horizontal and vertical manner. The horizontal axis goes from left to right whereas the vertical axis is authoritarian and the top and libertarian at the bottom. Using this model helps clarify the position of various ideologies and draw some comparison and contrast between them.

The distinction between **left and right** along the horizontal axis is a simple one, and as with several other ideological concepts finds its origins in the French Revolution. In the French National Assembly those who opposed the status quo and favoured a radical change to society sat on the left, whereas those who supported the King and the status quo sat on the right. To this day, the term left-wing is associated with a desire to radically change the basis of society, whereas the term right-wing is routinely applied to those who favour the status quo and in some cases the *status quo ante* (the way things were before). Whilst there is a good deal more to the left-right distinction, it does nonetheless offer a useful start for students of political ideology.

The **authoritarian and libertarian** axis is also a straight-forward one to understand and centres primarily upon the role of the state. Ideologies that belong on the authoritarian side of the spectrum prescribe a strong role for government in terms of securing their objectives. This may entail equality and social justice (socialism), national unity (nationalism / fascism), social order (conservatism) or the establishment of a theocracy (religious fundamentalism). In contrast, those ideologies associated with a libertarian outlook (such as anarchism and liberalism) believe that the concentration of power into the various agents of the state is undesirable and to be avoided. In order to grasp the reasons why, one has to understand the wider perspective held by that particular ideology. For instance, liberals believe that the power of the state must be curtailed because it represents a major threat to individual liberty. The only justification for state intervention is to maximise the concept of liberty. Anarchists go one stage further and claim that the state is a source of evil and must be abolished in order for people to experience genuine freedom. Anarchism represents the most extreme form of libertarianism and is as far away from fascism (the most hard-line form of authoritarianism) as one can get.

The horseshoe model strives to address a significant flaw with the conventional left-right libertarian-authoritarian axis. Ideologies of an authoritarian nature - such as fascism and a strand of socialism known as Marxism – are placed far away from each other on the left-right horizontal axis. This is because fascism is an ideology of the extreme right whereas Marxism is an ideology of the extreme left. However, this typology implies that the two ideologies are polar opposites with no common ground, yet in practise there are considerable similarities between the two in terms of the role of the state, the importance of propaganda, the lack of respect for human rights, the emphasis upon sacrifice for the greater good and the extent to which society is based upon collectivism. As such, the horseshoe model may be more appropriate in terms of our understanding of political ideologies. The horseshoe model has become much more widespread within ideological discourse in recent times. However, throughout this book the traditional left-right authoritarian-libertarian axis will be used because it still has considerable merit as a tool for learning.

The importance of Weltanschauung

Another important term to comprehend is Weltanschauung - a German word conventionally translated as *"world view"* – which has major epistemological implications for any academic inquiry. An exploration of Weltanschauung provides an appropriate starting point in terms of cultivating our understanding of ideology. Weltanschauung is the ideological prism from which we interpret events that surround us. Whilst that prism is not necessarily fixed it can close off the possibility of interpreting certain events from a perspective contrary to one's own Weltanschauung.

In order to fully understand each political ideology it is important to identify our own (and others) Weltanschauung. In doing so, we are armed with a conceptual toolkit by which to develop our understanding of political ideology. Both the ideological spectrum and Weltanschauung provide us with much-needed clarity in our search for a deeper understanding of ideology – beginning with the **predominant ideology** of our time.

CHAPTER 1
LIBERALISM

The core elements of liberalism

Political ideologies tend to be based upon an epistemological assumption of some kind, and liberalism begins with the assumption (as it cannot be proven in any meaningful objective sense) that **the individual is a rational actor**. The entire basis of liberalism as an ideology centres upon the conviction that the individual is a rational actor, and this gives liberalism much of its vibrancy and force of argument. From this basic starting-point, it is possible to trace the main elements of liberal ideology. But before we move onto the main elements of liberalism, we need to examine further the liberal supposition that the individual is a rational actor.

It is an article of faith amongst liberals that individuals are capable of exercising **free will** based on their own independent and reasoned judgement. This belief has found expression amongst several liberal theorists and many liberal-inspired movements and documents. Take the case of the 17th century English philosopher John Locke who opposed the dominant view within society that the *"divine right of Kings"* should facilitate an absolutist government. This view was

Core elements
Optimistic view of human nature
The individual is a rational actor
Humans are capable of exercising free will
We should be entrusted with as much freedom as possible

1

also shared by Enlightenment figures in France such as Voltaire and Diderot who championed reason and science over superstition and religious-inspired absolutism. Today, the belief that human beings are rational individuals finds expression within the Universal Declaration of Human Rights (1948), which is based on the assertion that human beings *are endowed with reason and conscience.* In these and several other examples, one can trace the liberal belief that the individual is a rational actor and are therefore not slaves to a higher form of being. It is here one can identify a stark contrast between liberalism and societies based upon religious fundamentalism (see Chapter 8).

According to the basic premise of liberalism – human beings act in a rational manner – a number of important elements take shape. The first is that liberals prescribe the view that human beings should be entrusted with as much freedom as possible. This has major implications for several issues relevant to *any* ideology. To give an example the student might be familiar with, the relationship between the individual and the state should be based firmly upon the freedom of the individual where he / she can conduct their actions unmolested by state intervention. Only when liberty itself is under threat is the state justified in taking action – a subject we will consider in greater depth later. For now, we need to identify the second core element of liberal ideology - **individualism**.

The 19th century liberal theorist John Stuart Mill succinctly observed that *"Over himself, over his own body and mind, the individual is sovereign."* This viewpoint best reflects the liberal conception of individualism. For liberals, individualism lies at the fulcrum of their belief system, providing a unifying element to all other aspects of liberal ideology. Whereas collectivism is based on the argument that we achieve more by our common endeavours, liberals centre their Weltanschauung firmly upon the individual. Within liberal thought there is also a clear rejection of the exalted position of a religious entity. Fundamentalist beliefs are anathema to liberals. Societies based upon religious fundamentalism (such as post-revolutionary Iran after the rise to power of Ayatollah Khomeini) have been some of the most illiberal regimes in history. Liberals do not support the view that religious beliefs should dictate the conduct of society. To do so would be counter to the liberal assumption that individuals are rational human beings. Religious beliefs are irrational by their very nature, in that they rely upon faith and superstition.

It is important to recognise that liberalism is grounded on the assumption that we are rational self-governing individuals capable of exercising our own free will and therefore we alone are best placed to decide what is in *our* interests. It is not for the state to decide what is in our best interests. Conservative notions of paternalism and Marxist dogma concerning the perfectibility of man have no place within the liberal agenda. Authoritarian societies based upon fascism or religious fundamentalism are also divorced from the liberal belief in rationalism. The inevitable consequence of the liberal perspective is a restricted role for the state in terms of its relationship to the individual, a point we shall analyse later.

From the essential starting point of the rational individual, a number of interrelated elements begin to emerge. These components of liberalism will shape the remainder of this Chapter. Please be aware that each Chapter is structured towards a consideration of issues that go to the very heart of each ideology – such as their view of human nature.

The liberal perspective on human nature

Unlike conservatives, liberals take an **optimistic** view of human nature. This is one of the major fault-lines between arguably the two most influential ideologies within contemporary political discourse. Whether one supports or disagrees with this optimistic view of human nature, one cannot deny that this argument inevitably flows from the liberal conception of individuals as rational actors. Liberal optimism about the motives behind human behaviour is firmly grounded upon the starting point of the rational individual. If the individual is a rational actor, then it logically follows that we can adopt a positive Weltanschauung of human nature. However, evidence to support or challenge the view that human behaviour is rational - and that we should be optimistic about human behaviour - is impossible to collate in any meaningful sense. There are simply too many variables to consider. It is ironic to note that for an ideology most closely association with secular beliefs, the liberal conception of human nature is essentially an article of faith. In order to be a liberal, one must simply 'buy into' an optimistic belief-system about human nature.

View of human nature	Ideology
Highly optimistic	Anarchism
Optimistic	Liberalism
Pessimistic	Conservatism
Highly pessimistic	Fascism

Within political discourse, labels are often attached to an ideology in both a positive *and* negative manner. In the context of the former, liberalism is the ideology most closely associated with the pursuit of happiness. Liberals strive to enable individuals to pursue their own conception of happiness provided their actions do not impinge upon the liberty of others. Unlike a relentless focus upon a sacrifice for the nation (as in the case of fascism) or the necessity of class struggle (as in the case of Marxism), liberalism is staunchly committed to the maximisation of individual happiness. Indeed, it is somewhat telling that in everyday language the very phrase 'liberal' implies positive virtues such as openness, generosity of spirit and trust in others. A moment's pause for thought will confirm that such an observation applies to *no* other ideology.

To its critics, to be a 'liberal' about human nature means little more than woolly-headed thinking resulting in dangerous consequences for society. Not surprisingly, this is an observation derived from those on the right of the political spectrum. Yet whatever view one takes on the liberal stance on human nature, it cannot be denied that such a positive view of human potential has formed the basis for a great many socially progressive ideas throughout history. Indeed without the characteristic liberal optimism about human nature it is unlikely that many of the most socially progressive policies would have ever been implemented. The inevitable consequence of this optimism is a firm belief in a better tomorrow. In contrast, conservatives are often criticised by their liberal counterparts for a misguided belief in a better yesterday.

Before we go any further, there are two important points to be made. Although liberals take a highly positive view of human nature, it is a view tempered by a degree of realism about humankind. Liberals acknowledge that individuals will on occasions act in an anti-social and criminal manner. Consequently, laws should be in place to deal with such behaviour and thereby protect individual liberty and freedom. As the 17th century English philosopher John Locke it credited with saying *"where laws do not exist, man has no freedom."* Thus unlike anarchists (see Chapter 6), liberals reject the view that freedom could flourish *without* the existence of a state. Liberals also reject the Marxist conception of the *"perfectibility of mankind."* According to the liberal perspective any change to the political structure of a society would not in itself lead to a utopian society. There is more on Marxism in Chapter 3. For now, it is merely worth noting that liberal optimism about human nature is more limited than that of anarchism and the Marxist conception of a Communist society.

The implications of liberal optimism about human nature can be seen in several policy areas, most notably in the area of social reform. The policies and arguments put forward by progressives everywhere are based to a considerable degree upon a positive view of human nature. According to this view the overwhelming majority of individuals are inherently good and can therefore be entrusted with as much freedom as possible. Whilst there should always be some limitations upon free will, the essential direction of government policy should always be towards maximising the concept of liberty for all. Social and ethnic groups should in no sense be excluded from this positive world-view. Liberals do not exclude minority groups and enthusiastically apply their conception of liberty on a universal basis, a point deftly observed by Wendell Wilkie who said that *"freedom is an indivisible word. If we want to enjoy it and fight for it, we must be prepared to extend it to everyone."* According to the liberal perspective no group of people are *less* rational than others – such is their optimism about human nature. As we shall explore later, other ideologies (such as fascism) are firmly opposed to the liberal world-view. One of the most poignant accounts of the need to apply human rights to all derives from the 20th century German theologian Martin Niemoller; *"First they came for the Jews and I did not speak out because I was not a Jew. Then they came for the Communists and I did not speak out because I was not a Communist. Then they came for the trade unionists and I did not speak out because I was not a trade unionist. Then they came for me and there was no one left to speak out for me."*

In British politics, the belief that individuals are rational actors was applied to both genders during the 19th century by liberal feminists such as John Stuart Mill and Mary Wollstonecraft. At a time when conservatives argued in favour of maintaining the status quo, a small but influential number of liberals claimed that women were rational individuals and therefore entitled to the same rights as men. As with a great many issues within political thought the same dividing-line can be observed today, particularly in American politics. As the reader will doubtless be aware one of the most controversial and important issues in the United States is abortion, with liberals in favour of a woman's right to choose and conservatives largely opposed. Liberals contend that women are rational individuals capable of exercising choice over such a vital issue. Whatever your views on the subject, it hardly needs adding that abortion is one of the defining issues of American politics to an extent unmatched within the democratic family of nations.

Liberal optimism about human nature and the universality of its application extends to their approach towards the treatment of criminals. Progressive reform of the criminal justice system is very much the prerogative of liberals. Rehabilitation of criminals is seen as both more effective and more humane. A 'liberal' penal policy is associated with a reformist stance on the treatment of prisoners, in contrast to a more authoritarian approach that may consist of lengthy custodial sentences or even the death penalty. One can also identify a contrast between liberals and authoritarians on the issue of prisoner's rights. At the 2005 General Election the Liberal Democrats were the only party to support the right of prisoners to vote in elections. Although a ruling from the European Court of Human Rights in 2006 enabling low-level offenders to vote has since made the Lib Dem policy somewhat redundant, it remains a clear example of the degree to which the liberal perspective takes an optimistic view of human nature. A further aspect to consider here is the liberal perspective on the causes of crime. For conservatives, this issue is relatively straight-forward. Human beings are prone to aggressive and selfish behaviour regardless of the political and economic structure of that society.

For conservatives, it is an immutable characteristic of human behaviour that members of society are inherently bad and will commit criminal acts. For liberals, the causes of crime are largely societal. Whereas a conservative is strongly in favour of tougher policies to deal with criminals and criminal behaviour, liberals contend that the way to reduce crime is to deal with the underlying social problems leading to criminal behaviour. Examples include the gap between the haves and have-nots, the existence of an underclass within society and the problem of relative deprivation. So whereas a conservative takes the view that criminal behaviour is the result of internal factors, a liberal is more likely to identify the causes of such behaviour as external.

The main strands of liberalism

Now that we have covered the core elements of liberalism and its perspective on human nature it is important to identify the two main strands within the liberal school of thought. The **two** strands of liberalism are **classical liberalism** and **social liberalism**. There are subtle yet significant differences between the two branches of liberalism – namely over the role of the state and their position within the political spectrum. However, it is important to note that what unites the two threads of liberal thought are the core elements of liberalism; namely a belief that the individual is a rational actor, an optimistic view of human nature and a firm commitment to individualism. The key difference between the two branches of thought is in the *means* by which they pursue the objectives of liberalism. As with all ideologies there is a degree of tension between the main strands of thought, and the debate within the boundaries of a particularly ideology can sometimes be as heated as that between the main political ideologies. In the context of liberalism, the debate is all the more animated because liberalism is one of the most difficult of all the ideologies to clearly demarcate its boundaries. As we will consider later, liberalism has been synergised with other ideologies to produce elements of thought such as liberal nationalism, liberal environmentalism, liberal feminism and individualist anarchism. As the dominant ideology of the modern era, it is hardly surprising to find that liberalism overlaps considerably with other ideologies.

The distinction between a classical liberal and a social liberal begins with their attitude towards economics. Classical liberalism is strongly associated with **laissez-faire economics** (a French term meaning *"leave alone"*) which stipulates that an economy works best when left to the market forces of supply and demand. State intervention will lead to inefficiency, bureaucracy and the misallocation of resources. The role of the state within the economy should therefore be limited to ensuring that contracts are honoured and that the market runs smoothly. The state may also have to provide merit goods such as clean air and clean water, but no more. For classical liberals, the role of the state is analogous to a **night-watchman**. The emphasis within classical liberalism is clearly upon a limited role for the state, which places this strand of thought firmly towards the right of the political spectrum. Yet unlike authoritarian perspectives on the right (such as fascism), classical liberals believe that the guiding principle of politics should be the maximisation of liberty. For proponents of this strand of thought, a market devoid of state intervention is the best means available for the maximisation of liberty. All ✦ classical liberals believe that **the freer the market, the freer the people**. Their commitment to the free-market is based on the premise that increased wealth within society benefits everyone. Unlike socialists, a more even distribution of wealth is a goal rejected by classical liberals.

Classical liberalism was at its height during the 18th and early 19th century when an influential body of scholars argued persuasively in favour of laissez-faire economics. These included classical economists such as David Ricardo (1772-1823) and a group of Manchester-based radicals such as Richard Cobden (1804-1865) and James Bright (1811-1889). Belief in the virtues of capitalism was the dominant view of the time and was underpinned by a *"survival of the fittest"* mentality (a theory associated with Herbert Spencer and Charles Darwin). Yet perhaps the most famous of all classical liberals was a Scottish economist called Adam Smith (1723-1790). Now immortalised on a £20 note, Smith is best known for his seminal work *'The Wealth of Nations'* (1776). It remains one of the most forceful arguments in favour of free trade, a point of central importance to all classical liberals.

Adam Smith defined an economic concept that fundamentally altered the means of production and provided the basis for a rapid expansion in global trade. In *the Wealth of Nations* he explained how the division of labour would ensure specialisation and economic efficiency. The resultant increase in output would in turn contribute towards the creation of wealth and thereby benefit all members of society. This would later prove the basis for the theory of trickle-down economics that characterised the Thatcher era of the 1980s. As we will consider later, socialists believe that the justification for trickle-down economics is merely part of the wider issue of exploitation within a capitalist economic system. As with several arguments within the realm of political ideology, there is always an alternative position to consider.

Socialists and classical liberals are strongly divided on the issue of economics and the role of the state within the economic realm. Classical liberals such as Adam Smith argue that the *"invisible hand"* of the marketplace will benefit everyone in terms of enhancing the concept of freedom, yet for socialists the state must plan the distribution of scarce resources in order to create a more equal society. Classical liberals justify their standpoint in terms of the democratic benefits of the free market and its association with fostering peace amongst nations throughout the world. According to the classical liberal school of thought, the profit motive enables firms to meet the needs of consumers. Over time, prices reach an equilibrium level decided upon by the interaction of thousands of people within the market. As such, the marketplace is based firmly upon the democratic will of the people. In terms of peace, the contemporary author Thomas Friedman (2005) has argued that a globalised economy based upon the principle of free trade is the best economic system available in terms of ensuring peaceful co-operation between different countries. To support his view Freidman claims that *"no two countries with McDonald's franchises have ever gone to war."* It is a modern-day illustration of an argument that can be traced back to the Manchester school of free-market liberals such as Richard Cobden who argued that free trade amongst the people of the world would create *"the bonds of eternal peace."* Adam Smith also advocated capitalism for the sake of freedom, a point advanced further by the 20th century classical liberal economist Milton Friedman (1980) who observed that *"history suggests that capitalism is a necessary condition for political freedom."* The German philosopher Immanuel Kant also believed that free trade would create a world without war, as did the French liberal philosopher Montesquieu who argued that *"the natural effect of commerce is to lead towards peace."*

That capitalism and democracy go hand-in-hand is arguably the most enduring aspect of the classical liberal school of thought. Such views have permeated to all areas of the world since the end of the cold war, when the Western nations led by the United States defeated their Communist rivals and instigated democratic change within the Soviet bloc. Whatever verdict one has upon the cold war, it is undoubtedly the case that the salience of capitalism as an economic system has grown significantly as a result of the West's victory. Even China, still nominally a Communist political regime, is as capitalist as any of the leading Western economies.

Whilst Adam Smith is rightly considered to be one of the leading figures within classical liberalism, he also believed that state intervention was justified in certain cases. For instance, he argued that *"the state has an interest in educating the young because the more educated they were, the less liable they were to delusion and enthusiasm."* Smith also supported progressive taxation on the basis of fairness and warned against the pernicious effects of unjustified levels of profit. Such arguments were taken up and developed further by social liberalism, a body of thought which emerged during the late-19th century and remained of major influence within the political process until the 1970s. In the contemporary era, such ideas have enjoyed a brief revival in terms of dealing with the credit crunch. Whether this continues to be a major aspect of economic policy, or a temporary response to a very serious economic problem, is impossible to say.

In the context of classical liberalism, such ideas enjoyed a revival during the 1970s and 80s when centre-right parties in the United States, the United Kingdom, Chile and New Zealand were heavily influenced by the ideas of the Austrian philosopher Friedrich Hayek (1899–1992) and the American economist Milton Freidman (1912-2006). Leading politicians such as Ronald Reagan and Margaret Thatcher were elected on a mandate to roll back the frontiers of the state via a bold policy package of privatisation, de-regulation, a reduction in direct taxation and the marketisation of the welfare state. This particular brand of economics had more in common with classical liberalism than conservatism, a point considered in the next Chapter on conservatism.[1]

Social liberalism differs to classical liberalism on an important premise, namely that **state intervention** in the economy and a **modest redistribution of wealth** via the taxation system is the best means to maximise the concept of liberty within society. Unlike classical liberals, those who put forward the social liberal argument are in favour of an active state. As such, social liberalism belongs on the left-libertarian axis. What distinguishes a social liberal from a socialist is their attitude to capitalism. All liberals are highly supportive of capitalism as the best means to achieve the core objective of liberalism; namely the maximisation of liberty. In contrast, socialists offer a critique of capitalism. [2]

For social liberals, an economy based upon laissez-faire economics with the state playing the role of a night-watchman cannot serve the core objective of liberalism. When left alone markets are prone to fail, which in turn holds negative implications for individual liberty. Furthermore, those with few resources within society are unlikely to enjoy liberty in any meaningful sense. As such, the state is justified in redistributing wealth to the less well-off on the basis of progressive taxation. This argument is based on a fundamentally different conception of liberty than the classical school. Central to this shift within liberal thought was an English radical called Thomas Hill Green (1836-1882). In ideological terms, Green developed the concept of liberty

---

[1] Milton Friedman came from a family that worked in what would now be called a sweatshop. To classical liberals such as Friedman, left-wing opposition to so-called sweatshops is based on a flawed analysis. Poorer countries need to develop along this basis in order to bring themselves up to (or near to) Western levels of GDP. Campaigns to boycott firms that use cheap labour will only harm the poor.

[2] Social liberalism goes under various guises including modern / new / progressive / welfare liberalism. For the sake of simplicity, social liberalism is used throughout.

towards a more substantive value. He argued that *"when we speak of freedom ... we mean a positive power or capacity of doing or enjoying something worth doing."* As liberty requires the actual capacity to act the state can and should contribute to freedom on the basis of some redistribution of income. He argued that a tax on inherited wealth was therefore justified in order for everyone to enjoy a life of liberty. Although Green was concerned that the state should never stifle individual self-direction, he claimed that liberalism should move on from the laissez-faire approach of the classical school of thought. The English economist Alfred Marshall (1842-1924) backed up Green's argument, claiming that a redistribution of wealth from rich to poor would enable the latter to enjoy a life of liberty. In America, the concept of what became known as positive liberty was further developed by the philosopher John Dewey (1859-1952).

During the late-19th century and early-20th century this new (or social) form of liberalism gradually eclipsed the classical liberal school of thought. One of the first manifestations of social liberalism within the UK was the Liberal government that won a landslide victory in the 1906 General Election. Leading figures in the party such as David Lloyd George and Herbert Asquith implemented a radical programme that laid the foundations for the modern welfare state. By the 1940s social liberalism had reached an important watershed. The two outstanding liberal theorists of that era were Sir William Beveridge (1942) and John Maynard Keynes (1973), both of whom laid the foundations for the post-war consensus. The former is credited with providing the blueprint for the welfare state. He was instrumental in the creation of a post-war consensus based around the provision of welfare on a comprehensive and universal basis from the cradle to the grave. Beveridge argued that the state should ensure that no-one fell below a certain level of poverty. Crucially, those who lacked sufficient means to fulfil their potential should be provided with some level of welfare provision. Beveridge outlined *"five evils"* in his best-selling report, each of which required a notable degree of state intervention. The problem of squalor would be addressed via low-cost social housing, want could be addressed via unemployment benefit, the problem of disease demanded a free at the point of use health service, the problem of ignorance could be addressed via a subsidised state education system and idleness required the maintenance of full employment. His report caught the spirit of the time and remained central to the expansion of the post-war welfare state within the UK.

By far the most influential theorist of the social liberal tradition was a brilliant economist called John Maynard Keynes (1883-1946). The Adam Smith of his day, the influence of Keynes was considerable and his ideas are still highly relevant in the modern era. For many, he is credited with saving capitalism from collapse because he offered a practical solution to the desperate economic situation of the 1930s. He turned conventional wisdom on its head by challenging the view of classical economists. Whereas they argued that a balanced budget, a firm commitment to the gold standard and a reduction in the level of wages was required to revive the economy; Keynes thought otherwise. The classical approach had led to an over-valued currency, a substantial rise in the level of unemployment and a sharp decline in real national income.

	Classical liberalism	Social liberalism
Ideological axis	Right-libertarian	Left-libertarian
The welfare state	Night-watchman role	State intervention is justified in order to maximise liberty
Economic policy	Laissez-faire capitalism	Mixed economy
Key figures	Smith, Cobden, Friedman	Keynes, Beveridge, Green

It is important for students to grasp that Keynes wished to *save* capitalism, because Keynes was of course a liberal and therefore supportive of capitalism. Yet unlike classical liberals, Keynes wished to expand the role of the government within the economy in order to bolster aggregate demand and therefore kick-start the economy from the depths of the Great Depression. Keynes argued that the government should fine tune the economy in order to meet its policy objectives. During an economic downturn the government should reflate the economy via a reduction in taxation and / or an increase in government expenditure. The state should therefore actively intervene in the economy to increase the level of aggregate demand. The cost of increasing state intervention would later be met by higher tax receipts as people spent their wages on consumer goods. Conversely, during a time of rapid economic growth Keynes argued that the government should deflate the economy by increasing taxation and cutting back government expenditure. Over the economic cycle governments should eventually balance their budget.

During the mid-1930s there was an acute need to kick-start the economy, and John Maynard Keynes magnum opus '*The General Theory of Employment, Interest and Money*' offered a timely and practical remedy. Rejecting the statist approach of more extreme ideologies such as Communism and fascism (both of which were popular during the inter-war years), Keynes provided a means to save capitalism in a manner comparable to Beveridge's blueprint for the five evils facing society. In retrospect, the influence of Keynes went well beyond his own political party and his native country. He was the towering figure of liberal thought during the mid-20th century and one of a handful of economists who could genuinely be credited with a lasting political legacy. Keynesian economics have of course been revived by Western governments worried about the fall-out from the credit crunch. Once again, it seems that Keynesian ideas are being implemented to rescue capitalism from another bout of market failure. Somewhat fittingly, he observed with characteristic foresight that *"the ideas of economists and political philosophers ... are more powerful than is commonly understood. Indeed, the world is ruled by little else."*

The role of the state

The role of the state is an absolutely central element towards our understanding of political ideology. Not surprisingly, the proper role and purpose of state intervention within society has fuelled considerable debate within the realm of ideological thought. In the context of liberalism, there are some over-arching comments to be made alongside a further exploration of the distinction between the two main strands of liberal thought. Yet as with all ideologies, the internal differences between the main strands of thought often generate the more interesting aspects of debate.

One general observation we can make with certainty is that *all* liberals wish to **protect the individual** from the abuse of state power. For liberals, the ability of the state to exercise power must be limited in some way. This serves one of the core elements of liberal thought, namely the belief in individualism. In terms of the relationship between the state and the individual, liberals will always side with the latter. The state undoubtedly has the ability to destroy the flame of liberty, a point borne out by several despotic regimes throughout the world today (including Zimbabwe, North Korea and China). So for liberals, the state must be curtailed if liberty is to be maximised and the rights of the individual are to be protected.

In terms of the proper role of the state, one of the most influential contributions within liberal thought derives from the famous English philosopher John Locke. He argued that government should be based upon the **consent** of individuals who have effectively entered into a contract with the state (1690). People therefore exercise their approval to be governed in return for the state protecting their life, liberty and property. Consent would usually be expressed through democratic means, although consent could also be merely tacit, taken as read from the behaviour of the governed. If the state were to violate this contract in any way, then the people were entitled to withdraw their consent. Crucially, the state was therefore the instrument through which citizens could protect their freedom. Locke's arguments are important simply because they have stood the test of time, with notions of legitimacy and consent central towards an understanding of liberal democracy.

After Locke, a number of leading liberal intellectuals such as Thomas Paine, Voltaire, John Stuart Mill and Thomas Jefferson argued that the exercise of state power should be based solely upon **legitimacy** and consent from the governed. Participation was also integral to the bourgeoning ideology of liberalism. As John Stuart Mill once observed, it is wrong for citizens to be reduced to the status of *"a flock of sheep innocently nibbling the grass side by side."* Individuals should participate within the democratic process, for without public participation 'democracy' is little more than a meaningless façade. For liberals, public participation greatly enhances the quality of representative democracy. Moreover, the ideal type of government is a representative one where power is exercised on the basis of legitimacy and consent.

For liberals, the state is essentially an organisation run by individuals whose authority derives from meeting the wants and needs of the governed. The divine right of Kings has no place within liberal ideology, and nor does the hereditary principle. During the 18th century the French philosopher Voltaire boldly declared that he wanted to *"Ecraisez l'infame"* (crush the infamy) because of the persecution of dissidents by religious clerics. As with many liberals, he believed that superstition leads to intolerance. From the same era the English radical Thomas Paine (1791) argued that *"the idea of hereditary legislators is as inconsistent as that of hereditary judges, or hereditary juries, and as absurd as a hereditary mathematician, or a hereditary wise man."* His argument is a useful illustration of the liberal stance on the role of the state and the exercise of power by the state. Paine was one of inspirations behind the American Revolution and it is worth noting that the famous slogan of the American rebels (*"no taxation without representation"*) is based firmly upon liberal hostility to the rule of an unaccountable elite. All liberals share Abraham Lincoln's belief that a little rebellion is a desirable thing, particularly when the ruling elite do not hold legitimacy from the people.

Liberals are highly supportive of restrictions placed upon the agents of the state. Those who exercise power must be **held to account** for their actions, either directly to the public or indirectly via elected representatives. Liberals are also strongly in favour of measures to strengthen and defend **human rights**. Such measures usually derive from constitutional safeguards, although the existence of a codified constitution is not in itself a guarantor of human rights. Nonetheless, liberals have always favoured codified documents strengthening the concept of human rights. Notable historical examples include the Declaration of the Rights of Man and the Citizen in post-Revolutionary France, the Bill of Rights in the United States and the United Nations Declaration of Human Rights. Liberals strongly believe that the citizen *needs* to be protected from a powerful state and that the means by which individuals can enjoy as much freedom as possible hinges upon the protection of human rights.

In the realm of welfare policy, social liberals have been instrumental in the creation of the **welfare state**, and today, the most vocal opponents of the marketisation of the welfare state derive from social liberals within the Liberal Democrats. For social liberals, the concept of liberty is enhanced by the provision of welfare services by the state. However, classical liberals take a very different view. There is significant friction within liberal ideology between those who favour a night-watchman role for the state against those who believe that the state can enhance the concept of liberty via some redistribution of wealth. Typical of the classical school is the German philosopher Wilhelm von Humboldt's (1767-1835) argument in favour of a minimal state in order to enable individuality and excellence to flourish. He also warned that a state that takes on an excessive amount of roles within a society will undermine individualism and the social bonds of mutual responsibility.

As a student it is important to chart the various areas in which ideologies cross over, and in the context of the role of the state, there is a degree of overlap between liberals and conservatives in terms of the effects of power. The 19th century English historian Lord Acton's observation that *"all power corrupts and absolute power corrupts absolutely"* is part of the liberal *and* conservative school of thought. Similarly, liberals agree with the conservative theorist Edmund Burke's observation that *"the greater the power, the more dangerous the abuse."* Similarly, both socialists and social liberals believe that the state has a role to play in terms of managing the economy, although the extent to which the state intervenes in the economy differs considerably. Finally, there are synergies of liberalism with many other ideologies. Frankly, it is very difficult to set an accurate boundary upon liberalism due to its considerable influence within political discussion. Typical of this synergy with other ideologies relates to the environmentalist movement. According to liberals within the green movement (so-called *"light greens"*), protecting the environment should have the same degree of importance as the protection of our human rights. Indeed, there is a close relationship between the two because the destruction of the environment represents a violation of our human rights. We should all have the right to breathe in clean air and drink unpolluted water.

Before we leave this section, we need to consider one of the most persuasive contributions to social liberalism in terms of the relationship between the state and the individual. The American philosopher John Rawls (1921–2002) work on the *"difference principle"* claims that – given certain assumptions about human rationality – we would choose to protect a set of basic rights when presented with a hypothetical choice in terms of distributing resources within society. Rawls (1971) also outlined two principles of justice;

> ➢ Each individual should have an equal right to the most extensive basic liberty compatible with a similar degree of liberty for others.
> ➢ Social and economic inequalities should be to everyone's advantage.

Rawls work on the concept of justice was challenged by the American philosopher Robert Nozick (1938-2002). Nozick argued in favour of an entitlement theory of justice. He claimed that if individuals are entitled to dispose of the resources they own, then whatever outcome results from those actions is – by definition – a just one. Nozick believed that the redistribution of wealth by the state constituted a form of slavery – since it represented an attack upon the rights of the individual – and thereby made individuals the *means* to an end. So whereas Rawls' argument would facilitate a role for the state in terms of ensuring social justice, Nozick claims that the state should allow an unequal outcome within society to arise. Rawls therefore belongs on the left-libertarian side of the political spectrum whereas Nozick belongs on the libertarian-right. The debate between Rawls and Nozick reflects the contested character of the concept of justice, one of many concepts that are up for debate within the realm of political discourse.

Liberalism and equality

The concepts of liberty and equality have often been presented as a zero-sum game (Jaeger, 1943). Conventional wisdom states that societies can have greater liberty *or* greater equality, but they cannot have both. Whilst this is an entirely plausible understanding of the concepts of liberty and equality, there is rather more to it than that. For example, it would be wrong to say that liberals are opposed to equality. For liberals, support for equality relates to **equality of opportunity**. In contrast, socialists are more favourable towards equality of outcome – particularly those further to the left of the political spectrum. The student also needs to be aware of a significant division between the two branches of liberalism on the issue of equality. Whereas classical liberals believe that the marketplace is the best forum for providing opportunities to enhance individual liberty, social liberals believe tha state needs to play a role in assisting disadvantaged groups. The objective of state assistance should always be to enhance the concept of liberty, and the state must limit its activities towards ensuring equality *of opportunity*. Too much state intervention on the basis of equality and social justice will undermine personal liberty.

Social liberals are in favour of measures designed to ensure equality of opportunity within society. Whereas they firmly **support capitalism**, a degree of state intervention in order to provide better life chances is considered both desirable and justified. Social liberals claim that laissez-faire economics with a night-watchman state cannot enhance liberty for *all* members of society. Those with less wealth should be assisted by the state. Social liberals of all parties have a lengthy record of promoting the rights of those individuals and groups traditionally at the margins of society (such as women, ethnic minorities, the young, etc.). Legislation designed to achieve a more equitable reflection of society within the workplace is closely associated with the social liberal perspective, as are laws that reflect an open and tolerant attitude to minorities (such as civil partnerships for same-sex couples). For liberals, state assistance may even take the form of affirmative action. In contrast, those on the right of the political spectrum consider affirmative action as just another form of discrimination. In reply, liberals claim that minorities are denied a fair chance in the workplace due to prejudicial attitudes. In order to assist individuals from disadvantaged groups smash through the glass ceiling the state needs to mitigate the effects of negative attitudes amongst employers. The debate over affirmative action is one of the most controversial issues within American politics and one of the few dividing lines between the two main political parties.

Both strands of liberalism believe that **inequality of outcome** is a natural and inevitable consequence of a smooth-functioning society. Individuals are endowed with different talents, abilities and levels of ambition and to construct a concept of equality that robs people of their individualism is incompatible with liberalism. John Maynard Keynes spoke for all liberals when he said that *"there is social and psychological justification for significant inequalities of income and wealth."* For liberals, an unequal distribution of wealth within society is the obvious consequence of a genuinely free society. Whereas social liberals believe that the state needs to play some role in terms of equalising opportunities, they do not believe that the state must distribute wealth and resources on an even basis. This is a major dividing line between social liberals and the various strands of socialist thought. For liberals, a government dedicated to equality of outcome would destroy personal enterprise and stifle creativity. A socialist society would result in crippling conformity and thereby entail a massive loss of personal liberty (Solzhenitsyn, 1963; Orwell, 1949). Furthermore, economic growth requires a system that allows what Keynes called the *"animal spirits"* of competition to function. As such, social liberals contend that the state must only redistribute a degree of wealth sufficient enough to ensure equality *of opportunity*.

It is undoubtedly the case that the issue of equality reflects a significant division between liberalism and socialism. Socialists are highly critical of laissez-faire economics due to its association with an uneven distribution of wealth. By the very nature of laissez-faire economics equality can never be achieved because resources are allocated on the basis of supply and demand. Yet for classical liberals, capitalism is by far the **best economic system** in terms of improving life chances. In contrast, a socialist-inspired alternative would simply result in a levelling down of society in order to achieve the goal of equality. Indeed some of the most vociferous opponents of raising the level of taxation upon individuals and families derive from the liberal perspective, particularly classical liberals from the so-called Austrian School of the mid-20th century such as Friedrich Hayek, Karl Popper and Ludwig von Mises. So in summary, liberals are in favour of equality in the sense of equality of opportunity. They are implacably opposed to an even distribution of wealth, although a small redistribution of wealth towards the less well-off is supported by social liberals on the basis of enhancing the concept of liberty. The liberal stance on the issue of equality is distinct from either conservatism or socialism. For conservatives, even a limited attempt at social engineering is undesirable, and for socialists, a capitalist economic system will always entail an unacceptable degree of inequality.

Features of a liberal democratic system
Protection of human rights
Plurality of pressure groups and political parties
Competitive multi-party elections
Free and fair elections
Separation of powers
Power should be limited (or checked)
Rule of law must prevail
Peaceful transition of power

The relationship between liberalism and liberal democracy

No ideology is as closely associated with democracy as liberalism, and there is a rich vein of liberal theorists that have advanced the cause of democracy throughout history. The extent to which liberals believe in democracy can be seen in the prevalent use of the term **liberal democracy**. Although a people's democracy was a term used within Communist regimes, no other political perspective is as closely attached with democracy as libera

Under a liberal democratic system, **eight features** are widely thought to be in evidence. Perhaps the most important is that human rights should be protected and enshrined. Legislative and constitutional safeguards must be in place in order to protect individual liberty and thereby avoid the excessive and arbitrary use of power by the state. Liberals everywhere are highly supportive of the concept of **constitutionalism** whereby safeguards are in place via the constitution to avoid decision-makers abusing their power. Those countries that have a lengthy history of democracy (such as the United Kingdom) tend to be more complacent about the concept of human rights, whereas those countries that have in living memory experienced the full horrors of a totalitarian regime (such as Germany) have more stringent laws in place to prevent the re-emergence of excessive state influence within society. Indeed, Britain is virtually alone within the world for its absence of a codified constitution, a point of contention for liberals amongst all the main parties.

Within a liberal democracy a plurality of pressure groups and political parties must be allowed to flourish in order that freedom of expression within society is maximised. For liberals, society must facilitate a marketplace of ideas. However, political parties and pressure groups must operate within the conventions of a liberal democracy. On this basis, liberals support restrictions upon extremist political parties and pressure groups – particularly those which advocate violence to achieve their political objectives. Furthermore, a society centred upon one belief system – as in the case of a theocracy or a Communist society - is the polar opposite of a liberal society.

A third aspect of liberal democracy is the existence of competitive multi-party elections where the people (or demos) are provided with a choice of alternatives and can therefore exercise their democratic right to vote. However, the existence of an election is not in itself sufficient criteria for a liberal democracy. Totalitarian regimes have regularly used the electoral process, and yet such elections have invariably been illiberal due to a lack of genuine choice. Moreover, people must be able to vote without impediment. In the context of UK politics, liberals also favour electoral reform based upon proportional representation. Support amongst liberals for proportional representation dates back to John Stuart Mill who believed that electoral reform would result in a more equitable balance of minorities within parliament. Liberals also claim that countries which adopt proportional representation are less likely to go to war than those based upon a majoritarian system such as the United States and the United Kingdom.

In terms of the distribution of power amongst the three branches of government (the legislature, the executive and the judiciary), liberals believe that each branch should be separate from the other. The view that the separation of powers is a prerequisite of a liberal democracy derives from the

18th century French theorist Baron de Montesquieu. His influence was far greater in the United States than in his native homeland. Montesquieu is the most quoted author in *'the Federalist'* (a seminal text that has never gone out of print!) and the political system of the United States has long been based upon the separation of powers.

Another element of liberal democracy is the idea that power should be checked or limited. Liberals firmly believe that all power has the potential to corrupt. In a liberal democracy power is dispersed throughout society right down to the local or regional level. A federal system as used in Australia, Germany, Canada and the United States is closer to this aspect of liberal democracy than a system based on a unitary structure such as the United Kingdom. Following on from the previous point, decision-makers who exercise power should be held to account and should be open in their activities. Accountability is a key concern for liberals. For liberals, the executive must be scrutinised in some way. As the people's representatives, the legislature is the most appropriate forum for this. In a liberal democracy, the actions of government should be as open as is practically possible. Although some level of government secrecy is permissible, liberals argue that excessive secrecy is incompatible with good government. Within a vibrant liberal society there must be a free flow of information and a degree of openness in terms of the state's activities. In the words of Jeremy Bentham; *"in the darkness of secrecy, sinister interest and evil in every shape have full swing."*

The penultimate element of liberal democracy concerns the rule of law. In a liberal democracy no-one is above the law. The police are citizens in uniform and members of the executive must not exceed their powers (known by the Latin term *"ultra vires"*). Furthermore, individuals must have the right to a fair trail regardless of social background, ethnicity, religion, sexual orientation and / or their political beliefs. In a liberal democracy people are also innocent until proven guilty. Any deviation from these guiding principles is inconsistent with liberalism. The only exception to the rule of law is war-time, when some curtailment of civil liberties may be necessary in the context of the threat to liberty from an enemy power. Finally, there should be a peaceful transition of power within a liberal democracy. Societies that do not have a peaceful transition of power cannot be classed as liberal democracies in any meaningful sense. Whilst this is hardly an issue within the developed world, there is a great deal of political unrest within certain parts of the world (such as Zimbabwe between the Movement for Democratic Change against supporters of the Zanu-PF leader Robert Mugabe). For those living in liberal democracies, the peaceful transition of power is often taken for granted.

The extent to which a political system matches these elements of liberal democracy differs widely throughout the world, and the extent to which a country's political system matches the criterion of a liberal democracy also fluctuates over time. For instance, the reforms instigated by the Labour government during the 1997-2001 Parliament (such as the Human Rights Act and the Freedom of Information Act) facilitated a greater level of democracy, but the government's shift towards authoritarian policies since 2001 has raised very serious concerns over the state of democracy within the UK (Raab, 2009; Kieran, 2007; Clarke, 2007; Atkins, 2007), with many claiming that Britain suffers from a considerable democratic deficit. Similar concerns have been raised about the United States (Wolf, 2008). Yet as with many aspects of political study, labelling a country as a liberal democracy is not entirely straight-forward. It would of course be ridiculous to say that Britain is *not* a liberal democracy simply because it has a fusion of powers amongst the three branches of government, and the fact that it is one of the very few countries in the world that lacks a codified constitution. Whilst it is relatively simplistic to say that neither Saudi Arabia nor North Korea qualify as liberal democracies, the debate arises when a country has certain elements of a liberal democracy. As such, it makes more sense to use the term liberal democracy in a comparative sense.

The individual and society

In terms of the relationship between the individual and society, liberals are firmly on the side of the individual. A political movement that prescribes collectivism to any degree is anathema to any true liberal. There is a particularly clear distinction to be made here between social liberals and social democrats. Whereas the former will adopt individualism as its credo, social democrats are – like all strands of socialist thought - favourable towards collectivist action to secure political objectives (such as social justice and equality).

Liberals have consistently championed the **rights of the individual** against those agents acting on behalf of 'society.' The most obvious agent is of course the state, although the role of religious institutions is another factor to consider. In the case of the former, liberals wish to protect the rights of the individual against the potentially illiberal exercise of power by the state. A manifestation of this point for liberals is their deep commitment to constitutionalism. A set of prescribed rights within a constitutional and legal framework is seen as a vital bulwark against the arbitrary exercise of power by the agents of the state.

In the case of a theocracy, liberals warn against the influence of mixing religion with politics. Throughout history, liberals have defended the rights of the individual to worship as they choose without being compelled to conform to the prevalent religious-based values of that society. During the Enlightenment era an impressive range of liberal theorists offered a direct challenge to the divine right of Kings and with that challenge contributed an important breakthrough in the salience of liberal ideology. In contemporary politics, the liberal stance against the potentially intolerant influence of religion within the political process is most visibly expressed within the United States.

In any society, a liberal will defend the right of the individual to express his or her beliefs even if the rest of society strongly disagrees with those views. As John Stuart Mill boldly declared *"human beings should be free to form opinions and to express their opinions without reserve."* Support for dissident beliefs is one of the most vibrant expressions of liberalism in action. As the philosopher Rosa Luxembourg once said *"freedom is always and exclusively freedom for the one who thinks differently."* For liberals, society must always facilitate the outsider. A society based around a slavish adherence to social conformity will stifle individualism. This would be to the detriment of all members of that society, not just the outsider in question. Perhaps the most eloquent expression of this view derives from John Stuart Mill who argued that ***"if mankind minus one were of one opinion, then mankind is no more justified in silencing the one than the one - if he had the power - would be justified in silencing mankind."***

Liberals claim that we can avoid dull conformity and stagnation of thought by exposing ourselves to the robust argument which inevitably derives from a **market of ideas.** In doing so, we can all benefit from the invigorating effects of new ideas and alternative viewpoints. As this benefits everyone, society has no more right in quashing the freedom of expression of an individual than the individual does of crushing the rights of other members of society. From a historical perspective, it is revealing to note that several ideas considered outside the realm of conventional wisdom (such as the Enlightenment during the 18th century and the emergence of Keynesian economics during the 1930s) have been championed by liberals.

Whilst it is the case that liberals will always side with the individual against the majority, there are inevitably limits to their support. Liberals will always endorse restrictions on free will if that individual is engaged in **illiberal behaviour.** This is to protect the liberty of various members of society, the overwhelming majority of whom are law-abiding and wish to enjoy their personal freedom without external restraint. Furthermore, our freedom of speech should be governed by the rules of a liberal democratic regime. It may therefore be permissible for the state – acting on behalf of society – to censor certain views if the impact of those views would be illiberal in content. One example would be the impact of expressing political views to a wider group of people with the intent on causing physical harm. John Stuart Mill argued that *"an opinion that ... private property is robbery ought to be unmolested when simply circulated through the press, but may justly incur punishment when delivered orally to an excited mob."* Property is robbery was a view widely expressed by anarchists during Mill's era, a point he doubtless had in mind when constructing that argument.

The objective of maximising liberty is one of the cornerstones of liberal ideology. Once again, this view is best articulated by John Stuart Mill. In his seminal text *On Liberty* (1859), John Stuart Mill argued that *"the only purpose for which power can be rightly exercised over any member of a civilised community, against his will, is to prevent harm to others. His own good, either physical or moral, is not a sufficient warrant."* An individual must therefore be free to pursue his or her own interests and activities provided they do not in any way harm others. It is not in the remit of the state – acting on behalf of majority rule - to decide what is best for the individual. The only possible justification for the state interfering in the lives of individuals would be in those situations where harm might arise. 'Offence' to others is not good enough. We should be free to express views that may on occasions cause offence to certain groups provided those views are in no sense resulting in harm to people's liberty. This extends to liberals defending views and thoughts that the majority of society may find distasteful.

Befitting a philosopher of his stature, John Stuart Mill's **harm principle** remains one of the most influential contributions to political ideology. He was motivated by a concern over the potential for societal norms and mores to stifle creativity and individuality. His argument rests on the supposition that societies need to renew themselves in order to prevent stagnation. Conformity stifles human potential and we should therefore always have a sphere of liberty that is immune from state intervention. Moreover, our sphere of liberty should be as wide as possible. The *only* limitation is if we harm the liberty of others. He also warned that *"those who are slaves to custom ... will never develop into rounded, flourishing individuals"* and argued that *"it is important to give the freest scope possible to uncustomary things, in order that it may in time appear which of these are fit to be converted into customs."* No conservative would concur with either of those views.

In terms of the relationship between the individual and society, liberals are firmly in favour of **toleration**. There are two main elements to consider here. The first is in terms of tolerating alternative lifestyles. Such thinking is guided by the long-standing liberal fear of the *"tyranny of the majority"* (an idea dating back to Alexis de Tocqueville but commonly attributed to John Stuart Mill). The second aspect concerns toleration of dissenting political voices. This

The Definitive Guide to Political Ideologies

tolerance even applies when such views challenge the conventional assumption of society, or when those views are contrary to the wider mores of that society. For liberals, the ability of the dissenter to express his or her viewpoint is of absolutely fundamental importance. The suppression of controversial views would only rob society of the desirability of constructive argument – which in turn helps us reconsider and reaffirm our own viewpoint. It is only via this process that ideas can truly develop. As John Stuart Mill observed; *"He who knows only his side of the case, knows little of that."* Thus in a truly liberal society all views should be tolerated *unless* they present a specific threat to the liberty of others. Such ideological coherence stems from a deep commitment to the desirability of pluralism and the requirement that people must be free to express their political views. As the French philosopher Voltaire famously declared; *"Monsieur ... I detest what you write, but I would give my life to make it possible for you to continue to write."* [3]

The liberal stance on lifestyle issues

The liberal stance on lifestyle issues flows neatly from the previous section. As a reflection of their deep commitment to individualism, allied to a concern over the tyrannical impact the majority may have over the minority, liberals are firmly in favour of the **right to choose**. However, this freedom is not absolute. Unlike anarchists, liberals argue that the state is entirely justified in placing certain restrictions upon individual's behaviour *if* such actions are contrary to the wider objective of maximising liberty within society.

Once again, the most important contribution within liberal thought on this issue derives from John Stuart Mill's harm principle. For Mill, society should never rob a person of their innate individualism. The *only* justification is to prevent harm to other people. Crucially, it is not the job of 'society' or the 'state' to decide what is in the best interests of the individual concerned. The implications of this succinct expression of liberalism are both far-reaching and unambiguous. Liberals firmly support the right of the individual to express their identity and pursue the lifestyle they choose without society inhibiting such freedom on the basis of morality. For liberals, we should adopt a stance of moral relativism and tolerate the widest possible spectrum of lifestyles.

The division between liberals and conservatives on lifestyle issues finds its most obvious expression within American politics. Conservatives in America

---

[3]   Voltaire also argued in favour of an enlightened dictator governing in the interests of the people, and dismissed the majority of the population as *"la canaille"* – the rabble. To modern sensibilities, such elitist thinking appears profoundly illiberal – and yet he remains one of the leading figures within liberal ideology.

argue that the termination of a pregnancy is morally wrong, with some hard-liners even claiming that *"abortion is the American holocaust."* Liberals however contend that women should have freedom of choice over their bodies and their lives. As the observant reader will no doubt be aware, the controversy generated on the subject does not travel well outside of America. Within other liberal democracies, abortion is usually considered to be a private matter and one largely outside the political realm. To many Europeans, the sight of Republicans labelling the pro-choice Barack Obama as a *"baby-killer"* during the 2008 Presidential campaign was uniquely American. Indeed, much of the ideological ferment within American politics centres upon issues of morality and lifestyle – the most important of which is undoubtedly abortion. On this controversial issue, the diving line between the pro-life and pro-choice viewpoint is as much of a theological issue as a political one. For those on the right of the political spectrum, liberals are guilty of hypocrisy over their stance on abortion. By championing the rights of women they have entirely ignored the rights of the unborn child.

Another important distinction between a liberal and a conservative within American politics is gun control. Conservatives believe that we have a duty to protect ourselves from those who wish to take our lives and possessions. This view reflects Edmund Burke's argument that *"all that is necessary for evil to triumph is for good men to do nothing."* In contrast, liberals take the view that we can best protect our liberty via restricting gun ownership. Ironically, the 'right' to own a gun is supported much more venomously by conservatives than liberals. Once again, Mill's harm principle casts valuable light on this apparent contradiction – as the right to gun ownership is an obvious threat to the liberty of others.

On a variety of issues that might come under the category of morality, liberals constantly favour an individual's right to choose. A good illustration is the issue of euthanasia (or assisted suicide). Liberals argue that if an individual of sound mind and body has decided to end their life then they should be allowed to do so. As with abortion, there is a trait of secularism within liberal ideology. The political views of liberals are rarely influenced by religious beliefs of any kind. For liberals, the private realm and the public realm should be entirely separate. A political regime centred upon religious beliefs will inevitably crush individualism and the right of people to decide what is in their best interests. Crucially, this does *not* mean that a society with a high level of religiosity cannot be liberal. For example, Catholic Spain was one of the first to allow gay couples to marry. Nonetheless, liberals reject the view of those on the right of the political spectrum that the political process should be governed by religious values, believing that religious dogma has been used to justify some of the worst atrocities in the history of humankind. Thus for liberals, social progress demands a decline in religious fervour within society. Such thinking dates back to Enlightenment figures such as Alexis de Tocqueville who predicted that *"religious zeal … will be extinguished as freedom and enlightenment increase."*

For liberals, the role of the government should be kept **separate** from that of religious worship. Combing the two is inconsistent with liberal teachings. Amongst liberal democracies, France and America are both illustrations of this point. In France, the Church and the state are kept firmly separate. In America, there is also a separation between the Church and the state. Moreover, there is no single established religion within the US. Unlike England, there is no Church of America. Liberal tolerance towards an individual's right to worship is one of the hallmarks of American society. Throughout history, those who have been persecuted for their religious beliefs have found refuge in the United States. Somewhat oddly, politicians in the United States are now routinely quizzed about their religious beliefs. Faith-based issues hold a level of political credence within America that is entirely foreign to most Europeans. An excellent illustration of this point occurred during the Iraqi war. The British Prime Minister Tony Blair (a man well-known for his Christian beliefs) wanted to end his address to the people with a reference to God. His emollient Press Secretary Alistair Campbell – fearful of how the media and the public would interpret such a comment – famously said that *"We don't do God here."* It is impossible to imagine such a comment from advisors close to the American President.

Whatever view one takes on moral issues, it is undoubtedly the case that the liberal emphasis upon individualism will inevitably result in **moral relativism**. It is not for society to dictate that a particular lifestyle is necessarily better than any other. For example, those who claim that a heterosexual relationship is morally superior to a homosexual relationship – perhaps based upon religious teachings – are taking a deeply illiberal stance. Similarly, it is illiberal to claim that marriage is the most desirable arrangement for two people in a committed relationship. For liberals, society must always tolerate individual choices within society because individualism is at the fulcrum of liberalism itself. The consequence of such thinking is a society made up of autonomous individuals who are free to chart their own course in life. The German sociologist Ferdinand Toennies (1855-1936) described this type of society as one based upon association (what he called *"Gesellschaft"*). He contrasted this type of society to one based upon community (what he termed *"Gemeinschaft"*). To opponents of liberalism, the emphasis upon individualism and moral relativism undermines societal bonds and results in a society based upon impersonal association. Such criticism derives from those on the authoritarian axis of the political spectrum, especially fascists and religious fundamentalists.

Basing a society upon an individual's right to choose is one the most distinctive features of liberalism. For society to accommodate individuality we must respect the right to worship as a person or group of people sees fit. In doing so, society will facilitate **cultural diversity**. This cosmopolitan approach is one of the more obvious manifestations of living in a liberal society. Basing a society around one set of religious beliefs is deeply illiberal and will inevitably lead to the tyranny of the majority. Diversity should always be the watchword of a liberal society. By maintaining tolerance and mutual respect the bonds of society will hold together, despite the warnings of those on the right of the political spectrum.

In everyday usage, to be 'liberal' on the subject of lifestyle issues is to adopt an open-minded approach to a variety of human relationships and forms of behaviour. A liberal attitude denotes a form of openness towards those living outside the sometimes stultifying norms and values of society. For instance, a true liberal would have no moral objection to any form of sexual behaviour between consenting adults provided no harm was being done. Over time, the liberal attitude has established itself as the predominant one within most of the Western world. For example, British society has become much **more liberal** on issues of morality and lifestyle choices. For liberals, considerable progress has been made in terms of the attitude taken towards those who adopt a lifestyle outside that of a nuclear family. This has been one of the most welcome trends within society and should not be cast aside in the desire amongst those on the right to return to traditional moral values. As the former Canadian Prime Minister Pierre Trudeau once said *"the state has no place in the bedroom."*

Order and hierarchy

Liberals and conservatives are divided on a wide variety of issues, but none more so than their attitude towards social order and hierarchy. For liberals, there is **no natural hierarchy** within society stemming from ascribed status. It is only via open competition on the basis of genuine equality of opportunity that the best people will emerge. Thus within liberal thought, there is a deep-seated commitment to **meritocracy**. Notions of aristocracy, the hereditary principle and the idea that an elite has a natural God-given right to power have no place within liberal ideology. Liberals have consistently been prepared to challenge the *ancien regime* in order to maximise the concept of liberty within society. Allied to a firm belief in individualism, liberals contend that hierarchy within society can only derive from concepts such as equality of opportunity and meritocracy. Moreover, those who hold political power must be held to account for their actions and derive their authority not from tradition or religion but from the consent of the governed. It is *only* via the route of consent that power and authority can be exercised in a legitimate manner. Consistent with this view, liberals from all political parties have consistently argued in favour of parliamentary reform. For example, the Liberal government of the early-20th century significantly curtailed the power of the unelected House of Lords, and during the 2005 election the Liberal Democrats campaigned in favour of an elected second chamber. The party also pledged to reduce the voting age to 16, extend primary legislative powers to the devolved assemblies, reform the voting system for Westminster from FPTP to STV (Single Transferable Vote) and to transfer powers held by unelected QUANGOs (Quasi-Non Governmental Organisations) to elected councillors.

Whilst liberals clearly belong on the **libertarian axis**, they differ to anarchists on the issue of order and hierarchy. Unlike anarchists (see Chapter 6), liberals believe that hierarchy and authority are a necessary condition of a free and liberal society. Thomas Paine spoke for liberals everywhere when he described government as *"a necessary evil,"* as did John Locke when he said *"wherever law ends, tyranny begins."* No anarchist could support either statement. For liberals, there will always be a hierarchy within society. Crucially, those with power must be held to account for their actions and must derive their authority from the people via the electoral process. Furthermore, power must be dispersed within society so that decisions are taken at the lowest-possible level on the basis of decentralisation. This is to avoid the abuse of power and thereby protect individual liberty from an authoritarian government.

As with hierarchy, the liberal stance on social order is unequivocal and rooted in the core assumptions of liberalism. Individualism and diversity must always come before social conformity, and the state must always side with individual rights. Authoritarian measures by the government can *only* be justified if they protect and uphold liberty in some manner. For instance, curtailment of civil liberties may be justified during times of war or when there exists a major threat to basic freedoms. However, the activities of the state must always be constrained by the desire to maximise the concept of liberty. So whereas the state is entirely justified in maintaining an army and a police force, the state must also respect people's privacy, and where ⌐
has a duty to address the threat of terrorism, the rights of indivi⌐
that society must always come first. In practice, striking the co⌐
between ensuring order and upholding civil liberties is a diffi⌐

act. One of the clearest illustrations of the need to balance social order against the need to protect civil liberties in the contemporary era is ID cards. Under the government's scheme an individual's right to privacy would be lost via the National Identity Register, a scheme which *will soon become part of the fabric of British life* according to the Home Office minister Liam Byrne. For liberals, opposition to ID cards is a matter of principle. It is illiberal to base the relationship between the state and the individual in such a manner, and those arguments put in favour of ID cards by the government hold little credibility amongst true liberals. Liberals do not share the government's view that ID cards will curb illegal immigration or reduce the number of bogus asylum seekers entering the country. Moreover, terrorists are highly unlikely to be deterred by ID cards. In fact, they may even take glory in people remembering their name – particularly if they are suicide bombers. On a more prosaic level, the scheme may make criminals out of those who either refuse to take out a card or (more plausibly) forget to amend their card. Finally, the argument that *"if you have nothing to hide, you have nothing to fear"* would never persuade a liberal. To quote the Longrider Blog on ID cards; *"Let me make this clear; my identity is just that, mine. It is not yours, it is not the state's, it is mine and mine alone. It is up to me to decide who will be privy to information about that identity. I will not, absolutely not, be fingerprinted like a criminal in order to satisfy your obsessive control freakery. This is not negotiable."*

Change or the status quo

For the purpose of clarity, the term status quo needs to be placed into its proper context. By status quo we mean the structure and workings of a liberal democratic system. By implication, one can also consider the stance taken by that ideology on reforming the existing system. As one would expect, liberals are deeply committed to the maintenance of a liberal democratic system. The main issue for liberals is the extent to which Britain conforms to the eight elements of a liberal democracy. On the issue of change, liberals are highly **supportive of reform** on the basis of greater political freedom and a more progressive society. Unlike conservatives, liberals tend to be optimistic about the prospects of reform, and many socially progressive policies are fundamentally shaped by liberal ideology. Liberals would also like to go much further along the path of democratic reform and thereby reinforce the concepts of freedom and liberty within a political system.

In the context of the UK there is much that would please a true liberal. The UK is a liberal democracy and capitalism reigns supreme as the dominant economic system of our time. Nonetheless, when we probe deeper there are significant elements of the UK system that a true liberal would oppose. For example, the Liberal Democrats are deeply committed towards electoral and parliamentary reform. Although the party was largely supportive of many of the libertarian measures taken by the Labour government during their first parliamentary term (1997-2001), the Lib Dems have become increasingly critical of the present government. For example, the Lib Dems have pledged to give more powers to the devolved assemblies and wish to locate decision-making power to the lowest possible level. Secondly, the party wishes to strengthen the Human Rights Act and the Freedom of Information Act, two of the most important constitutional reforms implemented by the Labour government. Thirdly, the party is supportive of electoral reform at Westminster – a move that would profoundly alter the character of party politics in the United Kingdom. In all these areas, the Liberal Democrats reflect the liberal belief in the dispersal of power away from the centre and support for a much more open political process. Greater regional autonomy and decentralisation have always been the hallmarks of liberal thought.

Liberalism's inherent optimism about human nature underpins their attitude towards reform. For liberals, the political structure can *and should* be improved on the basis of the fundamental principle of greater democracy. On this point, there is a very clear distinction between a liberal and a conservative. Whereas liberals believe that things can always be improved, it could reasonably be argued that conservatives base their approach upon a concern that things are likely to get worse.

Liberalism in contemporary politics

Liberalism is the **predominant** political ideology within contemporary politics and most academics would date the end of the cold war as the beginning of liberal hegemony (Fukayama, 1992). The defeat of Communism was a hugely significant historical event, and the resultant triumph of liberal democracy and capitalism remains the most profoundly important ideological event of recent times. Liberal values of individualism, tolerance, diversity, choice and personal freedom triumphed over Marxist concepts such as class solidarity, the dictatorship of the proletariat and an economic system based upon common ownership of the means of production. The woeful shortcomings of a planned economy and a closed society were graphically exposed via the Western media as the cold war came to an end. A truly epic contest for the very future of humankind between Communism and liberal democracy was won decisively by the latter. Today, most countries in the world could be described as either liberal democracies or in possession of many of the characteristics of liberal democracy, and liberal values have rarely been as widespread as they are today. Furthermore, capitalism is undoubtedly the foremost economic system within the global economy. Indeed, it is no exaggeration to say that we inhabit a world dominated by liberal values. Those parts of the world that do not in some way adopt to liberal values, or remain outside the globalised economy (such as North Korea), are very much in the minority. Whilst it would be going too far to claim that *"we are all liberals now,"* a great many of us within the world live in countries that could be categorised as liberal democracies. The majority of the world's population now live under democratic rule, a situation unthinkable even a generation ago. Moreover, capitalism is such a dominant economic system that to a significant extent there is no real economic alternative within the world today. From North America to South America, from Europe to Asia, from Africa to Australasia we are truly living in the era of **globalisation**.

Globalisation could be said to consist of four interconnected elements – the rapid growth in international trade, an increasingly flexible labour force, a significant increase in the power of Multi-National Companies (MNCs) and the ultimate victory of capitalism over a planned economic system. Whilst globalisation is not entirely new, the speed and extent of globalisation undoubtedly is. Whereas some commentators have claimed that globalisation represents *"old wine in new bottles,"* no-one denies its significance towards our understanding of world politics. As a process, globalisation is unquestionably the most momentous development of the modern era. There are several implications of this process for all the ideologies we will consider throughout. For now, it is sufficient to state that the process of globalisation entirely vindicates the core tenants of liberal thought. For example, the spectacular growth of India and China demonstrates the superiority of the free market over a statist approach to economic management. In both countries, the liberalisation of the economy under Deng Xiaping (China) and Manmohan Singh (India) is widely created with the rapid emergence of those economies. It is hard to refute the claim that the free market generates a level of wealth unobtainable under a planned economic system. Moreover, the spread of political freedoms to those parts of the world that had for many years suffered under the darkness of tyrannical regimes may well have created a more peaceful and prosperous world. Furthermore, the emphasis upon individual rights has proved itself to be a far more popular system than anything produced by ideologies based upon collectivist notions of social class (socialism) or national unity (fascism).

In the specific context of British politics, the two main parties have moved away from the ideological polarisation of the 1980s towards a more centrist approach. The shift towards the centre-ground undoubtedly reflects

The Definitive Guide to Political Ideologies

the predominance of liberal values within the political process. Nowhere is this clearer than in the case of the Labour party. After the electoral disasters of the 1980s the party eschewed many of its left-wing ideas and policies for an avowedly centrist position. Crucially, the party leadership has accepted the inevitability of globalisation and has in no sense attempted to reverse this trend. Revealingly, the adaptation of liberal values and policies by left-of-centre parties has also occurred throughout Western Europe (including France, Germany, Sweden and Italy). The shift within the Conservative party is more recent in origin, but it is clearly the case that the party is more centrist than at any time in recent history. Both main parties could therefore be described as liberal in their policy stance, and it is increasingly the case that British politics is becoming more consensus-minded. Perversely, this cross-party consensus actually limits the level of choice available to the electorate and undermines the market of ideas notion that reflects the importance liberals place upon pluralism. This phenomenon is particularly noticeable within American politics, where the Presidential campaign is more about the candidates than any noticeable ideological difference between the two main parties.

It would of course be very easy to overstate the extent to which both main parties are liberal. The increasingly authoritarian policies of the Labour government have undoubtedly angered many liberals, and the Conservative party is too traditional and moralistic on subjects such as multiculturalism and marriage to satisfy liberal sensibilities. Nonetheless, British politics is to a very significant extent dominated by the core tenants of liberal ideology. Whilst the Liberal Democrats remain highly unlikely to form a government, the political process itself is deeply influenced by liberal values.

Further quotes on liberalism

"Habeas corpus is the golden thread that links the Human Rights Act of 1998 with Magna Carta." Shami Chakrabarti

"The liberty of speaking and writing ... guards our other liberties." Thomas Jefferson

"I don't know exactly what democracy is. But we need more of it." Anonymous Chinese students during protests at Tiananmen Square in 1989

"The people of England regards itself as free but it is grossly mistaken; it is free only during the election of members of parliament. As soon as they are elected, slavery overtakes it." Jean-Jacques Rousseau

"All errors which a man is likely to commit against advice and warning are far outweighed by the evil of allowing others to constrain him for what they deem to be his own good." John Stuart Mill

"Globalisation is really about the transformation of space and time." Sir Anthony Giddens

"There is more to democracy than voting once every five years." Shami Chakrabarti

"A liberal is a conservative who has just been arrested." Tom Wolfe

"If a free society cannot help the many who are poor, it cannot save the few who are rich." John F. Kennedy

"The government of an exclusive company of merchants is, perhaps, the worst of all governments for any country whatsoever." Adam Smith

"To elect and to reject is the prerogative of a free people." Thomas Paine

"Freedom is how free your opponent is." Rosa Luxembourg

"You only have power over people as long as you don't take everything from them. But when you've robbed a man of everything he's no longer in your power – he's free again." Alexander Solzhenitsyn

Recommended reading

Atkins, C. (2007) *Taking liberties since 1997.* A detailed account of how the Labour government has eroded civil liberties since gaining power in 1997. Atkins takes a critical view of how the government has continually manipulated public anxieties over terrorism and crime in order to adopt illiberal policies.

Friedman, M. (1980) *Free to Choose: A Personal Statement.* A bold declaration of classical liberalism written at a time when governments in the UK and the US were actively engaged in a concerted attempt to roll back the frontiers of the state.

Friedman, T. (2005) *The World is Flat – A brief history of the twentieth century.* A detailed exploration of globalisation and its impact upon the economy and society. As with all liberals, Friedman takes a highly positive view of globalisation.

Goldberg, J. (2008) *Liberal Fascism.* A persuasive critique of the closed mentality of so-called liberals. Goldberg claims that an unquestioning mentality has build up around liberalism, and that liberals have been notably illiberal in their actions.

Hobhouse, L.T. (1911) *Liberalism.* One of the most influential accounts of social liberalism at a time when such ideas were beginning to replace the classical strand of liberalism.

Keynes, J.M. (1973) *The General Theory of Employment, Interest and Money.* Perhaps Keynes's most important work, this book is a timely account of how a significant degree of state intervention can resolve the scourge of unemployment. In order to properly assess the significance of his work it is important to place *'the General Theory'* in its proper historical context.

Locke. J. (1690) *Two Treatises on government.* The most important contribution within liberal ideology towards the social contract between the citizens and the state. Locke's work remains a template for the liberal perspective upon the role of the state and its relationship to liberty.

Mill, J.S. (1859) *On Liberty.* The most important contribution within liberal ideology from arguably the most influential liberal theorist of all-time. Mill's book remains a forceful expression of liberalism and is absolutely essential towards an understanding of liberalism.

Paine, T. (1791) *Rights of Man.* An epoch-defining work that did much to advance a more radical form of liberalism. Paine's work is primarily concerned with the need for a constitution and the importance of limiting the role of the state.

Popper, K. (1962) *The Open Society and its Enemies Volume 2 Hegel and Marx.* One of the most cogent arguments against the closed society of totalitarian regimes. Popper's work is not an easy read, but his arguments are delivered with moral clarity and great force.

Raab, D. (2009) *The Assault on Liberty : What went wrong with rights.* A right-wing critique of how the Labour government has undermined the whole notion of rights. Raab is also critical of judicial activism and the compensation culture; both of which tend to inflate the actual meaning of rights.

Rawls, J. (1971) *A Theory of Justice.* A philosophical account of the relationship between liberalism and social justice. Rawls is also championed by social democrats as well as liberals. In order to really understand Rawls one needs to contrast his work with Robert Nozick.

Smith, A. (1776) *The Wealth of Nations.* Despite the somewhat ponderous nature of the book, the Wealth of Nations remains one of the most seminal contributions to classical liberalism.

Tawney, R.H. (1969) *Equality.* Tawney's work is a persuasive account of social liberalism. His ideas have experienced something of a revival since the credit crunch.

Ideas for further discussion

What do liberals mean by the term liberty?
How do liberals view human nature?
What are the key differences between classical liberalism and social
    liberalism?
    Why are liberals divided over the role of the state?
In what sense are liberals opposed to equality?
Why are liberals supportive of the concept of liberal democracy?
What limits would liberals place upon individualism?
Why do liberals adopt a stance of moral relativism in relation to lifestyle
    issues?
To what extent are liberals opposed to the status quo?
To what extent is liberalism the dominant ideology within political
    discourse?

Key terms

Accountability A key concept within a liberal democracy consisting of
two related elements. The first element is where elected representatives are
answerable to the people. Accountability also consists of the government
facing scrutiny by elected representatives within the legislature, such as via
the committee system.

Big Brother society A term derived from the English author George Orwell
and his dystopian vision of society as outlined in '*1984.*' As the name clearly
implies, a Big Brother society has a wholly negative connotation. Recent
attempts by the government to curtail civil liberties and thereby implement
a tough approach to law and order have been criticised as a discernible shift
towards a Big Brother society (Raab, 2009; Atkins, 2007). The inherent
tension between order and liberty is a complex one for any government to
address, with major implications for the society we live in.

Capitalism An economic system based on the market forces of supply and
demand, private ownership and minimal state intervention. Virtually all
countries within the globalised economy could be classed as capitalist, although
the extent to which the economy is run on this basis differs considerably.
During the cold war, the economic system of capitalism was in ideological
conflict with Communism. Capitalism and liberal democracy triumphed in
the cold war and – according to the American theorist Francis Fukayama - we

The Definitive Guide to Political Ideologies

have now reached the *"end of ideology."*

Equality of opportunity Where individuals are provided with an equal chance in life regardless of social class, ethnicity, age, gender, sexuality or religion. All the main political parties support moves towards equality of opportunity, but the means by which they wish to achieve this goal differ considerably.

Freedom An expression of individual liberty closely aligned to the notion of a democratic society. In common with other democratic societies, Britain is a relatively free country. However, there are laws which limit our freedom in order to protect us from those who wish to do harm. The concept of freedom is strong within relatively open societies such as the UK, in which democratic ideals are upheld via the legal system and underpinned by societal norms and values.

Individualism A political stance applied to those who place an emphasis upon the individual as opposed to the collective. For example, the ideology of liberalism places the individual at the centre of its entire political philosophy.

Laissez-faire economics An economic system based upon the free market and minimal state intervention and derived from the French term translated at *"leave alone."* Critics of laissez-faire economics point out that an unfettered and unregulated market contributes to high levels of inequality and an unstable economic system (as in the case of major banks lending exorbitant amounts of loans in recent years, thereby contributing to the credit crunch that emerged during 2007). The most ardent supporters of this economic approach are classical liberals. Those on the left of the political spectrum are usually opposed to laissez-faire economies, believing state regulation to be a prerequisite of a fairer society.

Liberal democracy A synergy of two political concepts; 'liberal' freedoms alongside a 'democratic' method of electing representatives and the governing party. This democratic method involves periodic competitive elections in which almost all adults are entitled to vote. A liberal democracy is therefore liberal in the sense that the power of decision-makers is limited, and democratic in the sense that there is competition for power between politicians and political parties.

Mixed economy An economic system with a sizeable element of the private sector and the public sector. During the Keynesian era, governments operated on this basis. A mixed economy is most closely associated with social liberalism.

Moral relativism The view that one set of morals is no better or worse than another. Moral relativism is a manifestation of liberal views on lifestyle issues. Those on the right of the political spectrum believe in moral absolutism.

Open government The widespread availability of official records and official information to the general public. In a liberal democracy, it is argued that the public have the right to access information from the government. The aim of the Freedom of Information Act 2000 was to facilitate a more open form of government.

Participatory democracy A form of democracy in which citizens are actively involved in the decision-making process. John Locke favoured a form of participatory democracy in order to facilitate the moral betterment of individuals.

Pluralism A political philosophy influenced by liberalism in which power is dispersed within society amongst a variety of organisations. The dispersal of power avoids the creation of a dictatorship and helps to ensure that power is used for the good of society as opposed to one social group / ruling class. Pluralism is a key concept within a liberal democracy.

Rights An entitlement held by an individual or group. The concept of rights is related to the idea of responsibilities, or duties. For example the right to life involves a duty or responsibility not to take away another person's right to life. If you do end someone's life, you will have your rights and freedoms taken away via prison or capital punishment. There are many different types of rights – such as positive rights, legal rights, negative rights and moral rights.

Utilitarianism A political philosophy associated with 19th century liberal philosopher Jeremy Bentham. The most significant element of utilitarianism is the goal of attaining *"the greatest happiness for the greatest number."* To its supporters, a society based upon utilitarianism would provide the basis for a liberal utopia. To its critics, utilitarianism provides leaders with the ability to discriminate against minorities in order to protect the interests of the majority. For example, John Rawls believed that the application of utilitarianism to the concept of justice and fairness would always lead to majorities winning out over minorities. John Stuart Mill was also deeply concerned about the problems presented by the *"tyranny of the majority"* when trying to apply utilitarianism in practise.

Chapter 2
Conservatism

The core elements of conservatism

Conservatism is unique within the family of political ideologies. Unlike any other ideology, most conservatives would describe their political beliefs as a **state of mind** as opposed to an ideology in itself. It is from this distinctive basis that conservatism gains much of its character and content. In the words of the American political theorist Russell Kirk; conservatism is *"the negation of ideology."* Nonetheless, there are several core elements of conservatism we can readily identify.

As argued in Chapter 1, *all* ideologies are based upon an assumption of some kind. By far the most important premise within conservatism is that human beings are **irrational** and prone to aggressive and competitive behaviour. There is a chasm of difference between a liberal and a conservative on the absolutely fundamental issue of how to conceptualise human nature. Naturally, there are major implications that derive from conservatism's **pessimistic** stance on human nature. Their Weltanschauung on human nature presents a prism through which conservatives interpret the associated interaction of human behaviour. Consequently, the entire language and epistemological

Core elements
Pessimistic view of human nature
Belief in pragmatism
Organic view of society
Tradition
Importance of social order

tone of conservatism stands in complete contrast to liberalism. For example, conservatives refute the liberal view that individuals are rational actors who should be entrusted with as much freedom as possible. Conservatives also reject the liberal claim that society is a mass of autonomous individuals who should pursue self-regarding actions, as this will inevitably lead to selfish individualism in which people act with little or no regard for others. According to conservatives, the liberal emphasis upon tolerance and diversity will weaken – rather than strengthen - societal bonds. Conservatism can therefore be understood as the very antithesis of rationalist-based ideologies such as liberalism.

Conservatism centres upon a number of fundamental values, the most important of which is a belief in the virtues of **pragmatism**. There is a firm rejection of idealistic and untested projects such as the common ownership of the means of production, religious fundamentalism and the totalitarian democracy of fascism. Ideological dogma shaped by abstract reason is complete anathema to conservatives. In the words of the conservative theorist Michael Oakshott; *"to be a Conservative is to prefer the tried to the untried."* More than *any* other ideology, conservatism is a state of mind rooted upon a sense of tradition. Ultimately, conservatives tend to perceive themselves as the ones who uphold common sense values. However, this has not stopped conservatives employing abstract principles – such as authority and the free market – when considered practical to do so.

Another crucial element of conservatism is their **organic view of society**. As with other ideologies of the right, conservatism states that society is an organism which is constantly evolving. On the issue of change, politicians should always reflect upon the past and avoid implementing measures that mark a radical break with the traditions of that society. Utopian projects that promise a brave new world have absolutely no place within conservatism. In stark contrast to the more radical ideologies (such as Marxism, feminism and anarchism), conservatives are deeply sceptical of grandiose projects that go against existing social conventions. Conservatives also fundamentally disagree with feminists over the issue of gender relationships. Whereas feminists wish to change society due to the exploitative nature of the conventional nuclear family and the traditional mores of marriage, conservatives firmly believe that gender differences are both natural and inevitable. The conservative mindset is therefore deeply rooted in an organic view of society, which leads onto a preference for tradition and a degree of continuity with the past. Evolution, not revolution, is the watchword of a true conservative.

Conservatives firmly believe that society must preserve those institutions that have proved their worth from one generation to the next. As a consequence, conservatives are highly supportive of **traditional institutions** that reflect a nation's heritage (such as the Monarchy, the Church and the Constitution). Indeed, it is revealing to note that the term conservatism derives from the Latin *com servare* ("to preserve"). The conservative stance on the issue of reform presents a particularly sharp distinction from almost all other ideologies. According to conservatives, change is only advisable in order to strengthen and maintain those institutions.

Finally, all conservatives believe strongly in the importance of **order**. Without order, human beings would revert to a state of nature in which life would be *"solitary, poor, nasty, brutish and short"* and characterised by *"a war of all against all"* (according to the 17th century English philosopher Thomas Hobbes). Conservatives argue that those things which people have always cherished depend upon the maintenance of order within society. The very purpose of politics should therefore be to ensure social harmony. Those institutions that uphold harmony within society – such as the Church and the Monarchy – must be preserved in order to maintain social order. In short, social order is the leitmotif of conservatism. Revealingly, this is an observation which can be applied to conservatives in either a democracy or a dictatorship.

Conservatism can therefore be understood as a habit of mind centred upon a number of assumptions, the most important of which is a pessimistic attitude towards human nature. Secondly, pragmatism is always superior to a doctrinaire approach driven by a fervent ideological belief-system. There is also an unwavering belief amongst conservatives that society is an organism underpinned by an invisible contract between different generations. As the father of conservatism Edmund Burke (1729–1797) famously declared, society is a *"partnership not only between those who are living, but between those who are living, those who are dead, and those who are to be born. Each contract of each particular state is but a clause in the great primeval contract of eternal society."* In order to ensure order and social harmony, conservatives claim that we must uphold and defend those institutions and values that have proved their worth from one generation to another. Each generation is the custodian of accumulated wisdom, and each generation has a solemn duty to uphold and pass on that wisdom to the next generation.

The conservative perspective on human nature

Unlike liberals, conservatives are **pessimistic** about human nature. Conservatives also differ to socialists in their understanding of human nature. For conservatives, human nature is an immutable notion and therefore characterised by a set of factors that remain constant regardless of the economic or political system in question. We must therefore accept human imperfection and be prepared for it. It is this pessimism about human nature that provides conservatives with much of their ideological ballast. The habit of mind associated with conservatism rests firmly upon the need to keep human nature in check because of man's capacity for evil. Naturally, there are several implications to consider, the most important of which concerns the issue of order within society.

For conservatives, social order is of fundamental importance. Without the firm smack of government and a robust criminal justice system human beings would act in a hostile manner. Based on this important point, conservative politicians have consistently presented themselves as 'tough' on the issue of law and order. Conservatives also present themselves as hawkish on matters of foreign policy - following Edmund Burke's argument that we can only avoid war by restraining the various disorders that give rise to it – and routinely describe liberals as naïve in terms of their perspective upon human nature. For conservatives, it is foolish of liberals to centre their ideological stance so firmly upon an optimistic view of human nature.

Secondly, human nature **cannot** be transformed. A radical / revolutionary overhaul of the economic system will not diminish mankind's aggressive instincts and a totalitarian system based upon Communism would be a disaster because the political system would provide no check whatsoever upon the power of decision-makers (a point borne out by the experience of several Communist regimes throughout history). Furthermore, change on the basis of a liberal belief in co-operation amongst nation-states will not in itself make the world a more peaceful place – as the League of Nations and the United Nations have repeatedly shown. For a conservative, we should always be pessimistic about human nature. Political and social institutions must accept this truism and adopt accordingly. For example, we must have a strong and effective police force to ensure law and order within society, and in the context of foreign policy *all* conservatives would agree with the 4th century AD Roman military figure Vegetius who declared *"Let him who desires peace, prepare for war."* Idealistic and utopian projects based on fraternity, enlightenment values or fascism can never change the fundamental character of human nature, no matter how virtuous their intention. In the words of the German philosopher Immanuel Kant (1724-1804); *"from the crooked timber of humanity no straight thing was ever made."*

The third implication to consider here is that human behaviour is shaped by a degree of **competition**. Politicians must always recognise the power of self-interest over altruism, and any political or economic system that fails to recognise this important point is doomed to fail. Rather than trying to change human nature, the political and economic system must go with the grain of human nature. As such, conservatives are more favourable towards capitalism than any other economic alternative and prefer democracy over any other political system. Yet unlike liberals, they do not believe that democracy or capitalism is perfect, merely that both systems have shown themselves over time to be preferable to all other attempted alternatives. Moreover, conservatives have historically favoured a 'safety net' to provide for the less well-off. Unlike classical liberals, most conservatives claim that the state should be prepared for market failure and deal with it accordingly. Indeed, some of the most enthusiastic supporters of protectionism derive from the mindset of conservatism. This argument is more closely associated with the one-nation school of thought, a point that will be developed further in the next section.

As previously argued, whatever perspective is taken upon human nature it cannot be proven in any objective sense. It is also debateable whether or not there is such a phenomenon as human nature – a point discussed in greater depth by the French theorist Michel Foucault (1926-1984). Nonetheless, this does not allow us to discard the importance of human nature towards an understanding of political ideology. The point to remember is that liberals base their Weltanschauung upon an optimistic view, whereas the mindset of conservatism centres firmly upon a pessimistic stance. How to interpret and conceptualise human nature is of course a vital aspect of *any* ideology and in turn provides a rich source of ideas within Politics.

The main strands of conservatism

There are **two** main strands of conservatism – the **New Right** and the **one nation** school of thought. Of the two, the latter has been the most influential within British politics. Only during the 1970s and 1980s did the New Right have any notable impact upon the Conservative party and the wider political process. Since the 1990s, the New Right perspective has become less fashionable within the party itself, although this is by no means the trend within other countries. For example in the United States, the Republican Party adopts a strong element of New Right thinking.

The defining element of the one nation school of though can be summarised in one word; pragmatism. Followers of this particular strand of conservatism pride themselves on their **non-dogmatic** and **common sense** approach to politics. They claim that the core values and objectives of conservatism can only be achieved via a practical and non-ideological methodology. Unlike the New Right, one-nation adherents are characterised by a distinctly practical mindset (as opposed to a more right-wing ideological stance) and a degree of flexibility in their approach to politics. Due to the dominance of the one nation school of thought, conservatism itself is often characterised by a pragmatic attitude.

The second aspect of the one-nation school is the desire for **social harmony**. Whilst this goal is also shared by the New Right perspective, the very phrase *"one-nation"* reflects the centrality of social harmony to this particular school of thought. In order to secure harmony within society, one-nation conservatives strongly support those traditions and institutions that uphold the very fabric of society. It is highly unwise for a government or politician to ignore that which binds us together within a society. Based on this viewpoint, a number of one-nation Tories were critical of the radical policies implemented during Mrs. Thatcher's premiership (1979-1990). The one-nation school of thought is much closer to the writings of Edmund Burke than the New Right perspective, particularly his astute observation that *"the people have no interest in disorder."* Whereas Thatcher's period in office was characterised by ideological conflict with left-wing social groups (such as trade unions), one-nation Tories have often sought compromise with their ideological opponents in order to maintain balance and harmony within society.

An inter-related element of the one-nation school is the search for a **middle way**. In avoiding the extremes of a command economy and an unfettered free market, the middle way aims to gain the best of both worlds and ensure a degree of social harmony and stability. This approach gained much of its intellectual basis from moderate conservatives such as Hilaire Belloc, who in his seminal text *'The Servile State'* argued that both capitalism and socialism enslaved the masses. This particular aspect of one-nation conservatism was prevalent during the 1950s and early 60s, particularly under the Tory Prime Minister Harold MacMillan (1966). This pragmatic approach played a significant role in the party reaching out beyond its core electoral base. By presenting conservatism as the sensible alternative to the extremities of the political spectrum, MacMillan employed a strategy that paid impressive electoral dividends for him and his party. This moderate approach to conservatism was also exemplified in America under Dwight Eisenhower, in Germany under Konrad Adenauer and in France under Charles de Gaulle. It is here that one can trace further evidence for Russell Kirk's earlier observation that conservatism is the negation (or repudiation) of ideology.

The conservative preference towards a middle way could also be described as a reaction against political extremism. One of the most important intellectual contributions to this argument derives from the Austrian philosopher Karl Popper (1962) in *'the Open Society and its enemies.'* He argued that both Communism and fascism claimed to be in possession of the ultimate

	One-nation Tories	**The New Right**
Ideological axis	Centre-right	Further to the right than the one-nation school of thought
The welfare state	Provide a safety net	It creates a dependency culture and should be rolled back
Economic policy	Middle way between capitalism and socialism	Free-market capitalism
Key figures	Disraeli, Peel, MacMillan	Hayek, Thatcher, Rand

truth, and since the ultimate truth is beyond human understanding, both ideologies needed to distort reality in order to impose their ideas. Popper also claimed that institutions should recognise that a plurality of interests must be facilitated within an open society. In doing so, we can better understand the world around us. In contrast, a society based upon one universal truth cannot facilitate such understanding because it would refuse to allow any idea or argument to exist that undermines the basis of that particular ideology. The notion that one overriding theory is in possession of truth was also rejected by Isaiah Berlin. As someone who witnessed the Russian Revolution - and experienced German fascism as a Jew – Berlin claimed that totalitarian notions inevitably lead to mass slaughter.

It should be fairly obvious that there is a degree of overlap here between conservatism *and* liberalism. A common argument to both ideologies is that political extremism is intimately related to violence and the concentration of power. Sheer paranoia has also fuelled such leaders in the absence of anyone who might challenge their world-view. Even something as seemingly inoffensive as Mickey Mouse was banned in Communist countries because of its association with Western propaganda. In another example, the Romanian dictator Nicolae Ceauşescu (1918-1989) ordered the authorities to monitor his own children and all the members of his (and his wife's) family. He also employed a chemist to destroy his own excrement so that nobody could test his faeces to discover the state of his health!

The final aspect of the one-nation school derives from their attitude towards the welfare state. Unlike the New Right perspective, one-nation Tories believe that the wealthy have an obligation to those who cannot provide for themselves. It is morally right and entirely sensible for the government to provide for the welfare needs of its citizens. Rather than reverse the substantial increase in welfare provision bequeathed by the Attlee administration (1945-1951), conservatives from the one-nation tradition expanded the role of the welfare state. Increasing the role of the welfare state was based upon a sense of noblesse oblige amongst the Tory elite alongside hard-headed electoral considerations from the perspective of the Conservative party itself. To its supporters, the provision of a **safety net** reflects the notion of **paternalism** – where the state looks after its citizens. This view is not shared by the New Right who argue that any form of compassionate conservatism inevitably leads to big government (as in the case of the George Bush administration from 2000 to 2008).

The New Right is a body of thought that reflects a mixture of right-wing principles alongside a laissez-faire approach to economic policy. Whereas the one-nation school belongs on the centre-right of the political spectrum, the New Right is more hard-line and further away from the centre. Secondly, support within the New Right for the free market reflects a shared ideological ground with classical liberalism. As such, the term *neo*-liberalism is sometimes used to describe the New Right, particularly in American circles. In Britain, the term Thatcherism is also used in reference to its most important political figure.

The New Right emerged as a critique of the one-nation school and offered an alternative to each of the four core aspects of one-nation thought. Of those four elements, the most important from an ideological point of view was the first (pragmatism). As the name clearly implies, adherents to the New Right perspective are unashamedly **right-wing**. For them, pragmatism was merely a means by which the Conservative party acquiesced to the collectivist ethos of the post-war consensus. This point formed a centrepiece of the New Right mission to rescue Britain from creeping socialism. As one of its leading intellectuals (Sir Keith Joseph) boldly proclaimed, he only become a true conservative after the Tories lost office in 1974. According to Joseph and others, the Conservatives during the Heath / MacMillan era had become apologists for big government and state planning. The party needed to return to right-wing principles in order to restore Britain's economic status. Thus unlike the one-nation school, principles must come *before* pragmatism.

The distinction between the two main strands of conservative thought upon the issue of social order is one of *means* as opposed to ends. All conservatives believe that order is of paramount importance within society. Yet unlike the one-nation approach, the New Right believe that the Tories should maintain a set of core **principles** rather than seeking some watered-down compromise. This point was echoed most visibly on the issue of trade unions. Tories of the one-nation tradition believed that Conservative governments must co-operate with trade unions in order to ensure a degree of balance within society. The New Right however saw the trade unions as the source of Britain's problems. Spiralling wage inflation, a rigid labour market and an unworkable prices and incomes policy had lead to governments being increasingly dictated to by powerful union leaders. Only by weakening the role of the unions could Britain become economically competitive. If that meant confrontation with the unions, then that was the inevitable battle that needed to be won, a point graphically illustrated during the 1984 / 1985 Miners Strike.

The New Right perspective emerged during the mid-1970s, although its intellectual roots can be traced back further (Hayek, 1944). The core argument of the New Right was that previous Conservative governments had done nothing to roll back the frontiers of the state. In searching for a middle way, one-nation Tories had acquiesced to the spread of socialism within Britain. Each period of post-war Labour government had increased public expenditure, and Conservative governments had done much the same when in office. The Conservatives should therefore renounce their search for the middle way in order to reverse the exponential increase in the role of the state. One of the clearest examples of this point was **privatisation**. To one-nation Tories such as Harold MacMillan, the transfer of assets from the public sector to the private sector was akin to selling the family silver. To those from the New Right, privatisation secured a number of important objectives. First and foremost, it reduced the level of public expenditure. This helped to reduce the level of direct taxation and thereby stimulate economic activity. Secondly, it exposed previously state-owned industries to a greater level of competition. This helped to reduce prices and improve the level of choice available to the consumer. Few other policies are as clearly associated with the New Right perspective as privatisation. Furthermore, some figures on the New Right have even described taxation as a form of *"legalised theft."* It is here that we see why the New Right also goes under the label of *neo*-liberalism. It is rather fitting that one of the early champions of the New Right (Gerald Ford) paraphrased the classical liberal Thomas Jefferson when he said that *"If the government is big enough to give you everything you want, it is big enough to take away everything you have."* [4]

Unlike one-nation Tories, the New Right school of thought is highly critical of the welfare state. According to the American sociologist Charles Murray (1995) the welfare state creates a ***"dependency culture"*** where individuals are prevented from taking responsibility for their actions. The provision of welfare

---

[4]   Thomas Jefferson had argued that a *"government big enough to supply everything you need is big enough to take everything you have ... The course of history shows that as a government grows, liberty decreases."*

from the cradle to the grave enables the feckless within society to escape responsibility for their actions (including parenthood). The welfare state also makes lifestyles outside the nuclear family financially viable. Murray's arguments were grounded in the pioneering work of Friedrich Hayek (1944), who had warned that an expanding role for the state would lead to servitude for its people. Mrs. Thatcher was greatly influenced by Hayek and clearly agreed with the argument put forward by Murray. She implemented a series of measures designed to promote self-reliance and individual responsibility as an alterative to what she and others saw as dependency upon the state. Others from the New Right perspective argued that the welfare state had destroyed the bonds of mutual assistance amongst the less well-off and replaced it with an impersonal and technocratic bureaucracy. Whereas social liberals and socialists place a certain degree of faith into the hands of technocratic 'experts,' conservatives would concur with Edmund Burke's praise for *"the wisdom of unlettered men."* State provision of our welfare needs also leads to the incremental increase in the so-called *"nanny state."* Such moves represent the slippery road towards socialism and the clarion call for big government. Moreover, the welfare state undermines the traditional role of the family with the male as breadwinner and the female as care giver.

Before moving onto the next section, it might be worth explaining how the New Right differs to classical liberalism. As we have already considered, the New Right is liberal on the issue of economic policy. As with classical liberals, there is a strong preference for **laissez-faire economics.** One of the intellectual champions of the New Right (the Russian-born academic Ayn Rand) expressed this point very clearly. She promoted a moral case for free enterprise as it was the only economic system based on what she called *"objective reason."* She argued that *"the common good of a collective ... was the claim and justification of every tyranny ever established over men. Every major horror of history was committed in the name of an altruistic motive."* The New Right also shares common ground with classical liberals over the need for low direct taxation and their belief in the benefits of the trickle-down effect. According to the logic of the view, cutting the level of direct taxation on high-income earners would stimulate consumer spending and entrepreneurial activity. In the long-run, this would result in wealth cascading down to all income groups.

The New Right is essentially **illiberal** on the subject of lifestyle issues. Unlike liberals, the New Right does not celebrate cultural diversity. As with all conservatives, there is a strong preference for cultural homogeneity and a firm belief in the desirability of the nuclear family. Moral relativism will result in a search for hedonistic pleasure, lead us to ignore our responsibility ers and thereby undermine social cohesion. Society should return to a set of common sense values such as respect for authority and an acceptance of personal responsibility. The New Right (along with other conservatives) argue that a clear moral compass is a fundamental element of society, and that members of that society (particularly parents) need to reassert the immutable difference between right and wrong. In the words of the former Prime Minister John Major *"it is time to get back to basics : to self-discipline and respect for the law, to consideration for others, to accepting responsibility for yourself and your family, and not shuffling it off on the state."* Whilst the New Right accept that the relationship between rights and duties *is* an important one within liberal ideology, they argue that liberals over-emphasise the concept of rights and sideline the notion of responsibilities. Furthermore, the moral relativism of liberals has no place within the New Right perspective. So whereas a New Right conservative would agree with the classical liberal economics of Milton Freidman, they would totally reject some of his more radical libertarian ideas (such as the legalisation of all drugs).

The role of the state

The division between the two main strands of conservatism is stark in relation to the role of the state. For one-nation Tories the state acts as a **neutral arbitrator** within society and its primary function is to maintain social order. The state should not favour one social group over another. In terms of social policy, the state also has a **duty** to take care of all members of society. Crucially, this includes the provision of the welfare needs of those who cannot afford to provide for themselves or their families. The state must also **intervene** in the economy in order to deal with the damaging effects of market failure upon society, particularly in terms of preventing a violent uprising against the state. The government must also protect and preserve those institutions that have proved their worth over time, including the family and the Church. Finally, the state should play a role in **encouraging** those values that hold society together, such as respect for authority.

The New Right is simultaneously liberal *and* authoritarian in terms of how they prescribe a role for the state. In economic terms, the New Right believe as strongly in **capitalism** as any

	New Right perspective
Liberal	"Roll back the frontiers of the state" (Thatcher) Laissez-faire economics
Authoritarian	Firm emphasis upon law and order

classical liberal. Many of the leading lights within the New Right (such as Adam Smith, Milton Friedman, Friedrich Hayek and Ayn Rand) are also championed by classical liberals. In terms of the welfare state, the New Right perspective favours a **reduction** in the role of the state alongside a degree of moral absolutism. New Right scholars such as Charles Murray (1943 -) are critical of the legal neutrality of the welfare state and its failure to discriminate in favour of those families who stay together. As a result, the welfare state enables the underclass within society to escape responsibility for their children. The liberal character of the welfare state also facilitates moral relativism and a set of permissive values. Murray is passionately in favour of a renewed sense of moral vigour to deal with the problems facing American society, and his critique of the welfare state has found fertile ground amongst right-wing figures within the Republican party (such as Ronald Reagan and Pat Buchanan). Murray's argument is also supported by the right-wing academic William Kristol (1964 -) who argues that children born out of wedlock are the single most important social problem facing America whilst the 'liberal' welfare state refuses to discriminate against illegitimate children. Kristol is in favour of re-ordering the principles behind the welfare and taxation system in order to encourage marriage and stable families. In Britain, the impact of New Right ideology over the welfare state has not been as great. Whilst Thatcher instigated a degree of **marketisation** within the welfare state, she did not dismantle it altogether for fear of the electoral consequences.

In terms of law and order, the New Right perspective is firmly authoritarian. Whilst they concur with Lord Acton's famous observation about power, they believe that the state must be strong enough to deal with those forces within society that may undermine law and order. The **firm smack of government** was an important element of Tory governments influenced by New Right ideology, and in terms of how they dealt with the threat of crime and terrorism the Thatcher and Major governments of the 1980s and 1990s angered many liberals. Conservatives from the one-nation school of thought also criticised Tory leaders during that era for their apparent disregard for ancient civil liberties and for appearing to use the state to further their dogmatic cause. There is a certain overlap here between the actions of the Thatcher / Major governments *and* the Blair / Brown years – at least in terms of their authoritarian stance on the issue of law and order.

In order to understand the differences within conservative thought in terms of the role of the state it is useful to consider the historical context of UK politics. The New Right emerged in the mid-1970s when Britain faced significant economic problems. It was a decade characterised by a crippling level of industrial action, spiralling inflation and a significant brain drain due to punitive levels of taxation. The New Right prescribed a set of policies designed to restore Victorian values of thrift, individual responsibility and self-reliance. They argued that the state must no longer protect inefficient industries or try to micromanage the economy with a prices and incomes policy. The unfettered marketplace would allocate resources more effectively than the mixed economy. Within the New Right, great faith was placed upon what the former American President Ronald Reagan called *"the magic of the marketplace."* The same politician also said that *"the most terrifying words in the English language are 'I'm from the government and I'm here to help' "* – a particularly revealing quote in terms of the Weltanschauung of the New Right. But whereas the New Right believed that the role of the state must be curtailed in order for people to enjoy their economic liberty, it must also be strong enough to deal with the multifarious threats to social stability. Mrs. Thatcher's term in office was characterised by an *"authoritarian populism"* (Gamble, 1994) very much in tune with the opinions and prejudices of a significant swathe of the electorate. Over time, the confidence of New Right advocates increased as Thatcher and later Major secured four election victories over the somewhat moribund Labour party. In terms of the role of the state, Britain was transformed from its pre-1979 situation. Yet paradoxically, the proportion of national income taken from taxation barely changed. Under a government heavily influenced by New Right ideology, the level of taxation devoted to the police and the armed forces increased substantially whereas the level of state intervention in the economy drastically declined. The lasting legacy of New Right ideology was therefore a change in the *nature* of the role of the state as opposed to the actual level of state expenditure.

The historical significance of the one-nation school of thought is equally revealing. Conservatives dating back to Benjamin Disraeli and Sir Robert Peel aimed to unite the nation under certain core values such as support for the Empire, a sense of patriotism, support for the Church and a firm preference for traditional social mores. Extending the franchise and providing a safety net in order to mitigate the effects of unemployment were crucial elements of the one-nation perspective in the 19th century. By the 20th century Tory governments had broadly accepted the social democratic structure bequeathed by the Labour government of Clement Attlee, and by the 1950s the MacMillan government was building more council homes *and* putting more taxpayers' money into the socialistic National Health Service than the Attlee government. By the 1970s the one-nation approach had led to excessive state regulation of what the Tory Prime Minister Edward Heath once called the *"unacceptable face of capitalism."* Thus over time, the scope and scale of the state had increased massively under Conservative *and* Labour governments. However, it is important to note that the justification for state intervention differed according to which party was in government.

Whereas Labour were primarily guided by the concepts of social justice and equality, the Conservatives aimed for social harmony and a degree of stability within society. To many one-nation Tories, the unregulated free market was incompatible with fundamental conservative values. The experience of the 1930s had graphically illustrated how capitalism could result in mass unemployment – with the related problems of widespread social unrest and the growth in extremist ideology from both the left and the right.

The division between the New Right and the one-nation school in terms of the role of the state is a source of significant tension within conservative ideology. The Tory governments of Thatcher and Major were substantially different to the Tory governments of the one-nation era. The only shared ground was in terms of the importance of social order and the need for the state to deal with threats to the stability of society. One of the most important conservative philosophers in relation to the role of the state and the issue of social order remains the 17th century English philosopher Thomas Hobbes. He was one of the earliest contract theorists and he outlined a relationship between the people and those in authority that was later developed by the liberal philosopher John Locke. He argued that life in a state of nature was *"solitary, poor, nasty, brutish and short"* and that firm government was required in order to prevent mankind descending into a lawless and anarchic condition because *"covenants, without the sword, are but words."* He prescribed a strong role for the state to prevent this situation from occurring, calling this notion a Leviathan (1651). On close inspection of Leviathan, it is the people who constitute the figure itself. According to Hobbes, the people therefore provide legitimacy for an authoritarian approach to law and order. Moreover, he believed that the people had the right to disobey the authority of the state when their lives were under threat, thereby suggesting that authority is on loan from the people.

The fear of a brutish and anarchic state of nature, and the need for a strong response to those forces and elements which threaten social order, is an important component of the conservative mindset. From the one-nation school of thought Sir Robert Peel was the founder of the modern police force (hence the moniker Bobbies). The New Right perspective is equally uncompromising on the issue of order. Police resources and police powers increased substantially during the 1980s and 1990s with Thatcher herself often reviling in her depiction as *"the Iron Lady."* She also stood firm against the Argentine dictator General Galtieri and the Soviet leaders of the era, ridiculing the Labour party's unilateralist stance on nuclear weapons in a particularly effective campaign poster which showed an army figure adopting the surrender stance with the slogan *'Labour's policy on arms.'*

Conservatism and equality

On the issue of equality, conservatism offers an unequivocal position. Conservatives are firmly **opposed to equality of outcome**. For all strands of conservatism, a society based around the shibboleth of an even distribution of wealth and resources will result in a dystopian nightmare. During the cold war, many of the staunchest opponents of Marxism derived from the conservative perspective (such as Margaret Thatcher, Helmut Kohl and Ronald Reagan).

	Stance on equality
Liberalism	In favour of equality of opportunity
Conservatism	Opposed to equality of outcome, some support for equality of opportunity
Socialism	In favour of a more even distribution of wealth

Measures justified on the basis of equality mean confiscating the wealth of hard-working individuals and families. Such an approach is fuelled by the politics of envy and is ultimately self-defeating. Setting a high level of taxation will undermine economic growth, weaken the propensity for risk-taking amongst those who wish to get on in life and therefore undermine job creation. Many conservatives would agree with Abraham Lincoln's observation that *"You cannot help the poor by destroying the rich. You cannot lift the wage earner by pulling down the wage payer."*

The extent to which conservatives oppose an equitable distribution of wealth differs slightly in terms of what strand of thought we consider. The one-nation school of thought proclaims that some redistribution of wealth may be necessary to hold society together. In the words of the arch-Tory Samuel Johnson; *"a decent provision for the poor is the true test of civilisation."* Leaving the distribution of resources solely to the free market may result in social instability. The state must therefore bridge the gap between the haves and the have-nots in order to ensure we all feel a sense of belonging to society. This argument is attributed to the 19th century statesman Benjamin Disraeli and has to this day endured as a key tenant within conservative thought.

To supporters of the New Right, the provision of a 'safety net' is both unnecessary and undesirable. The welfare state is the cause of many problems within society. For one, it undermines individual responsibility. Benefits are too easy to obtain and too attractive to resist. A hand out is often seen as an entitlement, and claimants very often receive something for nothing. The welfare services are also bureaucratic and a burden on the tax-payer. Most importantly of all, the welfare state creates a *"dependency culture"* which traps people into poverty and therefore forces those families and individuals to become dependant upon the state. Claimants have little or no incentive to return back to work. Far from eradicating want and idleness, the welfare state actually discourages people from finding a job – damaging both the economy and the moral fabric of society. For New Right adherents, the welfare state is a stand-out illustration of the perennial problem facing policies grounded upon social reform; namely that good intentions often lead to perverse consequences. In order to improve the economy the state should leave the economy alone and ignore trying to re-distribute wealth more evenly within society. Welfare benefits should be reduced and become more selective. This would encourage people to work their way out of poverty, perhaps by accepting low wages in order to get back into the job market. Once in employment, the chance to keep most of their money, rather than losing it in tax, would provide a further incentive. This would help reduce the burden on the taxpayer and limit public expenditure. By facilitating tax cuts in the economy the level of consumer spending would rise and thereby generate demand for jobs. A flexible labour market would also improve the UK economy. [5]

The intellectual foundation for the New Right approach to the issue of equality and the distribution of wealth derives from scholars such as Ayn Rand and Robert Nozick, both of whom became very fashionable in right-wing libertarian circles during the 1970s. Ayn Rand argued that the welfare state is based on the mistaken premise that the redistribution of wealth is ethically superior to the free market. She argued that the origins of tyranny and corruption within society lie in the triumph of an altruistic creed and a spurious commitment to universal values. A society based upon individualism is both morally desirable and attainable. In a particularly evocative piece from her work, Rand (1957) warned that *"unless you discover that money is the root of all good, you ask for your own destruction. When money ceases to become the means by which men deal with one another, then men become the tools of other men. Blood, whips and guns or dollars. Take your choice – there is no other."* This right-wing libertarian stance was supported by Robert Nozick in his influential work *'Anarchy, State and Utopia'* (1974). He argued that progressive taxation violates the crucial principle that individuals ought to be seen as ends, treating them as means to the goals of equality and social justice. Such thinking guided the New Right's critique of those measures designed to implement socialism within society, particularly in terms of taxation.

---

[5] Even with far-reaching changes to welfare policy over recent years, the working poor can still find themselves in a worse financial situation than if they remain on benefits, and the system itself can incentivise claimants to stay on welfare.

The Definitive Guide to Political Ideologies

The conservative stance on the issue of equality has been subject to heavy criticism. Geoffrey Madan spoke for many on the left of the political spectrum when he described the *"Conservative ideal of freedom and progress* [as] *everyone to have an unfettered opportunity of remaining exactly where they are."* Others believe that an over-reliance upon the unfettered marketplace will result in unacceptable levels of poverty, a heightened sense of job insecurity and a significant gap between rich and poor. This argument was prevalent during the Thatcher era when the level of relative poverty and the gap between rich and poor substantially increased. Even one-nation Tories voiced objection to the North-South divide that was such a feature of British society at a time when New Right ideology was very much in vogue. Whatever views one has upon the rightward turn taken by Thatcher and her supporters during that time, it is unquestionably the case that governments no longer place as high a priority upon an equitable distribution of wealth as they did before Mrs. Thatcher came to power in 1979. As one of the main architects of the new Labour project (Peter Mandelson) memorably observed soon after Labour came to power in 1997, *"I am intensely relaxed about people getting filthy rich."*

On the issue of equality of opportunity, conservatives are also very clear. In the words of the British politician Iain Macleod; **"equality of opportunity means equal opportunity to be unequal."** Whilst conservatives fully acknowledge the virtue of equality of opportunity they also believe that society is profoundly unequal, and any attempt by the state to provide a more even distribution of life chances should be undertaken with considerable caution. State intervention in the name of equality of opportunity can *only* be justified if it upholds other objectives such as social order. Decision-makers must keep in mind that measures designed to ensure a more equitable degree of representation are merely another form of discrimination. As such, conservatives tend to oppose those measures taken under the guise of affirmative action (or positive discrimination). Opposition is particularly strong in the United States, where such measures often raise fears amongst white people at losing out to people from ethnic minorities in the job market. In the UK, the Conservative party claims to favour equality of opportunity but is sceptical about the supposed merits of state intervention to ensure a fairer distribution of life chances. The voluntary sector is often championed as the route by which to help people escape a life of poverty.

Conservatives of both main strands of thought believe that society is characterised by a **significant degree of inequality.** There are three reasons for this. To begin with, a natural hierarchy exists within society. Secondly, some individuals are simply better able to harness their talents within the marketplace. In addition, people have very different propensities for hard work and taking opportunities. As a consequence, equality can *never* be the goal of a true conservative, as it runs entirely counter to their world-view. Socialist-inspired attempts to create a more egalitarian society are doomed to fail because they do not recognise the innate desire amongst human beings to be different and express their own identity. People do not aspire to be equal, and it is wrong of a left-wing government to believe otherwise. Any large-scale programme of *"social engineering"* goes against the grain of human nature and leads to punitively high taxation and big government, and in the words of Samuel Johnson *"hell is paved with good intentions."*

Conservatives also claim that the issue of political correctness derives from a dogmatic need amongst hard-line liberals to ensure their version of 'equality of opportunity' becomes the official mantra of society. All conservatives are deeply opposed to the encroachment of political correctness upon our everyday lives. Critics from the right of the political spectrum claim that political correctness generates an illiberal mindset within society and a degree of intolerance towards less 'fashionable' views. The journalist Anthony Browne argues that *"political correctness is the dictatorship of virtue,"* a criticism that reflects conservative hostility to the new puritanism inherent within political correctness. Others claim that certain words and thoughts are prohibited in a desire to be PC, a point put forward by P.D. James who states that *"I believe that political correctness can be a form of linguistic fascism, and it sends shivers down the spine of my generation who went to war against fascism."* This point is elaborated further in the context of contemporary politics by the American-based academic Jonah Goldberg (2008) in his book entitled *'Liberal Fascism.'* This argument derives from the view shared by many conservatives that liberals are often intolerant - *despite* their claim to be highly tolerant. In the words of John McCarthy; *"inside of many liberals is a fascist struggling to get out."* Furthermore, political correctness generates a mindset which classifies certain groups of people as victims in need of protection thereby making true believers feel that no dissent should be tolerated. In the context of ideologies from all sides of the political spectrum such a mindset can be used to justify and perpetrate violence, thereby leading to disorder. As such, conservatives claim there is a degree of danger inherent within the use of political correctness by 'liberal' extremists.

Most political commentators would accept that there is a tension between liberty and equality. In terms of the dichotomy between these two fundamental goals conservatives place greater emphasis upon **liberty.** For conservatives, the freedom to do as we like with the wealth we create is far superior to abstract notions of equality and social justice. This view is particularly vociferous from the New Right perspective. During the 1980s Mrs. Thatcher was firmly committed to the creation of a property-owning democracy. This was an

The Definitive Guide to Political Ideologies

important element of Thatcher's electoral-winning coalition of support, enabling the Conservatives to reach out beyond their natural constituency. However, even conservatives from the one-nation tradition stress liberty over equality, agreeing with Edmund Burke's description of equality as a doctrine *"preached by knavery, and so greedily adopted by malice, envy, and cunning."*

Conservatives also believe that there is a **natural hierarchy** within society. There is an elite that possess both the necessary pedigree and background to offer leadership to the country. These so-called 'high Tories' argue that society functions best when it is structured around a clear sense of hierarchy. It is an approach that will contribute towards a more harmonious and orderly society than one governed by the socialist-inspired goals of equality and social justice. Underpinning this argument is Edmund Burke's stipulation that we should *"love the little platoon in society to which we belong."* It is from membership of that platoon that we gain our identity and social strata (i.e. in terms of our families and our local community). Attempts to create an abstract identity based around utopian notions are fundamentally flawed. According to the one-nation perspective, an organic society facilitates a naturally evolving and hierarchical order. Burke also argued that those entrusted with the responsibility of governing must exercise caution and show restraint when implementing decisions. The abuse of power will lead to chaos and disorder within society, the very antithesis of what a true conservative aims for. According to Burke the relationship between the governed and the elite is one based upon a sacred covenant that exists throughout the ages. Radical ideas and utopian myths will merely rob society of the benefits of tradition and accumulated wisdom. Another illustration of this point derives from the American sociologist William Sumner. He argued that communal folkways represent *"an amalgam of traditionally formed and sanctioned beliefs, myths and narratives that structure the moral and intellectual life of a community."* According to Sumner, these folkways reflect the very best of society. It is an argument very much within the mindset of conservatism.

The relationship between conservatism and liberal democracy

Unlike liberals, conservatives do not make a fetish out of democracy. Whilst conservatives in the Western world accept that liberal democracy is preferable to any other political system, this view is not shared by all conservatives. Within an autocratic system, conservatives have often warned against the desire for radical or revolutionary change on the basis of such an abstract concept as democracy. The only constant here is that conservatives often **favour the status quo** regardless of the political system in question.

As with the term 'ideology' itself, we need to begin with the French Revolution. Conservatives of that era sided with the King against those demanding radical change on the basis of liberty, fraternity and equality. Some years later the French royalist Charles Maurras (1868-1952) spoke for many conservatives when he warned that democracy would lead to the rotation of parliamentarians parasitic upon public money, diverting funds to projects for electoral purposes. He believed the electorate was fickle and unreliable, and that democracy itself was based on a hypocritical notion that everyone was somehow equal. Other conservatives warned of the destabilising effects of change on the basis of liberty leading the people, a view immortalised in the famous words of King Louis (*"après moi, la deluge"*). It is an observation that best reflects the conservative stance on changing a political system on the basis of greater democracy. For conservatives no system is perfect, and democracy does not by itself necessarily result in good government. The French Revolution plays another important role within conservative thought because it was the motivation for perhaps the most influential of all contributions to the ideology (or mindset) itself. Edmund Burke's *Reflections on the Revolution in France* (1790) warned that revolutionary change would lead to despotism and terror. As events transpired, Edmund Burke was proved correct in his argument. His short pamphlet serves to this day as a warning against the folly of change fuelled by abstract and idealistic notions.

In the more conventional parameters of political debate, conservatives are somewhat sceptical about the supposed merits of greater democracy. Within UK politics reform is often justified on the basis of democracy, but unlike liberals, conservatives believe that those who wish to change the existing system must convincingly prove that their alternative is somehow better. Simply changing the existing system on the basis of ill-defined notions of 'greater democracy' are highly unlikely to persuade a true conservative. This point has been most noticeable in the Conservative party's stance on elements of Labour's programme of constitutional, electoral and parliamentary reform (Bloor, 2007, Chapters 10-12).

Conservatives are also sceptical about the supposed merits of pluralism. Enabling pressure groups access to decision-makers can result in a cumbersome political process that generates a labyrinthine bureaucracy. For example, the American conservative Samuel Huntingdon (1927-2008) warned of excessive participation leading to overloaded government. Too much pluralism may also result in regulatory capture by powerful vested interests, particularly those pressure groups with insider status. Although conservatives agree that it is wise to provide proper ventilation for strongly held views within society, this may only be justified on the basis of maintaining order. The core values of conservatism may sometimes require the centralisation of power. This approach was particularly noticeable during Mrs. Thatcher's premiership. Today, the Conservative party is pledged to de-centralise power in order to reflect localism within Britain's unitary system. Such a major reversal of strategy does to some extent reflect the Tories predilection for pragmatism.

Whereas conservatives believe that human rights should be protected via legislative and constitutional safeguards, there must always be a balance between social order and individual rights. The conservative view on the proper balance between society and the individual has been expressed by several figures. For example, during the time of the French Revolution the diplomat and lawyer Joseph de Maistre argued that society should always be considered of more importance than the individual. Conservatives have consistently argued than an excessive emphasis upon individualism ignores the right of the majority to go about their daily lives in a peaceful manner. They argue that the culture of 'rights' tends to expand well beyond any degree of common sense. Over time test cases deliberately seek to extend the concept of rights, the use of judicial activism creates yet more legislation, rights become increasingly divorced from responsibilities and sporadic cases of disproportionate pay-outs leads to a compensation culture (Raab, 2009).

Conservatives also believe that the UK's uncodified constitution has proved its worth over time and that the fusion of powers amongst the three branches of government facilitates strong and effective government, as opposed to the liberal prescription of a separation of powers. Conservatives also support the existence of competitive multi-party elections because it enables the people to *"kick the rascals out"* (Edmund Burke). However, the electoral system used must reflect the traditions and character of that particular society. For many conservatives proportional representation does not reflect the character of the British people, and multi-party coalitions are (in the words of the 19th century Tory Prime Minister Benjamin Disraeli) *"unBritish."*

Whilst conservatives firmly believe that power corrupts and all power corrupts absolutely, they also see the dangers in adopting a system based upon checks and balances with no regard for the effectiveness of government. Britain must avoid the legislative-executive deadlock that has at times characterised the American system. Conservatives also believe that open government does not necessarily equate to good government. However, conservatives fully agree with liberals that the rule of law must prevail in a stable and orderly society. For example, Sir Robert Peel (the creator of the modern police force) once said that *"the police should always direct their action strictly towards their functions, and never appear to usurp the powers of the judiciary."* Judicial independence and judicial neutrality are also treasured by conservatives. Furthermore, any move towards judicial activism is firmly opposed by conservatives. Political issues should be decided by politicians accountable to the people, not by unelected and out-of-touch 'liberal' judges. This is one of the many criticisms offered by conservatives in relation to the Human Rights Act, which incorporated the European Convention of Human Rights into UK law and empowered the judiciary with the ability to declare a Bill incompatible with the Convention. Finally, a peaceful transition of power within a liberal democracy clearly matches the conservative mindset.

As one can see, the conservative perspective on liberal democracy offers only qualified support for its core components. In a wider sense, conservatives also offer support for the concept of democracy - albeit with a heavy dose of realism (or cynicism, as their opponents would claim!). So whereas liberals are passionately in favour of democracy, Tories such as Winston Churchill believe that *"democracy is the worst form of government except all others that have been tried"* and *"the best argument against democracy is a five minute conversation with the average voter."* Amongst conservatives, tradition on the basis of **accumulated wisdom** will always be preferable to idealistic notions of progress on the basis of greater democracy. Thus in terms of parliamentary reform or constitutional change, conservatives tend to favour the status quo even when the basis of authority itself is hereditary rather than democratic (as in the case of the House of Lords and the Monarchy). There is also a degree of scepticism within conservative thought over the supposed virtues of people power. Edmund Burke, the figure with the strongest claim to being the leading philosopher of conservatism, doubted the ability of what he called *"the swinish multitude"* to provide a sensible basis for government. He even went so far as to describe democracy as the *"despotism of the multitude."* There is a degree of overlap here with Burke's musings and those concerns voiced about democracy within Ancient Greece – such as Plato's fear over the actions of the unwise masses and Aristotle's warning that people would be swayed emotionally rather than thinking rationally. As one might expect, Burke's scepticism towards the concept of democracy is criticised by liberals. For example, Thomas Paine once said that Burke held *"prostitute principles"* due to his pragmatic / cynical stance on moves towards greater democracy during the late-18th century.

The individual and society

Unlike liberals, conservatives believe that the most successful societies possess a high level of cultural homogeneity, a strong emphasis upon personal responsibility and a widespread recognition of the duties we must perform for others. For conservatives, individuals can only flourish when they are part of a **cohesive and stable society**. In stark contrast, a liberal society based around excessive individualism undermines respect for others, results in parents ignoring their responsibility to properly socialise their children and ultimately leads to a variety of social problems. This analysis finds its modern expression in the Tory party's claim that Britain is now a *"broken society"* after a lengthy period of Labour rule.

Unlike liberals, conservatives are not concerned about the *"despotism of custom"* or the *"tyranny of the majority."* For conservatives, multiculturalism can be a recipe for very dangerous levels of tolerance towards those who pose a threat to social cohesion. The Daily Mail journalist Melanie Phillips' (2006) book *'Londonistan'* is a good illustration of this point. She argues that the authorities have failed to adequately deal with the growing threat of Islamic terrorism and have thereby provided a home for a subculture hostile to British (and Western) society. Thus in the context of cultural homogeneity and diversity, conservatives are very much in favour of preserving and building upon those factors which unite members of society together. Furthermore, they firmly believe that immigrants should integrate into the wider cultural norms and values of British society. Crucially, this benefits both society *and* the immigrant population. Society must be held together by a shared **consensus** over prevalent norms and values. The alternative would, quite literally, be anarchy.

Conservatives always offer a vigorous defence of those traditional institutions that have proved their worth from one generation to the next. The conservative mindset is - by instinct – favourable towards the nuclear family, believes that the kinship offered by the family unit is superior to anything offered by the welfare state and firmly supports the view that marriage should be between a man and a woman. The family is one of the cornerstones of society, and measures designed to strengthen the family have long been a feature of conservatism (such as tax breaks for married couples). Whilst progressive conservatives have tried to portray a more inclusive image of the party, this in no way detracts from the fundamental point that all conservatives favour traditional social mores.

As argued previously, social order is the core objective of conservatism. Conservatives claim that social disorder is likely to originate from the failure of individuals to take responsibility for their actions, or from the failure of parents to adequately socialise their children. Responsibility is ultimately down to the individual concerned. It is *not* the job of society (via the welfare state) to raise anyone's child. Conservatives also reject the popularised view from those on the left of the political spectrum that crime is caused by divisions within society. Furthermore, conservatives have no sympathy for those who blame 'society' for their behaviour because it reflects an excuse culture stemming from a mindset of victimhood. In the famous words of

Mrs Thatcher *"there is no such thing as society, merely individuals and families."* Revealingly, David Cameron has positioned himself away from Thatcher's oft-cited observation. During his victory speech in December 2005 he claimed that *"there is such a thing as society, it's just not the same thing as the state."*

The relationship between the individual and society has of course a direct impact upon the role of the state. On this issue, there is a degree of disparity between one-nation conservatives and the New Right. One-nation Tories believe that society should provide a basic minimum and should be able to deal effectively with market failure. The state should also supply merit goods for the whole of society regardless of a person's ability to pay. In contrast, the New Right claims that the marketplace is the appropriate forum to decide what society requires. As part of an aggregate of individuals we exert power and influence within the marketplace and, in doing so, society best provides for our wants and needs. During the 1980s and 90s the Conservatives radically diminished the role of the state in an attempt to empower individuals and turn them into owners of capital. Thatcher instigated a major expansion in share ownership, and millions of people became home-owners as opposed to council tenants. Once again, it is possible to trace a degree of overlap between the New Right and classical liberalism.

Whilst all conservatives acknowledge that the state has a role to play in terms of holding society together, there is a firm belief that the state must always be the **servant of the people**. In order to achieve this, parliamentary sovereignty must be upheld because Parliament itself is a key part of our shared natural heritage. Conservatives also claim that European integration undermines parliamentary sovereignty and therefore goes against the grain of British traditions and heritage. However, there is once again a slight divergence within the different strands of conservative thought. To the one-nation school, a degree of pragmatism is required on the subject of European integration. Many of the leading pro-Europeans within the party's history (such as Churchill, Heath, Heseltine, MacMillan and Clarke) have derived from the one-nation strand of conservatism. However, the New Right claims that European integration undermines parliamentary sovereignty and runs counter to several right-wing values (such as cutting the level of taxation). In the words of Mrs. Thatcher's 1988 Bruges speech; *"We have not successfully rolled back the frontiers of the state in Britain only to see them re-imposed at a European level, with a European super-state exercising a new dominance from Brussels."*

The conservative stance on lifestyle issues

Moral absolutism, as opposed to moral relativism, is one of the guiding values of conservative ideology. None of us should have the absolute right to do as we like, even if our actions cause absolutely no harm to others. A liberal approach based upon John Stuart Mill's harm principle would undermine the bonds of society and may even contribute towards lawlessness and anarchy. As such, conservatives firmly reject the trenchant individualism they associate with liberalism. For conservatives, a clear focus upon the difference between right and wrong is one of the central tenants of a stable and orderly society. Lord Acton spoke for many conservatives on this point when he said that *"liberty is not the power to do what we like, but the right to do what we ought."*

Conservatives also cherish those elements of society that contribute to social cohesion and have proved their worth over the course of time. As such, they are highly supportive of those religious values within society (principally Judeo-Christian principles) which best reflect Britain's national heritage. Conservatives believe that family values, individual responsibility, moral absolutism, respect for others and the need for hierarchy within society are all enhanced by a firm adherence to Judeo-Christian principles. A focus upon cultural diversity as prescribed by liberals can only weaken societal bonds, particularly when those cultural values stand in contrast to the wider Judeo-Christian values of society. Religious values can also help form a stronger bond within a family because *"the family that prays together stays together."* Furthermore, the state can and should reinforce the significance of religious values within society. So whereas liberals focus more upon the negative consequences of religion, conservatives tend to emphasise the positive aspects. This is an important point of divergence between a liberal and a conservative in terms of their stance upon lifestyle issues. Conservatives also reject the Marxist argument that religious institutions are an agent of false consciousness, believing that godless Communism is very much against the character of British (and Western) society.

The conservative stance on the role of the state and religion is best exemplified within the United States, particularly in regards to the Moral Majority. This religious-based movement campaigns in favour of school prayer, strongly supports faith-based initiatives and is morally opposed to gay marriage. Of these, it is the latter which is the most revealing in terms of the conservative stance upon lifestyle issues. For many on the right of the political spectrum, religious teachings sanction the act of marriage as that between a man and a woman for the procreation of children. In Britain of course, lifestyle issues of any kind rarely cause much political furore. The existence of so-called *"values voters"* that have formed such an important part of the Republican party's constituency of support are largely absent from British politics. Values voters have enabled Republicans to reach out beyond their natural base by appealing to less well-off voters, particularly those deeply opposed to abortion and gay marriage. For the British Conservative party, such a constituency does not exist. Britain is a much more secular society, and politicians tend to leave issues of a moral character to an individual's own conscience. There is no 'religious right' comparable to that of American politics.

In defence of conservatives, their stance upon lifestyle issues is fuelled not by ignorance or prejudice but on the basis of a long-standing preference towards those values and institutions that have proved their worth over time. It is entirely reasonable to claim that the nuclear family based upon a monogamous relationship has proved its worth from one generation to the next. Traditional values and institutions are a composition of the wisdom of all generations, whereas the liberal approach of moral relativism is linked to many social problems such as juvenile delinquency, drug addiction, alcohol abuse, anti-social behaviour and so on. Conservatives have also perceived liberals as *"aggressive secularists"* who both ignore and contribute to the moral decay of society. The ability of religious values and institutions to transform the lives of millions is a point emphasised repeatedly amongst conservatives, particularly within American politics where the role of religion holds far greater political salience.

Conservatives also argue that the Church has a valuable role to play in dealing with poverty and the effects of social / family breakdown. For conservatives, religion offers a much more effective route in tackling social problems than the welfare state. Solutions which derive from the local community (of which the Church often plays a central role) are more in keeping with the conservative mindset than those policies which require a major expansion in the role of government. An active role for the Church also helps to limit the growth of the state. Furthermore, religious institutions reinforce the traditional nuclear family. This is a major point of division between conservatives and socialists. The former often claim that those on the left of the political spectrum are hostile to traditional family values, although the validity of this charge is open to debate.

Order and hierarchy

Order is the central value and objective of conservatism. From that, all other elements of conservative thought can be understood. Without order, all those things which are precious to us (including our life and our liberty) would be under threat. Society itself is held together by a fabric that has evolved over generations, and order is a central element of that fabric. As such, order and hierarchy are essential to the **maintenance of stability** within a society. Having said this, there is a slight difference between the two main strands of conservatism over the *means* to maintain order within society. Whereas the one-nation school represents the triumph of **pragmatism over principle**, the New Right is more firmly **committed** to right-wing values and ideals. Perhaps the clearest illustration of this division derives from their stance on prison policy. The then Home Secretary (and later party leader) Michael Howard spoke for many on the right of the party during the 1993 party conference when he declared that *"prison works."* Tough measures are needed in order to keep human nature in check, and rehabilitation measures will ultimately fail to achieve their desired ends. The solution to crime is to enable the police to be strong enough to deal with crime and anti-social behaviour. In contrast, one-nation Tories adopt a more 'liberal' approach. For example, it was a government led by a one-nation Tory that presided over the abolition of the death penalty.

Both strands of conservatism strongly support the role played by the police within society. Police powers *and* police numbers should be increased to ensure law and order prevails. For example, in their 2005 election manifesto the party pledged to increase police numbers and remove the burden of excessive paperwork on the police. Conservatives firmly believe that the police represent the thin blue line between order and anarchy. Having said this, both liberals and conservatives agree on the need to ensure that the police are held accountable to the demos. David Cameron has even gone so far as to describe the police as *"Britain's last great unreformed public service"* and is in favour of replacing police authorities with directly-elected commissioners. He also believes that the police service would be improved by enabling Chief Constables to dismiss underperforming officers. On this particular issue Cameron reflects a distinct trait within conservative ideology that recognises the need to scrutinise the actions of those who exercise power.

The Labour government's increasingly illiberal policies have given a renewed sense of vigour to conservatives who champion individual freedom against the draconian power of the state. This was dramatically illustrated in May 2008 when the Shadow Home Secretary David Davies resigned his seat in order to fight the government on the issue of civil liberties. He reflects a long-standing tradition within the party that dates back to luminaries such as Winston Churchill, a leader who abolished ID cards in the early 1950s and even retained the principles of Magna Carta during war-time. For example, when the Nazi sympathiser Oswald Moseley was released from prison Churchill is quoted as saying that *"the power of the executive to throw a man into prison without formulating any charge known to the law and ... to deny him the judgement of his peers is ... the foundation of all totalitarian governments ... Extraordinary powers assumed by the executive with the consent of Parliament in emergencies should be yielded up when and as the emergency declines."* It is therefore important to be aware that conservatives are to some extent libertarian on the issue of order, principally in relation to those rights that have traditionally formed part of Britain's national heritage.

The contrast between conservatives and other ideologies on this issue offers further illumination. Take the issue of those factors which cause crime. Conservatives claim that a 'liberal' approach with its focus upon moral relativism, its optimistic view of human nature and its support for rehabilitation measures leads to the authorities being soft on crime. A lack of moral decency, the absence of a strong role model at home and a failure of parents and other agents of socialisation to teach children the difference between right and wrong is at the root of criminal behaviour. Policies designed to instil respect for authority, self-discipline, individual responsibility and moral decency have been shown to be the most appropriate methods available in dealing with crime. Crucially, the gap between rich and poor is *not a cause* of crime. Although the one-nation school believes that the provision of a safety net is a wise and prudent move from the ruling elite, there is a firm rejection of the argument derived from the left of the political spectrum that inequality and crime are in some way inter-linked. In addition, conservatives and anarchists are at polar ends of the libertarian-authoritarian axis in terms of the related concepts of order and hierarchy. According to the former, stability requires and demands respect for authority. This applies to all figures of authority ranging from teachers to the police. In stark contrast, anarchists believe that order can emerge spontaneously without the need for hierarchy. This is an argument which fuels their belief in the desirability of a stateless society, a utopian ideal that would make any true-blooded conservative recoil in horror.

In summary, conservatives often argue that society needs to return to (or retain) a set of **traditional values**, including respect for authority and a sense of hierarchy within society. This reflects conservative support for the status quo and a belief in the virtues of traditional values and institutions. Those organisations that instil a respect for authority and hierarchy (such as schools, the Church and the Army) are widely supported within the conservative mindset. These organisations most clearly reflect the conservative stance on order and hierarchy.

Change or the status quo

The conservative stance on the issue of change can sometimes confuse students of political ideology. Whilst it is entirely correct to say that conservatives are highly **sceptical** towards the desirability of change, they are **not opposed** to change in itself. Firstly, conservatives are irrevocably opposed to change for the sake of change. Secondly, it must always be the task of the reformer to persuade others of the merits of his or her case. Those who wish to defend the status quo should not have to rationalise their argument because they have tradition on their side. Conservatives will therefore always favour the status quo because that position best reflects the accumulated wisdom of previous generations. In everyday parlance, the conservative stance on reform or the status quo can be summarised as *"if it ain't broke, why fix it?"*

As with various issues we have considered in this Chapter, there is a certain contrast between the two main strands of conservative thought. The New Right perspective is much more supportive of change. The reforms instigated by the Thatcher / Major governments were very different to the stance taken by previous Conservative governments. In many ways, Thatcher herself was *anti*-conservative in her stance on the status quo. Her desire to transform British society from the social democratic consensus that had shaped the post-war era resulted in her adopting a strident and uncompromising approach to reform. On this issue at least, she (and to a lesser extent John Major) were not conservatives at all. Indeed, Thatcher could be described as a free-market anti-corporatist radical who fundamentally changed the character and content of British politics. Thatcher is therefore untypical of the conservative approach to the status quo.

For most conservatives, there is an undisputed merit in adopting a **cautious** approach to change. It is unwise for *any* generation to believe that they alone have the answers to the myriad of problems that face society. There is an inherent virtue in preserving and strengthening those institutions and values that have proved their worth from one generation to the next. Change may therefore be justified *if* it can be shown to build upon traditional institutions and values. In the words of Edmund Burke; *"a state without the means of change is without the means of its conservation."* This traditionalist and pragmatic stance has been criticised by both sides of the left-right spectrum. Many on the right have lamented at the inability of Conservative governments to turn back the clock and restore traditional values. For those on the left, the conservative preference for the status quo reflects a mindset hostile to social progress and other rationalist goals such as equality and democracy. Socialists also claim that conservatives try to justify a massive imbalance of power and wealth within society on the basis of tradition, and criticise their highly nostalgic view of the past.

In terms of their attitude towards reform, conservatives firmly reject grand utopian projects (principally those guided by abstract notions) in favour of incremental change. *"Evolution not revolution"* is the byword of a true conservative. For conservatives, the problem with embarking upon reform of traditional institutions is that it can easily unravel those delicate bonds which hold society together. Radical ideas that have yet to prove their worth within society are often the recipe for social disorder and chaos. This raises the question of *"when would a true conservative favour change?"*, and the answer to that question occurs when the reformist argument has shown that change will preserve traditional values and institutions. The conservative stance on this point was summarised by the maverick Tory MP Enoch Powell when he said that *"the supreme function of a politician is to judge the correct moment for reform."*

For understandable reasons, conservatives are often criticised for their irrational pessimism towards plans for reform. Within the conservative mindset there is an unmistakable belief that things could easily become worse rather than better. They do not share the liberal optimism in change, a point graphically identified by the American academic Carolyn Heilbrun (1926-2003) who argued that on the issue of social change *"conservatives always expect disaster, while revolutionaries confidentially expect utopia."* A conservative might therefore be depicted as someone who holds a deep sense of scepticism towards an agenda for change, particularly those which promise a utopian vision of society that cannot possibly be delivered, yet will also accept the need for piecemeal change when the alternative would ultimately weaken those traditional institutions. According to conservatives there is a tendency amongst politicians to promise far more than they can ever deliver, and a predilection amongst those of the current generation to ignore the lessons of the past. As such, there is a tradition within conservative thought dating back to the Scottish philosopher David Hume that is deeply sceptical towards those who offer a grand vision for society. Hume himself was opposed to social contract theorists such as John Locke because they outlined what society *ought* to be, as opposed to how society really functions. Amongst conservatives there is an inherent benefit in understanding the past and building on tradition.

Perhaps the most significant division of all between progressives and conservatives centres upon their attitude towards change. It would be entirely accurate to describe conservatives as supporters of the **status quo ante** - a Latin term for *"the way things were before."* Whilst progressives take the view that *"the past is another country,"* for conservatives there are important lessons to be gained from the past, a point they feel is often lost on radicals and revolutionaries. In the words of George Santayana; ***"Those who cannot remember the past are condemned to repeat it"*** – a quote which fully encapsulates the conservative stance on the issue of change. Continuity with the past is preferable to change guided by abstract ideals, and reform itself can only be justified in terms of strengthening those values and institutions that have proved their worth from one generation to the next.

Conservatism in contemporary politics

One of the oddities of modern British politics is that the most right-wing strand of conservative ideology has been highly influential in recent times under governments of both main parties, and yet the Tory party itself has gone through a lengthy period of opposition since 1997. Since coming to power over a decade ago Labour have implemented an economic and social policy shaped to a significant extent by New Right ideology. The Labour government has done a great deal to push forward a New Right agenda, and in several areas the Blair / Brown era has gone much further down the road of privatisation and marketisation than Thatcher herself (e.g. the Private Finance Initiative, charging students for Higher Education, foundation hospitals and so on). In the perceptive words of the conservative philosopher Roger Scruton *"Labour have accepted that Mrs. Thatcher was right."* As such, New Right ideology has been one of the most influential strands of ideology in the past 30 years. This observation can also be applied to the United States, where 'new' Democrats such as Bill Clinton did more to de-regulate and liberalise the economy (particularly the financial services) than Republican Presidents during the 1980s. The adaptation of low taxation, de-regulation and liberalisation of the economy has been the hallmark of many other economies throughout the Western world, and yet the latter point brings us to the most pressing economic and political issue of the modern era; the credit crunch. [6]

In response to the credit crunch several governments (including the UK and the US) have significantly expanded the role of the state both in terms of public expenditure via a fiscal stimulus to kick-start the economy and in terms of expanding the role of the state over the banking system, both of which

---

[6]   The New Right policy programme of cutting taxes, privatising public services, de-regulation and weakening the power of the trade unions has been described by the left-wing feminist author Naomi Klein as a form of *"McGovernment."* She argues that McGovernment represents a war against diversity and is biased at every level towards centralisation, consolidation and homogenisation. Her voice is a highly influential one within the alter-globalisation movement – a point considered in more detail during the next Chapter.

represent an obvious repudiation of New Right ideology. The meltdown of financial services puts the New Right in a very difficult position. The policy remedies that were fashionable in the 1980s and 90s now look highly dated, and few within the Conservative party argue publicly in favour of cutting taxes, privatising public services and de-regulation. Ironically, if the Tories win the 2010 General Election, they may have to implement exactly that sort of package in order to reduce the massive accumulation of government debt that has occurred over the past few years. So whilst the credit crunch widely discredits much of the New Right argument, the remedy may consist of even deeper cuts in public expenditure and taxation that that experienced during the 1980s.

As argued in the opening part of this Chapter, conservatism is a state of mind centred upon a small number of core values. In contemporary politics the conservative mindset finds deep resonance within Middle England, a mythical constituency highly prized by both main parties and often seen as the battle-ground in any election. Britain itself has been described by political scientists as having a conservative political culture (Almond and Verba, 1963), and there is much merit in this observation. Furthermore, the electorate appears poised to return the Conservatives to power. If that does occur (and opinion polls have been wrong in the past!), then the strand of conservative thought reflected by David Cameron will gain an unprecedented opportunity to shape the political process. The next General Election may also lead to the realignment of British politics in a manner comparable to the early-1980s, when the Labour party moved sharply to the left and the Conservatives shifted to the right. Whatever might occur in the foreseeable future, Britain is set for a fascinating political period after a lengthy and unprecedented period of Labour rule.

On a more global level, conservatism remains the **main ideological rival** to liberalism within the contemporary era. The contest between the two is often portrayed as progressives v. conservatives and is centered upon fundamental issues of ideology such as the need for change, cultural diversity and the role of the state. Of the two, liberalism is undoubtedly the more prevalent and influential within global politics. The argument that *"we are all liberals now"* has some validity in terms of the more inclusive tone and character of modern conservatism and the response by governments throughout the world to the credit crunch; which represents a return to social liberalism (and to some degree social democracy – a strand of thought we will consider in the following Chapter on socialism) alongside a move away from New Right ideology.

Further quotes on conservatism

"All conservatism is based upon the idea that if you leave things alone you leave them as they are. But you do not. If you leave a thing alone you leave it to a torrent of change." G.K. Chesterton

"A conservative is a liberal who has just been mugged." Unnatributed

"All modern revolutions have ended in a reinforcement of the State." Albert Camus

"Let our children grow tall and some taller than others if they have it in them to do so." Margaret Thatcher

"The people never give up their liberties but under some delusion." Edmund Burke

"Most stupid people are conservatives." John Stuart Mill

"The further you look back at the past the clearer you see the future." Winston Churchill

"The market has no morality." Michael Heseltine

"Might equals right, and what goes by the name of justice is merely whatever serves the interests of the strongest." Plato

"Loyalty is the Tory's secret weapon." Lord Kilmuir

"Paternalism is the greatest despotism imaginable." Immanuel Kant

"Marxists get up early to further their cause. We must get up even earlier to defend our freedom." Margaret Thatcher

"Nothing in politics is ever as good or as bad as it first appears." Edward Boyle

Recommended reading

Acton, Lord (1956) *Essays on Freedom and Power*. *Acton is championed by both liberals and conservatives for his views upon the corrupting influence of power. However, his views upon freedom and liberty are far more consistent with conservatism than liberalism.*

Bartholomew, J. (2004) *The Welfare State we're in.* A modern-day exploration of how the welfare state generates a cycle of dependency and thereby undermines individual responsibility. Bartholomew offers a scathing critique of how new Labour have squandered taxpayer's money and ultimately failed to deliver better public services.

Burke, E. (1790) *Reflections on the Revolution in France.* The most important contribution towards conservative ideology is - essentially - a note of caution against the French Revolution. Burke remains the key figure in conservative thought and his short pamphlet is perhaps the clearest introduction of all to the mindset of conservatism.

Hayek, F. (1944) *The Road to Serfdom.* A hugely influential book that was largely ignored during the time of its publication. Addressed to "the socialists of all parties," Hayek argues that the growth of state intervention will lead to slavery. Hayek remains a leading light within New Right ideology.

Murray, C. & Herrnstein, R. (1995) *The Bell Curve.* Charles Murray is best-known for his dependency culture argument, but in this book Murray and Herrnstein take a controversial right-wing look at human nature. Whatever your own personal views, this is a book bound to generate debate and intellectual stimulation.

Hobbes, T. (1651) *Leviathan.* Although it has been claimed that Hobbes offers an essentially liberal argument in terms of the social contract, he remains a figure widely associated with the need for a forceful state to keep human nature in check. On inspection of the cover you will see that Leviathan is actually made up of people, an important point to grasp when reading his work.

Jenkins, S. (2007) *Thatcher and Sons : A Revolution in three acts.* A favourable but not overtly biased account of how Thatcherism changed Britain and the manner in which she has influenced subsequent Labour Prime Ministers.

MacMillan, H. (1966) *The Middle Way.* A solid account of pragmatic one-nation conservatism and the need to avoid the extremities of left and right. Readers may be struck by the highly practical tone of the book.

Nozick, R. (1974) *Anarchy, State and Utopia.* The most important philosophical outline of libertarianism and one championed by both New Right conservatives and individualist anarchists. The debate between Nozick and Rawls is a hugely stimulating one within contemporary political philosophy.

Young, H. (1991) *One of Us.* A largely critical account of the Thatcher years and how the expression 'is he one of us?' came to symbolise the manner in which the inner circle surrounding Thatcher operated.

Ideas for further discussion

How important is tradition within the conservative mindset?
In what sense does the conservative view of human nature differ to the liberal perspective?
In what areas does the one-nation tradition differ to that of the New Right?
Do conservatives favour a strong role for the state?

Why are conservatives opposed to equality?

What is the conservative stance upon liberal democracy?

Why do conservatives emphasise our duties as opposed to our individual rights?

Why do conservatives adopt a position of moral absolutism on lifestyle issues?

What is the conservative stance upon authority?

Why do conservatives favour the status quo ante?

Is conservatism in decline?

Key terms

Authority At a basic level, authority consists of the right to rule. Individuals willingly obey commands because the exercise of power by a figure of authority is seen as legitimate in some way. This concept was explored in detail by the German sociologist Max Weber who argued that authority can be based upon charisma, tradition or rational-legal factors. Authority is closely related to the concept of power, yet when power is exercised without authority conflict may ensue.

Broken society A term used by the Conservative party to highlight a myriad of problems facing British society. They include a relatively high rate of teenage pregnancy, high levels of drug and alcohol abuse, a high ratio of absent parents (especially fathers) and the existence of over a million NEETs (Not in Education, Employment or Training) within British society. The Conservatives' solution to these problems is consistent with a right-wing approach to social policy, such as an emphasis upon family values and a financial reward for couples who remain married.

Cycle of deprivation Where families from one generation to the next live below the poverty line. In some of the more disadvantaged parts of the country there are children today who are the product of second / third generation poverty. The term cycle of deprivation reflects the view that *"the poor breed the poor."* The term is often used by those of the New Right who claim that the welfare state traps people into a life of poverty from which they become dependent upon state benefits.

Dependency culture A term associated with New Right theorists such as Charles Murray who argue that the welfare state undermines individual responsibility and effectively traps claimants within the benefits system with little or no incentive to escape. This argument was prevalent during the 1980s and 1990s, but has since fallen out of favour. It occurs when welfare claimants adopt a subculture of norms and values that make it difficult for them to return to work. They include a lack of self-reliance and personal initiative. The welfare state is therefore considered to be a *cause* – rather than a solution – to poverty.

Deserving poor A term used to differentiate between members of society who are poor through little or no fault of their own, as opposed to the *un*deserving poor. The term tends to be used by those on the right of the political spectrum and is reminiscent of a Victorian-era approach to poverty.

Family values A term widely used by politicians to emphasise the importance of the family within society and the desirability of traditional morality. Advocacy of family values is closely associated with the conservative perspective and has a great deal of political salience.

Hierarchy A term used to describe how social groups and individuals are stratified within society. The term can also be used in the context of organisations that have a hierarchical structure in order to delineate responsibility and confer authority to certain individuals. Anarchists are deeply opposed to hierarchy, whereas fascists believe strongly in the importance of hierarchy. Conservatives support the concept of hierarchy in terms of strengthening social cohesion.

Marketisation The use of market forces and market principles within the welfare state. As the term suggests, marketisation takes the private sector as its model. Opponents of marketisation claim that it represents the 'privatisation' of public services, whereas supporters claim that market-based reforms result in efficiency gains and a greater level of personal choice. Marketisation owes its ideological basis to the New Right.

Organic society A view largely associated with the conservative perspective in which society evolves via a contract between the living, the dead and those yet to be born. Conservative nationalists and fascists also take an organic view of society. In Emile Durkheim's work into *The Division of Labour*, he identified two main types of social solidarity – organic and mechanical. In an organic society, Durkheim argued that social solidarity is maintained by a complex web of relationships in which each individual contributes a different task in the division of labour. In doing so, a form of mutual dependence (or interdependence) is established amongst individual members of society. According to Durkheim, individuals are influenced by society in the same way that a puppet is controlled by the puppeteer. Friedrich Hegel perceived the organic society as an expression of what he called a *"universal will."*

Social cohesion Those factors which bind members of a society together. Social cohesion is based upon norms, values and mores. Without social cohesion, the result would be anarchy within society.

State of nature A term associated with the English philosopher Thomas Hobbes. He argued that in a pre-social state individuals have absolute freedom but are exposed to high levels of personal danger. In this state of nature life is *"nasty, brutish and short."* In order to remove this threat, individuals should enter into a social contract with each other whereby absolute freedom is surrendered to the state.

Undeserving poor Members of society who live in poverty as a result of their own actions. The term is used to differentiate between the deserving poor and those who are poor due to their own feckless behaviour.

Utopia An idealised form of society. The term derives from the 16th century English philosopher Thomas More, who named an imaginary island utopia from the Greek words meaning 'no' (ou) and 'place' (topos). The perfect society was therefore nowhere because it had yet to be created. The Marxist conception of a communist society could be classed as a utopia, as could the stateless society prescribed by anarchists. Fascism too could also be described as utopian. Within political discourse the term utopia is applied in a negative sense to criticise idealistic and impractical visions of a future society – particularly by conservatives. According to conservatives, utopian is often thought to mean idealistic and unachievable.

CHAPTER 3
SOCIALISM

The core elements of socialism

The most distinctive element of socialist thought derives from its **critique of capitalism**. Whereas liberals and conservatives claim that capitalism is the best economic system available, socialists believe there is a fairer alternative to an economic system based upon unfettered market forces and private ownership, although the extent to which socialists wish to reform or dismantle capitalism differs widely amongst the various strands of thought. Those on the centre-left of the political spectrum claim that it is possible to 'humanise' capitalism via state regulation, nationalisation, the welfare state, comprehensive education and by providing public services free to all according to need regardless of the ability to pay. Those further to the left of the political spectrum advocate a form of socialism where the state takes on a significant role in terms of distributing resources within society, whereas the most extreme strand of socialist thought (Marxism) predicts that a revolution led by the proletariat will overturn capitalism and replace it with an economic system based upon common ownership (called Communism). Whatever strand we consider, socialism is first and foremost a critique of capitalism.

Another core element within socialist thought is a desire to **transform society** for the betterment of humankind. All socialists share a deep commitment to change the existing order on the basis of a more egalitarian society, and whatever view one has about socialism, it is undoubtedly the case that a passionate belief in a more humane world lies at the very epicentre of socialist thought. This is most noticeable within Marxism, a distinct strand of socialist thought that prescribes a bold utopian vision of society in which class conflict would no longer exist and the state would simply *"wither away"* (Friedrich Engels). Much of the appeal of socialism – regardless of the strand of thought in question – derives from the pledge to create a more civilised society in which exploitation and social injustice would be consigned to the dustbin of history.

A third element we need to consider in relation to socialism is **economic determinism**. Both ideologies considered thus far believe that human nature is essentially the same regardless of the economic (or political) system in question. In contrast, socialists believe that human nature is shaped by the economic basis of that society. Capitalism fosters competition between people, generates class division and provides substantial economic rewards for those who engage in the very worst of human behaviour. Under capitalism those who own the means of production (the bourgeoisie) have a clear economic interest in perpetuating the exploitation of those who work the means of production (the proletariat). According to Marxists, it is the bourgeoisie that appropriates the surplus value of the proletariat. Workers are paid a mere fraction of the wealth they (and they alone) generate. A complete transformation in the economic system is therefore required in order to facilitate the best of human nature. In doing so, co-operation will replace competition and fraternity will replace exploitation. It scarcely needs adding that such views are criticised by conservatives for their reliance upon abstract concepts and by liberals for their flawed belief in the ability of the economic system to fundamentally alter human nature. Liberals and socialists are also at odds over their view of the individual. Whereas liberals base their entire ideology upon individualism, socialists contend that the individual is a product of society and their 'freedom' is largely determined by their social and economic background. Behaviour is therefore socially conditioned and thus malleable to a change in the economic system itself.

The fourth and final aspect of socialism is arguably the most important, and that is a firm belief in the twin goals of **equality and social justice**. In terms of equality, socialists offer a very different approach to social liberals. Whereas the latter are in favour of measures designed to ensure equality *of opportunity*, socialists are in favour of a more equal distribution of wealth and resources. Whilst the extent to which socialists advocate a more even redistribution of wealth differs considerably, all socialists are united in their

Core elements
Critique of capitalism
Belief in change and a better tomorrow
Economic determinism
Equality and social justice

belief in the benefits of a greater level of equality within society. On the related issue of social justice, socialists differ from social liberals in terms of state intervention. Whilst social liberals such as T.H. Green and John Maynard Keynes argue that a limited degree of state intervention is justified in terms of maximising the concept of liberty, socialists contend that the state must actively intervene in the marketplace in order to ensure social justice. This may take the form of common ownership of the means of production, regulation of the marketplace and the provision of a free at the point of use health service. Yet crucially, the unfettered free market *cannot* facilitate social justice according to the socialist viewpoint.

It should be relatively clear that socialism belongs on the left of the political spectrum, and in terms of the authoritarian-libertarian axis, socialism is commonly positioned on the former due to its association with a significant role for the state. Having said this, there are many socialists within the labour movement who would more accurately be placed along the libertarian axis. In the words of a notable theorist and practitioner of socialism (Anthony Crosland); *"in the blood of the socialist there should always run a trace of the anarchist and the libertarian."* There is even a branch of thought known as eco-socialism, although due to its relationship to environmental issues this branch of thought will be discussed later in the Chapter on ecologism. A similar observation can be applied to collectivist anarchism and its advocacy of anarcho-communism. For now, it is important to note that both supporters and critics of socialism claim that it is primarily an ideology of the authoritarian-left.

The socialist perspective on human nature

Socialism differs to both liberalism and conservatism in terms of its view of human nature. For socialists, human nature is far from immutable. Consequently, the optimistic-pessimistic continuum we have used so far is essentially redundant. According to socialists, human behaviour is **determined** by the economic system. As with other economic systems such as feudalism and imperialism, capitalism brings out the worst in human nature. The entire basis of the economy must therefore change in order to facilitate the best of human nature. Under a socialist economic system resources would be planned according to need rather than the ability to pay, and no longer would our lives be dictated to by the machinations of the unfettered marketplace. As such, the socialist perspective on human nature is grounded upon economic determinism and prescribes replacing capitalism with a system based upon the **common ownership of the means of production**.

Socialists criticise the liberal perspective upon human nature for its disregard of the economic system in question. In failing to locate their understanding of human nature *within* a social construct, they prevent the creation of a better society based upon social justice and equality. Socialists also criticise conservatives for their pessimistic acceptance of the status quo. Social progress will inevitably be curtailed by a negative stance on human nature, yet by locating their understanding of human nature to economic determinism, socialists can realistically claim to offer hope of a more humane world where no-one would suffer from poverty and exploitation. Yet to its many critics, socialism has repeatedly failed to translate good intentions into practise.

The socialist argument rests on the premise that human nature can *and should* be liberated from the destructive and corrosive character of capitalism. For conservatives, the very notion that human nature can itself be changed is a complete fallacy. For liberals capitalism is by far the best economic system available, both in terms of allocating resources and in terms of its beneficial effects upon society. By contrast, socialism prescribes a markedly different approach to understanding human nature to either of the ideologies considered thus far. To its supporters, socialism will free the workers from the chains of their oppression. Planning resources along the basis of the common good will enable resources to be distributed more effectively than they ever would under capitalism. In doing so, resources would be allocated to serve the needs of society as opposed to the wealthy minority. An economic system based upon these socialist principles would emancipate workers from the drudgery of work. Human nature would seek an altruistic form of reward instead of the empty lives experienced by those living under a heartless capitalist regime. Furthermore, working selflessly for the collective good is morally superior to the egotistical self-serving individualism fostered by capitalism.

In attempting to grasp the socialist perspective on human nature it is worth recalling Karl Marx oft-cited argument that *"the ideas of the ruling class are in every epoch the ruling ideas."* Thus the ideas which underpin capitalism (such as competition, exploitation, alienation and the desire for a high level of profit) serve the interests of the ruling class (the bourgeoisie). The same observation could be offered about other historical eras such as slavery and colonialism. Yet by transforming the economic system those ideas could be changed to bring out the very best in human nature. That in essence is the socialist argument.

Whatever your perspective on the ideology itself, the socialist perspective on human nature offers an intriguing thesis. It claims that the true potential of human beings cannot be fulfilled within an economic system based solely upon the profit motive. In a capitalist society workers are alienated from their jobs and experience exploitation at the hands of the bourgeoisie. Furthermore, the nation's resources are distributed unevenly and inefficiently – thus perpetuating division within society on the basis of social class. A socialist system is both necessary and desirable towards the task of releasing the communal and co-operative instincts of human beings. The most hard-line socialists even claim that an economic system based upon common ownership would resolve class conflict, liberate us all from oppression, signify the end of history and the dissolution of the state itself. In the words of the co-author of the Communist Manifesto (1848) Friedrich Engels; *"when freedom exists there will be no state."* This point is of course not shared by other strands of socialist thought – which leads us onto the next section.

The main strands of socialism

Each ideology consists of various strands of thought, which one might fully expect when considering the subjective and controversial nature of politics itself. However, it is undoubtedly the case that socialism has one of the most diverse ranges of all (Wright, 1995). Indeed, the very fact that socialism consists of three distinct strands as opposed to two (as in the case of liberalism and conservatism) is itself rather telling. The main difference between the three main strands centres upon how one might replace capitalism with a socialist economic system. Underpinning the debate over the *means* to achieve socialism is a different world-view as to what a socialist society should look like.

The three main strands of socialist thought are **social democracy**, **democratic socialism** and revolutionary socialism (or **Marxism**). As it is by far the most influential, it seems appropriate to begin with social democracy.

	Social democracy	Democratic socialism	Revolutionary socialism
Ideological axis	Centre-left	Left-wing authoritarian	Extreme left authoritarian
Means of change	Gradualist approach	Parliamentary means based on the support of the masses	Revolutionary in order to replace capitalism with a communist society
Key figures	Crosland, Giddens	Benn, Bobbio	Marx, Engels, Lenin

The Definitive Guide to Political Ideologies

Closer to the centre of the political spectrum than any other strand of socialism, social democracy has long been the dominant influence within the Labour party itself. Virtually all of the leading politicians within the party's history belong on the centre-left of the political spectrum, and Labour governments have always been much closer to social democracy than any other strand of socialist thought. In crude electoral terms the majority of voters belong near to the centre of the political spectrum, and social democrats have often claimed that their vision of a socialist society is the one most likely to provide a path to power for the Labour party itself. Having said this, there is much more to this moderate strand of socialism than simply one of electoral considerations.

The most important aspect of social democracy is the belief that capitalism can be **humanised** to benefit working people. A mixed economy enables us to create a society radically different to that which exists under free-market capitalism. It is here that one can trace a degree of overlap with social liberals. However, the *extent* to which the state plays a role within a society based around social democracy is considerably greater than that which would occur under social liberalism. Moreover, the aims of social liberalism are completely different to any strand of socialism. In addition, it is helpful to distinguish between the desire for a mixed economy and the radical alternative proposed by Marxists who prescribe a command economy where resources are allocated on a planned basis.

Following on from the previous point, **incremental change** is the most appropriate method available towards creating a society based around left-wing values of equality and social justice. For social democrats, revolution is neither necessary nor desirable. On this crucial point, there is absolutely no common ground with Marxists – a branch of socialist thought that advocates revolution *and* believes such radical change is inevitable. For social democrats, violent insurrection is not the right path towards socialism because the ends do not justify the means. This gradualist and restrained approach to change is best exemplified within the labour movement by the Fabian Society. Sometimes criticised for being too intellectual and elitist within an ideology that is at heart all about changing the existing order, Fabianesque ideas have exerted a great deal of influence within the party itself. For example, Clause 4 of the party's Constitution (1918) was written by two prominent Fabians (Sidney and Beatrice Webb). It committed the Labour party to *"secure for the workers by hand or by brain the full fruits of their industry, and the most equitable distribution thereof that may be possible upon the common ownership of the means of production, distribution and exchange."* Although Labour failed to live up to such idealistic objectives whilst in government, the 'old' Clause 4 proved a guiding principle of the labour movement (which incorporates the Labour party, the trade unions and pressure groups such as Compass and Red

Pepper) and to this day remains an important expression of socialist thought. The Fabian Society is the party's leading think-tank and gains its name from the Roman General Quintus Fabius Maximus (nicknamed *"the Delayer"*) who adopted a step-by-step approach to change. This gradualist approach to modifying the economic system in favour of working people reached its zenith during the Wilson / Callaghan governments of the 1960s and 70s. During the post-war era several other countries successfully adopted the social democratic path towards socialism, particularly Sweden. Rudolph Meidner and Gosta Rehn were responsible for an economic model that stood for over 25 years and was the basis for the high wage, high concentration of capital and low wage differential Swedish economy. The Rehn-Meidner model resulted in Sweden having a very egalitarian wage system so that wage differentials between professions remained low, and to this day, Sweden is the only country in the world where the state spends over half of national income. The Social Democrats have regularly been in office, and it has often been argued that *"all Swedes are social democrats."*

In the UK, the Labour leadership has watered-down the party's historical commitment to socialist objectives since the mid-1990s and replaced it with a set of ideologically incoherent policies. An assortment of New Right theory and third way ideology has characterised the Labour government's stance since coming to office in May 1997, and many within the labour movement have been dismayed at the government's lack of commitment to the goals of equality and social justice, even those traditionally on the right of the party (such as the former deputy leader of the party Roy Hattersley) who once described Tony Blair as *"the prophet of ideologically footloose politics."* For those on the left of the party - such as Tony Benn – new Labour is little more than *"a party within a party."* Nonetheless, in order to properly assess the ideology behind new Labour we need to consider the impact of the third way.

The third way is difficult to define, but intellectuals within this ideological tradition - notably Sir Anthony Giddens (1998) – describe the ideology as a **modified** version of social democracy which reflects the globalised world that we inhabit. The third way can be said to consist of six main elements;

> ➢ An acceptance that some of the reforms instigated and policies enacted by the Conservative governments of the 1980s and 90s were both necessary and desirable.
> ➢ An attempt to renew the central tenets of social democracy in relation to globalisation.
> ➢ A desire to rebalance the notion of rights and responsibilities towards a communitarian basis.
> ➢ An attempt to restructure the welfare state in order to provide

The Definitive Guide to Political Ideologies

practical benefit to those wishing to escape the poverty trap.
- ➢ A modest redistribution of wealth within society.
- ➢ A belief in the concept of stakeholding – where businesses have a responsibility to various groups, rather than just their shareholders.

During the early years of the new Labour project leading figures within the party often talked about the third way, but the term has been out of fashion now for several years. In retrospect, the third way was part of a wider attempt to re-brand the party and make it electable again after four consecutive defeats to the Conservative party. The third way is also based upon the oxymoron of the radical centre; both its greatest strength and the source of its main weakness. The contemporary author Will Hutton spoke for many when he described new Labour as an ideologically incoherent movement cherry-picking from both left and right. It therefore presents itself to the electorate as the party of enterprise and regulation, flexible labour markets and social justice, and most importantly of all change and no change (2002, p.14). Thus in trying to be all things to all people, new Labour has sidelined the values and objectives of socialism for the unprincipled pursuit of power.

There is much evidence to support Hutton's claim. Whilst new Labour have won three elections in a row, a feat unprecedented within the party's history, the party has done very little to overturn New Right orthodoxy in terms of welfare and economic policy. Socialists within the labour movement have been critical of the close relationship between the government and big business, with Gordon Brown's long-standing support for light-touch regulation of the financial services looking increasingly naïve in the context of the credit crunch. New Labour have also abandoned many of the concerns of working people, with four million voters having deserted the party since the 1997 General Election. Yet perhaps the most perceptive criticism of new Labour derives from its drift towards authoritarian and illiberal policies during the past few years. Liberals from all parties have claimed that the government has undermined civil liberties in an ill-defined war against terror and a desire to outflank the Tories by being tough on crime. In the words of the contemporary political scientist Ralf Dahrendorf *the third way is not about either open societies or liberty. There is … a curious authoritarian streak in it.*

It is perhaps too soon to offer a full assessment of new Labour and the third way. All we can say with certainty is that the third way instigated a renewal in social democracy during the 1990s when traditional socialist objectives of equality and the redistribution of wealth were watered-down for perceived electoral gains. It is also useful to place recent developments within the party into some sort of international context. Many centre-left parties have been shaped by the ideas of the third way, not least Germany where the SPD has been greatly influenced by *die neue Mitte*. Blair and Brown are certainly not alone in this trend, and in some countries new Labour's approach is actually admired (as in France by prominent politicians within the Parti Socialiste such as Segolene Royal). Moreover, new Labour have done more to advance the cause of social justice than they are sometimes given credit for, and whilst in government new Labour's record actually compares well to the Wilson / Callaghan era.

The second strand of socialist thought is democratic socialism. This branch of socialist thought is **more left-wing** than social democracy and stipulates that socialism can be achieved via **parliamentary** means. Britain's unitary structure and traditional notion of executive dominance provides the Labour party with the opportunity to build a socialist Britain on the basis of a clear mandate from the people. Crucial to this strand of socialist thought is the concept of democracy. For democratic socialists, the will of the people and the goals of socialism are **intertwined**. One of its leading intellectuals is the Italian theorist Noberto Bobbio, who argues that democracy must always be the defining value of socialism. Furthermore, the reordering of society upon the basis of providing for the majority of people is itself highly democratic.

Democratic socialists differ from revolutionary socialists on the issue of political violence. According to the latter, capitalism will be overthrown via a revolution led by the proletariat. In contrast, democratic socialists such as the theorist Karl Kautsky (1902) claim that the proletariat must emancipate itself through **democratic means** as opposed to revolution. As should be clear, the distinction between the various strands of socialist thought centres upon the *means* to achieve socialism. This observation also applies when we consider other ideologies that advocate a major transformation in the existing structures of society – such as feminism and anarchism.

Nowhere near as influential as social democracy, democratic socialism has nonetheless had some limited impact within the labour movement itself (particularly the trade unions). Many of its most prominent supporters have been deliberately marginalised by the party's hierarchy. Perhaps the clearest illustration of this point is Tony Benn, although modern-day examples include Jon Cruddas and John McConnell. The high-point for democratic socialism in the UK occurred during the early-1980s, when the party turned sharply to the left as a response to the failure of the Callaghan government to secure lasting benefits for working people. Labour's 1983 General Election Manifesto pledged a number of left-wing policies (such as unilateral nuclear disarmament, withdrawal from the European Community, abolition of private schools and a massive programme of nationalisation) and was memorably described by

The Definitive Guide to Political Ideologies

Gerald Kaufman MP as *"the longest suicide note in history."* Since the 1980s the party has moved further away from the left and towards the electoral centre-ground.

The third strand of socialism is widely referred to as Marxism. The key difference from other branches of socialist thought centres upon its **rejection of democratic methods** to secure socialism. Unlike social democrats and democratic socialists, Marxists advocate revolutionary change as the only means to overhaul capitalism. Merely tinkering with the existing economic system will never lead to a truly socialist society. For Marxists, the conventional political process will not facilitate a socialist society. This is based on the argument that capitalists will always infiltrate political parties and other elements of the labour movement with bourgeois values. As such, the proper path towards socialism must therefore negate the parliamentary route. Moreover, capitalism can never be 'humanised' as claimed by social democrats. For Marxists, any path other than the one prescribed by Karl Marx would fatally compromise the core goals of socialism. In simple terms - it is revolution or nothing! In the incendiary words of Karl Marx, *"workers of the world unite you have nothing to lose except your chains."*

Marxism also differs to other branches of socialism in terms of what it offers as an alternative to capitalism. Whereas social democrats prescribe a **mixed economy** and democratic socialists favour a high level of **state planning** in order to ensure economic development, Marxists believe that the only viable alternative to capitalism is **Communism**. The term communism predates Marx and derives from the French word *commune* (meaning a small village). Communists before Marx advocated a society run along the basis of a small community where wealth would be owned collectively as opposed to privately. Whereas capitalism is based upon private property, Communism is based upon the *common* ownership of the means of production. According to Marx a communist society would be based upon total equality. It would be a society without competition and with enough resources for everyone. It would be free from exploitation and class distinctions. There would be no division of labour, resources would be allocated on the basis of need and comrades would be free to engage in creative labour. Several regimes throughout the world have at some stage operated under the banner of Communism, although none have managed to fulfil the utopian vision outlined by Marx and Engels in the *Communist Manifesto* (1848).

The role of the state

Socialism is conventionally located on the left-authoritarian axis due to its association with a significant degree of state intervention, particularly in the economic realm. This reflects one of the central elements of socialism, namely a critique of capitalism which necessitates a search for an alternative economic system. Having said this, the extent to which the state should interfere within the economy in order to secure left-wing objectives such as equality and social justice differs greatly according to the strand of socialism in question. As such, we need to differentiate between each strand of socialism in order to enhance our understanding of the role of the state in socialist thought.

To fully understand the socialist perspective upon the role of the state we need to begin with the concept of economic determinism. Socialists claim that the role of the state under capitalism is to **maintain** the dominant position of the bourgeoisie and perpetuate the exploitation of the proletariat. As a solution, socialists advocate a change in the economic system itself. In replacing capitalism, the role of the state is of absolutely central importance. Socialism therefore offers a critique of the role of the state under capitalism, and advocates ways in which the state can be used to create a new society based around equality and social justice. Therefore, socialists offer a descriptive and prescriptive stance on the role of the state. In terms of the former, socialists claim that under capitalism the state reflects and reinforces the dominance of one class over another. The agents of the state protect the interests of the wealthy and powerful at the expense of the majority. In the words of Karl Marx; *"the executive is but a committee for managing the common affairs of the bourgeoisie."* On this point at least, there is little disagreement amongst socialists. Divisions only occur when we consider the *means* to achieve a post-capitalist society.

For social democrats, capitalism can be civilised by a significant degree of **state intervention**. This would include the redistribution of wealth from rich to poor via progressive taxation, the provision of welfare services free at the point of use, comprehensive (as opposed to selective) education, management of the economy via co-operation with the trade unions and so on. This moderate strand of socialism argues that capitalism can be tamed by a role for the state on the basis of a mixed economy. After a major expansion in government expenditure during the Attlee administration (1945-1951) some argued that capitalism had been fundamentally reformed along socialist lines (Crosland, 1956). In contrast, democratic socialists completely reject the view that capitalism can be humanised. Only a **major programme of nationalisation** will secure the objectives of socialism. Crucially, this major expansion in the role of state must gain legitimacy from the people and take full account of the need to maintain democracy within a society. It is imperative that the people be persuaded that socialism is morally superior to capitalism.

Marxists prescribe a radically different role for the state. To understand the Marxist stance, we need to go back to the concept of economic determinism. Under capitalism, the role of the state is designed to 'legitimise' the dominant position of the ruling class, to oppress those that threaten the status quo and to distort the reality of class conflict (thereby preventing the emergence of class consciousness). For Marxists, the state is ultimately an **instrument of class rule**. Under capitalism, the bourgeoisie dominates the proletariat. Yet under the dictatorship of the proletariat, the position would be reversed and the proletariat would thereby dominate the bourgeoisie. At this stage of history the state would abolish private property, control the means of production, distribute resources on the basis of the collective good, raise consciousness amongst the people and thereby build the foundations of a genuine classless society. When this particular stage of history is reached the state would no longer exist and people would receive resources on the basis of need. It would be a communist society where class differences would simply disappear. As such, the *only* means to secure a socialist society is for the state to operate on the basis of a communist economic system.

Critics of socialism argue that such an excessive reliance upon the state represents a threat to our liberty and basic freedoms. This argument derives from both the liberal and conservative perspective, and is particularly relevant to those societies based around the ideology of Marxism. Marxist societies have an unenviable reputation for state brutality, arbitrary surveillance and implacable opposition to liberal values. The Soviet regime alone killed almost 62 million of its own people, China's *"Great Leap Forward"* accounted for 20 to 30 million people and the Khymer Rouge in Cambodia went on a killing rampage that accounted for a quarter of the entire population. In the context of state surveillance, those who lived under such regimes were spied upon by the agents of the state such as the KGB in the Soviet Union, the Securitate in Romania and the ruthlessly efficient Stasi of East Germany. To this day no other population has been so spied upon by its own government as that of East Germany, where there was approximately 1 informer for every 6 people (Molloy, 2009). Moreover, there was a total disregard for human rights. Marx himself thought that rights epitomised a corrupt egoism that separated the individual from their real identity within society, a view epitomised by latter-day Marxists such as Vladimir Illyich Lenin who once said that *"Liberty is precious – so precious that it must be rationed."* There are many illustrations of the illiberal character of Communist regimes, such as the imprisonment of dissidents and the enforced collectivisation of labour. Furthermore, there were several attempts by the state to *"re-educate"* those labelled as class enemies. On occasions, such actions had a distinct racial overtone despite official pronouncements of equality and fraternity. For example, the Romanian authorities conducted a mass programme of enforced sterilisation of Romany Gypsy women, and Saddam Hussein ordered the destruction of the Kurdish people during his reign as Head of the left-wing Ba'ath party in Iraq.

In the context of British politics, many of those along the libertarian axis of the political spectrum have raised concerns over the degree to which new Labour has undermined civil liberties in several areas. Obviously of a very different character to totalitarian Communist societies, concerns have nonetheless been raised at the increased role of the state in our lives. From liberals this criticism is perhaps to be expected, yet conservatives are in a rather different position. The core value of conservatism is order, and throughout history Tory governments have often implemented authoritarian measures in order to deal with threats to stability within society. Nonetheless, conservatives have also criticised socialists for ignoring the essential character and unique heritage of the British people. This point was eloquently expressed by Winston Churchill, undoubtedly the leading figure within the Tory party of the last century, when he said that *"a socialist policy is abhorrent to the British ideas of freedom. Socialism is inseparably interwoven with totalitarianism and the object worship of the state. It will prescribe for every one where they are to work, what they are to work at, where they may go and what they may say."* In their defence, socialists believe that liberty itself is determined by the economic system, and only by changing the entire basis of capitalism can we experience genuine emancipation and thereby become the masters of our own destiny.

Socialism and equality

The core value of socialism is **equality**. No other ideology is as closely linked to the goal of equality as socialism, and greater equality is an absolutely fundamental goal for all socialists. Thus in order to understand the socialist stance on equality, we must once again begin with the concept of economic determinism. For socialists, wealth derives less from individual effort / ability and more from the individual's place within a capitalist society. The opportunity to acquire wealth within a capitalist society is largely based upon the circumstances of one's birth and the life chances presented to us. As an alternative, capitalism must be radically transformed in order to create a more **egalitarian society**. In basic terms, socialism stipulates that everyone has equal worth and should therefore receive a fair chance in life.

The means to secure the goal of equality differs according to the strand of socialism we might consider. For social democrats, a more even distribution of wealth on the basis of **progressive taxation** taken directly from source is both necessary and justifiable. For example, by the end of a lengthy period of cross-party consensus (1945-1979) shaped by social democratic values the level of income tax for top-earners stood at 83%, and tax levels on inherited wealth stood at just under 100%. Equality could also be achieved via a shift away from selective education towards comprehensive education. In doing so, social democrats believe that we can create a fairer society. Such attempts reflected a notable tradition within the labour movement including figures such as Robert Owen, Harold Wilson and Anthony Crosland; all of whom placed a high value on education as a means to create a better society.

Democratic socialists are also staunch supporters of equality, but unlike social democrats, they believe that the state must substantially increase its role within society and the economy. In doing so, the state could **redistribute wealth** on a much more even basis than that which would occur under capitalism. Unlike social democrats, they believe that only a major programme of wealth redistribution can ensure social justice and equality. They adopt a Robin Hood-style approach to taxation (taking from the rich to provide for the poor), particularly on unearned income such as inherited wealth. Once again, the key distinction between social democrats and democratic socialists centres upon the *extent* to which state intervention might occur. For the latter, the state has a dominant role to play. Equality can only be achieved when the influence of capitalism is marginalised. That said, both democratic socialists and social democrats agree that laissez-faire capitalism would distribute wealth and resources in an entirely uneven and unfair manner. The market simply cannot provide for all members of society (particularly those on low incomes) because the marketplace operates solely on the profit motive. Only the state can provide for all regardless of social background and thereby mitigate the effects of the 'free' market.

Marxists take a rather different view of equality and the means to achieve it. According to Marxist analysis, the economic system is defined in terms of the relationship to **the means of production**. Under capitalism, the dominant relationship within society is that which exists between those who generate the wealth (the proletariat) and those who own the wealth (the bourgeoisie). Marx also claimed that at each stage of history the economic basis of society was characterised by exploitation. This would inevitably lead to conflict and – in accordance with the dialectic concept – result in a new stage in history. On the basis of this analysis, Marx famously predicted the collapse of capitalism. He firmly believed that capitalism created its own gravedigger in the form of the exploited and down-trodden proletariat. Whilst admiring the rapid development of capitalism, Marx took the view that conflict was inevitable and that a new society would emerge from the ruins of capitalism. A communist society would be free from exploitation and would bring class conflict to an end. In other words, it would be a class-*less* society based upon **true equality**.

In order to achieve a society based upon equality, Marx predicted that a form of class consciousness would emerge amongst the proletariat. He predicted that the proletariat would only become revolutionary when they became fully conscious of their situation. Consciousness would therefore have to be raised amongst the exploited. Class solidarity would translate into collective action and class polarisation would occur – thereby increasing the numbers of those who understood the system to be based upon the exploitation of the proletariat. The exploited would then realise where its true interests lay. Prominent members of the proletariat (the *vanguard*) would lead the proletariat into revolutionary action. Perhaps the clearest example of this point is the role of Lenin during the Bolshevik Revolution, a man who once said that a revolution only comes about *"when those from above cannot cope anymore and those from below do not want to cope any more."*[7]

As is self-evident, there is a rich vein of socialist thought on the issue of equality and the means to achieve this particular goal. Marxism in particular offers a radical path towards a truly equal society, and it is Marxism that presents us with evidence of the ability or otherwise of socialist thought to secure its objectives. Critics of state planning claim that socialism can never achieve its aims. In the words of the classical liberal Milton Freidman, *"a society that puts equality – in the sense of equality of outcome – ahead of freedom will end up with neither equality nor freedom."* This argument certainly holds validity when applied to those societies which claimed to be 'Marxist.' The ruling elite in those countries enjoyed luxuries way out of reach for the remainder of society. Furthermore, wage differentials remained despite the Marxist prediction that resources would be allocated according to the maxim ***"from each according to his ability, to each according to his need."*** Other critics of socialist regimes – including the conservative philosopher Karl Popper (1962) - claimed that the state would have to constantly intervene in order to prevent people eroding the socialist principle of an even distribution of wealth. According to Popper, the redistribution of wealth is entirely inconsistent with

---

[7]   Latter-day Marxist intellectuals lived up to Marx's predictions in various ways. One of the most intriguing historical examples relates to the Italian theorist Antonio Gramsci who launched the newspaper *L'Ordine Nuovo* in Turin during the early 1920s. The aim of the newspaper was to show how a revolution could be achieved. Gramsci was later imprisoned by the Fascist leader (and former Socialist party member) Benito Mussolini to *"stop that brain from functioning."*

the innate character of human nature, and would thereby result in the state imposing an unacceptable degree of uniformity upon its people.

Thus far we have considered that which divides socialists, but there is a point of agreement in relation to the issue of the hereditary principle. Socialists firmly believe that we must become a meritocratic society in which privilege and wealth are no longer ascribed at birth but are open to all regardless of social background. Socialists believe passionately in the desirability of an **open society**, and the Labour movement was set up to fight privilege and the vested interests of the rich and powerful. On the issue of the hereditary principle, Britain is unique in that it retains an unelected second chamber containing over 90 hereditary peers. The existence of an unelected chamber with members ascribed their status from birth is anathema to socialist thinking. There have been repeated calls within the Labour movement to radically reform (or even abolish) the House of Lords altogether. Some socialists have also been critical of the elevated status awarded to the Royal Family, although this view is limited to mavericks within the labour movement and is in no way representative of mainstream opinion.

Whatever perspective one takes upon socialism, it is unquestionably the case that equality holds the same importance to socialism as liberty does within liberal thought and social order has within conservative ideology. The Labour movement has been responsible for many of the most far-reaching moves towards greater equality within society, most notably the Attlee government (1945-1951) that laid the foundations for the modern welfare state as we know it today. To its supporters, socialism has improved the lives of millions via a range of policies shaped by a passionate concern for social justice. Yet to its critics, the socialist addiction to equality is completely alien to human nature and can lead to damaging (even devastating) consequences for individual liberty. It can also lead to problems for economic growth, an argument put forward by classical liberals such as Ludwig von Mises and Friedrich Hayek. According to the economic calculation problem an economic system run on a planned basis will find it impossible to allocate resources in an efficient manner because of the absence of the price mechanism. In retrospect, this argument could be employed as an explanation for the failure of the communist economic system. [8]

---

[8] For those who lived under Communism in Eastern Europe the following analogy was often used -*"They were pretending to be working and the employers were pretending to be paying them."*

The relationship between socialism and liberal democracy

For socialists, 'democracy' within a capitalist system denies working people the chance to transform the economic system on a fairer and more equitable basis. Liberal democracy will always ensure that capitalism 'wins' because powerful economic interests are able to greatly influence the political process in a manner that runs counter to socialist objectives. The media also plays a significant role in determining the contours of political debate, often with the aim to discredit any genuine left-wing policy programme. Moreover, the parliamentary system itself acts as a significant barrier towards radical change on the basis of left-wing values. As a consequence of all these factors, Labour governments are heavily restricted in terms of their ability to implement a genuine socialist alternative to capitalism. Therefore, a wholesale **transformation of the economic system** is required in order to attain a society based around socialist values.

As one can see, the main element of the socialist critique centres upon the **lack of genuine choice**. Providing the electorate with a choice between two or more bourgeois parties was dismissed by Marx as *"the sophistry of the political state."* He claimed that true power was held by the apparatus of the state (the bureaucracy, the law-enforcement agencies, the legal system, etc.). Parties were mere agents of the ruling class, even if they avowed left-wing policies. Elections therefore provided little more than the illusion of choice. For evidence of this argument, one might consider the American President Barack Obama who spent $640 million during the 2008 Presidential campaign. This represents an incredible accumulation of political debt because his financial backers will doubtless expect something in return for their 'investment.' At the very least, Obama is highly unlikely to do much that would threaten the interests of big business. According to the socialist critique, the political process within a liberal democracy will always be heavily biased towards those who can buy influence. In the case of British politics, the Bernie Ecclestone affair soured the early optimism of the new Labour government, and for a Prime Minister once elected on the pledge that he was a *"pretty straight sort of guy,"* it was somewhat revealing that Blair left office with the cash-for-peerages scandal in the news. Furthermore, since 1997 new Labour have pushed forward an agenda shaped by the needs of capitalists (such as the maintenance of a flexible labour force, light-touch regulation of the financial services and tax loopholes for the very wealthy) – much to the dismay of committed socialists.

Secondly, **the media** plays a significant role in preventing the emergence of a genuine socialist alternative to the unregulated free market. Commercial television presents capitalism as the natural basis of an economy, with some stations promoting a particularly virulent pro-market anti-socialist viewpoint.

Socialism is also thwarted by the propaganda put forward by right-wing elements of the press. In the UK, the role of the media mogul Rupert Murdoch has been of considerable political importance. He has routinely engaged in attacking left-wing Labour figures and has at times appeared to influence New Labour policies. For example, Murdoch's firm opposition to European integration (and the damage he could do to the Labour government) was widely perceived to have dissuaded Tony Blair from taking the pound into the Eurozone. Since coming to office, Brown has been understandably concerned at the support shown by the Murdoch press for a resurgent Conservative party under David Cameron. In a political sense, Brown came of age during Murdoch's portrayal of Labour as a party dominated by the so-called *"loony left."* Perhaps it is not entirely coincidental that Brown has repeatedly argued in favour of flexible labour markets and open competition, policies very much within Murdoch's particular view of the world. Murdoch is just the latest in a long-line of right-wing press barons that have thwarted the emergence of a socialist Britain. For example, during the 1924 General Election the Daily Mail published the forged Zinoviev letter and helped bring to an end the first-ever Labour government; and in a particularly telling quote Lord Beaverbrook of the Daily Express once admitted that *"I run the newspaper purely for propaganda purposes."*

Socialists also claim that **the parliamentary system** itself can act as a barrier to the emergence of a workable and effective socialist policy programme. This is based on the argument that - whilst in government - the Labour party have often faced resistance from sections of the civil service. The former Cabinet Minister Tony Benn once argued that the civil service adopts a mentality that is firmly opposed to radical change and very much in favour of the status quo. During his period as a Cabinet Minister Benn claimed that certain projects were 'pigeon-holed' due to their left-wing nature. So despite the claim of civil service neutrality, the state apparatus works as a barrier against the creation of a socialist Britain. The concentration of power into the hands of the executive can also thwart moves towards socialism, as historically the Labour leadership has tended to be much closer to the centre of the political spectrum than many others within the labour movement. In recent years, this has been clearly demonstrated in the desire amongst the new Labour elite to keep left-wing MPs 'on message' and in the context of several controversial measures instigated by the government (e.g. over foundation hospitals, the Iraq war, cutting the level of incapacity benefit for disabled people and the Private Finance Initiative).

The socialist critique of liberal democracy is a particularly illuminating one within the realm of political ideology. Whilst conservatives offer a degree of scepticism towards our understanding of liberal democracy, socialists highlight several weaknesses within the most prominent of all political systems. For socialists, a liberal democratic system is one in which freedom and liberty is largely determined by a person's level of economic wealth. For example, the 'right' to set up one's own political party is largely limited to wealthy individuals such as Sir James Goldsmith in the case of the now defunct Referendum party. As Lenin himself once argued; *"Freedom in a capitalist society always remains about the same as it was in ancient Greek republics - Freedom for slave owners."* Marxists such as Gramsci go even further than other strands of socialism, claiming that the bourgeoisie maintain their hegemonic status via the spread of false consciousness within society. As you can see, there is a great deal to the socialist critique of liberal democracy to explore. Due to its relevance to order and hierarchy, the notion of false consciousness will be considered in more detail later.

Predictably, the remedy offered by the various strands of socialism causes considerable disagreement. For social democrats, the character and context of capitalism can and should be humanised. In doing so, society becomes fairer due to a more even spread of life chances. For democratic socialists, the state has a major role to play in terms of allocating resources within the economy. In doing so, the state can run the economy for the benefit of the majority as opposed to the wealthy minority. Crucially, both these strands of socialist thought are opposed to a violent insurrection. The aim of both social democrats and democratic socialists is to transfer power towards working people and their representatives (such as MPs, trade union leaders, etc.). Empowering working people is the guiding principle at work here. Democratic socialists also believe in a form of socialism from below and - in doing so - try to distinguish their position from revolutionary and authoritarian socialists. For example, democratic socialists are in favour of **workers control** in which firms are run in accordance with the will of the people employed by that firm.

Unlike other forms of socialism, Marxism is based firmly upon a historical analysis of class conflict. Marx was different to other political theorists in that he believed it was possible to predict when a revolution would occur. For Marx, capitalism was an exploitative economic system where the bourgeoisie managed to keep wages low and working conditions poor by retaining a reserve army of labour and refusing to raise wages due to the weak bargaining position of the workers. They also made workers redundant during periods of overproduction and kept wages deliberately low in order to maximise the level of surplus value for the bourgeoisie. But as profits increased, so too did the level of exploitation. Eventually, the extent of **exploitation** would instigate the gradual emergence of **class consciousness**. The workers view of the world, and the reality of that world, would become increasingly dislocated.

Working-class movements would become more militant in their actions and a revolution led by the proletariat would inevitably follow. So whereas Marx admitted that capitalism generated considerable wealth for the bourgeoisie, his analysis centred upon its effects upon the proletariat. The majority of people were effectively trapped in a state of poverty. For Marx, capitalism created the seeds of its own destruction and was therefore doomed to collapse. Naturally, liberal democracy would also disappear as history progressed towards the inevitable victory of the proletariat.

It is difficult to offer one over-arching comment in terms of the relationship between socialism and liberal democracy. Nonetheless, it is true to say that socialists do not share the liberal faith in the desirability of liberal democracy. The most obvious illustration of this point derives from Karl Marx who argued in favour of removable servants acting under continuous public supervision and of course the aforementioned dictatorship of the proletariat. Non-revolutionary socialists have also advocated a powerful role for non-elected and unaccountable technocrats to ensure the goals of equality and social justice. During the late-18th and early-19th century the French theorist Saint-Simon was one of the first to argue in favour of technocrats exercising power within a society. In the modern era, the belief that technocrats hold expertise and should therefore exercise power on behalf of society is best exemplified within the European Union. Two other Frenchman, Jean Monnet (1888-1979) and Robert Schuman (1886-1963), were both strong advocates of European integration on this basis. In the context of Communist states such as the Soviet Union, a powerful elite (the Politburo in the case of the Soviet Union) held power to ensure that progress towards socialism would occur. Once again, one can see a huge divergence between socialism and liberalism here.

The individual and society

Both social democrats and democratic socialists wish to transform capitalism along **non-revolutionary** lines. The aim of such change is to reorder the relationship between the individual and society along the lines of equality, social justice and fairness. Whereas social democrats advocate piecemeal change in order to tame the forces of unbridled capitalism, democratic socialists advocate state ownership of the commanding heights of the economy. Common to both these strands of socialist thought is a passionate desire to empower the individual (particularly working people) on the basis of creating a truly socialist society.

Marxists however take a more strident stance. First and foremost, Marxists claim that under capitalism (as with other economic systems) the relationship between the individual and society is based on **class conflict**. The proletariat are exploited by those who own the means of production and thereby experience alienation. According to Marxist analysis, there are three aspects to alienation within a capitalist society. Firstly, workers are separated from their own labour by forcing to sell their labour for low wages. Secondly, their own workplace is physically alien to them. Thirdly, the product of their labour has little or nothing to do with their labour. This analysis was based upon a study of the harsh conditions encountered by the proletariat during the Industrial Revolution - a system based upon free markets, open trade and a flexible labour market. Friedrich Engels believed that those who toiled away in the cotton factories of Manchester had reached the lowest stage of humanity, and Karl Marx memorably argued that *"the more formed the product the more deformed the workers, the more civilised the product, the more barbaric the worker, the more powerful the work, the more powerless becomes the worker."*

As with other strands of socialism, Marxism attempts to reorder the relationship between the individual and society. Yet unlike social democrats and democratic socialists, Marxists predict that a communist society will emerge in which the individual and society become one. Under this utopian vision **"the socialist state expresses the will of the mass of the workers, and the individual owes it absolute obedience."** There would no longer be a need for bourgeois concepts such as rights and individualism. To critics of Marxism (even those within the ideology of socialism!), this is a recipe for a totalitarian state dictating the lives of its inhabitants. From the liberal perspective, John Stuart Mill predicted that the proletariat (or those acting on their behalf) would centralise power and crush all opposition. They would be characterised by an insensibility to the suffering of others. The Russian gulags, the cultural revolution in China, the Khymer Rouge in Cambodia and the military actions of the Soviet Union firmly support Mill's observation. From a similar perspective, Rosa Luxembourg warned that the dictatorship of the proletariat would be replaced by the dictatorship of the party, which would in turn be replaced by the dictatorship of the central committee. Economic liberals also claimed that a Communist society would fail to reach its utopian end because it failed to understand the need for economic incentives. Once again, there is considerable evidence to back up this argument. A common failing to all Communist regimes was a lack of economic resources. None of those societies managed to provide a world of plenty, something of absolutely central importance to Marxist attempts to liberate the people from the exploitation and alienation that characterised a capitalist society. Indeed, it is perhaps ironic that an ideology that owes so much to such a brilliant economist should

The Definitive Guide to Political Ideologies

fall short in this crucial area. All the above points suggest that Marxism was bound to fail in terms of reordering the relationship between the individual and society. Inevitably, the counter-argument is that Marxism has *never* been attempted in the truest sense of the phrase. The problem faced by all those who tried to implement Marxist ideology (such as Stalin, Lenin, Mao, Castro, etc.) was one of applying high-minded theory to the reality of the political world. Secondly, such regimes seemed to replace one class structure with another. This argument reflects the Italian sociologist Vilfredo Pareto's argument about the *"circulation of elites."*

Of all the main strands of socialism, it is social democracy that has held the most influence within the labour movement. This moderate branch of socialist thought does not advocate a major change in the relationship between the individual and society. The main consequence of social democracy is a redistribution of wealth in order to fund programmes ranging from the National Health Service to comprehensive education. Democratic socialists however advocate a greater role for the state than social democrats. Yet crucially, the individual's position within society does not alter to anything like the same extent as that prescribed by Marxism.

Thus far we have concentrated upon the divisions within socialist thought, yet perhaps of greater significance is the distinction to be made between socialism and liberalism in terms of the role of the individual. Whereas liberalism is firmly grounded upon individualism, socialists take a **collectivist stance**. Many of the achievements associated with the labour movement such as the NHS (which has been described as *"the jewel in Labour's crown"* and to this day remains perhaps the most well-known illustration of socialism in practise) have been secured via collective action. For a party that was born out of the bowels of the trade union movement and created to provide an influential voice for the working-classes, the emphasis upon collectivism is to be expected. Socialists claim that the collectivist ethos of a socialist society enables the co-operative characteristics of human beings to flourish. As such, all strands of socialist thought argue that what we achieve together is of greater significance than that which we might achieve alone. In the words of the Labour party's constitution; *"by the strength of our common endeavour we achieve more than we achieve alone, so as to create for each of us the means to realise our true potential and for all of us a community in which power, wealth and opportunity are in the hands of the many, not the few."* These words are a succinct expression of how socialists prescribe the relationship between the individual and society. In contrast, rampant individualism is entirely incompatible with the values and goals of socialism because it generates competition alongside massive inequalities in terms of wealth and life chances.

The socialist stance on lifestyle issues

Supporters of socialism claim that their alternative to capitalism is **morally superior** because it facilitates the inherent goodness of human nature. For social democrats, the entire raison d'etre for changing the economic system is to 'humanise' capitalism. The very term *humanise* reflects their deeply-held desire to create a fairer society based around the concept of social justice. Democratic socialists put forward a radical programme of state ownership in order that the state may allocate resources on a fairer and more efficient basis. These aspects of socialist thinking can be found throughout history. For example, the Welsh social reformer Robert Owen argued that employing child labour was immoral. Owen was a key figure within the co-operative movement and one of the leading practitioners of socialism in action. Today, the alter-globalisation movement is passionately opposed to unbridled capitalism and the existence of sweat-shops in the third world. They argue in favour of fair trade as opposed to free trade. Those furthest to the left of the political spectrum (Marxists) believe that a communist society is morally superior to any other possible alternative, including that offered by other strands of socialist thought.

Behind these predictable divisions, there is a contentious debate within the labour movement over the impact of religion within society. For ethical socialists such as Eduard Bernstein (1961) and Tony Benn (1980), religious teachings are entirely consistent with many left-wing goals. As such, the potential impact of religion upon society is therefore considered in positive terms. Historically, an important relationship exists within the labour movement and religious organisations – particularly non-orthodox religions. Morgan Phillips oft-cited observation that *"the Labour party owes more to Methodism than Marxism"* offers a clear summary of this point. Moreover, religious organisations have engaged in a myriad of campaigns designed to advance the cause of social justice. The point to be made here is that religious values are consistent with many aspects of socialist thought, although they are by no means exclusive to socialism or indeed any other political ideology.

This positive view of religion is not shared by all socialists. Those further to the left of the political spectrum tend to view organised religion as an agent of oppression, particularly within a capitalist society. One of the most important contributions to this argument derives from Karl Marx who once described religion as *"the sigh of the oppressed creature, the heart of a heartless world, and the soul of soulless conditions. It is the opium of the people."* Religion is little more than a means by which the poor and exploited are given false hope of a better afterlife when their energies should be focused upon a complete overhaul of the existing regime here on Earth. Furthermore, some

The Definitive Guide to Political Ideologies

aspects of religion provide legitimacy for the unequal distribution of wealth and power within a capitalist society. Religion therefore presents us with the view that the existing class structure is both natural and in accordance with God's plan. For example, it was once common for children to learn the rhyme *"the rich man in his castle to the poor man at his gate. God made them, high or lowly, and ordered their estate."* Marxists such as Antonio Gramsci and Louis Althusser have also argued that religion presents bourgeois values in a hegemonic manner. Religion is therefore an important agent of social control used by the bourgeoisie to placate those at the bottom of society via the spread of false consciousness. In doing so, religion offers justification for divine justice whereas socialists believe passionately in social justice. [9]

Unlike either of the ideologies considered thus far, socialists do not take a particularly firm stance upon the issue of moral absolutism and moral relativism. In essence, socialism is based upon economic determinism. Morality does not play a major role within that analysis. The main contribution within socialist thought upon the issue of morality is the advocacy of what they believe is a morally superior system. Naturally, this argument is rejected by liberals and conservatives. According to the former, socialism divides people on the basis of class and sidelines individualism for the collective good. For conservatives, socialism is centred upon a utopian vision for society. There are several illustrations of this point. During the 19th century, a community in New Lanark was created along socialist lines by the social reformer Robert Owen. He argued that co-operation and enlightened planning was better than the destructive and exploitative character of capitalism. His was a community in which profit and social co-operation co-existed. Owen also tried unsuccessfully to establish a similar community in America. To conservatives, such experiments are symptomatic of socialism's reliance upon untested ideas and are therefore prone to failure.

The argument that socialism relies upon a utopian vision of a post-capitalist society also finds credence within Marxist thought. Marx himself described socialist thinkers that came before him – such as Saint Simon (1760-1825), Charles Fourier (1772-1837) and Robert Owen (1771-1858) – as utopian. He claimed they all viewed socialism as ethically desirable but offered no historical analysis on the possibility of change. By contrast, Marx developed what he called **scientific socialism**. He claimed there was an empirical basis to his analysis, outlining the historical circumstances through

---

[9]   Consistent with Marxist teachings, all forms of organised religion were banned in many Communist regimes. In some countries, organised religion reached a compromise with the Communist authorities whereas in other countries the Church mobilised the people against the state and provided protection for dissidents of that regime.

which socialism would be bought about. As the reader will doubtless be aware, conservatives are just as opposed to *scientific* socialism as they are to *utopian* socialism. For example, the philosopher Karl Popper argued that Marxism was a *"bogus science"* because it did not facilitate a genuinely scientific approach. Liberals too offer the same criticism of these somewhat different approaches to socialism.

Order and hierarchy

There are two main elements to consider here. The first is that social order and hierarchy within a capitalist society facilitates **mass inequality**, **poverty** and **exploitation**. Secondly, powerful vested interests maintain their dominant position via the spread of **false consciousness**, although this argument is more closely aligned to Marxism than the other strands of socialist thought. Socialists and conservatives in particular disagree substantially on the subject of order and hierarchy.

According to the socialist perspective, order within a capitalist society reflects and reinforces the relationship between the social classes. Within any society various agents of the state – such as the police, the judiciary and the Armed forces – enforce the law. As laws are based upon the self-interest of the ruling classes, those agents of the state exist as a means to oppress the masses. Socialists are therefore critical of the role played by those agents of the state in terms of maintaining order within a capitalist system. For example, the often-expressed view that *"property is nine-tenths the law"* inherently favours the rich at the expense of the poor. The agents of the state also protect the interests of the powerful elite, a point repeatedly demonstrated during alter-globalisation protests. Furthermore, the proletariat is marginalised within the criminal justice system. Socialist critics of the judicial system have claimed that the elitist social background of judges makes them highly unsympathetic towards left-wing groups and working-class movements. They claim it is often difficult for the proletariat to gain justice within the criminal justice system because of the exorbitantly high cost of employing a good lawyer. As a result, order within a capitalist system reflects and reinforces class conflict. A good example of this argument is the 1984-1985 Miners Strike. The left-wing National Union of Mineworkers (NUM) led by Arthur Scargill and the right-wing government of Mrs. Thatcher were locked in a battle of ideas that would determine the future course of industrial relations within the UK. The NUM claimed that they were defending working people from Thatcherism, whereas the government claimed that the miners union represented little more than the *"rule of the mob."* The clash of ideas between left-wing socialism and

New Right ideology defined the era in a manner rarely matched since, at least in the arena of industrial relations. The ability to mobilise agents of the state in such a politicised battle was a major instrument of social control for the government of the day, and Mrs Thatcher was certainly willing to use the police to deal with militant trade unions and therefore defeat socialism. The Miners Strike remains one of the most important periods in recent British political history, and perhaps vindicates the socialist *analysis* of how social order is implemented within a capitalist society.

The second point to consider is the concept of false consciousness, and for that we must once again employ Marxist analysis. In the words of Karl Marx *"the class which has the means of material production at its disposal ... also controls the means of mental production."* Thus under capitalism, Marx claimed that the ruling class (the bourgeoisie) has the means available to generate a false consciousness amongst the proletariat in order to prevent the emergence of class consciousness amongst the oppressed. Latter-day Marxists such as Antonio Gramsci extended this argument further, claiming that various elements of society (such as the Church, the media and political parties) serve to tie the people to a capitalist society by moulding public acceptance of the status quo. Marxists have always recognised both the desire and ability of the bourgeoisie to retain power, which is one of the reasons why Marxists advocate revolutionary change as opposed to non-violent means. It is also argued by latter-day Marxists that one of main reasons why the predictions offered by Marx have failed to materialise is down to the spread of false consciousness within capitalist societies.

Hierarchy under socialism can take many forms. Amongst those closer to the centre of the political spectrum, the need for hierarchy is of some importance. Democratic socialists also prescribe a degree of hierarchy in order for the state to allocate resources in accordance with socialist principles. But before we turn to Marxism, we must pause to reflect upon the **alter-globalisation movement**. This new social movement works on the basis of an elaborate web of contacts as opposed to more traditional hierarchal structures. This has enabled the alter-globalisation movement to be much more mobile in the face of powerful forces intent on defending the status quo than old-fashioned pressure groups. Alter-globalisation contains many elements of left-wing thinking, but unlike the three main strands of socialism it belongs firmly along the libertarian axis of the political spectrum. As the reader will doubtless be aware, Marxism prescribed an unmistakably authoritarian power structure. Quite frankly, some of the most brutal dictators the world has ever known have operated in Communist regimes. To a significant extent the various agents of the state ensured social order in a more violent and exploitative manner than that experienced in capitalist societies – which somewhat undermines the whole Marxist argument.

Change or the status quo

The socialist stance on the status quo is very straight-forward. First and foremost, socialism offers a critique of capitalism. As such, socialism is **opposed** to retaining the status quo. Secondly, socialism advocates a major **change** to the economic system in order to instigate a fairer society constructed around left-wing values of equality and social justice. On both these points, there is agreement amongst all strands of socialist thought. The only division within socialist thought is on the *means* to achieve a post-capitalist society.

Social democrats firmly believe that socialism can be achieved via a gradualist and non-revolutionary approach to change. This strand of thought has long been dominant within the party itself, and policy measures designed to create a more civilised form of capitalism have long been a feature of Labour governments. Even under the watered-down version of social democracy that characterises new Labour there has been some progress towards the goal of social justice. For example since 1997 the Labour government has;

> ➤ Introduced the minimum wage, a socialist objective which dates back to the founder of the Labour party Keir Hardie.
> ➤ Changed the tax and benefits system in order to lift 600,000 children out of poverty (and has pledged to end child poverty by 2020).
> ➤ Substantially increased the level of child benefit.
> ➤ Helped the unemployed get back to work via a New Deal programme paid for out of a windfall tax on the privatised utilities.
> ➤ Extended maternity leave.
> ➤ Cancelled some of the debt owed by third world countries to the UK.
> ➤ More than doubled expenditure on state education.
> ➤ More than trebled the level of resources allocated to the National Health Service.
> ➤ Expanded state provision of childcare via the Surestart scheme.
> ➤ Strengthened the rights of agency workers.
> ➤ Helped to increase the rate of employment of disabled people and reduce the pay gap between men and women.

All those measures listed above have to some degree helped to humanise capitalism. It is a strategy with a lengthy association to Labour in power and was memorably summarised by the former Cabinet minister of the 1940s and 50s Herbert Morrison who once argued that *"socialism is what a Labour government does."*

Democratic socialists believe that the state must control key aspects of the economy in order to implement a socialist agenda. Unlike social democrats, there is a firm belief in the ability of the state to **distribute resources more efficiently** than that which might arise from the marketplace. As such, democratic socialists merely wish to retain a small private sector. They believe that social democracy cannot change the character of the marketplace because of its association with a significant private sector. Yet in common with social democrats, the means to change the basis of society must be peaceful and non-violent. Democratic parliamentary means are more appropriate to the establishment of a socialist society than the dictatorship of the proletariat advocated by revolutionary socialists.

Marxists fervently believe that capitalism will collapse and that the creation of a communist society is **inevitable**. This is based upon Marx's Hegelian-inspired analysis of historical progress. Marx was a student of the famous German philosopher Friedrich Hegel and was influenced by him in three important areas;

> ➢ For Hegel, history was based upon a logical progression of events based upon the dialectic which entails the emergence of a new stage in history when *"a proposition is confronted by its opposite."* Marx agreed with Hegel's view, although he modified it slightly.
>
> ➢ Hegel argued that alienation occurred when the people's perception of the world differed to the reality of that world. Collective consciousness would move away from old perceptions. This would result in major social change in which a new consciousness emerged. Again, Marx agreed with this analysis - although he believed that social change occurred within the realm of economics and not in the realm of human consciousness. The stance taken by Marx could therefore be described as dialectic materialism.
>
> ➢ Based on the two propositions above, society was destined to reach the final end of the dialectic. It would be a society in which each individual's consciousness would be the same as the collective consciousness. Social conflict would therefore cease and we would reach *"the end of history."* For Marx, this would

be a communist society.

As one can clearly see, Marxism advocates the complete rejection of the status quo and believes that capitalism contains the seeds of its own destruction in terms of the oppressed and exploited. After the inevitable victory of the proletariat in the revolution, the position of the social classes would be reversed. However, the proletariat revolution would be the last. The dialectic process would end and the post-capitalist society would be classless in nature. Collective ownership of the means of production and an equal distribution of resources would bring to an end class conflict because everyone would have the same relationship to the means of production.

Socialism in contemporary politics

Due to the significant divergence of thought within socialism, it would seem appropriate to address the question in two stages. The first could be said to deal with socialism as expressed within the conventional political process. The second will focus upon Marxism, which for many years was a hugely significant ideology within global politics.

The labour movement experienced a slow decline during the 1980s. As the post-war consensus came to an end in the UK, the Labour party seemed to implode between moderates and hard-liners. Some of those on the right of the party remained to combat the rise of democratic socialism, whereas others (including prominent ex-Cabinet ministers) left to join the short-lived Social Democratic party. It was a grim decade for the Labour party, and by the 1990s the new Thatcherite consensus appeared firmly embedded within the political culture of the UK. Combined with a decline in class identification and a growing sense of **embourgeoisement** (*"The process by which a working-class person adopts middle-class values usually on the basis of increased wealth and / or a change in occupation"*) amongst the working-classes, socialism seemed to have little future in British politics. Trade unions also suffered greatly under the Thatcher onslaught, and to this day are merely a shadow of their former selves. The days when union leaders were invited round to Number 10 over beer and sandwiches - and could hold the country to ransom over the threat of industrial action - are a distant memory. Changes in the employment market have further weakened the role of trade unions, traditionally a key element of the labour movement.

Since the mid-1990s, a modified form of social democracy has held sway within the upper echelons of the party. Three consecutive election victories (two by a landslide) have given the party an unprecedented period of office, and yet at the time of writing, the entire new Labour project looks to be in terminal decline. It is also debateable to what extent new Labour have implemented a socialist agenda. Critics claim that New Labour have betrayed the cause of left-wing values, yet to its supporters the government has to some extent advanced the cause of social justice. However, few could claim that new Labour is firmly committed to the concept of equality – and as equality is one of *the* defining principles of socialism – this is a rather telling argument. For example, the gap between rich and poor has increased since 1997.

To complete our assessment of conventional socialism, we need to consider left-wing opposition to the process of globalisation. Socialism has experienced a significant fillip from the alter-globalisation movement with many people concerned about the damage done by an ideology of market fundamentalism (Sorros, 2008). Moreover, support for the alter-globalisation movement looks likely to increase due to the public's reaction to the credit crunch. One of the most prominent intellectuals within this movement is the feminist author and journalist Naomi Klein. Her exposé of sweatshops became the bible of the alter-globalisation movement (2000), and her analysis of disaster capitalism (2007) has gained her many political admirers.

An analysis of Marxism inevitably leads us towards a rather different conclusion. During the 19th and 20th century Marxism represented a major challenge to capitalism and liberal democracy, and yet since the end of the cold war Marxism has suffered an irrevocable decline. Whilst many of the parties that dominate Eastern Europe are Marxist in all but name, and communist parties do enjoy *some* electoral success in countries ranging from Italy to India, the political influence of Marxism has waned dramatically. Having said this, it could reasonably be argued that Marxist predictions have not *yet* materialised. Perhaps capitalism really is in its latter stages. The credit crunch is unquestionably the most serious economic crisis for many years – which does vindicate Marxist analysis of the inherently unstable nature of capitalism. Moreover, there are millions of people who have good reason to feel exploited within the capitalist system; not least women and children working in sweatshops. Are they the seeds of the next Marxist revolution? Will *"the wretched of the Earth"* rise off and throw off the shackles of the system - as predicted by the 20th century Marxist Frantz Fanon (1961)? The fascinating thing is that no-one really knows. What we can say with rather more certainty is *why* the proletariat have not yet overthrown the shackles of the capitalist system as predicted by Marx. There are several possible reasons for this.

According to those sympathetic to Marxist analysis (such as the Frankfurt School of the mid-20th century), capitalists have always subverted the entire culture of a society in order to prevent the emergence of a revolution. Capitalists can therefore control consciousness via their influence over various social agents such as the media, the education system and the political process itself. Typical of this view is the argument put forward by the German theorist Herbert Marcuse who predicted that capitalism would eventually control the entire culture of a society. In doing so, it would disguise its true nature and thereby ensure its perpetual hegemony. There is perhaps some validity to his argument. In today's consumerist society, the proletariat appear more interested in consumer goods than the overthrow of the bourgeoisie. Whether this is due to the spread of false consciousness, or a genuine reflection of what the people themselves actually want, is a question that will continue to divide those contributing to the debate over political ideology. It would seem that capitalism has managed to ward off the threat of world-wide revolution simply by modifying the worst effects of market failure, and by providing many more opportunities for people to fulfil their potential than Communism ever could.

Perhaps the answer to this question is more prosaic - in that the proletariat were simply bought off with a welfare state providing for everyone from the cradle to the grave alongside an inexorable growth in consumerism. Those who move up the social scale from working-class parents often exhibit a form of embourgeoisement which ultimately tends to thwart the emergence of class consciousness. As a consequence, when a person moves up a social class he / she loses their revolutionary potential – thereby completely undermining the Marxist argument. Furthermore, governments have used billions of taxpayers' money to bail out the financial institutions. This was once predicted by Lenin himself who so perceptively observed that *"capitalists can get themselves out of any crisis, so long as they make the workers pay."* Alas, most of us will be paying off that debt for many years to come. Ironically, capitalism may have been saved by the very people who are set to lose the most from the biggest financial crisis in living memory.

Further quotes on socialism

"The more governments concede to the demands of world capital, the more they have to suppress their own people." Tony Benn
"The poor have incontestable rights on the abundance of the rich." Turgot
"What is Communism? It is the longest road from capitalism to capitalism."
East European joke
"The worst thing about Communism is what comes after." Adam Michnik
"When I give food to the poor they call me a saint. When I ask why the poor have no food they call me a communist." Helder Camara
"One world with many worlds in it." Slogan of the Zapatistas of Mexico

"We are a poor country and we opted for socialist policies, but to build a socialist society you have to have a developed society." Julius Nyerere

"I suspect that if a sovereign government was to challenge global finance it would be seen as a crime against the World Bank and the IMF and the WTO, and it would come to be regarded as a rogue state." Tony Benn

"All animals are equal, but some are more equal than others." George Orwell

"A spectre is haunting Europe - the spectre of Communism." Karl Marx

"The 21st century will not be about the battle between capitalism and socialism but between the forces of progress and the forces of conservatism." Tony Blair

"The past weighs like a nightmare on the brains of the living." Karl Marx

"International relations is right-wing, like nature. The social contract is left-wing, like humanity." Regis Debray

"To be working class under Communism was to be on the winning side, defeating the enemies of the past and building the socialism of the future." Peter Molloy

"A man is the one who is much, not the one who has much." Karl Marx

"We are all socialists now" Front-cover of Newsweek Magazine February 2009

Recommended reading

Benn, T. (1980) *Arguments for socialism.* A succinct expression of how democratic socialism could transform society. Slightly dated, Benn's work remains a solid introduction towards an understanding of the left-wing socialist perspective.

Cohen, N. (2007) *What's Left.* An account of the inconsistencies within socialist thought and the failure of left-wing parties and movements to translate theory into purposeful action.

Crosland, A. (1956) *The Future of Socialism.* To this day the most important account of social democratic thought. Crosland believed that the Attlee government had managed to fundamentally change the character of capitalism, and that social democracy had shown itself to be both practical and fair.

Etzioni, A. (1995) *The Spirit of Community : Rights, Responsibilities and the communitarian agenda.* An author in the vanguard of the third way, Etzioni outlines the theory of communitarianism that proved a key influence upon centre-left parties in several countries – including the UK.

Giddens, A. (1998) *The Third Way : the Renewal of Social Democracy.* Giddens is the leading intellectual architect of new Labour and this short book offers an outline of how the third way represents a modification of social democracy in the context of the increasingly globalised economy.

Hutton, W. (1995) *The State We're In.* A left-wing critique of how support for the free market and privatisation has undermined the role of the state and the ability of government's to secure left-wing objectives.

Hutton, W. (2002) *The World We're In.* Hutton offers a critique of new Labour from a left-wing perspective, as well as outlining the problems with laissez-faire economics.

Klein, N. (2000) *No Logo.* The most important contribution thus far towards the alter-globalisation movement. Klein puts forward a devastating critique of how capitalism exploits those at the margins of society – particularly women in sweatshops.

Klein, N. (2007) *The Shock Doctrine : The rise of Disaster capitalism.* A superb critique of how radical right-wing ideas gain influence after the disorientating effects of a shock. Klein also outlines the relationship between the psychological impact of a 'shock' and the manner in which governments influenced by New Right ideology advance free-market capitalism.

Marx, K. & Engels, F. (1848) *Manifesto of the Communist Party.* The seminal socialist text and a template for a Communist society. An understanding of socialism would be incomplete without reading this engaging book.

Molloy, P. (2009) *The lost world of Communism.* A timely reminder of what life was like under Communism. Molloy looks at the negatives and the positives of life in Eastern Europe under the Communist banner.

Stiglitz, J. (2002) *Globalisation and its discontents.* An important work within the alter-globalisation movement and one highly critical of the Washington consensus and its impact upon severely indebted countries.

Toynbee, P. & Walker, D. (2008) *Unjust rewards.* A contemporary defence of socialist ideas and the need for greater equality in a world that has become much more unequal in recent years.

Wright, A. (1995) *Socialisms.* A detailed exploration of the various strands and sub-sections of socialist thought.

Ideas for further discussion

In what sense is socialism distinct from social liberalism?
What is unique about the socialist perspective upon human nature?

How do the three main strands of socialism differ in their attitude towards capitalism?

Does socialism always entail an expansion in the role of the state?

How does the socialist perspective on equality differ to that of a liberal?

Why are socialists critical of how liberal democracy operates within a capitalist society?

Why are socialists supportive of collectivism?

Why are socialists divided over the issue of religion?

To what extent are socialists opposed to hierarchy within society?

To what extent are socialists divided over the issue of change?

Does the third way represent a revival of socialism or the abandonment of socialism?

Key terms

Alienation The Marxist perspective takes the view that in a capitalist society the proletariat are alienated from their work. There are essentially four main aspects of alienation within the workplace, the most important of which is a sense of powerlessness. Workers have little or no say over how their work is conducted. Secondly, there is a lack of any meaningful employment due to work being dull, routine and pointless. Alienation is also a waste of human talent, where the skills and abilities of the proletariat are neither encouraged nor developed unless they might serve the wider interests of the bourgeoisie. Finally, there is a sense of isolation from other people. Alienation therefore occurs when the capitalist appropriates the product and the proletariat feels no connection to that product.

Alter-globalisation Whilst the term *anti*-globalisation is often used within political discourse, *alter*-globalisation is a more accurate and relevant term. The core aim of this world-wide movement is to change the whole basis of globalisation away from neo-liberal economies towards meeting the wider needs of humanity and in doing so provide a degree of social justice. The alter-globalisation movement is particularly concerned at the spread of economic imperialism by MNCs. The Marxist historian Eric Hobsbawn even claims that *"the most convenient world for multinational organisations is one populated by dwarf states or no states at all."* States which are politically independent are reduced to powerless agents within a global system dominated by the rich and powerful. Attempts by left-wing governments to radically distribute resources on a more equitable basis face the opposition of powerful forces, thereby reducing the impact of socialism as a force within political ideology.

Bourgeoisie A Marxist term used to describe the owners of capital. The term is commonly applied to the middle class or ruling class. According to the Marxist perspective those who own the means of production exploit those who work the means of production (the proletariat).

Class conflict A Marxist term used to describe the inherent struggle within society between the bourgeoisie and the proletariat. In *the Communist manifesto* (1848), Karl Marx famously argued that all hitherto societies were based upon class conflict. His emphasis upon social class has been widely criticised, even from within the Marxist school of thought, for its conception of social class as being derived from the means of production. Latter-day Marxists have often revised this concept. For example, the Chinese leader Mao Tse-Tung (1893-1976) identified the class struggle of the peasantry with that of the proletariat.

Class consciousness A Marxist term used to describe a particular stage along the course of human development at which the proletariat becomes aware of their exploitation at the hands of the bourgeoisie. Class consciousness eventually determines the realisation of Marx's prediction of a full-scale revolution, eventually leading to the *"dictatorship of the proletariat."* Marxists have often argued that class consciousness is deliberately thwarted by the ability of the bourgeoisie to emphasise differences within the working-class, thereby dividing the proletariat and preventing the emergence of a shared view on their exploitation.

Collectivism A belief that people can unite and work together in order to instigate social change and thereby create a better society. The term is associated with a left-wing political perspective and has a lengthy history within the Labour movement. Individualism is the opposite of collectivism.

Commonsense knowledge A term associated with Antonio Gramsci in the context of his understanding of an individual's dual consciousness. Gramsci argued that commonsense knowledge was potentially revolutionary, but was mitigated by that consciousness raised within wider society.

Communism An economic and political system prescribed by Marxists in which private ownership is replaced by common ownership of the means of production. In theory, a communist society allocates resources upon an equitable basis.

Communitarianism A political philosophy influential during the emergence of 'new' Labour in the mid-1990s. Communitarianism advocates a balance between rights and responsibilities and a combination of social justice alongside market-oriented economics. It is opposed to vigorous individualism and seeks to reinvigorate social democracy. Communitarianism emphasises the interest of communities and societies over those of the individual. According to this particular stance, political reality is always embedded within a community.

Co-operative A voluntary organisation characterised by the absence of private ownership. Co-operatives are owned by their members and run on the basis of a democracy. The term tends to be associated with those on the left of the political spectrum.

Cultural hegemony A Marxist term associated with figures such as the Italian writer Antonio Gramsci. He argued that a particular cultural view can be used and manipulated by the bourgeoisie to dominate other groups within society. Gramsci used the concept of cultural hegemony to explain why Marx's prediction of a revolution led by the proletariat had not occurred on a more widespread level.

Disaster capitalism A term used by the feminist author Naomi Klein (2007) to criticise the Bush administration's Machiavellian attempts to force through radical right-wing policies by exploiting a particular crisis situation. She claims that the 'shock' of major events (such as 9 / 11 and Hurricane Katrina) is manipulated in order to serve the interests of the ruling elite under the guise of 'freedom' and 'democracy.'

Dominant ideology thesis A term used by Marxists to explain why the proletariat remain passive and subordinate to the bourgeoisie. The ruling class within society establishes its own ideology as the dominant one within society, indoctrinating subordinates who therefore accept it as the 'truth.'

Dual consciousness When an individual holds two contradictory sets of beliefs at the same time. For example, the working-class may hold a set of beliefs derived from the education system that contrasts with a set of values acquired from the workplace. The term is associated with the Italian Marxist figure Antonio Gramsci.

Economic determinism A term used by Karl Marx in his influential study of the Industrial Revolution. He argued that society is based upon an economic system in which the various agents of social control are determined by the economic system itself. Within a capitalist society those agents of social control are designed to serve the interests of the bourgeoisie and the ruling class. However, latter-day Marxists such as Louis Althusser and Antonio

Gramsci have challenged this view. There is a useful distinction to be made here between voluntarism and determinism. The former suggests that people make history and that change is not inevitable. Determinism suggests that people do not make history. Change is inevitable because the forces that shape history are inevitable. Karl Marx was a student of Hegel and perhaps because of this he took a deterministic view of the world. However, to some degree Marx also believed that people could shape history; namely via a revolution led by the proletariat.

Egalitarianism A perspective associated with those on the left of the political spectrum, in which the government aims to ensure that everyone has a fair chance in life. Those who endorse moves towards a more egalitarian society claim that it would result in genuine equality and greater social justice. As a concept, egalitarianism is best understood in a relative sense.

Embourgeoisement A process by which a working-class person adopts middle-class values usually on the basis of increased wealth and / or a change in occupation. As the name implies, embourgeoisement represents the spread of bourgeoisie values within society. It can be thought of as the opposite of class consciousness and its existence continues to provoke debate within the social sciences.

False consciousness A term used by Marxists such as Herbert Marcuse and Ralph Miliband to describe the situation in which the proletariat fail to grasp the truly exploitative nature of capitalism. Agents of the bourgeois state generate a sense of false consciousness amongst the proletariat in order to maintain the existence of the capitalist system. False consciousness thereby prevents the proletariat from taking on their predicted role within society as agents of revolutionary change, and is therefore an important instrument of control as used by the ruling class. According to Ralph Miliband (1973), the media is the new *"opium of the people"* by acting as a hallucinatory drug to keep the masses subsumed.

Labour movement A term used to describe the Labour party and its affiliated organisations (such as trade unions, the Christian Socialist Movement, the Fabian Society and the Co-operative Society). The Labour movement advocates a society based upon greater equality and the concept of social justice. In order to achieve these objectives, the labour movement has taken a collective stance upon various issues – such as the withdrawal of labour during a strike.

Means of mental production According to Marxist analysis, the bourgeoisie control the means of mental production and thereby prevent the emergence of class consciousness amongst the proletariat. The bourgeoisie thereby maintain their hegemony within society by presenting values that suit their own interest. Agents involved in the process of mental production include the media, religious institutions and schools. The means of *mental* production may be contrasted with the means of *physical* production – with the latter distinction used by Karl Marx to differentiate between one social class and another.

Means of production A Marxist term in origin, the means of production can be used to categorise the social classes into the bourgeoisie and the proletariat. The bourgeoisie own the means of production and the proletariat work the means of production. Unlike the *mental* means of production, this term places its focus upon economic resources, and is sometimes known as the *"means of physical production."*

Proletariat A Marist term used to describe the working-class. The term derives from the Latin word *"proles,"* meaning offspring. Until Karl Marx popularised the term it often held a negative connotation. Karl Marx believed that the proletariat would lead a revolution within a capitalist society in response to exploitation at the hands of the bourgeoisie.

Reserve army of labour A Marxist term used to describe the ranks of the unemployed who – through the absence of any meaningful choice – are prepared to work for very low wages in temporary jobs. The existence of a reserve army of labour serves the interests of the bourgeoisie and exploits members of the proletariat. Work undertaken by the reserve army of labour is characterised by low-wages, low-status and poor working conditions.

Social justice Those policies and measures designed to ensure a more equitable distribution of life chances within society. The term tends to be associated with those on the left of the political spectrum, including social liberals and socialists. In modern parlance, it consists of various attempts made to address the problem of social exclusion and inequality within society.

Surplus value A Marxist term used to denote the monetary value of a proletariat's labour taken by the bourgeoisie in the form of profit. The worker is robbed of his or her life essence when their labour is converted into surplus value by the bourgeoisie.

CHAPTER 4
NATIONALISM

The core elements of nationalism

Nationalism is the most simplistic of all the ideologies we will consider. Whilst this may sound like a definite positive from the perspective of students (and teachers!), nationalism is perhaps the most difficult of all ideologies to offer any generalised comments. This is because nationalism relies so heavily upon our emotions. Without an emotional attachment to one's nation, the ideology of nationalism would not exist. Not surprisingly, nationalism is an inconsistent ideology that lacks intellectual clarity. In the words of the author Andrew Heywood there is an ***"ideological shapelessness"*** to nationalism (2007, p.158), and as Ian Adams (2001, p.80) rightly observes, nationalism is *"the simplest and most powerful of ideologies, but intellectually the weakest."* Nonetheless, there are three elements we can identify common to all forms of nationalism. They include a firm belief in the need to structure global politics around the concept of the nation-state, faith in the desirability of uniting a nation and an emphasis upon the nation as the only appropriate source of loyalty and identity.

The core belief of nationalism is that the nation is – and should always be - the basis of political organisation. The primary objective of nationalists is therefore the creation and maintenance of a **nation-state**. This can be achieved through either unification of disparate people or independence from foreign occupation. The process of unification *and* independence reflects nationalist thinking and has undoubtedly been a major factor shaping the

112

development of world politics. Yet whilst the nation-state remains a major feature of global politics, its significance to the modern world appears to be in decline.

Secondly, all nationalists aim to **unite the various members of a nation** together with a sense of common purpose. For the purposes of clarity, a nation can be defined as a group of people united by cultural and geographical factors. Crucially, those characteristics which constitute the nation will differ to that of another nation. In the words of the liberal theorist John Stuart Mill; *"a portion of mankind may be said to constitute a nationality if they are united among themselves by common sympathies, which do not exist between them and any others."* Sometimes these common sympathies are easy to identify, as in the case of religion. However, in an increasingly globalised world with a complex range of conflicting loyalties, many nations find it difficult to unite people together under a common national identity. One of the clearest illustrations of this point is Britain herself. Attempts to define what it means to be 'British' are often vague and ill-defined.

There are of course various unifying factors we might consider in the context of nationalism such as language, religion, cultural, ethnic / racial factors and a shared sense of heritage. What gives expression to a nation can be said to exist through all these factors. However, none of these symbols in themselves constitute nation*hood*. For example, English is the world's unofficial business language spoken by millions throughout the world, yet English-speakers do *not* constitute a nation. Religious beliefs do not in themselves reflect a sense of nationhood either, and cultural factors can often be difficult to identify. Ethnic / racial factors can also present problems, yet perhaps the most problematic issue of all is the notion of shared heritage. For example, our perspective on past wars may differ substantially according to our world-view. For instance, the acquisition of an Empire and the struggle for independence from the colonial power will inevitably divide people.

Core elements
The nation is the basis of political organisation
A desire to unite the nation
The nation should be the only source of loyalty and identity

Thirdly, the ideology of nationalism places the nation above all other potential lines of **loyalty and identity**. This raw appeal to our base emotions gives nationalism its unique appeal. Inevitably, nationalism is closely associated with the language of populism. Appeals to one's sense of nationhood rest upon national myths as opposed to any degree of rationality. Thus unlike rational-based ideologies such as socialism and liberalism, nationalism is widely considered to be an irrational and romanticist ideology. This argument is shared by both supporters and critics alike. Furthermore, the emotional character of nationalism is distinct from the pragmatism that lies at the heart of conservatism. Nationalism is therefore unlike any of the ideologies considered thus far, and yet it overlaps with every one of them. Once again, this is partly a reflection of the lack of intellectual clarity within nationalist ideology.

Due to its lack of intellectual consistency, nationalism is impossible to locate with absolute certainty along the left-right continuum. Although it is commonly identified along the right, some of the most powerful nationalist figures have been from the left (such as Joseph Stalin and Robert Mugabe). It is of course far easier to place nationalism along the vertical axis of the ideological spectrum due to its association with authoritarianism. An emphasis upon social order and a strong role for the state supports this assessment of nationalism.

It may help to further our understanding of nationalism with a brief consideration of what nationalism is opposed to. As the name clearly suggests, nationalism is the very opposite of **internationalism**. Nationalism also takes a **consensus** view of society - in contrast to conflict theories such as socialism and feminism. Equally, it may help us to consider those factors which are commonly linked to nationalism. For instance, there is a distinct emphasis on tribal sensibility. Much of nationalism's potency derives from a widespread assumption within a society that *'we'* as members of a tribe perceive ourselves to be different to others. Furthermore, those outside of our nation also recognise this. Furthermore, racialism can often find expression within nationalist ideology (as in the case of apartheid which was implemented by the South African National party between 1948 and 1994), although by no means all cases.

Throughout history, nationalism has always been one of the most **powerful** of all ideologies. In terms of its ability to mobilise people together it has few equals. This is particularly so when a nation is - or perceives itself to be - under threat. As one of the simplest and yet most intellectually weak of all the ideologies one might consider, nationalism offers several intriguing contributions to the discourse of political ideology. Thus before we go any further, it is important to recognise that the language of nationalism differs somewhat to the other ideologies considered thus far; beginning with its perspective upon human nature.

The nationalist perspective upon human nature

Unlike the optimistic-pessimistic continuum that aids our understanding of liberalism and conservatism, or the economic analysis offered by socialism, nationalism takes a very different view of human nature. For nationalists, human beings are divided by nationality and belong to a particular national group. Unlike liberalism's focus upon the individual or socialism's class-based approach, nationalism takes the view that human beings identify with a particular nation. As an inevitable consequence of this position, **the nation is the most legitimate construct** of political rule.

Once again, it is easier to identify that which nationalism is opposed to rather than what it actually stands for. Unlike liberals, the nationalist conception of the world is contained within the nation itself. The source of sovereignty is not the individual, it is the nation. And unlike socialists, the entire focus on nationalism is centred upon what unites us as opposed to what divides us. Therefore nationalism can be said to contribute two key arguments to the debate over human nature – that the nation is sovereign and that which drives the political process should concentrate upon the nation itself. These arguments are of course underpinned by a Weltanschauung whereby human beings are divided into different national groups.

As with nationalism itself, the argument that **the nation is sovereign** dates back to the French Revolution. Those famous revolutionaries brought together the state and the nation within an ideological context, and in doing so set an important historical precedent within international relations. Clause 3 of the 1789 Declaration of the Rights of Man states that *"the Nation is essentially the source of all sovereignty; nor can any individual, or any body of men, be entitled to any authority which is not expressly derived from it."* This was a bold expression of liberal nationalist thought, and one that remains fundamental to the nationalist perspective on the issue of sovereignty. Allied to this argument is the supposition that every human being belongs to a nation. Both our identity and sense of loyalty is shaped by a fundamental attachment to that nation, although that 'nation' could be a subjective emotion rather than an objective reality.

The main strands of nationalism

Nationalism is by far the most 'promiscuous' of all the ideologies we have considered thus far. Over the development of political ideology nationalism has forged links with liberalism, conservatism, fascism, religious fundamentalism and even socialism. Only anarchism and feminism entirely rule out a relationship to nationalism. In the case of the former, the connection between nationalism and the state rules out any link to anarchism. In the case of the latter, the centrality of gender to feminist analysis makes it an unsuitable vehicle for nationalism. The exceptional flexibility of nationalism is a clear reflection of its lack of intellectual clarity. Only an ideology grounded in collective emotions could ever manage to forge such a distinct path within ideological discourse.

Of all the hybrids and synthesis of nationalist thought, it is **liberal nationalism** that is the most significant. There are two reasons for this. One is the dominance of liberalism within ideological discourse – an observation which also holds for liberal feminism and liberal ecologism. Secondly, liberal nationalism is the oldest of all the ideological strands of thought – dating back to the French Revolution itself - and has over time emerged as the most important strand of nationalist thought; a position that remains to this day.

	Liberal nationalism	Conservative nationalism	Socialist nationalism	Far right-nationalism
Key figures	J.S. Mill, Rousseau	de Gaulle, Thatcher	Nyerere, Stalin	Mussolini, Hitler
Core elements	Right to self-determination, opposition to imperialism and a desire to facilitate social progress	Patriotism as a means to unite the nation, an organic view of society and a belief in national spirit	Reflects an accommodation between left-wing goals and nationalist rhetoric	Racialism and a desire to unite the nation along blood lines
Inclusive / exclusive	Inclusive	Inclusive	Inclusive	Exclusive

Liberal nationalism consists of three elements, the main one being **the right to self-determination**. Nations are sovereign entities entitled to express their liberty, most importantly the right to determine their own territorial boundaries. This right has been a very powerful catalyst for change throughout history and continues to fuel territorial disputes within international relations. The right to self-determination reached an important landmark shortly after the First World War when the American President Woodrow Wilson (1856-1924) gained support from the victorious allies that all nations should have a right to statehood. Since the end of the Second World War the number of nations exercising their right to self-determination has rapidly increased due to de-colonisation and the collapse of the Soviet bloc. Today there are almost two hundred sovereign nations, which is a testimony to the spread of the liberal nationalist conception of self-determination. Moreover, the cause of those 'nations' without a territorial state of their own (such as the Kurds, the Basques, the Québécois, the Catalans, the Chechens and the Bretons) is given greater legitimacy by the right to self-determination. However, the fervent wish of liberal nationalists such as the Italian theorist Giuseppe Mazzini (1805-1872) that the right to self-determination would bring about perpetual peace has never materialised. Self-determination remains the source of political disputes throughout the globe.

Secondly, liberal nationalism is opposed to the process of **imperialism**. The creation of an Empire is inconsistent with the liberal right to self-determination. A world centred upon liberal nationalist values is based upon each nation respecting the sovereignty of another. Having said this, liberal nationalists believe that the defence of a nation does not preclude the concept of collective security. Liberal nationalists recognise that nations must work together in order to protect their right to exist as sovereign entities. Some liberal nationalists even endorse supranational institutions - such as those that exist within the European Union – because those institutions can help to defend and protect liberal values.

Whilst nationalism is often presented within academia in a negative sense, supporters of liberal nationalism claim that it can facilitate **social progress**. This particular strand of nationalism is driven by the *"general will"* of the people. First articulated by the French philosopher Jean-Jacques Rousseau (1762), the demos (or people) express their identity and unity via the nation. The vitality of such an argument was expressed most dramatically during the French Revolution. The progressive nature of liberal nationalism is also reflected in their support for a civic duty upon individuals, and in the inclusive nature of their particular form of popular self-government.

One of the most influential of all liberal nationalists is John Stuart Mill. He argued that *"a necessary condition of free institutions is that the boundaries of governments should coincide in the main with those of nationalities"* and that *"free institutions are next to impossible in a country made up of different nationalities."* Mill also argued that the existence of a common sentiment of nationality enables effective government, although he was also concerned that this very same sentiment could be used to crush the spirit of liberty. Perhaps due to this concern, he stipulated that respect for the rights of the individual must always outrank national sovereignty. Conversely, some of the most powerful threats to national sovereignty derive from liberal beliefs (e.g. the universality of human rights). Liberal interventionism in the name of freedom and democracy is a common justification for the foreign policy of Western countries, and yet it is entirely **inconsistent** with the principle of national sovereignty. This is one of the many contradictions within nationalist ideology.

For an ideology born out of a violent revolution, nationalism can readily be applied to serve the key conservative objective of social order. As the leitmotif of conservatism is social order, and as nationalism is based upon the desire to unite the nation, there is a logical overlap between the two ideologies. Conservatives have often employed national myths and symbols in an attempt to unite members of a nation together, and have long seen the benefits of employing the language and sentiment of nationalism. This has been particularly important in attracting working-class voters to Conservative parties, and in offsetting the threat of revolution from the ranks of the disaffected. Yet for conservatives, the emphasis should be on patriotism as opposed to nationalism. The former has a positive and inclusive association, whereas the latter can be linked to political upheaval and violence. As the conservative French President Charles de Gaulle once said - *"patriotism is when love of your own people comes first - nationalism is when hate for people other than your own comes first."* The relationship between patriotism and nationalism is self-evidently an important one. Patriotism also underpins all forms of nationalism – but *not all* patriots are nationalists. For many people, patriotism holds absolutely no political significance whatsoever – it is merely confined to the sporting realm or celebrating the achievements of fellow countrymen and women. Few would call themselves nationalist either, choosing to associate themselves with the much more positive connotations of being a true patriot. Pride in one's nation and its collective achievement is *not* the same as holding a political belief in nationalism. Whereas many would claim to be patriotic, a lesser number would describe themselves as nationalist.

Secondly, **conservative nationalism** takes an organic view of society. Nations emerge naturally from the innate desire amongst human beings to live with others who possess the same characteristics and values. Thirdly, there is a firm belief amongst conservative nationalists that each nation is in possession of what Johann Herder (1744-1803) called a *"Volksgiest"* (**national spirit**) and Johann Fichte (1762-1814) described as a common culture. This gives conservative nationalism its nostalgic tone and anti-modernist quality, with a firm emphasis upon continuity with the past.

Other authoritarian ideologies have a close connection to nationalism. The exclusive character of nationalist ideology is firmly reflected within **fascism** (see Chapter 7). Fascists view the nation in organic terms and as a social whole. Nations are pitted against each other in a struggle for survival. Unlike conservative nationalism, there is a definite undertone of racialism within fascist ideology. Religious fundamentalists (see Chapter 9) also employ elements of nationalist thought in their particular set of beliefs, although the nation is defined solely on the basis of a religion and is therefore *pan*-national in character and content. Islamic fundamentalism is a clear reflection of this particular approach. Yet whereas fascism and **religious fundamentalism** overlap with nationalism, there are not separate strands of nationalist thought in the same manner as *liberal* nationalism and *conservative* nationalism.

The relationship between socialism and nationalism is a peculiar one. On first glance, the two ideologies are polar opposites. The class-based analysis of socialism is firmly internationalist. For those further to the left of the political spectrum, nationalism is an agent of false consciousness designed to divide the working-classes. Nations are therefore an artificial construct used by the bourgeoisie to prevent the emergence of class consciousness amongst the proletariat. Marxists such as the celebrated historian Eric Hobsbawn (1983) claim that nations are an invention used by the ruling elite as a method of social control to manipulate the masses. Furthermore, capitalism is an economic system characterised by international rivalry over scarce resources. Imperialism and colonialism are a form of class oppression driven by the profit motive of capitalists and the proletariat always pay a far greater 'price' during war-time than the bourgeoisie – particularly in the form of lives lost. War is seldom bad for business, and some of the most profitable businesses in the world economy gain their revenue from war in some manner. Several conflicts could be said to derive from competition between capitalist nations over valuable resources such as oil.

Despite this visceral critique of nationalism, it would be accurate to say that socialists have reached **an accommodation** with nationalism – particularly the revolutionary strand of socialism. Karl Marx may have argued that *"the working men have no country,"* and Friedrich Engels may have once described nationalism as *"national egoism"* - but socialist leaders have often found it useful to employ nationalist sentiment in order to mobilise the people. Stalin repeatedly used nationalist rhetoric to protect the motherland in the world's first socialist society, and African socialism was as much a reflection of quasi-nationalist ideology as it was a commitment to socialist values. In both cases, socialist leaders found it expedient to employ nationalist rhetoric in their attempt to unite the people against an external threat to socialism or in the exportation of socialist ideas to other countries. For example, the African *National* Congress successfully managed to unite different tribes together under the banner of anti-apartheid rule and a commitment to socialist ideology. Even centre-left political parties have repeatedly been willing to employ nationalist language and sentiment, particularly in recent years. Gordon Brown is a very obvious manifestation of this point with a repeated emphasis upon the concept of Britishness and his conference call for *"British jobs for British workers."*

In trying to identify various strands of nationalist thought another useful distinction derives from **inclusive nationalism** and **exclusive nationalism** (Dowds and Young, 1996). According to the inclusive strand of nationalism members of a community are encouraged to accept and uphold those cultural values that symbolise a nation. Liberal nationalism is of an inclusive character, as too is conservative nationalism. Furthermore, inclusive nationalists adopt the prevalent values and parameters of liberal democracy. In contrast, the more exclusive strand of nationalism believes that the nation is contained within a rigid territorial unit. Exclusive nationalism is commonly associated with non-democratic regimes, and can even take on a racist tone because that race is defined by blood lines. Evidence of this point is rife within nationalist movements that have emerged within Eastern Europe since the collapse of the Soviet Empire. After throwing off the shackles of an imperial power, these former captive nations have tended to experience a renaissance of nationalist feeling.

The role of the state

The role of the state within nationalist discourse is two-fold. Firstly, nationalists advocate the nation-state as the **only viable** political unit. This is a core belief amongst all nationalists. Secondly, the reach of the state within that nation is of a firmly **authoritarian** character. This may range from economic protectionism within a liberal democracy to a fully-fledged totalitarian regime (as in the case of the absolutist ruler of France King Louis 14th and his enduring one-liner *"L'etat c'est moi"*). Whatever the context, nationalism belongs on the authoritarian axis of the political spectrum.

The nation-state is the **fundamental** unit of governance within international relations. Since the Treaty of Westphalia in 1648 the idea that the state should govern the nation has remained an important objective for many nations, and the very concept of national sovereignty has been one of the remarkably few principles governing the conduct of global politics. Having said this, the centrality of national sovereignty has undoubtedly been undermined in recent years. Whilst reports of its death are greatly exaggerated, it is nonetheless true that the importance of the nation-state within international relations has experienced a steady decline. Globalisation, the influence of supranational institutions and the immense power of Multi-National Companies have all undermined the importance of the nation-state.

Within a society based upon the ideology of nationalism the role of the state is of central importance. The nationalist goal of uniting members of society together necessitates an active role for the various agents of the state. Having said this, the *extent* to which the state would play a role within society differs according to the particular strand of nationalism in question. The more inclusive character of nationalism is deeply concerned with maintaining liberty. Democratic means are therefore the only legitimate way in which to express **nationhood**. The means to advance the cause of nationalism must derive from the democratic process. For example, the Scottish Nationalist party (SNP) are pledged to hold a referendum on their cherished goal of independence by the year 2011. Theirs is a liberal strand of nationalism where the people must provide legitimacy for such a major constitutional change. Having said this, supranational institutions do have some role to play within liberal nationalism.

The more exclusive strand of nationalism can be used to justify a **non-democratic** role for the state. People may have to be coerced into upholding national unity – a trait that bears a very close relationship with the ideology of fascism. Exclusive nationalism also has an obvious relationship to an expansionist and aggressive foreign policy. The German philosopher Heinrich von Treitschke (1834-1896) spoke for many exclusive nationalists when he argued that *"a great expansion of the territory of the State is desirable in itself on grounds of national economy as well as for military reasons."* Once again, there is an obvious overlap here with fascist regimes and their search for *lebensraum* (or living space) amongst those people who have become divided by historical circumstance. This level of aggression is a very clear reflection of the emotional basis of nationalism. Consider the following words of the Italian patriot Giuseppe Garibaldi to his countrymen – *"Anyone who wants to carry on the war against the outsiders, come with me. I can offer you neither honours not wages; I offer you hunger, thirst, forced marches, battles and death. Anyone who loves his country, follow me."* It is impossible to imagine an inclusive nationalist expressing such barbarous sentiment. Moreover, the 'appeal' of such sentiment rests solely upon love of country. Nothing more, nothing less!

In terms of economic policy, there are no general observations one can apply to the ideology of nationalism. A regime based upon nationalism may adopt a planned economic system as in Cuba under Fidel Castro, a policy of self-sufficiency in the case of Tanzania under Nyerere or a largely free-market economy as Sri Lanka did under Ranil Wickremesinghe. The dependant factor is merely that which serves the interests of the nation itself. Once again, the malleable character of nationalism is very clear. Having said this, the authoritarian character of nationalism lends itself to an active role for the state within economic affairs. Similar observations can be made concerning the scope and scale of the welfare state within that society. Unlike socialism or liberalism, there is a distinct lack of prescriptive guidelines offered by the ideology of nationalism.

Nationalism and equality

Nationalism firmly rejects the emphasis upon equality that is so prevalent within socialism and feminism. The idea of class solidarity throughout the world or a gender-based analysis of society is equally abhorrent to nationalists. The emphasis of nationalism therefore rests upon the goal of **uniting people** within that particular nation. In order to achieve this, a degree of hierarchy and social order is required. Nationalism necessitates a purposeful sense of leadership from the societal elite. Without that leadership, it is unlikely that a nationalist regime could secure its objectives. Such leaders often portray themselves as embodiments of the national character and the nation's destiny. This applies to both democratic leaders (such as Jawaharlal Nehru in post-independence India) to undemocratic leaders (as with Suharto in Indonesia), and even those somewhere in between – as in the case of Vladimir Putin in Russia with his self-styled *"managed democracy."* In retrospect, Vladimir Putin (President from 2000 to 2008) filled the power vacuum that might otherwise have been met by a fascist politician such as Vladimir Zhirinovsky or the firmly authoritarian Gennady Zyuganov. Putin presented himself as a man of action who stood up for ordinary people, and his belligerent stance against Western powers was a major source of his appeal to a nation that has experienced considerable disorientation since the end of the cold war.

One of the core tenants of liberal nationalism is the right to self-determination. If a nation were not free, the citizens of that nation could not be thought of as free. Consequently, the people that compose a nation should be able to freely **consent** to place themselves under a government of their choosing and thereby exercise their right to govern themselves. This fundamental principle has driven many anti-colonial movements, particularly during the 1960s and 1970s when nationalist ideas spread rapidly throughout the Third World, and in the early-1990s during the collapse of the Soviet Empire. Liberal nationalism is firmly opposed to any form of imperialism and can therefore be described as a rejection of how right-wing ideologies view international relations. The Darwinist assumptions that lie behind fascism, religious fundamentalism and (to a much more limited extent) conservatism have no place within liberal nationalism. According to this chief strand of nationalist thought, there should be a degree of equal respect shown towards the various nations of the world. Institutions that recognise this ideal – such as those organisations that award an equal number of votes to each national representative – are consistent with the ideological assumptions behind liberal nationalism. Such views go back to the very origins of nationalism itself. For example, during the 18th century the German theologian Johann Herder (1744-1803) argued that nations should hold an equal value, thereby facilitating peaceful co-existence rather than mutual competition and warfare. Herder was also opposed to all kinds of tyranny and firmly rejected racialism as a world-view. In the contemporary era liberal nationalists are largely supportive of **European integration**, believing that vital national interests (such as the avoidance of warfare amongst nations who have traditionally been rivals) are facilitated by the mutual co-operation of the EU member states. Such states should be treated on an equal basis – as in the context of one commissioner from each of the member states.

Conservative nationalists such as Charles de Gaulle (1890-1970) recognise the need for nations to determine their own sovereign borders, but unlike liberal nationalists, they believe that equality between the nations of the world is an **abstract** goal and therefore undesirable. International relations is characterised by a struggle for power in which nations must defend themselves in order to preserve their sovereignty. Conservative nationalism was a powerful force throughout Europe during the 19th and 20th century. It fuelled the scramble for Africa amongst imperialist nations and was justified on the racialist belief in the *"white man's burden."* It also contributed to the outbreak of the First World War. In the context of modern British politics, conservative nationalists have focused much of their indignation upon the process of European integration. The gradual shift towards a federal United States of Europe is firmly opposed by many conservative nationalists. Within the party system, these views can be found amongst those on the right of the Conservative party (many of whom are members of the 'Better Off Out' campaign) and the UK Independence Party. The appeal of Euroscepticism is strong within Britain and is by far the most important expression of nationalist thought within England. In contrast the nationalist parties of Scotland, Wales and Northern Ireland are largely supportive of European integration. As with all conservatives, there is a strong emphasis upon cultural homogeneity underpinned by a somewhat reactionary and pragmatic mindset.

As an ideological mindset, exclusive nationalism is deeply **opposed** to any notion of equality. The appeal of exclusive nationalist rests upon a tribal sensibility that our nation is somehow superior to others. This aggressive strand of nationalist thought remains a key feature of modern politics. During the Bush era, many outside of America perceived US foreign policy as driven by a dogmatic view that what was right for America was right for the rest of the world. This was an outlook rooted in the American sense of exceptionalism and its *"manifest destiny"* to lead the world. One particularly illuminating observation is offered by the cultural critic Robert Hughes who describes the collective mindset of post – September 11th America as a form of *"patriotic correctness."* Even with a much more liberal President there are understandable fears that America might turn protectionist and put their own interests above all others in a desire to revive their domestic economy. If so, the consequences for world trade and the global economy could be very significant. A bout of beggar-thy-neighbour policies may even break out, just when the world economy needs a major increase in the level of trade. Due to the sheer power of the United States, the tone and character of how their nationalist interests are defined *and implemented* will have a massive impact on global politics, and there is undoubtedly a trace of exclusivity to the manner in which America does this.

As nationalism rejects equality as a guiding principle, it should not surprise the reader to find that the language of nationalism can take on a **chauvinistic** tone. A rise in nationalism is often perceived of as a threat to other nations, principally those which surround them. The Middle East has long been a hotbed of nationalist ideology reflecting the ethnic and religious conflict between Jews and Arabs. Northern Ireland is another illustration of how nationalist rhetoric can present a threat (either imagined or real) amongst opposing communities. These situations can generate a *"siege mentality"* amongst that nation which feels most threatened – such as the Protestants of Northern Ireland and the Jewish community within Israel. Of the two, it is the latter that has the most cause to feel under threat. The President of Iran Mahmoud Ahmadinejad has been reported as saying that Israel should be wiped off the face of the map, and the ruling party in the state of Palestine (Hamas) is committed to the destruction of the state of Israel. The exclusive character of nationalism within the Middle East holds particular salience because of its capacity to drag other actors (principally the world's only *hyper*power the United States) into a potential conflict. Revealingly, hope for a more peaceful situation may be found in the recent experience of Northern Ireland – where the two communities have put aside their differences for a more normal and peaceful existence. The language of nationalist politicians is now much more inclusive and liberal than during the troubles (1969-1993), particularly in the case of Sinn Fein who are now pledged to respect the equality of all peoples on the island or Ireland.

The examples of Arab nationalism and Irish nationalism highlight another relevant aspect of nationalist ideology – that of **victimhood**. A sense of being oppressed by a more powerful nation (usually an imperial power) can fuel a great deal of nationalist sentiment. Nationalist parties have long employed this sense of victimhood in order to promote their aims. In the context of Ireland, the presence of British forces continues to cause resentment amongst those communities that readily identify with an Irish Republican outlook. Britain has a lengthy history of dominance over Ireland and has rarely sought an equal relationship with its immediate neighbour. To hard-line Irish nationalists, the British should leave Ireland altogether. In the Middle East, Arab nationalists

The Definitive Guide to Political Ideologies

claim that the actions of the Zionist state of Israel are characteristic of an aggressive militaristic force. The language of victimhood can also be found in the case of separatists within the Basque region, the Albanians within Serbia (who gained independence in February 2008 to form the state of Kosovo) and the Tamil Tigers in Sri Lanka. Sometimes, that sense of victimhood applies to ethnic nations that have previously engaged in a form of imperialist activity – such as Russians within the Baltic States. In all such cases, the language of victimhood is often a prevalent feature within nationalist movements.

The relationship between nationalism and liberal democracy

Some nationalist movements and parties operate firmly within the parameters of liberal democracy. They tend to be inclusive in character and are based upon either liberal nationalism or conservative nationalism. For liberals, support for liberal democracy is an article of faith. For conservatives, liberal democracy has proved itself to be the best system available in terms of maintaining social order. In contemporary politics, this is the prevalent stance taken within the ideology of nationalism. In contrast, the more extreme forms of nationalism firmly reject the central tenants and philosophical underpinnings of liberal democracy. This particular brand of nationalism offers justification for undemocratic activities. Further away from the centre of the political spectrum, this hard-line version of nationalism is often hostile to the state itself rather than the values inherent within liberal democracy. In such cases, the state often upholds a colonial influence over 'their' nation.

Those parties which operate firmly within the parameters of liberal democracy believe that the goals and objectives of their particular movement *can* be facilitated within the prevalent rules of the game. Obvious examples from the United Kingdom include the Scottish Nationalist party, Plaid Cymru and the Social Democratic and Labour party within Northern Ireland. Support for liberal democracy amongst such parties is less ideological and more tactical. Such parties believe that they can achieve independence (or a much greater degree of autonomy) via the pursuit of democratic means. Another illustration of this approach includes the Parti Québécois in the French-speaking province of Canada. These inclusive nationalists believe that independence / greater autonomy can and should be achieved via popular consent.

Nationalist movements that adopt non-democratic means to achieve their aims can be found throughout the world. The Irish Republican Army, the Euskadi Ta Askatasuna (the Basque separatist movement) and the National Front for the Liberation of Corsica have all employed deeply undemocratic means to achieve their nationalist aspirations. In various ghettos of the Catholic community within Northern Ireland the IRA have long operated as a paramilitary organisation engaged in illegal activities. The political wing of the Republican movement (Sinn Fein) is one of wealthiest political parties in Europe, gaining a great deal of funding via criminal activities. In addition, ETA have continued their terrorist campaign against the Madrid-based government despite several concessions made to the Basque nation. These and other exclusive nationalists believe that their goals *cannot* be secured via the normal democratic process, perhaps due to the majority of people being opposed to the break-up of the territorial unit. In the case of Irish nationalism, the partition of Ireland and the gerrymandering of various constituencies make any talk of 'democracy' little more than a meaningless word to hide the colonial character of British interference in Ireland. Irish nationalists believe that true democracy can only be achieved by the removal of an occupying colonial force intent on protecting Unionist hegemony in the six counties.

The opposition of more extremist nationalist groups towards the basis of liberal democracy is often based upon the *status* of the territory itself. In other words, it is not liberal democracy they are opposed to but the basis of the state itself. Such groups invariably portray themselves as fighting for the freedom and liberty of an oppressed nation, and these claims should at least be taken seriously by those who wish to develop their knowledge further. The well-known aphorism that *"one person's terrorist is another person's freedom fighter"* offers a very good insight into how the political world operates. This often extends into pan-nationalist movements (e.g. pan-Slavism and pan-Arabism) who aim to unify a disparate nation under a common home. Their rallying cry for unity can often appear highly aggressive to 'outsiders' who cannot share in that nation, and yet to its supporters such calls are often viewed as defensive and essentially peaceful. As with several aspects of political discourse, the conclusion reached is entirely dependent upon the Weltanschauung one adopts.

The individual and society

The three key elements of nationalist thought are a firm belief in the need for a nation-state, the desire to unite a nation and an emphasis upon the nation as the only appropriate source of loyalty and identity. Thus according to nationalist ideology, the relationship between the individual and society will be dominated by the latter. Nationalism is **collectivist** rather than individualist. Having said this, liberal nationalism strives to protect the individual from the tyranny of the majority – specifying certain boundaries

The Definitive Guide to Political Ideologies

in terms of the relationship between the individual and society. As with all ideologies, there are certain nuances that a student needs to be aware of.

For all nationalists, the nation-state is the only legitimate political entity in which a nation should be bound together. The individual gains a sense of identity from that nation and may be called upon by the ruling elite to offer sacrifices for the wider needs of the nation – principally during times of war or economic crisis. Consequently, the relationship between the individual and society is effectively determined by the needs of the nation. In recent times, the US President Barack Obama has called upon all Americans to make sacrifices for the collective good – particularly those at the top who will *"have to chip in a bit more."* His call for sacrifice is backed up by a trade policy shaped by **economic nationalism** (or protectionism).

Nationalism rests upon emotional appeals to loyalty and belonging in a manner virtually unique within ideological discourse. Whilst this could legitimately be employed as a criticism of nationalism, it also reflects the main strength of the ideology itself. Thus at its most pervasive, nationalism provides a strong sense of affiliation and a secure identity to a demos searching for both. In an era dominated by globalisation identity politics are becoming increasing important - and nationalism has a tradition of filling that vacuum – particularly during times of rapid change. National identity gives us a firm sense of who we are in an increasingly globalised world. This is perhaps nationalism's most important contribution to the debate within political ideology over the proper relationship between the individual and society.

Few other ideologies (with the exception of fascism) place loyalty to a society as highly as nationalism. The emphasis is upon our **responsibilities** to the nation, as opposed to the exercise of inalienable human rights, is fundamental to the nationalist credo. Having said this, there are subtle distinctions within the various strands of nationalism on this point. Crucially, liberal nationalists believe that the rights of individuals should never be sacrificed for the needs of the nation. Their inclusive form of nationalism is – like all other branches of liberal thought – preoccupied with the maintenance of individual liberty. This view has of course always been rejected by conservative nationalists. During the 18th century the French royalist Charles Maurras advocated a form of *"integral nationalism"* where individuals lose their identity within an all-encompassing nation, and nationalist theorists of the same era - such as Herder and Fichte - took a similar line in the context of the German nation. The collective needs of society must always triumph over the liberal conception of inalienable rights. Moreover, those cultural bonds that unite the nation are far stronger than anything a government could engender. Socialist nationalists have routinely enforced sacrifices upon their people for the wider needs of society, principally amongst leaders in the developing world such as

Julius Nyerere (Tanzania) and Jawaharlal Nehru (India). Remarkably few socialist regimes have managed to unite the citizens without some form of nationalist rhetoric, despite the obvious ideological tension between socialism and nationalism.

Nationalist parties and movements further away from the centre of the political spectrum take a much more **illiberal** view of the relationship between the individual and society, and the Weltanschauung of such groups can provide justification for highly undemocratic actions. Illustrations of this point include terrorist groups campaigning for national independence such as the Tamil Tigers in Sri Lanka and Basque separatists in Spain. Extremist political movements within an existing nation can also adopt a highly illiberal stance – as in the case of India with the nationalist BJP and the more extremist group the Sri Ram Sena (SRS). The SRS are committed to the establishment of a state built upon *"Hindutva"* (or Hinduness) and thereby rid India of all legacies of foreign influence – such as Christianity. The SRS was founded by Pramod Mutalik and has been linked to violent attacks on Christians in India. In the UK, the British National Party is another obvious example to consider. Its right-wing populist message feeds off alienation amongst working-class voters in areas characterised by white flight and parallel lives. As with other hard-line nationalist parties, the BNP scapegoats what it sees as 'outsiders' for the problems facing society. In one particularly evocative paragraph from its 2005 General Election manifesto, uncontrolled immigration was linked to no less than 16 separate problems facing British society.

Our nation can of course provide us with a **sense of identity**. This can be an important aspect of who we are and how we relate to others. It can even be our master status, although for many people, national identity has little political significance. Nonetheless, nationalism does provide the individual with a collective sense of belonging to a wider whole. For liberal nationalists, this may form the right to self-determination. For conservative nationalists, this is an important unifying and stabilising force within society. For socialist nationalists, appeals to the nation can be used to mobilise the people towards the achievement of left-wing objectives. Social justice and equality can bring disparate tribes together in the search for a common cause – as in the case of the African National Congress in South Africa. Amongst the more exclusive forms of nationalism, our collective sense of belonging can form the basis for undemocratic and illiberal activities.

All of us are born into a nation. That nation may not have a state, or may exist within a disputed territory, but that does not alter the fact that all of us are born into a nation. It may simply be an accident of birth, or it may form an abiding love for fellow countrymen and women. It may even be a mixture of several cultures, a point addressed in a later Chapter on multiculturalism.

Whatever the situation, nationalism puts forward an important contribution towards our understanding of the relationship between the individual and society. Within nationalism, the relationship between the individual and society is essentially viewed from the prism of the state, rather than the individual. Furthermore, that individual is a member of a wider collective group, and that one's identity derives from an attachment to that particular nation.

Change or the status quo

It is entirely in keeping with the shapeless ideological character of nationalism that it can be either reactionary or revolutionary depending upon the aims of the nationalist movement in question. There is an extraordinarily vast difference in terms of tactics and outlook within nationalist movements such as ETA, the UKIP, Plaid Cymru, the SNP, the PKK and the Real IRA. Offering any overarching comments on the issue of change or the status quo applicable to such a vast range of groups may at first sound problematic. Fortunately, there are at least a few observations we can make – principally if we consider the content of that particular type of nationalism.

As an ideological movement, nationalism dates back to the revolutionaries that fought against the absolutist rule of King Louis the 14th in 1789. Influenced by the concept of the *"general will"* derived from Jean-Jacques Rousseau's work on the social contract, the very origins of nationalism are deeply revolutionary and firmly committed to the overthrow of the ancien regime. Rousseau's argument that *"obedience to the general will enhances liberty"* provided intellectual substance to the mobilisation of that vitally important revolutionary movement. According to Rousseau's argument, everyone is obliged to obey the state because it represents the general will (in other words, what *everyone* wants). At the time, the notion that popular self-government should derive from the people was a very radical idea, and throughout history, the goals associated with liberal nationalism have found an obvious home amongst revolutionaries committed to exercising the right to self-determination. Indeed, the revolutionary character of nationalism has traditionally been one of its most distinctive features. For example, the Italian theorist Giuseppe Mazzini founded the revolutionary movement 'Young Italy' during the 19th century on the belief that self-determination was bound up with notions of social progress, and the division of people into national groups was akin to the division of labour under capitalism. He also argued in favour of guerrilla warfare against the oppressive power, a tactic since used by several nationalist movements throughout history. Amongst the myriad of independence movements that swept the developing world during the 1960s and 70s, the tactics of nationalists were often revolutionary. These actions found their intellectual grounding in the work of the left-wing intellectual Frantz Fanon (1925-1961) who justified the need for violence as a response to Western colonialism.

Nationalism and political violence can make obvious bedfellows, and the fervour by which groups may hold nationalist beliefs can provide irrefutable justification for political violence. Mob mentality can also play a factor in the armed struggle against the status quo - and it is these characteristics that cause deep concern for conservative nationalists. Unlike other strands of nationalism, conservative nationalists believe firmly in **social order** and thereby **defend the status quo**. Within the UK, conservative nationalism is an important element along the right of the political spectrum. For example the UK Independence Party and some on the right of the Tory party wish to protect the national interest against the inexorable process of European integration. They argue that sovereignty should be returned to the nation-state and that the proper level of decision-making power should always be the nation-state, not some entity called 'Europe.' This strand of conservative thought is reactionary in character and opposed to any further erosion of national sovereignty to a European superstate. For them, a federal United States of Europe stands firmly against the traditions and national heritage of the British (particularly English) people. The UKIP and Eurosceptic Tories support the withdrawal of the UK from what they see as a socialist bureaucratic enterprise fundamentally at odds with the British national character.

Nationalism in the developing world has held a strong element of **anti-colonialism**. This may range from protests against the ruling regime (as in Tibet against the Chinese authorities) to civil disobedience in a manner that owes much to the peaceful tactics of Mahatma Gandhi. Such actions are grounded within both liberal nationalism and socialist nationalism. However, some of the most violent nationalist regimes could also be associated with liberal nationalism and socialist nationalism. Furthermore, nationalists within such countries search for those factors that may unite their people together – perhaps via mythology or religion. Ironically, the very existence of Empire amongst European states was itself fuelled by nationalism. Thus one could argue that the ideology of nationalism has perpetuated itself over time.

Defence of one's national interest can often take on a militaristic **aggressive** tone with China and Russia being leading examples of this point in contemporary international relations. In the context of China, there is an old saying that *"the shadow of China is greater than China itself."* The seemingly inexorable rise of China as an economic and political power looks set to be an increasingly significant development within global politics, and one of the core principles behind Chinese foreign policy is the aim to restore national pride after the so-called *"century of humiliation"* at the hands of hostile powers. The academic Robert Kagan observes that pride in China's growing international status has become a source of legitimacy for the ruling oligarchy of the Chinese community party, and that a form of popular nationalism has grown since the 1990s (2008, p.30). We can already find evidence of autocratic actions by the Chinese authorities over internet censorship and the issue of Tibet – with the latter causing huge controversy within liberal democratic regimes in the run-up to the Beijing Olympics of August 2008. Russian nationalism also strives to restore national pride after the collapse of the Soviet Union in the early 1990s. Russia's military and economic resources have been mobilised in an aggressive manner against those states who fail to toe Moscow's line. The West is understandably nervous about the true intentions of the Russian government, particularly given the West's reliance upon Russian gas and energy supplies. Furthermore, there are potential sources of conflict between the two. To Russia, NATO and EU enlargement presents a clear danger to their traditional sphere of influence. What appears a fundamentally democratic process to Western European countries is seen as contrary to the national interests of Russia.

Some nationalist movements strive for **independence**, whereas others are content with a degree of political autonomy. Nationalism does not therefore always equate to full-scale separatism. Consequently, the *extent* to which nationalists wish to change the existing power structure of a society differs widely. The degree to which nationalist movements and parties aim to secure independence often reflects a wider sense of nationalist feeling within that nation. Thus in the context of the UK, Scottish nationalism has always been stronger than Welsh nationalism, a point reflected in the greater powers given to the Scottish Parliament relative to the Welsh Assembly. Change can also be secured via peaceful means – as in the example of Czechoslovakia in 1993, where the nations of Slovakia and the Czech Republic split on peaceful terms during the velvet revolution. In stark contrast, the savage practise of ethnic cleansing within the former Yugoslavia during the early to mid-1990s was one of the darkest episodes of contemporary European history. An even more tragic illustration of humankind's capacity for hate-fuelled destruction occurred in 1994 when the genocide in Rwanda between Hutus and Tutsis killed half a million people in the space of just a hundred days.

Nationalism in contemporary politics

Nationalism is *"alive and well"* - or in *"terminal decline"* - depending on the evidence chosen to back up either of these assessments. In the context of British politics, nationalism is in good health. Since 2007 the SNP and Plaid Cymru have been the majority parties in their respective legislatures, and the Northern Ireland assembly is now governed by a multi-party coalition which includes Irish nationalists such as Sinn Fein alongside the main Unionist parties. Even English nationalism has grown due to a backlash against what some voters see as preferential treatment towards non-English countries. If the people of Scotland vote for independence in a referendum, nationalism will gain another hugely significant victory, and the structure of the United Kingdom will change beyond recognition.

Further afield, nationalism still has the muscle to **divide** people. Beside the obvious flashpoint of the Middle East there are a whole range of disputes centred in some way upon the controversial issue of national identity and territorial politics. Take the case of the linguistic cleavages at the heart of Europe; with Belgium split between the French-speaking Walloons region and the Dutch-speaking Flanders region. France and Spain also contend with significant linguistic cleavages. Further afield, Africa has long been a hotbed of ethnic and nationalistic rivalries, a problem compounded by the patchwork of inappropriate boundaries placed upon it by European imperialists. In the Far East there are considerable ideological tensions between North Korea and South Korea. In South Asia the region of Kashmir is a disputed territory contested by two nuclear powers (India and Pakistan) that fought three wars in the space of a generation. Various other disputes from around the globe underline the continued vitality of nationalism within contemporary international relations. There is virtually no area of the world where disputes over territory do not exist; such is the continued importance of nationalism and national sovereignty.

In the context of the current economic crisis, there is a definite undercurrent of nationalist ideology to the growth of **protectionist measures**. This is one of the most serious threats to the prosperity and peace of the world we inhabit. If countries turn inward in the face of globalisation the result will almost certainly be a reduction in global trade. This will have a very serious knock-on effect for people's livelihoods. A zero-sum game mentality might ensue causing considerable hardship for many people, and the economic form of nationalism that characterised the 1930s may well return, possibly with the same devastating results. It is already the case that wars are being fought over access to natural resources and in the use of economic measures to secure foreign policy objectives. Nationalism could therefore be said to be thriving within contemporary politics and *"the nation-state remains as strong as ever"* (Kagan, 2008, p.3).

The arguments that suggest nationalism is in terminal decline are also persuasive. After the seemingly inexorable rise of the nation-state, academics have speculated that we are approaching the era of **post-Westphalian politics**. National sovereignty has been greatly eroded by globalisation, European integration and the growth in the scope and scale of international organisations. Of these, it is globalisation that presents the most momentous challenge to the continued salience of nationalism.

The nation-state faces a very serious challenge to its relevance within the political process in an era increasingly dominated by the process of globalisation. Borders are much more permeable and porous than in previous generations, and those issues that now face countries throughout the world are largely trans-national in character (e.g. pollution, crime, terrorism, swine flu and the credit crunch) and therefore require a degree of co-operation between states. States have a responsibility not just to their own citizens, but to others within the international community. No longer can nation-states successfully close themselves off from the international community, and those that do (such as North Korea) seem destined to face very serious problems such as mass famine. Globalisation has also spawned a spectacular rise in the economic power of Multi-National Companies (MNCs), which once again undermines the political significance of nationalism. The economic policies of several nation-states are hugely influenced by the power of MNCs, and several smaller nation-states have a GDP far below the economic wealth of the top MNCs. Nation-states are increasingly regulated to the status of powerless bystanders within the era of globalisation, and even the more powerful nations can be hugely affected by a process which is out of their immediate control.

European integration has also changed the contours of nationalism within the European states. Countries previously dogged by bloody conflicts have voluntarily surrendered many aspects of their national sovereignty. The EU has fostered a habit of co-operation amongst former allies and displayed the benefits of deeper integration within areas traditionally the sole responsibility of national governments (such as defence and foreign policy). Member states have pooled sovereignty in the desire to create an ever closer union and the EU has grown substantially from just six original members to twenty-seven. Moreover, the success of European integration in terms of avoiding war and generating a peaceful co-existence amongst neighbouring states has been copied by many other international organisations (such as the ASEAN, Mercosur, the OAU, etc.). On refection, it seems somewhat ironic that the continent that gave birth to nationalism and national sovereignty should be the one that may signal its eventual demise.

International organisations such as NATO, the United Nations and the APEC have legitimised international co-operation and spread universal liberal values (such as the protection of human rights) throughout the world. These organisations (particularly NATO) have even used military force to implement such ideas. The combined effect of such organisations is to undermine the capacity of nationalism to secure its objectives. Furthermore, dictators whose appeal rests primarily upon nationalism have been removed via the actions of these international organisations.

To its supporters, nationalism provides a sense of kinship and affiliation with a wider whole, and is therefore a powerful mobilising force within politics. To its opponents, nationalism is inherently divisive and aggressive. A more reflective assessment might suggest that nationalism can also be rather insular (as in the case of Scottish nationalism) and somewhat modest in its aims (as in the case of Welsh nationalism). Whatever the case, nationalism remains one of the main ideologies one might consider. Whether it maintains this status in an era of globalisation is very much an open question.

Further quotes on nationalism

"Patriotism is your conviction that this country is superior to all other countries because you were born in it." George Bernard Shaw

"Patriotism is a survival from barbarous times which must ... be eradicated by all means." Leo Tolstoy

"Nationalism is the starkest political shame of the twentieth century." John Dunn

"No nation is fit to sit in judgement upon any other nation." Woodrow Wilson

"I would rather be British than just." Ian Paisley

"There is no room in this country for hyphenated Americanism." Theodore Roosevelt

"Nationalism is an infantile disease [and] *the measles of mankind."* Albert Einstein

"The first man who, having enclosed a piece of ground, bethought to himself of saying 'This is Mine', and found people simple enough to believe him, was the real founder of civil society." Jean-Jacques Rousseau

"When the language of its forefathers is lost, a nation, too, is lost and perishes." Adolf Arvidsson

"The great nations have always acted like gangsters, and the small nations like prostitutes." Stanley Kubrick

Recommended reading

Anderson, B. (1983) *Imagined communities : Reflections on the origins and spread of Nationalism.* A consideration of those somewhat elusive elements that constitute a nation.

Dowds, L. & Young, K. (1996) *"National Identity"* in *British Social Attitudes* (13th **report**). A sociological perspective that details the distinction between inclusive nationalism and exclusive forms of nationalism.

Fanon, F. (1961) *The Wretched of the Earth.* A Marxist exploration of the psychological character of imperialism, and a call to arms for oppressed nations. Fanon was hugely influential amongst left-wing figures who believed that colonial rulers could only be removed by political violence.

Rousseau, J-J. (1762) *The Social Contract.* Rousseau belongs to a variety of ideologies and should not simply be confined to nationalism. That said, his work on the social contract was hugely influential within the emergence of nationalism and the French Revolution. His work on the general will is particularly relevant towards an understanding of liberal nationalism.

Sen, A. (2006) *Identity and violence.* A modern-day reflection upon the relationship between multiculturalism and nationalism.

Ideas for further discussion

To what extent does nationalism represent the 'politics of the heart' as opposed to the 'politics of the head'?

How does the nationalist perspective upon rights differ to that of the liberal perspective?

Just how different are the main strands of nationalism?

What is the role of the state within a society based upon nationalism?

What is the nationalist perspective upon the concept of equality?

What is the attitude of nationalists towards liberal democracy?

What is the relationship between nationalism and conservatism?

What is the nationalist perspective upon the issue of social order?

In what ways would nationalists change the basis of a liberal democracy?

Is nationalism still relevant within world politics?

Key terms

Apartheid A method of social stratification based upon a person's race. Apartheid means *"separateness"* in Afrikaan and was practised within South African society until 1994. Since then South African society has developed on a more multicultural basis. Apartheid is a clear illustration of a closed society.

Chauvinism An exaggerated sense of national superiority. Jingoist in tone, it is commonly associated with conservative nationalism.

Colonialism The settlement of a foreign country via an imperial power causing the separation of the indigenous population from the settlers. The term is often used interchangeably with imperialism.

Diaspora Where a nation is scattered across different states and subject to a ruling regime outside that nation. Nationalists have often tried to unite a nation experiencing diaspora - as in the case of the Jewish nation before the creation of Israel.

Ethnic conflict A territorial and political dispute contested along ethnic lines, as opposed to the more common historical setting of a war between two or more countries. In recent years the trend within international relations has been towards conflicts centred upon ethnicity. Examples include conflict in the former Yugoslavia, the Chechen region of Russia, Rwanda and the political dispute between Armenians and Azerbaijanis.

Ethnic group A group within society that shares a distinct ethnic culture and identity. Cultural identity is often expressed in terms of religion, language, attitude and / or a style of dress. The term also has currency within the field of social differentiation.

Ethnocentric A world-view based on a particular ethnic perspective. A great deal of what we understand by the political world derives from a Westernised standpoint. Ethnocentrism holds clear epistemological relevance and is of major importance within the social sciences.

Failed state A state in which there are no political institutions that claim sovereignty within that territory. Failed states can often provide a haven for terrorist organisations and other extremist groups, particularly those shaped by religious fundamentalism (e.g. the Taliban in Afghanistan). As such, the 'West' may increasingly rely upon liberal interventionism in order to prevent the spread of fundamentalist beliefs within those states. This may even entail a greater use of pre-emptive action.

Imagined community A community whose members do not know each other but who share a common sense of belonging created on the basis of imagination. The clearest example of an imagined community is a nation.

Imperialism The imposition by force by an external power over another country's territory. Many countries throughout the world have been part of an Empire at some point in their history.

Myth A narrative account of the sacred which embodies collective experiences and represents a collective conscience. Myths are an important element of national identity and can act as a means of social cohesion (as in the case of the *"frontier mentality"* in the United States or the *"Dunkirk spirit"* in the UK).

National identity An emotional attachment to what is considered to be one's nation. For most members of a society, national identity is a relatively straight-forward matter. However, due to the greater movement of people throughout the world the whole issue of national identity has taken on a more complex dimension. The extent to which members of a particular society feel an emotional attachment towards their nation has a major impact upon the degree of social cohesion. Attempts to generate a feeling of national identity include the use of national symbols and an emphasis upon the concept of citizenship.

Nations A community of people who share a common national identity. In the context of British society it can at times be relevant to discuss the *English* nation, the *Scottish* nation, etc. It is important to recognise that a race is not necessarily a nation.

Nation-state A theoretical concept which suggests that a particular nation should inhabit a particular state. The nation-state is a fundamental concept in terms of how a society is governed and how national territory is defined within international relations. The concept dates back to the Treaty of Westphalia in 1648, and continues to shape independence movements throughout the world. Many political commentators claim that the era of the nation-state is in terminal decline. However, citizens of a nation-state often hold a strong emotional attachment to their perceived nation. Another important point to consider is that a state is an objective reality, but a nation may not be. Most nations have formed a state, and most states are composed of one dominant nation. Furthermore, the very character of nationalism has changed. National prestige is no longer bound up with notions of conquest and Empire, and may in the future take on a much more inclusive nature.

Neo-imperialism A modern manifestation of Western imperialism. For example, the alter-globalisation movement has accused Western governments and Western-based multi-national companies of treating majority world countries in a neo-imperialist manner. The term neo-colonialism is also used in this particular context.

Patriotism A firm attachment to – or love of - one's national identity. Unlike nationalism, patriotism does not entail extremist politics. Within political discourse nationalism has a largely negative connotation, whereas patriotism has a more positive connotation due to its unifying impact upon various members of society. Patriotic behaviour is also seen as much less threatening than nationalistic behaviour.

Parallel lives A term derived from the Ouseley report (2001) into that summer's race riots within several northern cities. The term was used to describe the absence of any meaningful contact between white people and Asians within such cities, thereby contributing towards prejudice and negative stereotypes about the 'other' community. The existence of parallel lives is clearly a major barrier towards social cohesion between white people and Asian people.

Self-determination A notion derived from liberal nationalism in which a nation or community has the right to form its own political structure. Self-determination has influenced many nationalist movements throughout history. It claims that a nation should achieve statehood and determine the manner in which they are governed.

Territory A geographical area usually outlined by the boundaries of a country, or nation. There are several territories throughout the world where two or more ethnic groups / nations contest its sovereignty. A clash over territory often reflects a division in terms of national and ethnic identity.

White flight A demographic trend in which white people move out of an area in response to an increasing number of people from ethnic minorities having moved into that area. White flight reinforces the problem of *"parallel lives"* within several parts of the country (particularly the East End of London and certain northern cities), and thereby contributes to the creation of ghettos.

Xenophobia A hatred of foreigners formed on the basis of ignorance and racial prejudice. It could be argued that xenophobia manifests itself in the context of exclusive nationalism.

CHAPTER 5
FEMINISM

The core elements of feminism

First and foremost, feminism offers a **critique** of a patriarchal (male-dominated) society. Feminists argue that females are subjugated within a patriarchal society. Following on from this critique, feminists advocate change in order to **emancipate females** and thereby create a better society. However, the *means* to achieve this goal differs amongst the various strands of feminism. There is an obvious parallel here with socialism – both in terms of an attempt to create a better society and in terms of disagreement amongst its followers over the means to achieve its aims.

Core elements
Critique of patriarchy
Aim to emancipate women and create a better society

Due to its critique of the status quo and its desire to overhaul the existing structure of society, feminism can be located on the left of the political spectrum. Feminism does not prescribe a strong role for the state and advocates greater freedom for women (and to some extent men). As such, feminism can also be placed along the **libertarian axis**. Having said this, there are considerable differences between the three main strands of feminism – which can of course be charted along the political spectrum. As the name implies, liberal feminism belongs nearer the centre of the political spectrum. Socialist feminists are further away from the centre, and the strand of feminism furthest away from the centre is called (appropriately enough) radical feminism.

	Main demands	Predominant strand	Key figures
1st wave	Votes for women and to change the view that wives were the property of their husbands	Liberal	Wollstonecraft, J.S. Mill
2nd wave	Equality between the genders and greater sexual freedom for women	Radical and socialist	Greer, Millett
3rd wave	Facilitate a wide spectrum of choice, and ensure equality of opportunity	Liberal	Klein, Wolf

All strands of feminism share two basic characteristics - a critique of a patriarchal society, and a desire to transform society from its patriarchal basis. However, students need to be aware that feminism has been categorised into three distinct **waves**. These are not strands of feminist thought but simply a reflection of major changes in the demands and objectives of feminists. More than any other ideology, feminism has changed to reflect the circumstances of the time. Crucially, the two basic elements of feminism have remained constant throughout. Before we move onto the issue of human nature, it is important to note that feminists differ to socialists on the issue of equality. Whereas all feminists wish to improve the status of (and choices available to) women, they do *not* all seek equality. Radical feminists differ greatly to other strands of feminist thought in their desire to reorder society upon a **gynocentric** basis. Thus not all feminists believe in equality – although feminists are often thought to be strongly in favour of equality between men and women.

Feminists argue that patriarchy is both easily recognisable and curiously invisible, managing to dominate women without causing sufficient hostility towards it. Typical of such observations is that offered by the contemporary philosopher Julia Kristeva (1941-) who argues that western culture and thought has repressed the value of the maternal. It has also been argued that patriarchy relegates women to the domestic realm and then deliberately undervalues that realm of society. For instance, Dale Spender in her book *'Man Made Language'* (1980) argues that male language is considered more important and powerful than women's language. This has given men and unfair advantage within the public realm, which would therefore explain male dominance of the political sphere. Spender also found that men often cut off women in conversation and that women's words are only given intermittent attention by men. As a consequence, what women look like is considered important within a patriarchal society because what women say is not. Another illustration of this point derives from Simone de Beauvoir who famously argued that *"women are not born, they are made"* to serve the needs of a patriarchal society.

The feminist stance on human nature

Human nature has traditionally been a principal area of academic inquiry within ideological discourse. During the Enlightenment, several (male) figures such as David Hume and Voltaire argued that human nature exists as an immutable concept and developed theoretical assumptions based upon that standpoint. All the ideologies considered thus far (liberalism, conservatism, socialism and nationalism) have postulated coherent ideas about human nature. In contrast, feminists have not preoccupied themselves with the question of human nature. The entire basis of feminist analysis is focused upon gender, and issues surrounding human nature do not play a central role comparable to say liberalism or conservatism. Nonetheless, certain strands of feminist thought have offered some contribution towards how we might understand human nature.

The two core elements of feminism are a critique of patriarchy and the desire to emancipate women. Based on the first of those points, feminism criticises aspects of **male behaviour** and seeks solutions based to a greater or lesser extent upon feminine qualities. This view is most strongly associated with a branch of thought known as **essentialism**. Essentialist (or difference) feminists contend that women's innate nature is superior to men's. Men are the destroyers of life, whilst women are the creators of life. Women are also linked to the natural rhythms of mother nature, whereas men are attached to an artificially created culture. In the words of Germaine Greer men are condemned to act in a competitive manner, a view backed up by the controversial activist Andrea Dworkin who once said that *"Men love murder. In art they celebrate it. In life, they commit it."* However, such bold statements are by no means shared by all within the feminist movement. Liberal feminists believe that the somewhat belligerent tone of radicals and essentialists is ultimately self-defeating for the women's movement. For example, liberal feminists contend that men are not innately bad. Men are redeemable and have an important role to play in the creation of a better society. Socialist feminists also believe that men can play a key role in building a better world, particularly those men who are exploited by the capitalist economic system. The consequence of such divergence of thought makes it difficult to summarise the feminist position on the topic of human nature. Unlike any other ideology, there are no over-arching generalisations one can offer about the feminist perspective upon human nature. Such divergence will become much clearer once we consider the various strands of feminist thought. [10]

Main strands of feminist thought

As previously mentioned there are **three** main strands of feminist thought. Of these, the most influential is **liberal feminism**. During the first wave of feminism, liberal feminists such as Mary Wollstonecraft (1792) and John Stuart Mill campaigned in favour of extending the franchise to females. Their argument was based firmly upon liberal principles – namely that women were rational human beings and should therefore be entitled to the same voting rights as men. Liberal feminists of the first wave also challenged the misogynist argument that wives were the property of their husbands. To the modern reader, such arguments must seem highly outdated. Indeed, the view that women are incapable of making rational judgements due to their irrational nature dates all the way back to Aristotle. Nonetheless, it cannot be denied that the first wave of feminism secured important goals in the emancipation of women. [11]

Liberal feminism is based on the view that women are rational actors entitled to inalienable and universal human rights. As such, legislative and employment measures must be implemented in order to prevent the discrimination of females on the basis of sexist attitudes. During the 1970s the Equal Pay Act and the Sex Discrimination Act were instigated after pressure from feminists to ensure equality of opportunity for women. In contemporary society, the focus of liberal feminism centres upon protecting the rights of female workers (especially the disproportionately high numbers of women in part-time work) and helping women break through the glass ceiling in order to compete on an equal footing with men. Liberal feminists also campaign in favour of a greater number of women in powerful political and economic positions. Liberal feminists argue that the governance of society would be

---

[10]   Due to the specific assumptions and character of eco-feminism it is more appropriate to consider this branch of thought within the Chapter on Ecologism.

[11]   Jean-Jacques Rousseau even argued that women should never be taught to reason. He claimed that women were always able to use their emotions to manipulate men, and that if they were taught to reason they would have far too much power over men!

improved significantly by a more inclusive attitude to women. These benefits would also apply to the economic realm. Access to education and career opportunities must also be broadened to benefit women.

Another core value for liberal feminists is to facilitate a diversity of lifestyles amongst women. A society governed by liberal feminism should enable women to maximise the choices available to them in which restrictive notions of femininity are replaced by a more liberal attitude. Above all, the guiding principle should always be **choice**. These arguments have recently come to prominence during the third wave of feminism. Liberal feminists claim that second wavers such as Germaine Greer (1970) and Betty Friedan (1963) imposed a restrictive concept of femininity. The argument that women should have as wide a choice as possible over their lives, instead of being limited by the more collectivist notion of the second-wavers, is an important area of divergence within feminist discourse. As one might expect, liberal feminists are firmly individualist. Liberal feminists also wish to dismantle all those barriers that prevent women enjoying a fulfilling life. One of the most significant contributions from modern-day liberal feminists derives from Naomi Wolf (1991). Her best-selling book *'The Beauty Myth'* illustrates how society constructs a concept of femininity that is ultimately designed to oppress women. Females are made to feel insecure about their bodies for their 'failure' to confirm to the feminine ideal. Wolf calls this ideal the *"iron maiden,"* and as with other liberal feminists she aims to empower women from the oppressive nature of a patriarchal society.

As their name clearly implies, **socialist feminists** such as Charlotte Perkins Gilman (1860-1937) believe that equality between the sexes is the most appropriate means towards the emancipation of women. For them, the causes of oppression within a patriarchal society derive from inequality amongst the social classes. Capitalism and patriarchy are linked, and under a free market economic system women are exploited by men. Work undertaken by women is underpaid, undervalued and even unpaid (e.g. housework). Women are often recruited on a part-time basis and given less employment rights than their male counterparts. They also tend to be in less stable employment. In Marxist terminology, women represent the *"reserve army of labour"* and face a life of alienation and exploitation under capitalism. Thus in the words of Irish labour leader James Connolly *"the worker is the slave of capitalist society, the female worker is the slave of that slave."* There is an obvious parallel here with other aspects of socialism – such as economic determinism and a critique of capitalism. [12]

---

[12] Studies have also shown that the only professions in which women consistently earn more than men are modelling and prostitution (Wolf, 1991).

Another important element of socialist feminism relates to **collectivism**. Unlike liberal feminists, this strand of feminism believes that the goals of the feminist movement can only be secured by a collectivist approach in order to redress the power imbalance within a patriarchal society. By doing so, women can liberate themselves from the oppressive nature of patriarchy. Throughout this strand of thought one can trace a strong desire amongst socialist feminists to liberate women (and men) from the confines of gender identity. In doing so, the self-esteem and expectations of females will match that of their male counterparts. For example, the French philosopher Simone de Beauvoir argued that true equality between men and women would only be possible *"when the socialist society is realised worldwide, when there would no longer be men and women but only workers equal with one another."* Although de Beauvoir had an uneasy relationship with the feminist movement as a whole, she remains the most influential of all socialist feminists.

Socialist feminists also claim that the nuclear family reflects and reinforces patriarchy in a number of ways. Firstly, it maintains the dominant position of the bourgeoisie by enabling rich fathers to pass on their wealth in the form of inheritance to their sons. The family also relieves some of the pressure a male proletariat may feel at work. In doing so, the prospect of revolution within society is weakened. Thirdly, the family is a unit of consumption which helps the bourgeoisie maintain a profit. Finally, mothers are expected to undertake the main responsibility for nurturing children and taking care of male workers. The bourgeoisie therefore gain a healthy supply of workers without paying for costly health-care schemes. The emancipation of women must therefore entail a re-examination of the role of the family.

Radical feminism represents the most extreme strand of feminism. Unlike the other two strands of feminism, radical feminists are very much outside the mainstream of the political spectrum. For radical feminists, the means to achieve the goals of the feminist movement entail a complete transformation of society. Females should dominate the private realm *and* the political process. Radical feminists have also tried to change the way people think about issues such as rape and the patriarchal structure of marriage. The views of radical feminists such as Andrea Dworkin have not always ingratiated themselves to other feminists (or indeed other females). For example, Dworkin once argued that *"all men are potential rapists"* and that *"seduction is often difficult to distinguish from rape. In seduction* [at least] *the rapist bothers to buy a bottle of wine."* Within feminist discourse there is considerable divergence over such issues. For the majority of feminists (and females), the views of radical feminists are simply counter-productive to the women's movement as a whole. Critics also claim that radical feminists are too militant in their demands and deeply unrepresentative of what women actually want. It has also been claimed that they posses a degree of hostility towards men (known by the term *"misandry"*). Indeed within American politics, the pejorative term *"feminazis"* has been directed against radical feminists – particularly from those on the right of the political spectrum. For these and other reasons, radical feminism is the least influential of all the three main strands of feminist thought.

The term *radical* derives from the Latin word for *"root,"* and radical feminists locate the root cause of women's oppression in patriarchal gender relations; as opposed to the legal-political-workplace emphasis of liberal feminists and the class-based analysis offered by socialist feminists. Only via opposing stereotypical gender roles and the patriarchal oppression of women can society be reordered and therefore saved from the destruction caused by men. It is important to note that radical feminists believe that *both* men and women must be saved from the tyranny of patriarchal rule. Unlike other strands of feminist thought, the role of males is entirely secondary within radical feminism. Whereas liberal feminists believe that men can assist progress towards feminist goals, and socialist feminists place their faith upon a key role for the male proletariat, radical feminists do not specify a role for men within society. As with radicals of any ideology, they remain very much on the margins of political debate with little opportunity to frame the contours of debate. Their principal contribution to feminism is in terms of raising consciousness amongst women about the extent of their oppression and in their advocacy of women-only communes.

	Liberal feminism	Socialist feminism	Radical feminism
Ideological axis	The strand of feminism nearest the centre	Left-wing	Furthest away from the centre
Means to emancipate women	Constructive engagement with the political process	Radical / revolutionary	Complete transformation of society from its patriarchal basis
View of men	Men are redeemable and have a key role to play	The male proletariat have a revolutionary role to play	Men are the enemy

Leading figures	Klein, Wolf, J.S. Mill	de Beauvoir, Gilman	Hanisch, Dworkin

Although *not* a strand in itself, it is important to consider essentialist feminists such as Lynne Segal and Susan Griffin. Essentialist (or difference) feminists celebrate women's superior virtue and spirituality, contrasting such values to the male world of violence and destruction. For example, the psychologist Carol Gilligan (1936-) claims that women develop a fundamentally different and superior moral psychology to their male counterparts. Essentialist feminists advocate that women should celebrate their differences to men as opposed to striving to be like men. For essentialists, the objective of the women's movement must eschew a form of genderless equality in a manner associated with socialist feminists. Instead, the template for women should be **womanhood** – not personhood. This outlook provides an important contribution within feminist discourse over those issues surrounding motherhood. The essentialist stance within feminist discourse also has obvious implications for the issue of equality.

The role of the state

All feminists view the state as an instrument of patriarchy that must be transformed in order to satisfy the goals of the feminist movement. The state has always been firmly within the public sphere, and the dominance of males within this sphere both reflects and reinforces the patriarchal structure of society. The main difference between feminists over the role of the state is in terms of how to reorder society. As one might expect, liberal feminists believe that the state can facilitate reform within a liberal democratic structure. Socialist feminists view the state as an instrument of class rule designed to protect and advance the interests of the bourgeoisie whilst simultaneously acting as an instrument of patriarchy. Of all three branches of feminist thought, radical feminists are the most implacably opposed to the existing structure of the state. They believe that the state itself is a creation of a male world-view and therefore needs to be transformed in order to create a more female-centred construct of society and politics. Their approach is the most uncompromising within feminist discourse. As one can see, the division over the role of the state within feminist ideology centres solely upon the prescribed means towards the emancipation of women. This is a common trait within other reformist ideologies such as socialism, ecologism and anarchism.

Within the three main strands of feminist thought, the stance taken on the role of the state also bears relevance towards their perspective on liberal democracy. As with all other elements of liberal thought, the premise of liberal feminism is that a political system centred upon pluralism and people power will facilitate social and political change. Many of the most substantial gains of the feminist movement have derived from the democratic political process, thereby giving considerable weight to the liberal feminist approach. For socialist feminists, the principal objection is the relationship between liberal democracy and capitalism. For them, the state within a capitalist system will always side with the rich and powerful. Democracy itself is largely meaningless when the distribution of power is so uneven. As with all other manifestations of a socialist viewpoint, changing the economic system is of paramount importance. Radical feminists also believe in fundamental and far-reaching change. The entire basis of liberal democracy, including the role of the state within that system, must be transformed. For those feminists closer to the centre of the political spectrum, the strategy of radical feminists is both unrealistic and contributes towards a highly negative image of feminists.

Feminism and equality

Equality is widely considered to be a central goal for the feminist movement, but the reality is rather more complex. In order to assess the relationship between feminism and equality, it is necessary to distinguish between the three main strands of feminist thought – as each one offers a rather different perspective. Essentialists also have an intriguing contribution here. Due to their influence within the political process, it seems appropriate to begin with liberal feminists. As with all elements of liberal thought, the emphasis is upon **equality of opportunity** rather than equality of outcome. This is an absolutely fundamental distinction between a liberal and a socialist, and one that has obvious resonance towards our understanding of feminism as an ideology. According to liberal feminists, the political process and wider society needs to remove those barriers which hold back the progress of women. These include the glass ceiling, the glass cliff, the media and gender socialisation.

The glass ceiling is a sociological concept with important political implications. For many women, the glass ceiling is an everyday reality that denies them an equal opportunity in life. Much of the focus of liberal feminism has centred upon helping women smash through the glass ceiling. Legislative changes designed to prevent discrimination, the use of quotas to bolster the number of women in the workplace and female-friendly changes to working practises are all examples of attempts to help women break through the glass ceiling. A term less widely used within ideological debate is glass cliff which can be defined as those situations where women are promoted into risky, difficult jobs because the chances of failure are quite high. Women are deliberately placed into such positions due to a desire within a patriarchal firm to see ambitious women fail. Furthermore, this deters other women from applying for promotion within that institution. Both the glass ceiling and the glass cliff are instruments of patriarchy, and liberal feminists believe we should remove these barriers towards women's emancipation, thereby ensuring the key objective of equality of opportunity.

The objectification of women via the media is an important issue within feminism. The tendency to objectify the female body and present women as sexually available for the gratification of men is widely viewed as a very powerful instrument of patriarchy. This objectification of the female form is a means by which males oppress females; thereby lowering the self-esteem of women and trivialising what women are capable of. There are also major double standards between males and females in their media portrayal. Moreover, the media presents a myth of beauty designed to punish women (Wolf, 1991). Websites devoted to 'celebrating' anorexia - and countless articles commentating upon the body weight of female celebrities - are good illustrations of this point. The high number of teenage girls reading such material illustrates the all-pervasive and curious nature of patriarchy. According to Wolf the beauty myth permeates other facets of society, thereby leading to women being under attack in five areas – work, religion, sex, violence and hunger. She boldly states that women should have *"the choice to do whatever they want with their faces and bodies without being punished by an ideology that is using attitudes, economic pressure and even legal judgments regarding women's appearance to undermine* [women] *psychologically and politically."*

One of the main contributions from feminism within ideological discourse concerns the politics of **gender**. According to feminists, the manner in which girls are socialised into the feminine gender is designed to oppress women. From an early age, girls are socialised into accepting a passive and submissive role within society. In her seminal study of this issue, the liberal feminist Ann Oakley (1972, 1974) claims that parents use verbal appellations and canalisation in order to present a construct of femininity which ultimately serves the needs of a patriarchal society. Verbal appellations are those phrases which shape a child's behaviour, and they may often have a specific gender-context, such as *"brave boy"* or *"pretty girl."* Canalisation occurs where parents 'channel' their children towards toys appropriate for that child's gender, such as toys designed for girls that mimic household appliances and replicate the responsibility of caring for a young baby. Oakley argued that the use of canalisation is deliberate, in that girls and boys are given a view of gender that presents the subordination of the woman (particularly the housewife) as both natural and inevitable. As a result, males retain their dominant status and females are constrained to a subordinate status. [13]

Socialist feminists take a more strident view of equality. Whereas liberal feminists favour equality of opportunity, socialist feminists believe that **genuine equality** should be the goal of the women's movement. The emancipation of women requires a more left-wing approach than that advanced by liberal feminists. Their critique of society centres upon the twin evils of capitalism and patriarchy; which socialist feminists claim are inter-linked. Equality is therefore at the fulcrum of the socialist feminist prescription to improve society. Of all the three main strands of feminist thought, socialist feminism is the most committed to equality. Some socialist feminists – such as Charles Fourier (1772-1837) and Robert Owen (1771-1858) - have even advocated free love and communal living in order to create a truly equal relationship between men and women.

Whereas socialist feminists believe that men (in the form of the proletariat) have a key role to play in the betterment of humankind, radical feminists tend to see men as the problem. Radical feminists argue that women can only free themselves from the shackles of patriarchy via a complete disassociation with men. Those institutions which formalise the relationship between men and women are deeply patriarchal (particularly marriage and the conventional nuclear family). According to Andrea Dworkin – perhaps the most prominent of all radical feminists - *"marriage is an institution developed from rape as a practise"* and *"intercourse as an act expresses the power men have over women."* As a prescription, Dworkin advocates complete freedom for women from the conventional norms and mores of marriage. Some radical feminists (such as Sheila Cronon) have even gone as far as to call for the abolition of marriage, which she describes as *"slavery for women"* because husbands gain an unpaid servant via marriage. As an alternative to marriage, radical feminists prescribe women-only communes and in some cases lesbianism.

To summarise, liberal feminists favour a degree of legal and political equality between men and women, but believe that women can only achieve true emancipation via the widest possible **choice** over their lives. If a woman chooses to be a stay-at-home mother and takes her husband's surname she

---

[13] A great deal of research has been undertaken on the issue of gender (de Beauvoir, 1949; Sharpe, 1976 & 1994, Mead, 1949; Wolf, 1991), all of which suggest that femininity is ultimately a social construct. According to such research there is nothing natural - or inevitable - about behavioural differences between the genders.

is in no sense of the phrase *"selling out the sisterhood."* Socialist feminists view equality within a social and economic context. An equal distribution of wealth and life chances is required in order to meet the objectives of the feminist movement. Radical feminists however wish to free women from all instruments of patriarchy including marriage. Equality with men is not the goal of radical feminists. They believe that women should be the dominant sex. Equality and feminism is therefore not synonymous, despite the popular myth that the two are inexorably linked.

Beyond the three main strands of feminist thought, there is an intriguing contribution to consider from the essentialists. In the context of feminist thought, essentialism claims that true equality between the genders is largely **meaningless** in terms of meeting the goals of the feminist movement. Women should simply celebrate what makes them different to men. Nowhere is this difference clearer than in terms of motherhood. Whereas radical feminists wish to liberate women from the traditional burden of responsibility associated with raising a child, essentialists argue that motherhood should be a celebration of what makes women different to men. After all, it is only women who have the capacity to give birth. Gender ultimately reflects fundamental biological differences, and essentialists stipulate that women should fully embrace those biological differences. Their stance is contrary to the desire amongst some feminists to transcend biological differences and thereby construct an identity centred upon a genderless personhood. In addition, a small number of post-feminists have questioned the whole assumption behind biological differences. For example some women may choose not to have children, or perform the role of a surrogate, or are simply not attract to men.

The majority of feminists disagree with the essentialist stance on the issue of equality. For instance, the American author Kate Millett (1934-) believes that the relationship between men and women should be based upon **androgyny** in which people possess both masculine and feminine characteristics and qualities. Gender differences are based primarily on nurture and are there to serve the interests of patriarchy, particularly the traditional view that women are more suited to the task of caring for children. She argues that men and women should ultimately be judged as individuals, and gender should never be our master status. The construct of the male-female relationship should be both genderless and equal. This is a profoundly egalitarian argument which rejects the biological determinist argument of the essentialists. Yet for essentialists, women should celebrate what makes them different to men and should never strive for an androgynous ideal. To do so would be to deny what makes a woman distinct from a man. In practical terms, this means women should be free to wear what they like without being subject to a certain code of dress via notions of sisterhood. This is something of a fault-line between second wave feminists such as Andrea Dworkin (who eschewed conventional notions of femininity in her appearance) and third wave feminists such as Naomi Klein (who tends to gain a disproportionate amount of comments from journalists about the appearance of her hair – a subject no male intellectual is likely to experience and one that exposes a revealing double-standard).

The perspective taken on this debate rests upon the importance one might attach to gender differences. If one believes that such differences are designed to oppress women then it logically follows that we must completely overhaul those social constructs. However, if one believes that gender differences actively celebrate the essential character and spirit of femininity then true equality between men and women is both meaningless and undesirable. Whatever path taken, feminists have done more than any other ideology to elevate the importance of gender within political discourse.

The relationship between feminism and liberal democracy

The relationship between feminism and liberal democracy centres solely upon the issue of change. There are significant and predictable differences between the various strands of feminist thought. As with socialism – an ideology that feminism bears certain parallels with – much of the debate generated focuses upon *how* to achieve the goals of the feminist movement. There is considerable divergence within feminist thought ranging from reformist strategies to outright revolution to the complete rejection of the conventional political process within a liberal democracy.

Liberal feminists firmly believe that the position of women can and should be advanced by a **constructive engagement** with the political process. The emancipation of women from the confines of a patriarchal society requires feminists (and females) to change the system from within. As with all elements of liberal thought, the assumption here is that a society based upon liberal democracy enables change via peaceful means. Consequently, liberal feminists have advanced their aims through pressure groups and political parties. Prominent examples of the former include the American organisation NOW (National Organisation for Women) - which was created by the celebrated feminist Betty Freidan – and the Fawcett Society in the UK. These are mainstream organisations that highlight issues of a *liberal* feminist character (e.g. the low number of women within the political process and the extent to which the glass ceiling holds women back). In the context of political parties, liberal feminists do not gravitate towards any one particular party. Having said this, the liberal progressive quality of this moderate strand of feminism finds a more welcoming home within the Labour party and the Liberal Democrats. In contrast, the Conservative party has often been considered unsympathetic to feminism. Whether this situation will change in the immediate future remains to be seen. [14]

Socialist feminists take a less sanguine view of liberal democracy. For them, the root cause of female oppression is **capitalism** – an economic system closely bound up with liberal democracy. According to this strand of thought, capitalism ultimately damages the position of women. In the words of Friedrich Engels, capitalism bought about *"the world historical defeat of the female sex."* Furthermore, the bourgeois family underpins the oppression and subjugation of women. Feminists should prioritise the class war above the gender war in order to liberate women from the confines of a patriarchal / capitalist society. Unlike liberal feminists, socialist feminists wish to radically overhaul the liberal democratic structure of society. Most socialist feminists are revolutionary, as opposed to the reformist agenda of liberal feminists.

Radical feminists believe that the cause of female oppression derives from **the family**. It is from this basis that patriarchy reproduces itself within all spheres of life such as education, employment and politics. Fundamental change is therefore required in order to achieve the betterment of humankind. Systems based upon liberal democracy and Marxism have ultimately failed to liberate women. On the latter point, there is a point of disagreement between radical feminists and socialist feminists. For radical feminists, gender divisions are the most politically significant of all social cleavages. This is true within all political systems – including liberal democracy. One of the most prominent theorists within this tradition - Kate Millett (1970) - describes government itself as *"a patriarchal institution whereby half the populace which is female is controlled by that half which is male."* The economic and political structure of that society ignores the real problem. Only by radical change can feminists achieve emancipation because **men are the enemy**.

The individual and society

Feminism offers a gender-based analysis of society. As such, it naturally follows that the most important relationship within society is that between

---

[14] Betty Friedan did much to initiate what became known as second-wave feminism and has rightly been described as the *"mother of women's liberation."* The National Organisation for Women campaigns on a number of liberal feminist issues (e.g. amending the US Constitution in order to guarantee equal pay between men and women and to outlaw discrimination on the basis of gender).

men and women. A great deal of feminist discourse has centred upon a critique of the relationship between men and women and a prescription for a different approach. Radical feminists have even gone so far as to call for women to remove themselves from any relationship with men, although this separatist approach has been criticised by other feminists as impractical and dogmatic. For liberal feminists, individualism must always be the guiding principle. Socialist feminists advocate an equal relationship between men and women based upon personhood. Finally, those who adopt the essentialist stance argue that women should celebrate that which makes them different to men. Women should be female-centred, as opposed to being concerned with adopting masculine behaviour in an attempt to be more like men. These difference feminists claim to subscribe to a pro-woman position free from the collectivist character of other strands of feminism.

Whatever strand of thought we might consider, all feminists agree that the conventional relationship between men and women (particularly that between a married couple) reflects and reinforces the oppression of women. Feminism is ultimately grounded upon a firm critique of patriarchy. Disagreement and division arises on the possible solutions to this problem. Perhaps the most obvious illustration of this point is the ideological chasm that exists between liberal feminists and radical feminists. According to the former, much of the attitude displayed by radical feminists is openly hostile towards men. For instance, Dworkin's infamous description of all men as *"potential rapists"* has drawn vociferous criticism from liberal feminists. If all men are *potential* rapists, surely it follows that all women should perceive themselves as *potential* victims of rape? Furthermore, this hatred of men (or misandry) provides ammunition for those who wish to undermine feminism, particularly from those on the right of the political spectrum. Misandry also betrays the real needs and desires of women, as does the adaptation of a *"victim mentality."* The liberal feminist Naomi Wolf has even described Andrea Dworkin as a *"victim-feminist,"* and the outspoken author Camille Paglia (1990) has challenged the assumption that females should ever think of themselves as victims. In contrast, radical feminists assert that males are motivated by more sinister motives than females. Marilyn French goes one step further than Andrea Dworkin in terms of labelling men. For her *"all men are rapists, and that's all they are. They rape us with their eyes, their laws and their codes."* Susan Brownmiller (1975) adds that men have created an ideology of rape that creates a conscious process of intimidation. Women are therefore kept in a state of fear and men rape simply because they can. Even men who do not rape women benefit from the fear and anxiety that rape causes.

Criticism of males and masculine behaviour can be found within all strands of feminist thought. Typical of this element of feminist thinking is the observation offered by Rosa Luxembourg, who declared that *"all war is male."* In addition, the author and social critic Germaine Greer believes that *"women have very little idea of how much men hate them."* Difference feminists take a particularly strident stance on the issue of gender, believing that women are culturally and behaviourally superior to men. Humankind can only be rescued via the transferral of power from men to women. Crucially, this would liberate both women *and* men. On a less extreme level, feminists have called for men to change their behaviour in order to facilitate the goal of women's emancipation. For example, in the domestic sphere men should adopt the same level of responsibility for housework as women. These so-called symmetrical families (Willmott & Young, 1973) would relieve much of the burden that at present falls disproportionately upon women. Underpinning such arguments is the view that both genders are equally capable of caring for a child. Therefore, there is absolutely nothing biologically determined or natural about traditional gender roles.

The feminist stance on lifestyle issues

Perhaps the most famous slogan within feminism is *"the personal is the political."* Cited to the radical feminist Carol Hanisch, this slogan personifies a concerted attempt by feminists to address the status of the private realm within political discourse. Indeed, no other ideology has done more to elevate the private realm within ideological debate as feminism. The main contribution we need to consider is an attempt by feminists to politicise the private realm and thereby promote those issues of most concern to women. Secondly, feminists have been divided over certain lifestyle issues – thereby exposing significant tensions within the feminist movement.

Traditionally the public sphere (such as politics and employment) has been the preserve of men, whereas women have been confined to the private realm centered upon the family and housework. The public sphere has always gained more serious attention, whereas the private realm has been marginalised. This process has been to the obvious detriment of the status of women within politics, with issues of deep concern to females having been sidelined due to male-bias within the political process. Feminists have tried to address this problem by re-defining what we might consider to be 'political.' In the words of Kate Millett, politics consists of *"power-structured relationships* [and] *arrangements whereby one group of persons is controlled by another."* She offers an understanding of the term 'politics' which inevitably widens the manner in which we perceive the political realm. In addition, Simone de Beauvoir (1949) argued that the masculine is represented as the positive or the norm whereas the feminine is routinely depicted as the other and therefore inferior. Women are therefore the *"second sex"* and face considerable limitations upon their freedom. Once again, we can identify an attempt to politicise the private realm by challenging the traditional 'public' man / 'private' woman dichotomy. It is here that feminism has changed the contours of the political process, having politicised what was previously located outside the political realm. In contemporary politics, there is undoubtedly a concerted attempt within the political process to address issues located in the private sphere.

Another important contribution towards **the politicisation of the 'private' realm** derives from Betty Friedan (1963). She argued that the feminine mystique is a cultural myth that reflects the patriarchal structure of society. Women were prevented from fulfilling their potential in life (especially in the public realm) due to the confines of this cultural myth. She also argued that society must address the deep sense of unhappiness amongst those women who feel trapped by the boundaries of the domestic or private sphere. Friedan undoubtedly touched a nerve amongst many women, highlighting the frustration and misery of stay-at-home wives confined to the private sphere. She did much to raise awareness of what she called *"the problem with no name."* In her later work (1983), Friedan argued that *"today the problem that has no name is how to juggle work, love, home and children."* She has also argued that the feminist movement needed to reconcile the achievement of personhood with a woman's need for love.

Feminists have also argued that the division between 'private' woman and 'public' man has limited the progress of females and feminine values within the political process. For instance, there is a marked tendency for political parties to pick 'safe' candidates, which tends to favour men over women. Secondly, those female politicians who have successfully climbed the greasy pole have routinely displayed masculine (rather than feminine) characteristics. Mrs. Thatcher was widely depicted as *"the Iron Lady,"* the former Israeli Prime Minister Golda Meir was known as the *"Chariot of Israel"* (and was once described as *"the only man in the government"*) and Hillary Clinton is unmistakably hawkish on the issue of foreign policy. One can also trace a revealing double standard here. During the Clinton era it was commonly observed that Bill was allowed to cry, but Hillary was not. The sight of a powerful man showing his emotions was considered to be a positive, whereas any display of emotion from Hillary leads to questions about her suitability for political life. There are many other illustrations of undue hostility directed unfairly at women within the political realm. During the 2007 French Presidential campaign Segolene Royal was labelled a bad mother with one of her male rivals in the Socialist party raising the question *"who will look after the children?"* if Royal was to become President of France. In Spain, the high number of females within Jose Zapatero's Cabinet led the Italian Prime Minister Silvio Berlusconi to describe that Cabinet as *"too pink."* I think the reader would agree that it's unlikely a male-dominated Cabinet would ever be described as *"too blue."* Even Mrs. Thatcher met with considerable resistance amongst the male Tory hierarchy despite the undoubted electoral success she bought to the party. [15]

In direct contrast to the feminist argument, the traditional division between 'public' man and 'private' women is seen as **natural** and **inevitable** by those on the right of the political spectrum. According to conservatives, gender divisions reflect the wider needs of society – especially children. It is therefore both natural and desirable for men to take on the role of breadwinner and women to take on the role of care giver. Men and women are suited towards different roles, and each much perform that role to ensure order and stability within society. Some on the right even claim that feminists have undermined the moral fabric of society by encouraging women to place employment over motherhood. Rising levels of crime, welfare dependency and drug addiction have been blamed upon feminists who prescribe roles that go against the norms and values of society. This backlash against attempts by feminists to 'politicise' the private realm and provide women with a sense of empowerment over their lives has been particularly virulent within the United States. The attempt to re-assert traditional gender roles by neo-conservatives reflects the degree to which feminism has contributed to American society, and could therefore be viewed as a back-handed compliment. Another aspect of this backlash concerns what Naomi Wolf describes as the beauty myth which is designed to make women feel *"worth less"* in order to counteract the way feminism had begun to make women *"worth more"* (1991, p.18).

To feminists the most important lifestyle issues are motherhood, the sex industry and abortion. In all three cases, feminists have been divided. In the case of motherhood, the American author Megan Basham (2008) in her book *Beside Every Successful Man : A Woman's Guide to Having it all* claims to speak for the majority of mothers who want to work fewer hours (or give up work altogether) whilst their children are young. In order to achieve this, Basham argues that wives should concentrate on helping their husbands become more successful in their careers. In doing so, the couple are more able to cope financially with the pay cut to the mother. At the core of Basham's argument is the view that women have a more communal concept of success, and a great deal of that can be applied to relationships. Her views can be

---

[15]   Charlotte Whitton is quoted as saying that *"whatever women do they must do twice as well as men to be thought half as good."* Somewhat sardonically, she added *"luckily, this is not difficult."*

The Definitive Guide to Political Ideologies

seen as a reflection of the essentialist argument and have gained Basham support amongst the religious right in America, a group that has published the *'True Women Manifesto'* which claims that men and women are designed to reflect God in complementary and distinct ways. This Biblical notion of **complementarianism** consists of a counter-revolution against second wave feminism. In reply, the contemporary journalist Leslie Bennetts (2007) warns women that stepping out of the workforce for even a short period of time will damage their earning's potential, and that women should maintain the gains of feminism. Any return to the notion that *"behind every great man is a great woman"* would represent a massive step-back for the women's movement.

In relation to female politicians, the issue of motherhood has always been a contentious one. In essence, one's view rests upon how we view the role of a mother to a child, particularly during an infant's early years. Leading politicians such as Rachida Dati and Sarah Palin have either sold out the sisterhood by returning to work soon after giving birth, or are empowering figures who demonstrate that women really can have it all. Dati's return to work was particularly controversial because she had given birth by caesarean section. Many feminists argue that the traditional concept of the female's role consists of a double burden for women. Moreover, being a mother can greatly damage a woman's financial health and employment prospects, particularly if they stay at home for a lengthy period of time. The long-hours culture also deters mothers from seeking promotion at work, and the pay and grading system often devalues *'soft skills'* that society largely associates with feminine characteristics. Those who put forward the essentialist argument claim that women should celebrate that which makes them unique. For them, motherhood provides a reward that goes beyond anything men could experience within the world of work. The superior qualities of females – such as empathy and a high level of emotional literacy – should be the basis of celebration and pride.

The sex industry exposes another major fault line within feminist ideology in terms of lifestyle issues. Second wave feminists claim that pornography represents the **objectification** of women and is therefore an instrument of patriarchy. This argument is most closely associated with the radical feminist Andrea Dworkin (1991) and her study into the effects of the porn industry. Third wave feminists have however taken a more nuanced view of the sex industry. They have argued that women *can* be the ones in control, and *if* they have freely chosen to work in the sex industry, they should be free to do so. They are in no sense betraying feminism simply by exercising their choice to work in the sex industry. Indeed, some women may find it empowering. Furthermore, pornography is also sold to females and much of the taboo surrounding females exploring their sexuality has been removed. Although this argument is not shared by all third wave feminists, there is undoubtedly a division over this particular issue. It should be easy for the student to trace an undercurrent of liberal feminist thought within this argument. As with *all* aspects of liberal thought, the guiding principle is one of **moral relativism**.

On the issue of abortion, the right to choose has long been an article of faith for many feminists. Women should be in control of their fertility and society must respect the right of a woman to terminate her pregnancy, if that is her choice. Naturally, this argument owes much to the liberal strand of feminist thought. However, there has been a limited degree of revisionism on this lifestyle issue. It must also be added that a great many women are involved in pro-life campaigns, especially in the United States. *These and other questions generated within the realm of lifestyle choices are further compounded by the argument that "one woman's emancipation may be another woman's idea of oppression." For instance, a Muslim who covers her body would to some feminists be seen as a sign of oppression, yet in reality she could be experiencing a sense of liberation from the widespread objectification of the female form. From the other extreme, a woman working in the sex industry may be considered truly liberated (or firmly oppressed) amongst feminists.*

Change or the status quo

As with socialism, change is the very credo of feminism. The critique of patriarchy inevitably leads towards demands within the feminist movement for change. However, there are substantial differences between the **reformist** approach taken by those closer to the centre of the political spectrum and the more **hard-line** stance taken by radical feminists. The issue of female suffrage is a very clear illustration of the distinction between the various strands of feminist thought on social change. The direct action of the suffragettes was a definite reflection of radical feminism, whereas the Declaration of Sentiments written by Elizabeth Cady Stanton (1815-1902) deliberately drew upon the language of liberal feminism. In order to fully understand the relationship between feminism and change we once again need to differentiate between the various strands of feminist thought.

There are two main elements to the liberal feminist stance on the issue of change. Liberal feminists believe that their goals can be achieved via engagement and activity with the conventional political process due to the plurality and openness of the liberal democratic system. Both pressure groups and political parties facilitate the pursuit of feminist goals. For example, since 1997 the Labour government has extended maternity leave, expanded state provision of childcare via the Surestart scheme and has closed the pay gap between men and women. Thus despite male-dominance within the political process, it is both possible and desirable for the feminist movement to achieve change via the democratic process. Liberal feminism takes a reformist approach and campaigns on a myriad of issues such as a more equitable representation of women within the political and economic realm and more crèches within places of employment. Secondly, liberal feminists believe that true emancipation requires the fullest possible range of choices for women. Change must therefore be guided by moral relativism and individualism. As with all liberals, there is deep concern over the tyranny of the majority. Change must therefore be accompanied by an absence of conformity upon women. Unlike radical feminists, liberal feminists believe that women must have the fullest possible range of lifestyles in order to liberate women from the shackles of a patriarchal system.

Socialist feminists prioritise **the class war** over the gender war. Change must therefore be revolutionary if women are to secure the goals of the feminist movement. Equality between men and women requires the overhaul of capitalism and the reordering of society along the basis of a more even distribution of wealth. According to this line of thought, the conventional family structure reflects the economic domination by men over women. Centred on Marxist assumptions of class consciousness and economic determinism, society should be transformed from one based upon private ownership to one based on common ownership of the means of production. Freedom from the confines of a bourgeois conception of the family would thereby ensure the objective of female emancipation, in contrast to the situation in a capitalist society in which men have effectively enslaved women and condemned them to the domestic sphere. Once again, it is possible to trace the private – public sphere distinction that is so important to feminist ideology.

Radical feminists believe that the root cause of female oppression is the family, and the first step towards reordering society should be to change the conventional mores of the family. Simone de Beauvoir even called for the abolition of the family (although she is more commonly associated with the socialist strand of feminism). Underpinning the radical feminist stance on change is their attitude to men. Unlike other strands of feminist thought, radical feminists see men as the enemy. It has even been argued that men would not be necessary within a society based upon radical feminism, thereby reflecting a sense of **separatism**. This redundant male theory stands in direct contrast to the view amongst liberal feminists and socialist feminists that men are redeemable (citing evidence of recent trends such as househusbands and symmetrical families).

Radical feminists have also demanded change in the realm of sexual relations. In her best-selling book *The Female Eunuch* (1970) Germaine Greer argues that females are socialised into accepting a passive role. This has not only repressed their true sexuality but also their more adventurous side. According to her analysis, the widespread stereotype of the eternal feminine works as an instrument of patriarchy. She also argues that *"women will* [only] *be free when they have a positive definition of female sexuality."* Greer's call for a **sexual revolution** remains one of the boldest and most influential contributions from the ideology of feminism. Today, most would accept that women are far more liberated in their pursuit of sexual pleasure than previous generations – yet feminists still claim that society has a long way to go before women are freed from the constraints imposed by patriarchy. For example, Naomi Wolf (1997) argues that women must reclaim the legitimacy of their own sexuality by shattering the polarisation of women between *"virgin"* and *"whore."*

As with all ideologies committed to change, much of the ideological debate derived from feminism is located amongst its followers. For instance, the focus of liberal feminists upon an agenda that reflects the needs of white, middle-class women has faced criticism from within the feminist movement. In class terms, socialist feminists argue that liberal feminists have ignored the economic basis of sexual inequality. In race terms, black feminists such as bell hooks (the avoidance of capital letters is deliberate!) have argued that the women's movement has sidelined the unique needs of black women. She is part of an offshoot of feminist discourse described as **black feminism** – a view much more prevalent within America than the UK. Black feminism portrays sexism and racism as interlinked, highlighting the complex nature of those disadvantages that face black women. In other words, emancipation for black women cannot be achieved without a fundamentally different agenda to that put forward by liberal feminists (most of whom are white).

Feminism in contemporary politics

Feminism has made a significant contribution to ideological discourse by facilitating a study of politics and society from a **female-centred perspective**. Feminism has also widened the palate of ideological language, especially in the context of gender. An issue formerly the preserve of the private realm and thereby divorced from political discourse is now an established part of academic inquiry. Indeed, the politicisation of gender is perhaps feminism's most important legacy within ideological discourse. In a more direct sense, feminism has empowered the lives of many women. The glass ceiling has been broken by many females, most obviously in the case of Mrs. Thatcher in the political realm. Feminists have even managed to reclaim negative words in an expression of identity politics. During the 1990s, a major underground movement associated with underground music bands strived to present previously negative insults in a positive light. Those concerts provided an exhilarating experience that went well beyond music, and as someone who attended them myself, I can definitely say that they were as much about politics as they were about music. The sight of 'riot grrrl' bands such as Huggy Bear and Bikini Kill demanding that men go to the back of the audience so that women could experience what it was like at the front, and the prevalence of fans writing negative labels of women on their arms, was very liberating for women (and perhaps for those men who felt restricted by the conventional construct of masculinity). The tradition of embracing negative slurs continues in modern-day India, where a campaign based in Bangalore by the self-styled 'Loose and Forward' women involves posting a pair of pink knickers to the Headquarters of Hindu extremists.

Having said all this, feminism as an ideology has not dated particularly well. It reached a high point during the 1960s and 70s when significant gains for women were achieved in the political and economic realm, yet over time, feminism has lost some of its driving force. The goals of the feminist movement have to some extent been achieved, with most women experiencing a level of choice and opportunity unavailable to previous generations. Based on this view, it has been argued that we have reached a post-feminist paradigm and therefore gone beyond feminism. Another important question to consider here is *"do feminists speak for the majority of women?"* A great many women reject the feminist argument (Sommers, 1994), with some of the most powerful political figures being deeply opposed to feminism (such as Margaret Thatcher and Golda Meir). The latter once claimed that *"women's liberation is just a lot of foolishness. It's the men who are discriminated against."* This leads onto the view that feminism has perhaps gone too far, and it is the position of men that we should be concerned with.

Another interesting development within contemporary discourse is a questioning of the supposed 'achievements' of feminism. For instance, the English writer Julie Burchill argues that *"the freedom women were supposed to have found in the sixties largely boiled down to easy contraception and abortion – things to make life easier for men."* The traditional focus of feminists upon the right of women to choose an abortion has also been subject to a degree of revisionism. In addition, the hope amongst feminists that society would be improved if women were in charge has been challenged by the American writer Katie Roiphe who raised the following point; *"has anyone on earth ever been nastier, more brutal, than little girls? … The hierarchies between women are so rigid, so patrolled, so absolute, it seems ludicrous to pretend that women in power would be more democratic, more inclusive* [and] *more generous to those who are less fortunate."*

In the contemporary era, feminists have offered conflicting insights into the state and condition of feminism. The celebrated third wave feminist Naomi Wolf rejects the possibility of a universal female agenda, and the outspoken social critic Camille Paglia has raised serious questions for the feminist movement as a whole. She has accused feminism of generating a victim mentality amongst women and claims that *"if civilisation had been left in female hands, we would still be living in grass huts."* Paglia also adds that *"there is no female Mozart because there is no female Jack the Ripper"* – an enigmatic observation perfectly designed to cause controversy and generate animated debate. In contrast, Germaine Greer boldly claims that *"it is time for women to get angry again."* She argues that patriarchy has the capacity to reproduce itself and that women have been tricked into accepting a **phoney degree of equality**. She also believes that feminism remains as relevant as ever due to the continued existence of patriarchy.

In summary, the divisions within feminism are perhaps greater than any of the ideologies considered thus far – even socialism. The existence of liberal feminism, socialist feminism, radical feminism, essentialism and black feminism reflects a highly eclectic ideology. Some have even speculated that we have reached a post-feminist paradigm. In response to this point, feminists rightly claim that society still has a long way to go before the goals of the feminist movement have been fully secured. For an ideology bound up so closely with the issue of gender, perhaps the last word should go to the Burmese human rights campaigner Aung San Suu Kyi who observed that *"in societies where men are truly confident of their own worth, women are not merely tolerated but valued."*

Further quotes on feminism

"Woman, even more than the working class, is the great unknown quantity of the human race." Keir Hardie

"I myself have never been able to find out precisely what feminism is: I only know that people call me a feminist whenever I express sentiments that differentiate me from a doormat or prostitute." Rebecca West

"High heels are a conspiracy against women." Unnatributed

"A woman without a man is like a fish without a bicycle." Gloria Steinem

"There is more difference within the sexes than between them." Ivy Compton-Burnett

"The philosophy of women is not to reason but to feel." Immanuel Kant

"Men look at women. Women watch themselves being looked at. This determines not only the relations of men to women, but the relation of women to themselves." John Berger

"Fat is a feminist issue." Susie Orbach

"Feminism is the theory, lesbianism is the practise." Ti-Grace Atkinson

"The better the treatment of women, the more civilised the society." Charles Fourier

"As a woman I have no country. As a woman I want no country. As a woman my country is the whole world." Virginia Woolf

Recommended reading

Brownmiller, S. (1975) *Against Our Will : Men, Women and Rape.* A radical feminist perspective upon the impact of rape within society and its relevance to patriarchy.

de Beauvoir, S. (1949) *Le deuxième sexe.* A seminal text within socialist feminism. Simone de Beauvoir argues that women are the other sex and this sense of otherness works to their disadvantage.

Friedan, B. (1963) *The Feminine Mystique.* The classic second wave feminist text, Friedan remains influential amongst American feminists. This book should be read alongside the Second Stage (see below).

Friedan, B. (1983) *The Second Stage.* Freidan updates her work upon *"the problem with no name"* to claim that women face a new set of boundaries and challenges. She also argues that much more needs to be done in order to satisfy the aims of the feminist movement.

Greer, G. (1970) *The Female Eunuch.* In her best-selling book Greer argues that women need to reclaim their sexual identity from the confines of patriarchy. Not only will this lead to sexual liberation but will also enable women to become more adventurous in their personal lives. Under patriarchy women have been treated - and perceived of - as eunuchs.

Millett, K. (1970) *Sexual Politics.* The leading exponent of how men and women need to adopt a genderless and androgynous persona in order to fulfil the goals of the feminist movement.

Oakley, A. (1972) *Sex, gender and society.* A sociological account from a liberal feminist as to the importance of gender roles within a patriarchal society.

Oakley, A. (1974) *The sociology of housework.* A sociological study of how children are socialised into accepting the oppression of females as both normal and inevitable. She claims that the family has a vital role to play within the wider structure of patriarchy.

Sommers, C.H. (1994) *Who stole feminism? How women have betrayed women.* Sommers offers an insightful account of the relationship between feminism and the everyday lives of women. She is largely critical of how feminists have tried to push forward their agenda.

Spender, D. (1980) *Man Made Language.* A superb account of how language operates as an instrument of patriarchy. Spender shows that men routinely cut women off in conversation and that more weight is given to men's words.

Watkins, S.A., Rueda, M. & Rodriguez, M. (1999) *Introducing feminism.* A brief introduction to the main aspects of feminism, this book offers a generalised coverage of feminism.

Wolf, N. (1991) *The Beauty Myth.* The classic third wave feminist text. Wolf argues that the notion of beauty is used to oppress women and make them feel worth less when feminism has made them feel worth more.

Wolf, N. (1997) *Promiscuities.* Continuing a line of argument first put forward by Germaine Greer in the Female Eunuch, Wolf claims that women need to assert their sexual identity in order to experience true emancipation.

Wollstonecraft, M. (1792) *Vindication of the Rights of Woman.* The classic first wave text from a key exponent of liberal feminism. Her work is particularly relevant from a historical perspective as to why feminism developed as an ideological and political movement. Her work also has relevance to the ideology of liberalism.

Ideas for further discussion

What are the main elements of feminist ideology?

In what sense do feminists seek to change human behaviour?

What differences exist between the three main strands of feminism?

What would be the role of the state within a society based upon feminism?

To what extent do feminists support greater equality between men and women?

What is the feminist stance upon liberal democracy?

What differences exist within feminism over their attitude towards men?

Why have feminists focused so closely upon the private sphere?

What approaches are advocated by feminists towards securing change within a patriarchal society?

Are we now at the post-feminist stage?

Key terms

Emancipation Liberation from discriminatory attitudes. The term is linked towards moves by women and ethnic minorities to secure greater freedom over the conduct of their own lives.

Emasculate Where power and status is withdrawn from the male on the basis of changes to gender roles. The term has formed part of the backlash against feminism, particularly in the United States, and tends to derive from the right of the political spectrum.

Empowerment When an individual or social group gains a greater influence over their own lives and society as a whole, as in the case of the feminist movement which aims to empower females. The term can be used in a variety of settings.

Exploitation The means and method by which a social group manipulate and take advantage of another social group. The term is usually employed by Marxists and feminists. The former claims that in a capitalist society the bourgeoisie exploit the proletariat, whereas feminists claim that in a patriarchal society it is men who exploit women. The term can also be applied to the method by which the trading system operates within the global economy. Those campaigning for a fairer trading system argue that powerful multi-national corporations exploit workers within the majority world, often with the collusion of Western governments.

Feminazis A highly derogatory term used to label radicals in the feminist movement. The term is American in origin and employed by those on the right of the political spectrum to highlight the more extreme examples of feminism.

Gender Those social and behavioural characteristics associated with masculine behaviour and feminine behaviour. Socialisation along the basis of gender forms a key aspect of identity and a major determinant upon human behaviour. There are several illustrations of how we are socialised into a particular view of gender, such as the concept of canalisation (Oakley, 1972 & 1974). Gender undoubtedly has massive implications for our understanding of society (de Beauvoir, 1949; Mead, 1949). One thing clear about gender is its sheer diversity within various societies, which strongly suggests that there is nothing universal about masculine / feminine values. For example, adult males in Tchambuli society act in a manner usually associated with females, and adult females act in a manner often associated with masculine behaviour. Amongst the Nigerian Wodaabes, the women hold economic power and judge men in beauty contests.

Glass ceiling A term used to describe those barriers which face women and ethnic minorities aiming for promotion in the workplace. Having said this, the term can be applied to other disadvantaged groups. The word *"glass"* refers to the subtle and covert character of this form of discrimination, whereas the phrase *"ceiling"* is a reference to the limitation it places upon upward mobility.

Glass cliff Where women are promoted into risky, difficult jobs because the chances of failure are quite high. Women are deliberately placed into these positions due to a desire within a patriarchal institution to see ambitious women fail. The driving force behind the glass cliff is undoubtedly sexism and misogyny.

Male-dominated society A term used interchangeably with a patriarchal society. Certain professions may also be described as male-dominated, particularly those in which social, political and economic power is concentrated into the hands of a small male elite. The degree to which society / a profession is male-dominated can be assessed by statistical evidence, yet it often makes more sense to consider the term *masculine*-dominated when striving towards a deeper understanding of politics and society.

Misandry A prejudicial hatred of men. Radical feminists have often been accused of misandry.

Misogyny A prejudicial hatred of women. Feminists claim that certain aspects of a patriarchal society reflect misogynistic attitudes amongst men.

Motherhood penalty A term used to describe those considerable financial penalties suffered by working mothers. For example, according to research published by the Trades Union Council in March 2008, the gender gap in terms of pay more than trebles when women reach their 30s (a time when many women have reached the stage of motherhood). The long-hours culture also deters mothers from seeking promotion at work, and the pay and grading system often devalues *'soft skills'* largely associated with feminine values.

Patriarchy A term used to describe the dominance of men with positions of power and the exploitation of women. The term is exclusively associated with the feminist perspective.

Redundant male theory A view prevalent during the 1970s amongst radical feminists who claimed that society could and should be transformed along the basis of feminine values. Within such a society most males would effectively become redundant with no real purpose. The redundant male theory exists at the margins of feminist thought and could in no way be presented as part of mainstream feminism.

Sisterhood A collective term used by feminists to emphasise the need for unity amongst women in terms of advancing the feminist cause. Since the emergence of third wave feminism the term has become rather less common. To third wave feminists, the notion that women were betraying the sisterhood simply by exercising their own free will imposed a rather restrictive concept of femininity.

CHAPTER 6
ANARCHISM

The core elements of anarchism

Anarchism is the most fascinating and thought-provoking of all the political ideologies one might consider. Anarchism is unequivocally uncompromising, wonderfully eclectic and unapologetically utopian. As a body of thought, anarchism dates back to the Cynics of Ancient Greece and according to one of its principal proponents *"stands for the liberation of the human mind from the dominion of religion: the liberation of the human body from the dominion of property* [and the] *liberation from the shackles and restraints of government* [it is] *the philosophy of a new social order based on liberty unrestricted by manmade law; the theory that all forms of government rest on violence, and are therefore wrong and harmful, as well as unnecessary."* More importantly, anarchism offers the promise of deep intellectual interest for both students and teachers of Politics due to its *"salutary effect upon awakening thought"* (William Godwin). [16]

Essentially, there are two core elements of anarchism. The first is a bold assertion that individuals must possess **absolute and unrestricted freedom**. This view is based upon a fundamental commitment to liberty as a political value. For anarchists such as Joseph Labadie *"liberty is the solution to all social and economic questions."* This deep-seated belief in liberty places anarchism on the extreme edge of the libertarian axis. Anarchism thereby confronts the

---

[16]   The lengthy quote derives from the American anarchist Emma Goldman (1869-1940).

prevalent Weltanschauung amongst political ideologies, all of whom justify a role for the state within society in order to enhance human existence. For anarchists, we can only realise the goal of a truly utopian society when – and only when – we are freed from the confines of the state.

The second element of anarchism is a belief that *any* form of political authority is unnecessary and evil. Naturally, this manifests itself in implacable **opposition to the state**. All anarchists share an abhorrence of the criminal, illegitimate and violent actions of the state. As a body of thought, anarchism offers a firm critique of authoritarianism in all its forms. Anarchism thereby takes the Jeffersonian argument to its final conclusion, a view best articulated by the words of the American theorist Henry Thoreau (1817-1862) who said *"that government is best which governs not at all."*

As you will have no doubt deduced, the two main elements of anarchism are mutually reinforcing. According to anarchists, the only way we can have complete freedom is via the abolition of the state. In doing so, we would exist in a state of nature characterised by harmony where individuals would be left to their own devices without any state interference. We alone would govern ourselves. To its manifold critics, such a world would be either totally impractical or one characterised by lawlessness and chaos. The anarchist writer Joseph Sobran acknowledged this point when he said that *"the measure of the state's success is that the word anarchy frightens people, while the word state does not."* It is difficult to say whether this is due to the process of socialisation or our own innate desire to gain the protection of the state. To borrow from Marxist terminology, it may even be a manifestation of false consciousness. Whatever the reason, the word 'anarchy' is widely perceived in a negative sense – conjuring images of lawlessness and sporadic acts of violence. Inevitably, this will constrain the ability of anarchism to win over hearts and minds. Yet to its supporters, the ability to govern ourselves would free us all from the unnecessary and unnatural evil that is the state.

Core elements
Absolute freedom / extreme libertarianism
Political authority is unnecessary

Anarchism offers by far the most far-reaching challenge to our conventional understanding of the political world. More than any other ideology, anarchism turns the whole political world upside down, a not inconsiderable feat considering the degree to which conventional assumptions govern the parameters of ideological debate. Existing on the fringes of **extreme libertarianism**, the ideology of anarchism makes a unique contribution to our understanding of the world around us. However, its political impact seems destined to remain negligible. Anarchism requires a leap of faith considerably greater than any other political ideology. Moreover, the ability of anarchists to persuade others of their argument is largely confined to a small group of idealists.

Anarchist perspective on human nature

Anarchism holds a **highly optimistic** view of human nature. The only other ideologies that come close to this view are liberalism and socialism. But unlike liberals, anarchists believe that we can only be free when we are free from man-made laws. In regards to socialism, the ideology of anarchism claims that human nature cannot be understood on the basis of economic determinism. For anarchists, it is the existence of the state that thwarts the emergence of the positive character of human nature. This is true of *all* societies where a state exists. Even a communist society necessitates the existence of a state during the transition period known as the dictatorship of the proletariat. Thus according to anarchists, we should view human nature in a very positive manner and construct a society based around the argument that we must liberate ourselves from the state itself.

According to anarchists, the human spirit will thrive once we are **liberated** from all forms of hierarchical rule and state-imposed order. It is the state that crushes the human spirit and enslaves us to a level of perpetual dependency in a world characterised by domination and subordination. Human nature can only be free once we create a stateless society and abolish all government. In a world of unrestricted free will the natural goodness of human nature would come to the fore.

The language and flavour of anarchism is far more **spiritual** than other ideologies (with the obvious exception of religious fundamentalism). This holds clear implications for the anarchist perspective on human nature. It is a world-view based upon the spiritual bonds amongst human beings and other components of the natural world. As such, anarchism marks a radical departure from all other ideologies we have considered thus far, and is as far away from conservatism as any ideology could be. Perhaps the clearest contrast to consider here is that between the conservative philosopher Thomas Hobbes and the ideology of anarchism. To the former, a state of nature would be a nightmarish hell. People need the state in order to protect and defend their liberty. Yet to anarchists, a state of nature would release the enlightened life-force of human beings. The human condition would be elevated once the unnatural boundaries imposed by the state were removed. Whatever your thoughts so far, it is a bold and controversial assertion that goes right to the heart of how we view human nature and the political realm.

Main strands of anarchist thought

Although anarchism is regarded as unique within ideological discourse, there are at least two ideologies it has some relationship with. Anarchism takes both socialism and liberalism to their anti-state conclusions. It has been described as a synergy of *"ultra-liberalism"* and *"ultra-socialism"* (Heywood, 2007, p.178), a point which will become clearer when we consider the two main strands of anarchist thought - individualist anarchism and collectivist anarchism. These are the **two** main strands of anarchist thought. There is also a link between nihilism and anarchism.

The difference between the two main strands of anarchist thought is relatively simple to comprehend. **Individualist anarchism** belongs on the libertarian-right of the political spectrum, whereas **collectivist anarchism** belongs on the libertarian-left. Individualist anarchists believe that human nature is governed by egoism, whereas collectivist anarchists believe that human nature is fundamentally co-operative. Anarchists from the former tradition stress concepts such as voluntary trade and free-market capitalism, whereas collectivist anarchists believe that co-operation can be facilitated by concepts such as mutual aid. The two main strands also differ over the issue of private property.

	Individualist anarchism	**Collectivist anarchism**
Ideological axis	Right-libertarian	Left-libertarian
Influential concepts	Time store, total solitude	Mutual aid, anarcho-syndicalism
Key figures	Warren, Stirner, Godwin, Rothbard	Kropotkin, Bakunin, Proudhon, Sorel
View of private property	Essential characteristic of liberty	All property is theft

Individualist anarchism takes liberalism to its extreme anti-state ending. Individualist anarchists expand Mill's observation that the individual is sovereign to its ultimate conclusion. Yet whereas the famous liberal theorist stipulated certain restrictions upon free will, individualist anarchists believe that human beings should have **full autonomy** over their lives. Concerns about self-regarding actions and the harm principle have absolutely no place within anarchist thought. This is one of the main distinctions between liberalism and individualist anarchism. According to liberal ideology, the state must place some limits upon our freedom in order to enhance and maximise the concept of liberty within a society. Yet according to anarchists, the ideology of liberalism enables the state to hide its true intentions behind seemingly necessary measures. Governments routinely present restrictions upon personal liberty as in *our* interests when the reality is completely different. For anarchists, this is little more than deceit exhibited by those with authority because the state has absolutely no right to intervene in our personal conduct, and any attempt to do so is done by those corrupted by power.

Individualist anarchism also departs from liberalism on the issue of man-made laws. They reverse John Locke's famous dictum (*"without laws, man has no freedom"*) in order to justify their argument that we do not need the state. All laws are restrictive of some freedom; therefore we need to remove laws and the apparatus that goes with those laws. The various elements of a liberal democracy will lead us towards the maintenance of a state, thereby enabling the state to impose its coercive stranglehold over our liberty. No restriction whatsoever on the individual can ever be justified, even the night-watchman role stipulated by classical liberals. For individualist anarchists, an unbridled version of capitalism is the only appropriate economic model for a stateless society.

Unlike the main ideological perspectives, there is no towering intellectual within the anarchist tradition. There is no figure comparable to a Mill (liberalism), a Burke (conservatism) or a Marx (socialism). Thus to understand anarchism it is necessary to consider a wide range of eclectic and idiosyncratic thinkers. The first and perhaps most important of all individualist anarchists is the English philosopher William Godwin (1756-1836). He argued that human perfectibility could be achieved once we were bold enough to free ourselves from the shackles of the state (1793). In order to achieve this goal Godwin advocated a decisive role for education in order to transform human consciousness from its reliance upon the state. In a **stateless society** we would live in accordance with universal moral laws and chose to co-exist peacefully without the need for a state.

Godwin took the liberalist assumption of the rational self-interested individual to its final conclusion. He said that we are all capable of exercising our own consciousness and our actions should only be influenced by the laws of nature. The reasoning behind this argument is simple – there is and can never be any possible justification for the existence of a state. By replacing the state, Godwin advocated a world governed by natural laws without any political institutions. Such a society would enable human beings to live in

The Definitive Guide to Political Ideologies

harmony with one another. Most anarchists have a particular model in mind when constructing their view of a stateless society. In the case of Godwin, he advocated a society of small producers united in co-operation. Partly because of this, Godwin accepted the need for small-scale private ownership. This is a common theme running through the individualist anarchist strand of thought. For anarchists on the right of the political spectrum, the **ownership of private property** is an essential manifestation of freedom.

The German anarchist Johann Caspar Schmidt (1806-1856) departed from Godwin's argument on the issue of violence. Schmidt argued that the state should be destroyed via revolutionary means. The advocacy of violence cuts through anarchist thought; belonging neither to one strand or another. Within such an eclectic body of thought, this is perhaps to be expected. Schmidt can also be differentiated from Godwin on the issue of egoism. Under the assumed name Max Stirner (1843), he argued that human nature was driven and motivated by **egoism** within a truly utopian society. The individual should be the centre of his or her moral universe and therefore free to act regardless of laws, social conventions and religious beliefs. In common with latter-day anarchists such as Ayn Rand, Stirner was highly critical of all forms of socialism. Once again, this highlights another common trait amongst individualist anarchists. According to this strand of thought, socialism necessitates a significant role for the state and is fundamentally opposed to individual expression and unrestrained free will.

Around the same time, this emerging body of thought was developed further by America's very first anarchist theorist Josiah Warren (1798-1874). Unlike Godwin and Schmidt (or Stirner), his contribution was rather more practical. Warren (1852) is best known for outlining a concept called **time store** in which individuals enter voluntarily into an unregulated contract based on the exchange of labour time. The word voluntary is of course highly important, because any element of coercion would necessitate the existence of a state. Under this scenario, economic activity would operate on a system of bartering in which a person's labour could be exchanged for the promise to return labour in kind. In reflecting his individualist beliefs, Warren claimed that *"genuine anarchism is consistent Manchesterism"* – a reference to the Manchester school of classical liberals such as Richard Cobden and James Bright. Indeed, Warren was one of the first to link individualist anarchism with a genuinely free-market. He also practised what he espoused, thereby grounding anarchism on a more practical path.

The American author Henry David Thoreau (1817-1862) also put his anarchist principles into practice. He took individualism to its very extreme by living a life of simple and unbridled **solitude**. Whereas Warren advocated an economic system based upon a laissez-faire approach, Thoreau lived by the principle of laissez-faire which he later described in his book *Walden* (1854). Thoreau's uncompromising attitude and bold commitment to the anarchist cause marks Thoreau out as one of the most notable figures within the ideology of anarchism. Thoreau's lifestyle centred upon the argument that he had willingly chosen to withdraw from all contact with the state – and for that matter all forms of social convention (including religion). He lived the life of a hermit in the woods of Massachusetts in a state of nature. Thoreau built his own cabin by Walden Pond, a mile from his nearest neighbour, and lived there for more than two years. He spent the time earning a living only by the labour of his hands, whilst a stream of people visited him to find out what life as a hermit was actually like. Revealingly, what happened to Thoreau could be seen as exposing the true character of the state. Thoreau adopted a strategy of civil disobedience that led to him being arrested for his refusal to pay tax, despite claiming nothing directly from the state. He argued that the American government was acting in an immoral manner due to the practise of slavery and in conducing bloody warfare against foreign countries. More than any other anarchist, Thoreau exemplifies the **leave me alone** approach unique to this particular ideology, an approach also taken by latter-day anarchists such as Allen Thornton who asks *"give me only the same respect you pay the badger and the blue jay, and leave me alone."* Thoreau's remarkable commitment to the ultimate sovereignty of the individual remains one of the noblest illustrations of anarchism in practise.

The American theorist Benjamin Tucker (1854-1939) also deserves a mention within the strand of thought known as individualist anarchism. Tucker was supportive of a truly open market-place in which anyone could set up a business, where land belonged to those who worked it, where no-one could create a monopoly and no-one could be exploited. Unlike conventional notions of capitalism which entail an obvious role for the state, Tucker argued that **anarcho-capitalism** provided the means by which one might realise the goals of anarchism as an ideology. Tucker was also instrumental in the publication of the journal *Liberty*, an influential outlet for radical ideas during the late-19th and early-20th century.

Over time, support for a genuine free-market has become the most influential aspect of individualist anarchism. This was best exemplified during the mid to late-20th century when anarcho-capitalism experienced something of a revival. The ideas of figures such as Ayn Rand (1905-1982), Robert Nozick (1938-2002), David Friedman (1945-) and Murray Rothbard (1926–1995) became influential within radical right-wing think tanks. Amongst neo-conservatives in the US radical ideas previously relegated to the fringe of right-wing political movements and parties gained a level of acceptance unimaginable in previous years. In their desire to curb state

The Definitive Guide to Political Ideologies

interference in the market-place, neo-conservatives were ready to adopt some of the ideas put forward by individualist anarchists of the era such as Murray Rothbard (1978) who boldly declared that various activities of the state could (and should) be transferred to the private sector, a point also taken up by Nozick. Such ideas found an even-more receptive audience in the Libertarian party, which regularly puts up candidates for the Presidency of the United States. In terms of pressure groups perhaps the best-known is the Ayn Rand Institute. The stated goal of the Ayn Rand Institute is *"to spearhead a cultural renaissance that will reverse the anti-reason, anti-individualism, anti-freedom, anti-capitalist trends in today's culture. The major battleground in this fight for reason and capitalism is the educational institutions—high schools and, above all, the universities, where students learn the ideas that shape their lives."*

For a body of thought so eclectic and idiosyncratic, it is difficult to identify common traits. More than any other ideology, anarchist thinkers and activists offer a patchwork of ideas with one overall thread – implacable opposition to the state. Nonetheless, it is possible to outline at least three elements of the individualist anarchist body of thought. The first is that the individual is absolutely sovereign. Secondly, an anarchist society would entail the ownership of private property. Thirdly, anarcho-capitalism is the most appropriate economic model available in a truly stateless society. In the eloquent words of Murray Rothbard; ***"capitalism is the fullest expression of anarchism, and anarchism is the fullest expression of capitalism."*** He justified his support for anarcho-capitalism by the argument that *"everyone earns according to his productive value in satisfying consumer desires under the free market. Under state intervention and the re-distribution of wealth, everyone earns in proportion to the amount he can plunder from the producers."* For Rothbard and others like him, state intervention within the economy was the moral equivalent of a *"protection racket."* Such arguments underline beyond any doubt that individualist anarchism belongs firmly on the right of the political spectrum.

Whereas individualist anarchism takes liberalism to its anti-state conclusion, collectivist anarchism takes socialism to its anti-state conclusion. Collectivist anarchism can be understood as a form of **state-*less* socialism** in which human beings are naturally co-operative and wish to work together for the communal good. We are social animals who wish to co-exist peacefully in a world where collective responsibilities emerge spontaneously. There are three main elements of collectivist anarchist thought. One is opposition to private property. Secondly, collectivist anarchists believe that a society based upon social justice can only be achieved once we free ourselves from the oppressive actions of the state. In order to achieve this, collectivist anarchists advocate a type of anarcho-communism in which everyone performs their responsibilities within a commune.

Collectivist anarchists tend to adopt the view that *"all property is theft"* – thereby rejecting any 'liberal' association with private property. Whereas the acquisition of property is an expression of liberty for those on the libertarian-right, the ownership of property equates to a form of exploitation according to those on the libertarian-left. For collectivist anarchists, *"private property is impossible because with it society devours itself."* Thus unlike individualist anarchism, there would be no private ownership of property within a society based upon collectivist anarchism. This is one of the most important distinctions between the two main strands of anarchist thought.

Secondly, collectivist anarchists argue that the state will always corrupt the expressed goals of socialism. The only route towards genuine equality and social justice is to discard the state altogether. Collectivist anarchists re-word Marx's famous dictum (*"from each according to his ability, to each according to his need"*) and create a vision of society based from each according to his ability, to each according to his work. For collectivist anarchists, the state can *never* act on behalf of the proletariat as predicted by Marxists. The state would impose a form of authority as equally abhorrent and evil as anything witnessed under a capitalist regime. For collectivist anarchists, state socialism is an oxymoron and Marxists are entirely wrong to assume that the state would simply die away under a communist regime. This was an important point of departure between followers of Marx and followers of Bakunin when the latter was expelled from the International Working Men's Association.

The most influential theorists within this tradition of thought are Peter Kropotkin (1842-1921), Pierre-Joseph Proudhon (1809-1865), Mikhail Bakunin (1814-1876) and to a lesser extent Georges Sorel (1847-1922). Kropotkin's main contribution towards anarchist thought was the concept of **mutual aid** (1914). Kropotkin believed that our collective energies could be harnessed for the common good of humanity. To support this view, he claimed that the concept of evolution underlined the need for animals and humans to work together. This represented a radical challenge of the prevalent Darwinist view of evolution of the time. Kropotkin claimed that co-operation was the highest stage of human evolution, and that by engaging in the process of mutual aid, human beings would ensure their development and progression as a species.

Pierre-Joseph Proudhon admired the small communities of peasants and craftsmen and used them as a model for his beliefs. As with Bakunin, Proudhon believed that violent action was necessary to achieve an anarchist utopia. He was involved in the revolutionary insurrection that occurred in Paris in 1848 and throughout his life aimed to make anarchism a genuine mass movement. His main legacy to anarchism is the following well-known contribution – *"to be governed is to be watched over, inspected, spied on, directed, legislated, regimented, closed in, indoctrinated, preached at, controlled, assessed, evaluated, censored, commanded; all by creatures that have neither the right, nor the wisdom, nor the virtue."* He is also credited with the argument that *"all property is theft."* [17]

The Russian anarchist Mikhail Bakunin is one of the most fascinating characters within ideological discourse. As with Max Stirner, Bakunin believed that anarchism could only be achieved via **revolutionary means**. Bakunin is also atypical of anarchists in that he took a strictly atheist standpoint and based his anarchist beliefs on empiricism. He also did a great deal to carve out a trajectory for collectivist anarchism after his expulsion from the International Working Men's Association in 1872 for opposing left-wing participation in parliamentary elections. Throughout his life, Bakunin was active in several revolutionary movements and argued forcefully against the all-pervasive power of the Church, believing that religious values underpin the need for authority and therefore the existence of the state itself. Bakunin argued that *"the abolition of the Church and the State must be the first and indispensable condition of the true liberation of society."* Such views found a receptive audience within Catholic societies where the role and influence of organised religion is far greater than that of Protestant societies. Bakunin's hostility to organised religion was also shared by the individualist anarchist Max Stirner and by the left-wing figure Leo Tolstoy. For Tolstoy, a more liberated form of religion requires the complete negation of the state – thereby avoiding the need for the government which, in Tolstoy's words, consists of *"an association of men who do violence to the rest of us."* Once again, there is such a wide range of views within the ideology of anarchism. For many anarchists, spiritual beliefs are of fundamental importance, whereas for others such as Bakunin, religion is bound up with the notion of unchallengeable authority.

Whereas Bakunin agreed with Marx on the negative implications of religion, he firmly disagreed with Marx on the need for a state. Bakunin argued that the state was a totally inappropriate vehicle for the creation of a society based upon social justice and equality. He believed that a communist society would merely replace one ruling elite with another. There would be a rotation of elites that would ultimately be just as corrupt as each other. Bakunin also departed from Marx on the need for leaders to raise awareness amongst the exploited and specifically rejected any role for the intellectual in terms of social change. Consistent with anarchist principles, Bakunin argued

---

[17] In response to the argument all property is theft; Emma Goldman once said that the theft is done without danger to the robber!

that social change arises spontaneously from amongst the consciousness of the exploited. Bakunin also claimed that human beings would raise their consciousness above selfish interests. He advocated common ownership of the means of production, although he was prepared to accept private ownership of the means of consumption.

The French anarchist Georges Sorel believed that the trade union movement offered a vehicle by which to advance the anarchist cause. He claimed that the workers could be mobilised into conducting a general strike – what he termed a *"revolution of empty hands."* This form of **anarcho-syndicalism** is an important aspect of collectivist anarchism, marking a key departure from individualist anarchists who reject a role for the trade unions. Anarcho-syndicalists such as Sorel have often been associated with the use of political violence in mobilising the industrial working-classes. Such acts of violence would entail a heavy-handed response from the state, thereby exposing the true character of the state to a wider populace. In response, the people would therefore mobilise against the state and join the anarchist cause. Anarcho-syndicalism gained influence during the Spanish Civil War and has also played a role within anarchist movements in France and Italy. However, anarcho-syndicalism has gained little success in Britain, where the labour movement has been characterised by the use of peaceful means to achieve broadly socialist ends. [18]

Before we leave this section there are a small number of **nihilists** – such as Sergei Nechaev (1847-1882) and Pisarew – who are often classified within the anarchist tradition. Nihilists are opposed to any form of social order and literally believe in nothing. Sharing little in common with either strand of anarchist thought, nihilists do not share the same level of optimism over human nature as other anarchists. However, their virulent opposition to the state provides nihilists with a link to the ideology of anarchism, as does their rejection of all social conventions. Furthermore, anarchism has permeated other ideologies in order to create a hybrid perspective – such as anarcho-feminism and eco-anarchism. As with other ideologies that offer a critique of the status quo and a prescribed path of action, the main source of intellectual ferment within anarchism centres upon *how* to achieve change. The seemingly inevitable fragmentation of anarchist thought has led to calls for *"anarchism without adjectives"* – but this is highly unlikely to occur within an ideology as eclectic as anarchism.

---

[18]   Anarchists believe that the state is the key agent of violence in society, a point made clear by Randolph Bourne (1977) who said that *"war is the health of the state."*

Role of the state

As with several other political terms, the word *'anarchy'* derives from the Greek language. Anarchy can be translated to mean ***"without rule"*** and thereby entails a world without man-made laws and without government. Anarchism rejects the conventional view that we need a state in order to protect liberty. It also claims that the state cannot facilitate reformist goals such as equality or social justice. These are arguments which deserve further investigation.

The principal justification for the very existence of the state is to protect our possessions and our lives. Under the conventional notion of citizenship, agents of the state have a responsibility to protect their citizens. In a liberal democracy or a dictatorship, the over-riding justification for the very existence of a state is to protect its people. Yet in the words of Emma Goldman (1969); *"the most absurd apology for authority and law is that they serve to diminish crime. Aside from the fact that the State is itself the greatest criminal, breaking every written and natural law, stealing in the form of taxes, killing in the form of war and capital punishment, it has come to an absolute standstill in coping with crime. It has failed utterly to destroy or even minimise the horrible scourge of its own creation."* Laurance Labadie adds that *"governments and the military purport to protect the public from enemies, and if there were no enemies they would have to invent some, for the simple purpose of rationalising their existence."* From the contemporary era, Jacob Halbrooks puts forward another thought-provoking argument on this subject;

> *"When people say Hitler killed six million Jews they are placing the blame entirely on a single individual. But what of the millions of Germans who actually did pull the trigger on Jews? What of the millions of Germans who called the Gestapo to report their neighbours? What of the millions of Germans who used the electoral process to secure themselves a national socialist police state? The Holocaust indeed resulted from much more than the actions of one man; it was the combined result of millions of people who directly or indirectly used the state to aggress upon, enslave, and kill others. Hitler was not the root of the problem. He was merely the symptom of a larger disease inflicting a great many people. That disease was statism."*

Secondly, anarchism insists that the state is wholly inappropriate to secure the cause of social reform. Whereas socialism and feminism strive to reorder society via mobilising the various agents of the state, anarchism declares that the state must be **destroyed** in order to liberate the human condition. Any restriction on the individual by the state is immoral and absolutely all forms of government are evil and unnecessary. Emma Goldman spoke for anarchists everywhere when she said that *"all government is tyranny. It matters not whether it is government by divine right or majority rule. In every instance its aim is the absolute subordination of the individual."* Goldman adds that true freedom will only arise in a society where human beings exercise control over the work they perform. In doing so, they can unleash the creative energies within them and thereby benefit society as a whole. Her argument is symptomatic of the wider anarchist position on the state. Amongst anarchists, there is a passionate desire to place human behaviour and activity beyond the reach of the state. In freeing ourselves from the state, human behaviour will demonstrate its truly enlightened state. A stateless utopia would enable us to achieve a more humane and just world governed only by nature itself. For anarchists, human nature is benign with absolutely no need for the state to constrain liberty. A state of nature is (by definition) natural and good, whereas any form of state rule is unnatural and oppressive. We must therefore rid ourselves of government and the various agents of the state. It is *only* the state that corrupts human behaviour. Anarchism is therefore fundamentally opposed to the German philosopher Friedrich Hegel's widely accepted assertion that human nature requires a state both in terms of security and freedom.

To critics on the authoritarian side of the political spectrum, anarchists are hopelessly naïve in their assumption that violence and anti-social behaviour would somehow dissipate once we remove the state. Such a world would lead to chaos, lawlessness and yet more violence. In reply, anarchists claim that behaviour that deviates from the norms of an anarchist community can be dealt with by reasserting Labadie's opening gambit that the solution to all social problems is liberty. Notions of equality and humanity should also play a part. This argument was clearly expressed by Peter Kropotkin who declared *"no more laws! No more judges! Liberty, equality and practical human sympathy are the only effective barriers* [by which] *we can oppose to the anti-social instincts of certain among us."* Moreover, social order can arise from below and therefore does not need the state. Any deviation from this argument would simply cause yet more violence and thereby entrench the position of the state itself.

Anarchist opposition to the state is of absolutely defining importance. In the stirring words of Pierre-Joseph Proudhon; *"Whoever puts his hand on me to govern me is a usurper and a tyrant; I declare him my enemy."* He spoke for many anarchists when he declared that *"My conscience is mine, my justice is mine, and my freedom is a sovereign freedom."* Anarchists also employ Lord Acton's observation about power (*"all power corrupts, and absolute power corrupts absolutely"*) to its absolute limit. Yet on the issue of the state, arguably the most important intellectual contribution from anarchist ideology derives from the challenge it lays down to conventional justifications for the existence of the state. The libertarian activist Jacob Halbrooks lays down this provocative challenge to all statist ideologies; *"show me the government that does not infringe on anyone's rights, and I will no longer call myself an anarchist."* At the very least, it is an intriguing contention that is very difficult – if not impossible - to adequately answer.

Anarchism and equality

Anarchism does not place as high an emphasis on equality as other reformist ideologies such as socialism or feminism. In terms of the liberty-equality continuum, anarchists will always side with liberty. In the succinct words of Benjamin Tucker; ***"As a choice of blessings, liberty is the greater; as a choice of evils, liberty is the smaller."*** Nonetheless, there is some support for equality amongst anarchists. In order to address this point, we need to distinguish between the two main strands of anarchist thought upon the issue of equality and its relationship to liberty.

Individualist anarchists view the unbridled **marketplace** as the best means to achieve absolute liberty. Under this laissez-faire system, everyone should have an equal opportunity to acquire possessions and exchange their labour on a free basis. Collectivist anarchists also view equality of opportunity as integral to their beliefs, yet crucially, they firmly oppose any attempt to redistribute wealth and resources in a manner consistent with egalitarianism. The anarcho-communist Peter Kropotkin believed that workers would co-operate on a spontaneous basis to produce goods and services, thereby meeting the needs of everyone within that society. He called this system *"free communism"* in order to distinguish it from the statist path of socialism. Kropotkin and other collectivist anarchists oppose the socialist desire for a more equal distribution of wealth because of its axiomatic need for a state apparatus. Self-governing communes, rather than state-enforced socialism, can thereby fulfil the goal of anarchism. The means of production will be shared, and political equality will be achieved on the basis of direct democracy. [19]

Anarchism is a utopian political creed based upon a highly optimistic view of human nature in which rational individuals will choose to live together in a state of harmony and peace. Anarchism also stipulates that the state is evil

---

[19]　This being anarchism, there is of course a caveat to add. Some anarchists have voiced opposition to the majoritarian nature of direct democracy, claiming that it can impede individual liberty. In common with liberals, there is a fear that *"the tyranny of the majority"* would suppress individual rights.

and unnecessary. This argument has obvious and significant implications for the concept of equality. Wherever political power is exercised, a form of **inequality** operates. Notions of state-imposed order and man-made laws are inherently hierarchical. Consequently, true equality *cannot* be achieved in a system with a state or government. Anarchism therefore offers a firm critique of societies that operate with a state. It is a stance that marks a clear departure from socialism, an ideology that anarchism was in competition with for much of the 19th century.

One of the principal problems in reconciling anarchism with equality is in terms of translating principles into practice. Despite professing to a credo of individual autonomy, it seems virtually inevitable that power struggles will emerge within any anarchist movement. This is partly because hierarchy is so ingrained within the process of socialisation, and acceptance of authority and the need for hierarchy is a key part of that socialisation. Moreover, anarchist groups operate on the basis of core activists leading (or manipulating) followers and fellow travellers. An unequal distribution of power is therefore inherent within anarchist groups, just as it is within all groups. Perhaps power cannot be distributed in any meaningful sense without some form of equality? At the very least, the maintenance of equality within anarchism seems improbable. [20]

The individual and society

Central to anarchist philosophy is a fundamental belief in **individualism**. For anarchists, any action taken by the state is restrictive of liberty in some form. Therefore, the state itself is a threat to our individual liberty. Acting on behalf of 'society,' the state has the resources to subordinate the will of the individual. Consequently, the state has absolutely no justification for its continued existence. Although not an anarchist himself, the radical liberal theorist Thomas Paine's argument that *"society is produced by our wants and government by our wickedness"* encapsulates the anarchist position. The relationship between the individual and society is therefore straight-forward; the individual is sovereign and the state must be destroyed. Whereas the *means* to achieve an anarchist utopia is a point of contention amongst anarchists,

---

[20]   After the failure of the anarchist uprising at Lyons in 1870, Bakunin summarised the position taken by the anarchists involved. *"We wish, in a word, equality – equality in fact as corollary … of liberty. From each according to his facilitates, to each according to his needs; that is what we wish sincerely and energetically."* Whilst these words offer clarity, they do not in themselves resolve the complex relationship between anarchy in theory and equality in practise.

the desire to rid society of the state is a common thread throughout anarchist thought. Liberating human nature from the corrupt and evil practises of the state would enable society itself to flourish. The benign and enlightened character of human nature would be revealed, people would co-operate with each other and order would emerge spontaneously. Concepts such as time store and mutual aid would form the basis of meaningful contact between individuals.

Perhaps the most potent argument against anarchists (and one raised repeatedly by students) is the impracticality of reordering society along anarchist lines. In the words of James Madison (1751-1836) *"if men were angels, no government would be necessary."* It is precisely because men (and women) are not angels that government *is* necessary and desirable. There are, however, answers offered by anarchists on the issue of maintaining order without the need for a state. The celebrated American anarchist Benjamin Tucker addressed this fundamental issue in two ways. Firstly, he argued that rational human beings could resolve their differences via **reasoned discussion**. Secondly, he firmly believed that a mechanism could be found through which the independent actions of free individuals could be brought together into harmony with one another. He advocated a form of **market exchange** in order to achieve this (a view also supported by another individualist anarchist Josiah Warren). From the collectivist school of thought, Proudhon believed that society could be reordered on the basis of spontaneous order and enlightened rational interests. In a stateless community, Proudhon claimed that *"public and private consciousness, formed through the development of science and law, is alone sufficient to maintain order and guarantee all liberties."* In doing so, there would be no need for the state. Whether such answers are convincing is very much open to further debate. In the case of the Christiania anarchist community in Denmark there have been riots, a shooting and a murder since it was set up in the early-70s.

The relationship between anarchism and liberal democracy

Liberal democracy has shown itself to be the most successful of all political regimes in terms of maintaining peace, prosperity and the support of the people. Basing legitimate authority upon the consent of the demos has worked in virtually all parts of the globe, and academics have even speculated that the victory of liberal democracy during the cold war has resulted in *"the end of ideology"* (Fukayama, 1992) – a point addressed in more detail during the final Chapter of the book. For now, we need to outline why anarchists are opposed to the most prominent of all political regimes.

As one might expect, anarchists claim that the process of voting has enslaved the people into meekly accepting the need for and existence of the state. Some of the most eloquent arguments within the anarchist tradition relate to their view of liberal democracy. Benjamin Tucker once described the act of voting as a *"device for ascertaining on which side force lies and bowing to the inevitable... It is neither more nor less than a paper representative of the bayonet, the bully and the bullet."* The modern-day anarchist Butler Shaffer (author of an article entitled *'Why I do not vote'*) added that *"when we vote in an election, we are declaring, by our actions, our support for the process of some people ruling others by coercive means."* Another modern-day writer Joseph Sobran observes that *"democracy has proved only that the best way to gain power over people is to assure the people that they are ruling themselves. Once they believe that, they make wonderfully submissive slaves."* The 19th century individualist anarchist Dr. Marx Edgeworth Lazarus went even further with his opposition to democracy when he said that *"every vote for a governing office is an instrument for enslaving me."* No other ideology offers such a powerful riposte to liberal democracy as anarchism.

Anarchist objections to liberal democracy are exactly the same as their objections to any other political system centred upon the existence of a state. In providing a sense of legitimacy for the government we are effectively giving ammunition to our oppressors. Liberal democracy is therefore dangerously flawed in its assumption that the people give consent to be governed because that in itself entails the need for a state. As Benjamin Tucker made clear *"an anarchist is anyone who denies the necessity and legitimacy of government."* Liberal democracy is ultimately based upon an elaborate façade which hides the true character of the state, which for anarchists is both evil and unnecessary because all power corrupts. There is absolutely no need whatsoever for a hierarchal relationship between free individuals within an anarchist utopia.

The anarchist stance on lifestyle issues

In terms of lifestyle issues, anarchists take libertarian principles to their very extreme. Anarchists advocate a form of total individualism in which the only restraint upon our behaviour is our own conscience. The message to our would-be oppressor (the state) is simple; leave me alone to conduct the lifestyle of my choice. This applies to all aspects of personal behaviour, including sexual conduct. On this particular point, there are a number of anarchist theorists who advocate a form of **free love**. This movement was prominent during the 1850s amongst theorists such as Dr. Marx Edgeworth Lazarus, Charles Fourier and John Humphrey Noyes. Noyes was the founder of the Oneida

Society in New York which viewed that the traditional format of a marriage as hierarchal. Closely tied to the free love movement is a group of anarcho-feminists such as Mary Gove Nichols, Victoria Woodhull and the celebrated figure Emma Goldman. They challenged the prevalent societal mores of the time in calling for the right to marry in accordance with romantic desires free from state interference. However, they did not call for promiscuity or multiple partners – unlike the free love movement. In a succinct expression of anarchist beliefs entitled *'Love v. Marriage'* (1852), Lazarus argued that marriage as an institution was a form of *"legalised prostitution"* that oppressed both women and men by allowing loveless marriages contracted for economic or utilitarian reasons to take precedence over true love. Calls for free love resurfaced during the 1960s when sexual behaviour and attitudes to sex experienced a major transformation, although by that time such ideas were promoted by feminists rather than anarchists.

More than any other ideology, anarchism will always find it difficult to translate principles into practise. Enabling individuals to lead a life of absolute autonomy is all very well, but what would such a society look like in practise? In answer to this point, there are several **experiments in anarchism** that we might consider – all of which are revealing in terms of the anarchist stance on lifestyle issues. The social experiments of Josiah Warren (Utopia, Modern Times and Village of Equity) provide some clues as to how an anarchist community might operate; as did the Oneida Community set up by Humphrey Noyes in 1848. Around the same time, mutual credit banks were set up in France and Switzerland in accordance with Proudhon's beliefs. In more modern times, the Freetown Christiania community in Denmark is a self-governing neighbourhood near the Danish capital of Copenhagen. Christiania has been a semi-legal independent community run along anarchist lines since 1971. In these and other scenarios, the anarchist commitment to libertarian principles is implemented and the realm of lifestyle choices is wide-ranging.

Change or the status quo

The over-riding issue to consider here is the division between **pacifists** and **revolutionaries** within anarchism. It is a division that cuts across the established strands of anarchist thought. On the pacifist side, anarchists such as Benjamin Tucker and Joseph Labadie insist that peace is essential to the anarchist code of behaviour. Benjamin Tucker claimed that *"a true anarchist must constantly endeavour to disassociate his imagination from sanguinary dramas of assassination and revolt,"* and Joseph Labadie argued that *"the killing of* *another, except in defence of human life, is ... authoritarian, and therefore, no anarchist can commit such deeds. It is the very opposite of what anarchism stands for."* In contemporary politics, the maintenance of peaceful means to achieve the aims of anarchist ideology can be found within New Age religious and Buddhist teachings (Buddha means *"the enlightened one"*). Most anarchists are pacifists, believing that the state is the sole perpetrator of violence within a society. For them, one of the most important moral arguments in favour of anarchism is the eradication of (state-imposed) violence.

Perhaps the most celebrated revolutionary within anarchist thought is Mikhail Bakunin. As an unapologetic agent provocateur, Bakunin once said *"Let us put our trust in the eternal spirit which destroys and annihilates only because it is the unsearchable and eternally creative source of all life. The urge to destroy is also a creative urge."* Support for *"propaganda of the deed"* has also been tacitly endorsed by anarcho-syndicalists such as Georges Sorel (1950). He argued that political violence should be viewed as a means to demoralise the ruling classes and ignite popular rebellion against the government. In the contemporary era, a small number of anarchist groups within the alter-globalisation movement engage in a violent form of direct action. They reflect a long-standing tradition within certain anarchist groups towards political violence (such as the Baader-Meinhof gang, the Italian Red Brigade, the Angry Brigade in the UK and the extremist organisation Movement against the Monarchy). Nihilists have also been associated with random acts of violence, although their only link to anarchism is opposition to both the state and hierarchy.

The advocacy of violence amongst a number of politically active extremists exposes a certain lack of coherence and consistency within anarchist thought. If human nature is naturally peaceful, surely violence cannot naturally arise from it? In reply, anarchists who support political violence insist that the social condition of humans must be improved by revolutionary change before the state can be abolished. Much the same way as Marxists prescribe a *"dictatorship of the proletariat"* before the state withers away, there are a certain number of anarchists who believe that *"propaganda of the deed"* is required before we can rid ourselves of the state. Even if the overwhelming majority of the population wished to live according to anarchist principles, the agents of the state are unlikely to simply disappear voluntarily without a fight. It could therefore be argued that violence against the state is required in order to make people conscious of the truly repressive nature of the state itself. More prosaically, the use of political violence can be counter-productive for any political movement – including anarchism.

Within academia, Stanley Hoffman (1995) has argued that anarchists have tended to confuse 'the state' with 'the government', but this is to confuse force with constraint. The state exercises force, whereas the government does not. As such, it is possible for stateless societies to have governments. Thus by embracing the concept of government, Hoffman believes that anarchists are presented with a realistic path towards a genuinely stateless society. Hoffman's work is widely recognised as an attempt to resuscitate anarchist theory in the modern era, although the premise of his argument is by no means accepted by all anarchists. Once again, it is very difficult to offer much in the way of generalisations about anarchism (e.g. during his later work Pierre-Joseph Proudhon accepted the need for a minimal state in order to assist in the creation of a truly anarchist society). More than *any other* ideology, anarchism is defined by what it is opposed to as much as any coherence over how to achieve its fundamental objectives.

Anarchism in contemporary politics

In order to assess the true impact of anarchism within contemporary politics, it might be useful to make a historical analysis. Over time, the influence and impact of anarchism has been sporadic to say the least. During the mid to late-19th century anarchism was in competition with socialism for the hearts and minds of the dispossessed, but socialism established itself as the more popular of the two ideologies. Anarchist movements held some degree of influence between the 1880s and 1930s, briefly holding power in parts of Spain during the Civil War (1936-1939) before being dealt a decisive blow by Franco's forces. The more violent elements of anarchism caught the headlines during the 1890s and 1970s, and there have been times when anarcho-syndicalism has been influential amongst trade union movements within Spain, France and Italy. Moreover, a number of small-scale experiments in anarchism have taken place. Yet in the modern era, the influence of anarchism is largely limited to that of certain elements of the alter-globalisation movement, a new social movement of a disparate and fragmented nature. Only in the activities of a few renegade activists could anarchism be said to have a political impact any wider than its immediate circle of followers. Invariably, such activities gain media attention – but those activities are short-lived and can hardly be said to constitute a meaningful force for social change.

Without the ability to organise or mobilise a mass of people the impact of anarchism will always be debilitated. Unless anarchism can penetrate a wider social movement – most likely via the anarcho-syndicalism route – then the opportunity for anarchism to influence contemporary politics is negligible. In the UK, anarcho-syndicalism has never really taken off because of the support within the trade union movement for mainstream socialism. Compared to other left-wing movements in continental Europe, the trade unions have never truly embraced a libertarian agenda.

On the more positive side, anarchism may be able to tap into widespread anxieties about the direction of globalisation. There is undoubtedly an appeal amongst outsiders to "do your own thing" – particularly those opposed to notions of hierarchy and authority. Furthermore, there are several pressure groups that reflect some commitment to anarchism; principally those with an anti-capitalist message. One of the most interesting examples of this point concerns the group Reclaim the Streets who have been at the vanguard of a new form of protest, combing a street party atmosphere with a serious political stance. Such groups are, however, resolutely outside the political mainstream and will surely remain so because no politician or political party wants to associate with anarchist groups. Perhaps anarchism will always be a victim of its own belligerence, doomed to a world of outsider status amongst pressure groups.

Anarchism offers a thought-provoking challenge to our deep-seated assumptions, and this is arguably its most important contribution to ideological discourse. Anarchism undoubtedly awakens thought amongst those contesting the realm of political ideology, providing guiding principles that will always have some appeal amongst those with a libertarian outlook. It raises questions that no other ideology does, and prescribes a utopian vision that can inspire and horrify to similar effect. Even its detractors would accept that anarchism offers a world-view that takes its principles to their absolute extreme. So whereas ideological discourse would be much duller without anarchism, its impact within contemporary politics remains where it always has been – **firmly and forever outside the mainstream.**

Further quotes on anarchism

"Under a government which imprisons any unjustly, the true place for a just man is also a prison." Henry David Thoreau

"Man is born free, and yet everywhere he is in chains." Jean-Jacques Rousseau

"Anarchism is a game at which the police can beat you." George Bernard Shaw

"Slaves become so debased by their chains as to lose even the desire of breaking from them." Jean-Jacques Rousseau

"The more perfect civilisation is, the less occasion has it for government." Thomas Paine

"The state is only people - and, generally, the least competent of people. They are the ones who cannot innovate, only steal. They cannot reason, only kill.

The Definitive Guide to Political Ideologies

They are brutes who see the greatest efforts of mankind as loot to seize and control." G.K. Chesterton

"Two feelings [are] inherent in the exercise of power … contempt for the masses, and, for the man in power, an exaggerated sense of his own worth." Mikhail Bakunin

"The government of the world I live in was not framed, like that of Britain, in after-dinner conversations over the wine." Henry David Thoreau

"The world has enough for everyone's need, not for everyone's greed." Mahatma Gandhi

"The social revolution is seriously compromised if it comes through a political revolution." Pierre-Joseph Proudhon

Recommended reading

Bergman, P.M. & Powell, W. (2002) *The Anarchist cookbook.* A useful opening text for anyone keen to develop their knowledge of anarchist thought.

Godwin, W. (1793) *Enquiry concerning political justice.* One of the first and most important contributions towards anarchist thought. Godwin remains a leading exponent of individualist anarchism.

Goldman, E. (1969) *Anarchism and other essays.* Emma Goldman is the dominant figure within anarcho-feminism and her work could therefore be considered relevant towards two separate ideologies. Goldman puts forward an intriguing account of how anarchism could operate in practise.

Hoffman, S. (1995) *Beyond the State.* Hoffman did much to update the work of anarchism to the modern era. Hoffman argued that it is entirely possible for a stateless society to have a government, thereby making anarchism relevant to a new generation of students.

Kropotkin, P. (1914) *Mutual Aid.* Kropotkin did much to advance the practical side of anarchism. In this book Kropotkin develops his view on mutualism and makes a worthy contribution to the strand of thought known as collectivist anarchism. An understanding of anarchism is incomplete without some consideration of Kropotkin's work.

Rand, A. (1957) *Atlas shrugged.* Rand is one of the leading proponents of right-wing libertarianism and has – like Nozick – been championed by both New Right conservatives and anarchists. Rand's classic work is a tale of how bureaucratic parasites steal from the talented and hard-working in order to maintain their grip on power by manipulating the easily-led masses. 'Atlas shrugged' is her best-known work.

Rothbard, M. (1978) *For a New Liberty.* Murray is an exponent of anarcho-capitalism. He famously argued that *"capitalism is the fullest expression of anarchism, and anarchism is the fullest expression of capitalism."* A contrast with earlier individualist anarchists is particularly illuminating.

Sorel, G. (1950) *Reflection on violence.* Sorel advocates anarcho-syndicalism and *"propaganda of the deed"* in order to advance the cause of anarchism. As with Bakunin, Sorel believes that political violence is entirely justified. The division between pacifist anarchists and violent anarchists is an intriguing one for students to consider.

Stirner, M. (1843) *The Ego and His Own.* Writing under an assumed name, Schmidt argued that human nature is driven by egoism and that violence is needed in order to establish an anarchist utopia. Like Rand, he is highly critical of state socialism.

Thoreau, H.D. (1854) *Walden and civil disobedience.* An inspirational figure within the anarchist movement, Thoreau exemplifies the *"leave me alone"* attitude of the true anarchist. He lived a life of solitude on Walden Pond and claimed that the American government was acting in an immoral and illegal manner over the issue of slavery and in conducting war with foreign powers.

Warren, J. (1852) *Equitable Commerce.* Like Kropotkin, Warren did much to advance the practical side of anarchism. Warren outlined the concept of time store in which the exchange of labour would provide the basis for a stateless society.

Ideas for further discussion

Why are anarchists committed to the abolition of the state?

How does the anarchist perspective upon human nature differ to that of the liberal perspective?

What are the differences between individualist anarchism and collectivist anarchism?

What is the anarchist stance upon the concept of equality?

What is the anarchist critique of liberal democracy?

Why are anarchists so committed towards individual freedom?

What is the anarchist position upon lifestyle issues?

To what extent are anarchists divided over the issue of political violence?

Is anarchism still relevant within contemporary politics?

The Definitive Guide to Political Ideologies

Key terms

Anarchy A condition in which no laws are enforced and individuals would pursue their own interests regardless of any wider obligations towards other members of society. Conservatives argue that anarchy would completely undermine social cohesion and in doing so result in a state of nature characterised by *"a war of all against all"* (a quote attributed to the English philosopher Thomas Hobbes). Individuals would be 'free' to commit any activity they so desired, even murder. Anarchy is the very antitheses of how the behaviour of individuals is shaped in contemporary society - where behaviour is influenced by the norms, mores, values and laws of that particular society. Individualist anarchists advocate a system of fair and equitable exchange based on reciprocity and a voluntary form of contract. This can be thought of as *"a market without state intervention"* which drives prices to their wage costs; thereby eliminating profit or interest. Firms would compete over workers just as workers compete over firms. Collectivist anarchists take a more left-wing position.

Mutual aid An anarchist term used to describe the ability of people to co-operate with each other in a stateless society.

Statism A belief in the need for a powerful state to exert control over members of society. Statism is strongly associated with the authoritarian side of the political spectrum. Anarchists are deeply opposed to statism.

Syndicalism A term used to describe a political movement with the avowed aim of transforming a capitalist society through co-ordinated action on the industrial front. Trade unions would provide the means of both overcoming capitalism and of running society in the interests of the majority. Syndicalists have argued that the labour movement (principally the trade unions) can capture key industries and the state in order to promote the cause of socialism. A general strike would pave the way for a better society.

CHAPTER 7
FASCISM

The core elements of fascism

Fascism is an ideology of the **extreme right** consisting of a number of inter-related elements. In no particular order these components are ultra-nationalism, totalitarianism, authoritarian corporatism and the necessity of physical strength and moral vigour as a source of the leader's legitimacy. Fascism takes an exclusive form of nationalism to profoundly illiberal (and sometimes racist) levels. Throughout history fascism has been repeatedly (but not exclusively) associated with racist beliefs, although in the contemporary era fascists have tried to distance themselves from any trace of racism. Fascists also believe passionately in the benefits of totalitarianism. Indeed the term totalitarian was invented by Italian fascists to describe their drive to nationalise the masses. Authoritarian corporatism represents a third way between capitalism and corporatism where economic resources are run by the state for the benefit of the nation. Furthermore, the leader of a fascist society is one that emerges from a power

Core elements
Ultra-nationalism
Totalitarianism
Authoritarian corporatism
Vigour / strength as a source of legitimacy
Romanticist assumptions
Critique of rationalist ideologies

struggle. His legitimacy derives from military conquest and heroic action as opposed to the ballot-box.

In addition to those elements listed above, fascism is **romanticist** to its very core. As a body of thought, fascism completely rejects the Enlightenment view that individuals are rational actors and that politics and society should reflect this liberal assumption. The fascist critique of rationalism is two-fold. According to fascists, rationalist assumptions ultimately lead to the separation of a nation. It breads ideas and ideologies that divide people such as feminism (on the basis of gender), socialism (on the basis of social class) and capitalism (on the basis of wealth). Rationalist assumptions also enable liberals to apply human rights on a universal basis which is entirely misconceived and contrary to the Darwinesque world-view of fascists. The romanticist stance taken by fascists is reflected by a propensity towards employing populist measures and messianic language. More than any other ideologues, fascists eulogise their world-view in terms of a struggle. From Hitler's *Mein Kampf* to the modern-day concept of jihad, the notion and language of personal toil lies at the very epicentre of fascist thought.

Students often find it easier to identify what fascism is opposed to rather than what fascism actually stands for. For example, fascists are deeply critical of the liberal emphasis upon individualism and the socialist emphasis upon social class. Either approach will ultimately weaken the unity of purpose that is absolutely central to the fascist Weltanschauung. Fascists also attack rival right-wing ideologies (such as conservatism) for their failure to recognise the need for decisive action and for their willingness to reach a compromise with sectional forces in society such as the trade unions. Fascists also claim that feminism undermines the natural structure of the family and thereby prevents society from functioning effectively. The ideology of feminism is also attacked for its failure to recognise the worthiness of militaristic endeavours and bravery. Such criticisms of other ideologies have led some commentators to describe fascism as *"a negative ideology"* (Passmore, 2002).

Whereas fascism is unquestionably an ideology of the extreme right, it is revealing to note that a high proportion of its leading figures have either been former members of socialist parties (e.g. Moseley, Mussolini) *or* have led parties with socialism in its name (e.g. Hitler). Furthermore, the most important contemporary manifestation of fascist beliefs (Islamo-fascism) often employs the language of the left against the imperialist and neo-colonialist attitudes that characterise 'the West.' In terms of the horizontal axis, fascism is as **authoritarian** as any ideology could get!

Fascist perspective on human nature

Both conservatism and fascism could be said to take a pessimistic view of human nature. However, that is where the similarity between these two right-wing ideologies ends. Fascism offers a much **darker** - and somewhat sinister - view of human nature than that offered by any other ideological standpoint. The grounding behind the fascist viewpoint on human nature derives from a world-view in which some races are superior / inferior to others. At the heart of the fascist perspective on human nature is that a racial hierarchy exists with the 'chosen' people at the very top and lesser races further down the scale. At the very bottom of the scale are sub-humans. Superior races are entirely justified in using sub-humans to serve a higher purpose. Sub-humans have absolutely no entitlement to rights whereas superior races that have proved their worth in some manner can effectively do what they wish to inferiors. Such thinking led directly to the Holocaust and other fascist-inspired atrocities against 'lesser' people. Liberalist notions of universal human rights have no place whatsoever within fascist ideology, nor does any concept or idea associated with humanist values (such as social justice or Communism).

The application of such disturbing views is not consistent to all fascist regimes. For example, the Italian regime led by Benito Mussolini did not share Adolf Hitler's hysterical anti-Semitism, and many Italian troops refused to co-operate with German requests to round up Jewish people and other 'inferiors.' Whilst there was a degree of racism in Mussolini's attitude towards North Africa, the Italians did not engage in the same level of racism as the German Nazis. Other regimes implemented racist policies to a greater or lesser extent, but to really examine the devastating impact of racism to fascist teachings we need only consider the Nazi German regime. The virulent racism that fuelled Nazi Germany was inspired by Count Gobineau (1816-1882) and Houston Chamberlain (1855-1927). Both men believed that races could be defined on a hierarchal basis with the Aryan people at the very top. In order to secure their rightful place Aryans had to beat their sworn enemies – the Jews. The Aryan people had no other choice but to confront the considerable threat of a world-wide Jewish conspiracy in order to maintain their very survival. Throughout much of his political career Hitler was advised by Chamberlain, and during his formative years Hitler was undoubtedly influenced by the Ostara Society which sought to purify the Aryan race of contamination from racial inferiors, socialists and liberals.

On the issue of leadership, fascists contend that human beings need to be mobilised via a firm emphasis upon power and the renewing effects of **struggle**. Human nature can purge itself from decadent behaviour by engaging in a Darwinesque struggle for power and status. Human existence

The Definitive Guide to Political Ideologies

itself is - and always will be - characterised by an enduring struggle where human beings need a strong leader to rescue them. Without proper order and meaningful purpose, human beings are prone to degenerate activity and physical inertia. A fascist society would therefore be based upon the politics of the will where respect for the strong would be restored after a period of decadent liberalism in which the needs of the weak were considered paramount by politicians desperate to gain and retain power.

In the contemporary era, Islamo-fascism provides an intriguing illustration of how fascism views human nature. According to their Weltanschauung Muslims are superior to *"the infidels"* (non-believers) and require a clear sense of spiritual purpose in order to fulfil their true destiny. As with German Nazism, there is a strong sense of quasi-religious / spiritual language to such proclamations which firmly reflects the romanticist element of fascist ideology. With the exception of religious fundamentalism, few other ideologies rely so heavily upon divine-like language as fascism. Once again, this illustrates the sinister undertones of fascism because presenting fundamentally racist beliefs in a spiritual manner is surely to pervert the true nature of religion itself. Perhaps the most well-known illustration of this point is the use of the Swastika; a symbol commonly associated with the Hindu religion that was later adopted and modified by the Nazis. It remains one the most bizarre ironies of politics that a symbol of peace should be distorted into a symbol of such manifest evil.

Main strands of fascist thought

Somewhat unique within the ideologies we have considered thus far, fascism has **no ideological tension** amongst its followers. What divisions exist amongst its followers have more to do with rival groups struggling for power. Fascism is about physical action, not intellectual discussion. Consequently, we should not be surprised to find a dearth of ideological tension within fascism. Part of the reason for the paucity of intellectual debate over what is the correct path for fascists to follow is the absence of the norms and practices associated with liberal democracy. Discussing the proper conduct of political activity is fundamentally at odds with the ethos of fascism. More than any other ideology fascism is driven by the leader, and an ideology that relies so heavily upon the direction taken by the leader is never going to generate ideological discussion. As one might expect, there are significant differences in the manner in which fascist ideology has been implemented by various regimes. For example, the Peronist regime in Argentina allowed a form of democracy to exist and did nothing to quash likely political opponents (such as trade unions). It also abandoned authoritarian corporatism soon after gaining power. In Europe, the German Nazi regime was far more racist than its most obvious counterpart (Italian Fascism). Even within the contemporary manifestation of fascist thought (Islamo-fascism), there are widespread differences of emphasis according to the leader in question.

Although they are not strands in themselves, it is revealing to offer some comparisons between certain Fascist regimes. In the context of Fascist Italy and Nazi Germany there are five distinct elements which suggest a difference of strategy and emphasis;

> Fascism in Nazi Germany was much more cultural in inspiration than Italian fascism. Hitler viewed German culture as superior to all others, but Mussolini was less concerned with cultural values.

> Hitler was frenzied in his anti-Semitism, whereas Mussolini was far more pragmatic in his view of Jewish people.

> According to Hitler, the state was *"a vessel"* for implementing a particular world-view. In contrast, Mussolini's conception of the state was much closer to fascist ideology. His conception of the state was totalitarian and based upon authoritarian corporatism. Unlike Hitler, Mussolini typified a voluntary and all-embracing form of fascism.

> Whereas Hitler brutally repressed any rival source of power Mussolini reached an understanding with the Catholic Church and the Monarchy, a situation copied by later-day Fascist regimes in Latin America. This may reflect little more than political realism on behalf of fascist regimes. Forming an alliance or maintaining an agreement with such powerful forces within society is merely *realpolitik*.

> Mussolini was more modernist than Hitler. Il Duce was influenced by futurists such as the Italian writer Filippo Marinetti (1876-1944), whereas Hitler invoked images of a glorious Germanic past and the traditional links between the German peasantry and the land.

It is also worth reflecting upon the argument that Germany and Italy may well have been uniquely suited to the development of fascism. Notions of national destiny were promoted long before Hitler and Mussolini came to power via intellectuals such as Garibaldi in Italy and politicians such as Otto von Bismarck in Germany. Furthermore, many Germans and Italians felt that they had missed out from the imperialist expansion of European powers during the 19th century. Fascism also received a more sympathetic audience in Germany and Italy because its people had been divided by historical and geographical circumstance. Emotional appeals to *"lebensraum"* (German for breathing space) and the unity of the Italian people found a receptive audience that would have been absent in other comparable countries.

In the modern era, Paul Berman (2003) and Christopher Hitchens claim that there are six similarities between the European fascism of the inter-war years and the Islamo-fascism of today;

> ➤ A feeling of rage at the humiliation suffered by their people at the hands of hostile powers.
> ➤ Recalling an earlier golden age as a source of inspiration.
> ➤ A desire to revive the glory of that particular age via totalitarian means. Berman and Hitchens describe this element as *"a fanatical determination to get on top of history after being underfoot for so many generations."*
> ➤ A belief that they are under threat from a Jewish conspiracy backed by a powerful Israeli lobby in the United States and the world's financial system.
> ➤ A desire to clamp down on decadent and degenerate behaviour. This is most noticeable in the case of women in Islamic theocracies who should *"dress modestly"* and be limited to the domestic sphere in order to avoid inappropriate contact with men.
> ➤ The necessity of political violence in order to restore the rightful position of the Muslim people.

The link between Islamo-fascism and earlier Fascist regimes is particularly revealing in terms of the role played by **religion**. There is unquestionably a quasi-spiritual element to fascist ideology. For example, the German Nazism of the inter-war years took the form of a *"substitute religion"* (Burleigh, 2001) and relied a great deal of mysticism. Hitler also placed great faith in Tarot cards and believed the Swastika had mystical properties; a trait somewhat at odds with the widespread perception of the man as a master tactician prone to rapid military advances. In the contemporary era Islamo-fascism is a very obvious illustration of this point – a phenomenon that began with the Iranian revolution of 1979 and led to overthrow of the autocratic Shah and his replacement with the spiritual figure Ayatollah Khomeini. Fascist leaders also take direction from higher spiritual guidance. For example, Hitler based decisions on astronomy whereas Khomeini decided to send troops into neighbouring Iraq on the basis of religious instruction.

Before we move onto a consideration of the role of the state, it is important to recognise that fascism is a political movement centred upon action as opposed to an intellectual process. The 'proof' of what is the right course of action to take derives from action on the battlefield, *not* from the eloquence of mere words. Fascism is much more of a political movement than an intellectual body of thought. *"Action not talk"* (the slogan of the Italian fascists under Mussolini) is the hallmark of fascism. Faith in the wisdom of the leader and the need to unite members of society together for a greater purpose lies at the very centre of fascism. The masses should adopt a slavish devotion to the state, and the benevolence and wisdom of the leader should never be questioned. As an inevitable consequence there is a striking degree of intellectual weakness within fascist ideology. This may remind the reader of nationalism, and yet even nationalism presents contesting strands of thought (such as liberal nationalism and conservative nationalism). Indeed, there are no theoretical strands of fascist thought to consider. An ideology that relies so heavily upon ultra-nationalism, totalitarianism, authoritarian corporatism, romanticism and the necessity of physical strength and moral vigour as a source of the leader's legitimacy is never going to present ideological tensions.

Role of the state

Fascism is a deeply authoritarian ideology that prescribes a **totalitarian role** for the state. It is the duty of the state to direct the people towards fascist goals. Only the state can mobilise the people towards the realisation of a truly fascist society. Indeed, it is impossible to imagine a fascist society being created without an authoritarian role for the state. In the words of the influential Italian philosopher Giovanni Gentile (1875-1944); *"everything for the state; nothing against the state; nothing outside the state."* Gentile's observation also holds significance for those aspects of ideology we will consider later – such as lifestyle issues and the relationship between the individual and society. As with Karl Marx, Gentile was inspired by the philosophy of Friedrich Hegel – principally the Hegelian argument that individuals express their collective will and consciousness via the state. They therefore seek an ideal state and an ideal leader, an argument with obvious applicability to fascism.

As with other totalitarian regimes, there is considerable reliance placed upon the need for propaganda to ensure the people remain in line. Amongst the various illustrations of fascism in action, the Nazis are widely considered to be the leading proponents of **propaganda**. The 'truth' was presented in accordance with the Fuhrer's wishes and undoubtedly had a major impact upon German society of the time. In the words of Adolf Hitler; *"all propaganda*

The Definitive Guide to Political Ideologies

has to be popular and has to accommodate itself to the comprehension of the least intelligent of those whom it seeks to reach" and *"the broad mass of a nation ... will more easily fall victim to a big lie than to a small one."* In stark contrast to the pluralist character of liberalism, fascism is monistic. In other words, it is an ideology centred upon a belief that there is one theory or doctrine capable of uniting a society together. Fascism therefore adopts a fundamentalist approach to politics. This is why Islamic fundamentalists are depicted as promoting an ideology of Islamo-*fascism*.

From a historical perspective, there is a notable degree of divergence as to how the state operated within fascist regimes. Whereas the state was *"a vessel"* under the German Nazis, the Italian leader Mussolini regarded the state as the supreme ethical ideal for his brand of Fascism. Mussolini placed great faith in the ability of the state to unite the Italian people and restore the glory of Imperial Rome. His stance reflected that of the celebrated Italian nationalist Joseph Mazzini, who believed that national unity could only be achieved via an authoritarian state. Mussolini was also much more consistent than Hitler in his adherence to fascist ideology. For example, he based his economic policy firmly upon **authoritarian corporatism** – an economic system that represents an alternative to free-market capitalism and a planned economy. Fascists argue that the free-market cannot facilitate the true patriotic character of the nation because it divides workers from bosses, whereas a communist system would inevitably lead towards an egalitarian society fundamentally at odds with the elitist structure of fascism. Corporatism thereby enables the state to take the lead in organising economic resources, incorporating organised interests into the mechanism of government and thereby benefiting all of society. However, in terms of *how* the economy operated – particularly during the Second World War – both Hitler and Mussolini adopted a policy of mass industrialisation. Other examples of fascism place less of an emphasis upon mass industrialisation and corporatism. For example, Islamo-fascism is less concerned with mobilising the state to secure economic objectives, believing that the promotion of religious teachings should be the guiding principle of a utopian society free from the degenerate disposition of the modern world.

Consistent with fascist ideology there is only one party and one leader. Dictatorship, not democracy, is the trademark of a fascist regime. Whereas legitimacy derives from the electorate within a liberal democracy, a fascist regime derives legitimacy from the heroic acts of its leader. The leader is truly the **embodiment** of the nation itself. In Weberian terminology, his authority derives from charismatic and divine-like qualities; unlike the rational-legal basis of authority within liberal democracies. This basis of legitimacy and authority reflects the deeply illiberal foundations of fascist ideology. The terms *"popular autocracy"* or *"totalitarian democracy"* can be employed to describe the role of the state within the realm of the political process. According to fascists, parliamentary government only leads to feeble politicians failing to implement stability and order within society. It is therefore revealing to note that fascism has tended to gain in popularity within 'democracies' suffering from instability (such as the Weimar Republic). Fascism has also been widely practised in those societies where the military has traditionally played a dominant role in politics – as in Latin American countries such as Argentina, Chile and Brazil.

Fascism marks a concerted attempt to reorder the world around notions of past glories, spiritual / ethnic purity and national vigour. Central to the construction of a fascist society is a totalitarian state headed by a man of destiny capable of uniting the nation due to his unique qualities. Not surprisingly, fascist societies often exist on a **cult of personality** encapsulated by the leader; be it the Generalissimo in Spain, the Ayatollah in Iran, Il Duce in Italy, the General in Chile, die Fuhrer in Germany or the Conducator in Romania. The leader plays a role best described as somewhere between a father figure for the nation, a deity worthy of religious worship and a military overlord. No other political system concentrates so much power and authority into the hands of a leader. This is partly why there is a degree of divergence over *how* the state operates within a society. For example, Hitler viewed the state as a servant of the nation. By mobilising the agents of the state to expel foreigners and persecute inferiors Hitler believed that the concept of racial purity would be strengthened – thereby ensuring the survival of the Aryan people and the glory of the Third Reich. Inevitably, Hitler's Weltanschauung entailed a forceful role for the state. Other fascist regimes adopted a similar role for the state, albeit with a degree of divergence over tactics. Yet one thing we can say is that the individual is nothing and the state is everything. In the words of the Italian Fascist leader Benito Mussolini (1883-1945), *"the state is absolute, individuals and groups are relative."* In Nazi Germany, Hitler added that *"the state must not become a servant of the masses, but their master!"*

Fascism and equality

Consistent with the description of fascism as *"a negative ideology,"* it is somewhat easier to describe what fascism is opposed to than what it actively stands for – especially in the context of equality. First and foremost, fascism is implacably opposed to the left-wing goal of equality. Socialism's appeal to sectional / class interests, and its inherent internationalism, is anathema to fascists. Furthermore, the centrality of equality and social justice towards the achievement of a socialist society is deeply alien to fascist ideology. Socialism is roundly criticised by fascists for subverting the natural patriotism of the working-classes and for trying to divide society between two monolithic social classes (the proletariat and the bourgeoisie). Strident opposition to socialism has often played a key role in the popularity of several fascist figures including Hitler, Pinochet, Franco and Mussolini.

Fascists are also implacably opposed to feminism, and an exploration of why fascists are opposed to feminism provides us with a useful insight into the fascist Weltanschauung. To begin with, fascism is deeply hostile to what *they* portray as 'feminine' characteristics such as deviousness and manipulation. It is also revealing to note that the label *"unmanly"* has been routinely employed against their political opponents. Furthermore, fascism adopts an overtly macho stance and presents a somewhat idealised view of masculinity. For fascists, society should be driven by masculine virtues. In order to achieve this fascism seeks to champion masculine qualities such as heroism, obedience to authority, virility, bravery in battle and physical strength. Indeed fascism takes it name from the Italian word *"fascio"* (meaning a bundle of rods tied around an axe) which was used in Imperial Rome to denote power and authority. The symbolism at work here can be summarised as strength through unity, because a single rod can easily be broken whereas a bundle is very difficult to break.

The concept of an **übermensch** is another very clear illustration of this idealisation of masculinity within fascist ideology. The notion of a man of destiny emerging from a struggle for power to rescue the nation derives from the hugely influential German philosopher Friedrich Nietzsche (1887). He argued that an übermensch is endowed with qualities that place him above all others. He alone is capable of inspiring the nation into heroic endeavours, and the nation itself is best exemplified by the heroic actions of that leader. In later years, the existentialist philosopher Martin Heidegger added that people needed a sense of direction that could only be obtained from a strong leader, leading him to endorse aspects of the Nazi German regime.

Fascism takes a highly **elitist** and **hierarchal** view of society. Within a fascist society the masses are expected to follow orders given by their superiors. Men are conscripted into the army and expected to do their duty to the nation. There is no room for dissenting voices because a leader has demonstrated that he (and he alone!) is in possession of the necessary attributes. The leader and the various agents of the state are able to mobilise the masses for the glory of the nation. Crucially, it is for the elite to decide what is in the best interests of the nation because only the elite have the power and authority to know where the destiny of that nation lies. The relationship between society and the individual under fascism is always dominated by the needs of society. There is absolutely no room for the concept of equality within a fascist society.

Fascism also stipulates that human beings are **divided into races** and exist in a Darwinian struggle for survival in which the strong will prosper at the expense of the weak. One of the most extreme illustrations of this point derives from the practise of **eugenics** within Nazi Germany. This entailed the sterilisation of the unfit and the provision of financial rewards to encourage the fittest people to reproduce. The practise of selective breeding was justified on the basis of strengthening the blood lines of the chosen people, whereas the unfit were little more than parasites living off the hard work of the chosen nation. As such, inferior people had to be destroyed by the Aryan race. The social Darwinist writer Houston Stewart Chamberlain added a veneer of 'scientific' study to the practise of eugenics, and Hitler was a great admirer of Chamberlain's theories. The barbaric practise of eugenics clearly underlines the deep hostility amongst fascist regimes to any notion of equality. However, other fascist regimes suppressed minorities without recourse to eugenics. For example, General Franco banned the use of the Catalan language and other symbols of Catalan identity.

In the contemporary era, Islamo-fascism reflects a Darwinist view of society. As with other branches of fascism, radical Islamists conceive of a world in which the strong will prosper at the expense of the weak. The 'strong' are characterised by a degree of moral purity and adopt a virtuous lifestyle, whereas the 'weak' are morally decadent and are not prepared to fight for their beliefs or values. The strong are closer to the teachings of God whereas the weak place hedonistic materialist pleasure above any higher life purpose. Such language generates division between believers and non-believers, a point explicitly recognised by some Western politicians such as the US Republican Mike Huckabee who once argued that *"either Islamo-fascism must disappear from the face of the earth, or we will."* The existence of Islamo-fascism also holds relevance to the ideology of religious fundamentalism and will therefore be considered in more detail during the following Chapter.

The relationship between fascism and liberal democracy

There are two elements to the fascist perspective on liberal democracy. The first is a robust critique of liberal democracy, and the second is the fascist conception of how a leader might acquire legitimacy and authority in the absence of liberal democratic institutions. Both elements underline the profoundly illiberal content of fascist ideology.

Fascists are scathing in their **critique** of liberal democracy. Elections merely permit an ignorant mass of people to choose mediocre representatives, and from a process of unprincipled bargaining and manipulative deception a leader emerges who is too feeble to give proper direction and leadership to the nation. The inevitable result is chaos and instability. As a political system, liberal democracy is inherently flawed because it generates diversity amongst members of the nation. It also permits decadent behaviour within society due to its emphasis upon individual rights and moral relativism. Moreover, the pluralist character of a liberal democracy enables conspiratorial forces to exert influence over weak politicians more concerned with their own careers than the moral health and continued survival of the nation. As a consequence, the entire ethos and structure of a liberal democratic system ultimately weakens the strength of the nation by its focus on cultural diversity and its celebration of extreme individualism. Rather than gaining a sense of loyalty to their nation, the broad mass of the populace lead disparate lives with no real sense of purpose. A society that promotes self-interest above any concern for the common good will ultimately divide (rather than unite) the nation. Individualism is therefore soundly rejected with the fascist concept of society.

In order to restore the moral vigour of the nation from the decadence of liberal democracy, fascists believe that a leader will emerge that embodies the popular will of the people. This übermensch has the aura of **a savour** – be in from Communism, an international Jewish conspiracy, moral decay or Western influence – and has the ability to inspire people to perform heroic deeds. He will resurrect the spirit of the nation from its seemingly permanent moral decay and its recurring problem of corrupt and feeble politicians. In practise, some leaders (e.g. Hitler) have managed to effectively mobilise their nation into combat – whereas others (e.g. Mussolini) have struggled to do so. Nonetheless, what remains constant within fascist ideology is the role played by this man of destiny. The concept of the übermensch is vitally important towards an understanding of fascist ideology, in that it provides justification for a leader in a comparable manner to how the democratic process provides legitimacy within a liberal democracy. In a fascist regime the leader is truly the embodiment of the nation itself. It is also worth noting that popular legitimacy is bolstered considerably by victory in wartime (as in the case of the Blitzkrieg from Nazi German forces) and can suddenly be lost via defeat in wartime (as in the case of General Galtieri after the defeat of Argentine forces over the Malvinas - or Falklands Islands - at the hands of British forces in 1982).

The critique of liberal democracy from Islamo-fascists is an important feature of contemporary international relations. Fascism consists of an attempt to define a new world order in which the weak and morally corrupt nature of liberal democracy – with its emphasis on hedonistic debauchery and egotistical individualism - is rejected in favour of a utopian vision of society inspired by a mythical notion of the past. However, in the context of Islamo-fascism; this utopian society takes on an overtly religious tone. Radical Islamists wish to eradicate the corruption of Western influence (including Christianity and globalisation) from the Muslim world. Islamo-fascism represents the entire reversal of Enlightenment thought and with it much of the basis of the modern world. It is an ideological movement that represents a hostile reaction to the manner in which the West has corrupted, infiltrated and polluted the Islamic world. The desire of Islamo-fascists to effectively turn back the clock may be impossible, but that does not negate the influence of such ideas amongst those willing to listen. Islamo-fascists contend that moral vigour, social order and a renewal of their nation is preferable to the morally decadent, lawless and decaying Western world with its flawed belief in the virtues of liberal democracy.

The distinction between a fascist society and a liberal democracy can be seen most clearly in relation to referendums (or plebiscites). In a liberal democracy the purpose of a referendum is to assess the will of the people and enable them to directly influence the political process. The wishes of the people are thereby respected and enforced by the appropriate bodies. Democratic governments tend to hold referendums on matters of major constitutional significance. Within a fascist regime plebiscites are deeply illiberal. For example, plebiscites were called in Nazi Germany to enable the authorities to persecute minorities and thereby strengthen their grip on power. The purpose of calling a plebiscite was simply to demonstrate the degree of support its people had for the elite. Such referendums were also deeply **illiberal** in that they deliberately targeted minorities.

The relationship between fascism and liberal democracy presents us with further insights into the character of fascist ideology. Fascism emerged from deep anxieties about the advance of liberal democracy, and throughout its history fascism has largely appealed to those who feel a tangible sense of resentment at losing out from the spread of liberal democratic values. Fascism has always fed off popular disenchantment at liberal democracy, and that practise continues in contemporary politics. It might therefore be claimed that the spread of fascism bears some relationship to the 'failure' of liberal democracy to win over hearts and minds (particularly in the case of Islamo-fascism). Another revealing distinction concerns the issue of freedom. According to liberal theorists such as John Stuart Mill the individual should be free to do whatever he / she wants provided those actions do not in any way harm the freedom of others. Under a fascist regime the conduct of individuals is to some extent limited to those activities specified by the appropriate authorities. Some of these activities may serve no obvious political purpose. For example, many fascist regimes have placed great store in the value of sporting activity because it benefits the health of the nation, fosters a sense of unity amongst its people and serves to underline the importance of struggle and battle. On a more political level, party membership in a fascist regime acts much like the concept of citizenship within a liberal democracy. Yet unlike a liberal democracy, citizenship within a fascist regime is only prescribed to those from the chosen nation.

Fascists believe that liberal-rationalist assumptions about the universality of human rights are entirely flawed. The leading philosopher of fascist ideology – Friedrich Nietzsche - believed that universalism served to undermine **respect for the strong**. Fascists also believe that allowing people to do whatever they wish will result in **moral decay**. As such, fascism is opposed to the moral relativism of liberal ideology. In addition, there are several other illustrations of fascism's illiberal character. Within a fascist society opposition to the leader means opposition to the nation itself, a standpoint with dangerous consequences for dissidents. Fascism is also entirely discriminatory - favouring their chosen nationality over all others. Fascism also targets the bourgeois indifference and ivory tower existence of the liberal elite. The feats of ordinary men and women are widely celebrated in contrast to the 'failure' of the cowardly liberal elite.

As discussed earlier, one of the core elements of fascism is a form of ultra-nationalism. Yet whereas nationalism can be inclusive and pluralist, particularly within the parameters of a liberal democracy such as the UK; fascism is neither inclusive nor pluralist. Although fascist parties and politicians have gained power via the liberal democratic process (e.g. Italy), the ideology of fascism is entirely incompatible with the main tenants of liberal democracy. Some fascist organisations are even banned in liberal democratic regimes, especially Islamo-fascist parties such as Hizb-u-Tahir and the British Jihadi Network. However, most democratic countries permit the continued existence of these extremist parties and pressure groups, placing their faith in the ability of the demos to reject those that promote the politics of hate. Of all the ideologies we might consider fascism is the most illiberal – a point which leads neatly onto the next section.

Individual and society

Fascism is as **collectivist** as liberalism is individualist. Under fascism, there is absolutely no room whatsoever for individual rights akin to a liberal democratic society. Individualism cannot exist within the fascist conception of the world because fascism is an ideology rooted upon a totalitarian role for the state. Each member of the chosen race has a part to play in restoring that nation's past glories. It is the leader of the state that embodies the will of the people within a fascist society. As Hitler once said *"the majority can never replace the man"* – and in the words of the Nazi party slogan - *"Ein Reich, ein Volk, ein Fuhrer."* Fascism promotes a very strong sense of duty which seeks to replace the egoism of liberalism, the unmanliness of conservatism and the sectionalist nature of socialism with a much higher moral purpose. Ultimately, fascism champions the values of self-sacrifice and discipline. In doing so, people gain a sense of fulfilment from their lives with those duties defined in relation to the needs of the nation. There are three aspects to consider here; gender, the economic sphere and society itself.

In the context of gender the man must be heroic, physically strong, be of pure moral fibre and forgo hedonistic pleasure in favour of proving his qualities in the field of battle. In contrast, the woman must be nurturing, caring, maternal and must avoid tempting the opposite sex away from their ultimate purpose. Men must fight and show virility whereas women must give birth to and raise pure-bred children. In making these observations, fascism undoubtedly reflects a highly reactionary state of mind, one that wishes to reassert ultra-traditional norms and values. As the Italian leader Benito Mussolini once said **"war is to men what maternity is to women."** Adolf Hitler adopted similar sentiments, locating his view of the genders in the context of Germanic traditions.

In the economic sphere, the nation's resources should be allocated for the benefit of everyone in that chosen nation. The economic system favoured by fascists is authoritarian corporatism; which represents **an alternative** to both capitalism and Communism. One of the earliest cases of this point occurred in Italy, when the Chamber of Fasces and Corporations replaced the Italian parliament in 1939 in order to centralise power into the hands of the state. The leader of the British Union of Fascists Oswald Mosley was a great admirer of Mussolini's corporatism and advocated a similar policy to deal with the very serious economic crisis facing Britain in the 1930s. Authoritarian corporatism involves the enforced transferral of power from the people to the state, and once again one can trace the profoundly illiberal content of how fascists conceptualise the relationship between the individual and society. However, there is a degree of divergence within contemporary fascist parties and politicians on this issue. Modern-day fascist leaders such as Gianfranco Fini and Jean-Marie Le Pen are much more supportive of the free market. Nonetheless, for a fascist regime to be ideologically coherent and consistent the economy should be run along corporatist lines. Under fascism a totalitarian state will suppress sectional organisations (such as trade unions and small businesses) for the greater good.

In the somewhat broader context of society itself, fascism is firmly rooted in the idea of an organic society unified along the basis of cultural ties (what the Nazis called **Volksgemeinschaft**). Thus in common with conservatives, fascism is based firmly upon an organic view of society. However, there are significant differences between these two ideologies. To begin with, fascism is dogmatic whereas conservatism is not. The language of fascism is also prone to a level of mysticism that one would never associate with conservatism. Furthermore, fascism is both utopian and undemocratic. The issue of property also divides fascists from conservatives. Whereas the latter seek to protect property rights, fascists believe it is entirely justifiable for the state to seize the property of 'undesirables.' Fascism is also based upon an exclusive sense of nationhood whereby those who cannot demonstrate a blood connection are excluded from society. The French theorist Maurice Barres believed that the peasantry exhibited French*ness* via their centuries-old attachment to the land, whereas the German Fuhrer Adolf Hitler placed great store in the spirit of *volk* amongst the German people. Allied to the fascist conception of an organic society is a Darwinesque world-view in which the nation can only retain its superiority via engaging in a struggle for supremacy and dominance over weaker nations. If that nation wishes to remain fit enough to survive then it must purify itself from the contamination of inferior people. It must also be in a state of permanent readiness in order to fight its enemies.

The relationship between a fascist leader and the masses is one characterised by domination and subordination. Throughout history, fascist leaders have routinely exhibited a degree of contempt for the lives led by the masses within a democratic regime. The people need to be stirred from their decadent slumber by an übermensch, and a vigorous policy programme is required in order to ensure that the masses become mobilised and thereby fulfil their natural destiny. This may take the form of fighting against an invading army, modernising the nation's economy or restoring the glory of that nation from corrupt and hostile forces. As an inevitable consequence, the relationship between the individual and society will always be dominated by the needs of the latter. As the fascist leader Benito Mussolini once said *"the Italians are a race of sheep"* who must follow his lead. He was also explicit in the need for national myths to unify the Italian people; describing his credo by the following words; *"Our myth is the nation, our myth is the greatness of the nation. And to this myth, this greatness, which we want to translate into a total reality, we subordinate everything else."*

The fascist stance on lifestyle issues

Fascists seek to **politicise all aspects of life**. It is therefore entirely consistent with fascist ideology for the state to intervene in the private realm and dictate the lifestyle adopted by the masses. There is absolutely nothing outside the proper domain of the state, an observation that even applies to sexual conduct. For instance, under the Italian fascist leader Mussolini it was a crime to impede the fertility of the Italian people. On a more sinister level, the Nazi German regime actively engaged in the practise of eugenics - a political objective which dates back to the work of Plato in Ancient Greece.

In the context of gender roles, fascists prescribe an **ultra-traditional role** for men and women. The use of propaganda within fascist regimes such as Nazi Germany idealised masculine characteristics such as bravery and heroicism. The fascist man was expected to do his duty for the nation – a role which entailed military action and fathering children. In addition, women were encouraged to abandon the public sphere in terms of employment and post-16 education in order to return to their rightful place in the domestic sphere. In the desire of the authorities to ensure that a woman's place was confined to the home, fascist regimes actively celebrated the contribution made by women to the health of the nation. Interestingly, many women actively engaged in fascist movements without any form of coercion. Those women opposed to the advance of feminism were particularly keen supporters of fascist parties and leaders.

Not surprisingly, fascism is deeply hostile towards homosexuality. Sexual practices outside the 'norm' of society are depraved and contrary to nature itself. Same-sex relationships would also negatively affect the ability of the chosen nation to reproduce. However, it has been claimed that fascist distaste for homosexuality may be a reflection of suppressed sexuality, an argument given credence by the homoerotic nature of some of the activities encouraged by the state. In the context of Islamo-fascism, there is a religious connotation towards their stance against homosexuality, believing such behaviour to be contrary to God's teachings. In the UK, the British National Party (BNP) describes homosexuality as an abnormal practise which should not be promoted. They have also pledged to offer financial incentives for white couples in order to aid reproduction.

There is a very clearly defined **insider-outsider model** applicable to fascist societies. Those on the outside face discrimination on every level. The totality of life within a fascist regime demands conformity to the will of the leader. For fascists, rights are not universal amongst all of humankind – particularly in relation to ethnic minorities who are invariably depicted as a threat to the ethnic / national majority. A minority is therefore abandoned to suffer from what liberals call the *"tyranny of the majority"* within the fascist conception of the world.

Change or the status quo

The fascist stance on the issue of change is **contradictory**. In one sense, fascists seek to impose a strong sense of order and to foster a belief in the virtues of discipline amongst the masses centred upon a hierarchal structure within society. However, fascists also seek to organise rebellion against those politicians holding power within a liberal democracy. Fascism is therefore both reactionary *and* radical on the issue of change. Albeit a right-wing ideology, it does not share conservatism's faith in preserving the status quo, particularly in the context of a liberal democracy. Fascism is a curious mix of an anti-establishment attitude alongside support for authoritarianism, seeking to replace democracy with a totalitarian regime.

At heart, fascism reflects a **deeply reactionary** mindset amongst its followers. Past glories are celebrated and eulogised in a manner unique within ideological discourse. With Hitler it was the bravery of the Teutonic Knights and the unique *volk* spirit of the German nation that moulded his vision of a Third Reich that would last a thousand years. For Mussolini, Imperial Rome was his inspiration. For Islamo-fascists it is the historical contribution made by Muslims towards the process of civilisation (before the West 'corrupted' Islam). Yet whatever the particular context of fascism, there is a very noticeable backward-looking element to it. The reactionary attitude of fascists can also be identified in their view of gender roles. Progressive notions derived from liberal / feminist / socialist ideology are firmly rejected by fascists. In the contemporary era, an illustration of this point is the opposition of Islamo-fascists towards the gains made by women in the public sphere. After the Ayatollah gained power in 1979 Iranian women were purged from the judiciary and the teaching profession. Women were also obliged to wear scarves in public and husbands were allowed to divorce their wives without the permission of the courts. More recently, the Taliban regime in Afghanistan prohibited the education of females because it was *"un-Islamic"* and denied women a range of basic human rights. In earlier fascist regimes, the gender roles were ultra-traditional and represented a reaction against the progress made by the feminist movement up until that time. Fascism's reactionary outlook can also be linked to their hostile attitude towards homosexuality, mixed-race relationships and 'degenerate' art.

On the subject of change, fascism also has a deeply **radical tone**. The desire to overhaul the existing liberal democratic regime is a historical feature of all fascist regimes. In order to achieve fundamental change, political violence has often been a feature of fascist regimes. The most obvious historical examples are Adolf Hitler's rise to power in Germany and Mussolini's emergence as the Italian leader. However, other cases one might consider are also revealing. For example, during the early-1970s Auguste Pinochet came to power in Chile after a coup d'etat against the existing regime. The leader of Chile at the time was democratically elected by the people. His name was Salvador Allende, and he was a Marxist. Pinochet's seizure of power was supported by the United States (a country which had of course fought *against* fascism during the Second World War). The emergence of Juan Peron in Argentina is another illustration of the willingness of fascist figures to use the military to secure their aims.

Unlike conservatism, fascism is fundamentally opposed to the status quo within a liberal democracy. Fascism is an ideology that provides justification for the use of political violence to restore order within society and enable that nation to regain its moral vigour. Fascists claim that they are the only ones prepared to take the necessary measures to save the nation from terminal decline. This apocalyptic language is prevalent today in the words of radical Muslim mullahs and in the tone adopted by contemporary fascist parties in Western Europe. Fascists portray themselves as possessing the necessary bravery to overhaul the existing regime. They propose action, whereas others merely talk. In the words of the academic Kevin Passmore (2002, p.30), fascism represents a *"manly revolution."*

Before we leave this section, it is worth noting that an ideology so closely related to violent change routinely justifies its actions by the use of defensive language. To fascists, it is other ideologies (such as liberalism and socialism) that indoctrinate the easily led, weaken the racial purity of the chosen nation and thereby deny people the chance to fulfil their destiny. It is others that instigate war and conflict, as in the case of a Zionist-led conspiracy or the omnipresence of Western hegemony underpinned by American military might. Whether any of these claims are valid is of course a highly contentious point. However, what we can say with absolute certainty is that the message of fascism has always been couched in the language of physical strength, which is a particularly strong hallmark of fascist ideology on the issue of political change.

Fascism in contemporary politics

It is impossible to provide too many generalised comments as to the state of fascism in contemporary politics. It is only possible to offer conclusions about separate countries. So to properly assess the position of fascism within contemporary politics it would seem appropriate to begin with the country in which the ideology first originated (Italy). The Northern League was created in 1992 and its leader Umberto Bossi has repeatedly employed fascistic language by stereotyping the industrious 'European' northerner against the lazy 'African' southerner. The party has gained ministerial seats in coalition governments, as too has the Alleanza Nazionale (AN) party led by Gianfranco Fini. Whereas Bossi has achieved some degree of electoral success it is Fini that has firmly re-established fascism as a political force in Italian politics, gaining the lofty position of Deputy Prime Minister in 2001 when the AN formed part of a right-wing coalition led by Silvio Berlusconi. Fini represents a revival of fascism *and* a degree of revisionism in fascist thought. For example, he has denounced anti-Semitism and has adopted a more centrist and inclusive tone. However, he has also demanded that school textbooks be purged of Marxist bias, making it an offence to 'distort' Mussolini's war record. Furthermore, Fini has repeatedly tried to scapegoat minorities (especially gypsies) and has routinely used quasi-racist language to gain electoral support.

Elsewhere in Europe fascist parties and politicians have gained electoral representation in France, Belgium, Austria, Denmark, the Netherlands and Switzerland. Even in the UK, a country with little history of extreme right-wing politics, the British National Party has gained a number of council seats in disaffected working-class areas. Revealingly, many of the fascist parties in Europe have adopted the more inclusive tone and moderate style of the Italian AN. One exception to this rule is the leader of the French National Front Jean-Marie Le Pen. He supports the revisionist interpretation of the Holocaust, has warned the French about the Islamisation of their country and has advocated policies of national preference in order to discriminate in favour of French people. He shocked the political world by coming second in the 2002 Presidential election, the same year that both Jorg Haider (Austria) and Pim Fortuyn (the Netherlands) also gained considerable electoral support at the ballot-box. The common theme throughout these cases was public concern over immigration and a sense of disaffection with the 'liberal' elite of those countries.

The main element of fascism within contemporary politics is undoubtedly **Islamo-fascism**. As with all other facets of fascism; it is an ideology that holds its strongest appeal amongst those with little stake in society. It provides a sense of self-respect, pride in oneself and a feeling of belonging. It also provides an outlet for those who wish to scapegoat 'others' for the decline of 'their' nation. It is an ideology that aims to generate a sense of superiority and attachment to a great nation (even when that nation is defined by religion or race). Throughout history fascism has always tended to gain its followers from the disaffected, and at the time of writing its core message shows no sign of disappearing.

In summary, fascism emerged after the First World War as a reaction to the spread of liberal democracy and socialist ideology. It reached its zenith during the inter-war years, but it has never really gone away. History has repeatedly shown that fascism holds its strongest appeal amongst social groups searching for a stable identity in a world subject to rapid change. They tend to perceive themselves to be under 'threat' from hostile groups and as suffering from a weakened sense of national / ethnic identity. Furthermore, fascism tends to appeal within those societies that experience significant disorientation due to the viscidities of the global economy and international relations. The lessons of history show that in an era dominated by the process of globalisation the appeal of fascism looks set to remain. It would therefore be complacent to believe that fascism is a dead ideology. The prevalence of xenophobia and racism, the recent growth in Islamophobia, the clash of civilisations (Huntingdon, 2002), the spread of radical Islam and widespread anxieties within Western societies over immigration and multiculturalism all provide a residue of potential support for fascism. Having said this, there is also good reason to believe that the political impact of fascism is greatly limited. As an ideological movement, fascism owes a huge debt to the characteristics and activities associated with war, and for that reason alone the potential impact of fascism is constrained in an era where democratic nations tend not to engage in warfare with each other to secure their aims.

Further quotes on fascism

"We must leave exactly on time … From now on everything must function to perfection." Benito Mussolini (to a stationmaster)
"Fascism is itself less 'ideological,' in so far as it openly proclaims the principle of domination that is elsewhere concealed." Theodor Adorno
"Fascism was a counter-revolution against a revolution that never took place." Ignazio Silone
"The century of democracy is over." Benito Mussolini
"Fascism should more appropriately be called corporatism because it is a merger of state and corporate power." Benito Mussolini
"Fascism is capitalism in decay." Lenin
"Fascism is not defined by the number of its victims, but by the way it kills them." Jean-Paul Sartre
"Il Duce was the greatest Italian statesman of the twentieth century." Gianfranco Fini

"Fascism is not in itself a new order of society. It is the future refusing to be born." Aneurin Bevan

"Fascism has a tradition of honesty, correctness and good government." Gianfranco Fini

Recommended reading

Burleigh, M. (2001) *The Third Reich : A new history.* Burleigh's excellent historical account of German Nazism provides a rich source of knowledge for Politics students. His work focuses more upon the practise of Fascism than the actual theory.

Hitler, A. (1998) *Mein Kampf.* Hitler's outline of his 'struggle' offers an insight into the world-view of one of the most important figures of the 20th century. Students do however need to distinguish between a fascist world-view and the one that is personal to Hitler himself. A contrast with Mussolini is particularly revealing.

Mussolini, B. (2006) *The Doctrine of Fascism.* A more useful account of fascist theory than Hitler's Mein Kampf, Mussolini's book offers perhaps the best description of fascist ideology.

Nietzsche, F. (1887) *The Genealogy of Morals.* More than any other intellectual, Nietzsche offered a theoretical basis for the fascist concept of a superman rising above all others to demonstrate his leadership qualities.

Passmore, K. (2002) *Fascism : A very short introduction.* An excellent introduction to fascism for any student, Passmore's book is part of the Very Short Introduction series. For students entirely unfamiliar with fascism, this book offers the most accessible introduction to fascist ideology.

Ideas for further discussion

What are the main elements of fascist ideology?

In what ways does the fascist perspective upon human nature differ to that of other right-wing ideologies?

To what extent is it appropriate to use the term Islamo-fascism?

Why are fascists so committed towards the implementation of a totalitarian society?

Why are fascists opposed to equality?

Why are fascists critical of democratic regimes?

Why are fascists opposed to individualism?

What is the fascist stance upon lifestyle issues?
To what extent do fascists support the status quo ante?
Is fascism still relevant within contemporary politics?

Key terms

Circulation of elites A term used by the Italian sociologist Vilfredo Pareto during his research into the impact and significance of elites. He observed that membership of an elite is open to change over time. Mussolini was greatly influenced by Pareto.

Islamo-fascism A controversial term equating fundamentalist Islam with the European fascist movements of the early-20th century. The term Islamic fascism was identified by the French philosopher Michel Onfray who observed in his *Atheist Manifesto* that the 1979 Islamic Revolution *"gave birth to an authentic Muslim fascism."*

Populism A form of political rhetoric characterised by a direct appeal to the people and popular opinion, as opposed to implementing a coherent ideology. Populist measures include a tough approach to law and order and a reduction in the level of immigration.

Racialism A belief that racial differences hold some degree of political significance. Racialism is associated with both fascism and exclusive nationalism.

Racism An irrational and prejudicial view that one racial group is either superior or inferior to another. Both Nazi Germany and apartheid South Africa were based upon racist ideology. In recent years, displays of overt racism have become less socially acceptable. However, the existence of covert racism remains a significant problem within society. Fascism and exclusive nationalism often contain a strong element of racism.

Romanticism The term is often contrasted with the liberal notion of rationalism and depicts emotional appeals to the greater good of the nation. Romanticism is associated with fascist ideology and rests significantly on mythology.

Totalitarianism A power structure within society characterised by dictatorship as opposed to democracy. Totalitarian regimes suppress individual rights such as freedom of speech and exert a significant degree of social control upon their members. Throughout history there have been several examples of totalitarian societies, although their numbers are now in decline. A totalitarian regime can be based upon a left-wing ideology, a right-wing ideology or a theocracy. All totalitarian regimes are authoritarian, although it has been argued that liberal democracy is itself a form of totalitarianism. According to Hannah Arendt, totalitarian regimes administer terror and psychological manipulation via a highly organised bureaucracy. The aim is to make real an abstract ideological understanding of the world and to destroy all existing human solidarities in the name of that particular ideology. Another intriguing contribution to the debate over totalitarianism derives from the Marxist Herbert Marcuse (1898-1979) who described liberal democracy and capitalism as a new form of totalitarianism. This was a fashionable argument at the time amongst the New Left, and still has credence within the alter-globalisation movement.

übermensch The fascist concept of a superhuman derives from the philosopher Friedrich Nietzsche. This superman emerges from a power struggle within society and is capable of inspiring the nation into heroic endeavours. He is characterised by outstanding leadership qualities. The concept of übermensch provides justification for fascism in a comparable manner to how the democratic process provides legitimacy for the concept of liberal democracy. Nietzsche also believed that God is dead and that humankind must take total responsibility for its own future.

CHAPTER 8
RELIGIOUS
FUNDAMENTALISM

The core elements of religious fundamentalism

First and foremost, religious fundamentalism can be said to represent the **politicisation of religion.** This is an absolutely crucial distinction between fundamentalist thought and all other existing ideologies; especially liberalism which insists upon a clear separation between the religious sphere and the political realm. Secondly, fundamentalism is a body of thought that offers one truth. Whilst this is not entirely unique within ideological discourse, the source of that truth undoubtedly is. For religious fundamentalists, the truth derives from the word of God (or whatever word is used for that religion's God or Gods). The source of truth is therefore **unchallengeable** and **unchangeable**. Some things do not have to be proven in a scientific sense, and some things simply cannot be justified via reasoned debate. The correct path in life derives from a sacred body of text, and it is right that those teachings should govern both politics and society. In common with fascism religious fundamentalism takes a monistic approach; a point that has obvious links to *Islamo*-fascism.

The core objective of religious fundamentalism is to construct a **theocracy** in which religious teachings and religious instruction play *the* defining role within society. Inevitably, this will entail a strong role for the state. As such, fundamentalism can be located along the authoritarian part of the political spectrum due to its insistence that the agents of the state are mobilised to ensure strict religious adherence within society, and for its absolutist stance on political issues. However, in terms of the left-right continuum there is no agreed consensus. Advocacy of traditional social mores and a belief that society is organic imply an ideology of the right, and yet a strong emphasis upon altruism and social justice suggests a left-wing bias within religious fundamentalism. What we can however say with certainty is that the term fundamentalism refers to a narrowly defined set of beliefs that form the basis of an increasingly important political movement.

Religious fundamentalism consists of a **reaction** against the moral decay,

Core elements
Politicisation of religion
One source of truth
Aim to create a theocracy

Godless secularism, rampant consumerism and a widespread sense of anomie within the modern world. Only by returning to God's teachings and reinstating fundamentalist principles and ideas can we ever hope to rescue humanity from the afflictions that characterise the modern world. Consequently, religious fundamentalism is an ideology that is both anti-modern *and* anti-liberal. The core objective of religious fundamentalism is therefore to roll back the tide of liberal-rationalist values such as secularism, individualism and moral relativism in order to restore the word of God to everyday life. It is important to note that this objective is shared by Christian fundamentalists (despite the fact that liberalism is pre-dominant within the Christian world and is to some extent perceived of as a reflection of Western values) along with all other strands of religious fundamentalism.

As with nationalism and fascism, religious fundamentalism reflects the politics of the heart as opposed to the politics of the head. It is a deeply **romanticist** ideology that adopts a complete rejection of liberal-rationalist assumptions. Furthermore, the rhetoric of fundamentalism is essentially backward-looking. The progressive language adopted by liberals and socialists is entirely absent. For many religious fundamentalists, 'progress' invariably represents a deviation from God's teachings – particularly in the arena of lifestyle issues.

There are three core elements in the appeal of religious fundamentalism. The first is a widespread perception that secularisation and / or a 'foreign' religion pose a threat of some kind to the moral and spiritual health of the people. The second is a general distaste for the omnipresence of liberal values such as cultural diversity, moral relativism, consumerism, sexual permissiveness and the separation of religion and politics. The third element in the appeal of religious fundamentalism is a tangible perception that the corrupt elite are actively promoting both liberal values and that of the 'foreign' way of life.

Fundamentalists have a tendency to contrast the corrupt and degenerate elite with the morally decent lifestyle of 'ordinary' God-fearing people. In America, considerable hostility is directed at the Washington-based liberal elite that protects the legality of abortion, prevents school prayer and defends the rights of sodomites. In the Arab world, it is the Westernised elite who are to blame. They have become hedonistic and soulless creatures corrupted by the instant gratification of a Western lifestyle. A particular source of controversy is the Saudi Royal Family; who have maintained a close relationship with the United States for well over 50 years. To many Islamo-fascists, the United States is the *"Great Satan."*

As the observant reader will doubtless be aware, the term fundamentalism is widely used in a negative sense. The atheist Richard Dawkins has used the term to characterise religious fanatics who cling to an entrenched position that defies reasoned argument or evidence to the contrary. They adopt positions that cannot be 'proven' in a scientific sense and often employ irrational arguments to justify their beliefs. Criticism has also derived from religious figures themselves. For example, the Rabbi and professor Elliot N. Dorff (1988) argues that we would need a perfect understanding of the ancient language of the original text in order to implement a fundamentalist programme. As this necessitates human interpretation, and that humans are fallible creatures, it is therefore impossible to follow the indisputable word of God. We can only achieve a *human* understanding of God's will. Take the case of the well-known Biblical phrase *"an eye for an eye."* This phrase could easily be used to justify the death penalty in cases of murder. However, it is a point of contention whether or not this short passage provides divine justification for such punishment. Other elements of the Bible imply that God alone will take judgement upon our behaviour (which may therefore be used to justify the abolition of the death penalty) leaving a form of divine justice to take effect. In reply to these and other criticisms, some fundamentalists have claimed that liberal-secularism is itself dogmatic. In a broader sense, many religious groups believe that they are often under attack from an aggressive form of secularism, particularly in Western societies where liberal norms and values are so prevalent.

The religious fundamentalist perspective on human nature

Religious fundamentalists believe that their sacred text must be interpreted literally and without deviation. Interlinked with this argument is the view that adopting a pious approach to religion is the only true path by which to conduct one's life. Any alternative is contrary to God's teachings and is therefore **morally wrong**. This argument applies to both fellow believers who compromise their religion in accordance with prevalent liberal social mores, and those who follow a different religion altogether. As such, those individuals who are devout and adopt a literal interpretation of God's word represent the best of human nature and thereby provide a blueprint for all others to follow.

Unique within ideological discourse, religious fundamentalism is underpinned by an unmistakable and unshakeable belief that God is on their side and will punish those who do not follow their moral code. That punishment may occur in this life and / or the next. The only constant is that punishment will be delivered with vengeful righteousness from a higher being. Following on from this, the commitment to the cause amongst religious fundamentalists is of a very different character to that adopted by other ideologies. More than any other ideology, religious fundamentalists are **dogmatic** in their political outlook. Religious fundamentalists are self-consciously aware of their place within the natural order of things and believe passionately in the need to convert others to their way of thinking. The obvious starting point is fellow believers who are less devout than fundamentalists. Furthermore, religious fundamentalists believe that a strict adherence to religious teachings holds the key to solving a myriad of social problems ranging from crime to family breakdown.

Unlike all other ideologies considered thus far, religious fundamentalism goes well beyond conventional assumptions within ideological discourse about the tenants of human nature. The only comparable stance within ideological discourse is ecologism which takes a philosophical view of the web of life within the natural environment (a point we will consider in the following Chapter). But whereas fundamentalism certainly adopts a philosophical approach, it is of course an ideology shaped exclusively by spiritual beliefs. Thus in the context of human nature, religious fundamentalists believe that devotion to the sacred word of God is the only method by which to release the **goodness** of human nature and curb the wickedness of human nature.

The broader perspective taken by religious fundamentalists in relation to human nature needs to be located within the spiritual conflict conducted on this Earth between good and evil. Human beings are in a state of struggle between the forces of darkness and light, and in order to ensure that good triumphs over evil, it is essential that the laws and mores of that society be governed by the one source of truth. Holy texts offer a clear moral outline as to what behaviour is deemed good and what behaviour is considered evil. According to the Weltanschauung of religious fundamentalists, the sinful ways of human beings can only be cleansed via the adaptation of a clear moral compass derived from the word of the almighty. Moral absolutism is the code of behaviour that we must *all* follow. Whereas moral relativism presents us with a smorgasbord of choices, religious fundamentalism either limits those choices or effectively decides them for us. Under liberalism we have the freedom to engage in pursuits that others might view as foolish, perverse or wrong. Under a theocracy, the people do not have that freedom because the desire amongst fundamentalists to interpret holy texts in a literal sense inevitably leads to moral absolutism. The answer to societal problems lies in the application of holy literature, which is and always will be the authentic and authoritative word of God. Theirs is an orthodox stance in a globalised world increasingly governed by the moral relativism of liberal thought. Strict fidelity to fundamental principles is the means by which we can do right on this Earth and implement God's will. Life itself is merely an ends to a higher purpose, and to concern ourselves with liberal-secular notions of choice ahead of religious observance is contrary to God's will and thus leads to amoral / immoral behaviour.

Main strands of religious fundamentalism

Unusually within ideological discourse, the various strands of fundamentalism derive from the context of that particular religion as opposed to the position taken along the political spectrum. We must therefore abandon any pre-conceived ideas of conservative fundamentalism or socialist fundamentalism in favour of Islamic fundamentalism, Christian fundamentalism, Hindu fundamentalism, Judaist fundamentalism and so on. What divides these various types of fundamentalism is merely a theological distinction as opposed to a conventional political / ideological one. Nonetheless, such distinctions can offer further insight into the features of that particular type of religious fundamentalism.

Most Christian fundamentalists believe in the concept of free will, in that every person is able to make their own choices, albeit with consequences. Ultimately, God will bring those who disobey without repentance to justice. This is based upon the commands of Jesus in the New Testament in relation to any kind of revenge (*"Vengeance is Mine, sayeth the Lord"*). Judaist fundamentalism is broadly similar, but they do not believe that it is wrong for a person (and by implication a government) to take vengeance. On this basis, the imposition of a death penalty would be justified under Judaist fundamentalism but not Christian fundamentalism. Hindu fundamentalists wish to transform the entire basis of Indian society away from its official policy of secularism towards a fully-fledged Hindu state. In contrast to all other strands of fundamentalism, Sikh fundamentalism is closely associated with the political goal of an independent nation-state and separation from India. Finally, Islamic fundamentalism is a broader movement than other strands of religious fundamentalism. Islamic fundamentalism stipulates that Muslims should restrict themselves to literal interpretations of their sacred text and advocates the replacement of secular law with Islamic law (as in the case of Iran after the 1979 Revolution). They believe that the Koran is the unadulterated word of God as revealed to Mohammed, and that the Koran should form the basis of that society.

Christian fundamentalists depict themselves as *"born again evangelicals,"* whereas Judaist fundamentalists are known as Haredi *"Torah-true"* Jews. In Islam, there are fundamentalists engaged in jihad against the spread of a Western culture that suppresses authentic Islam and the *God-given* (or Shariah) way of life. Yet despite these categorisations, there are a great many similarities between the various strands of fundamentalism. Such groups insist on a sharp boundary between themselves and the faithful adherents of other religions, and also between their sacred view of life against the secular world. They also believe that since religious scripture is considered the word of its God(s) no person or government has the right to challenge or change those words. The truth always derives from that sacred text. The problems of the world derive largely from secular influences, and that the path to peace derives from implementing the original message of their particular religion. In the words of Peter Huff; *"fundamentalists ... despite their doctrinal and practical differences, are united by a common worldview which anchors all of life in the authority of the sacred and a shared ethos that expresses itself through outrage at the pace and extent of modern secularisation."*

Role of the state

For many people, religion offers a sense of morality by which to conduct one's life and therefore prescribes what one might consider to be right and wrong. However, fundamentalists go much further than mainstream believers. Religious fundamentalists believe that the word of God must be the basis for societal mores and its legal / political system. As an inevitable consequence, the state offers an effective means by which to implement a fundamentalist conception of society. Fundamentalism therefore takes a deeply **authoritarian** stance on the role of the state, a point graphically exemplified in the case of the Taliban in Afghanistan and the post-Ayatollah regime in Iran (Satrapi, 2006). However, religious fundamentalism also offers a firm critique of the role of the state within a liberal democracy. From the perspective of religious fundamentalists, governments within liberal democracies such as the United

States are often **hostile** towards such groups. From the perspective of religious fundamentalists, the government can often be a considerable bulwark against the promotion of a fundamentalist agenda.

Common to all strands of fundamentalism is the belief that the agents of the state provide a highly useful instrument by which to implement the teachings of their sacred text. In the context of Afghanistan, the Taliban regime operated on the basis of a theocracy. Under this authoritarian regime those who committed adultery were stoned to death and significant restrictions were placed upon freedom of speech. In relation to women, the stated aim of the Taliban is to create *"secure environments where the chasteness and dignity of women may once again be sacrosanct."* In practice, this means forcing women to wear the burqa in public, preventing women going to work and denying girls an education after the age of 8. Females could only be treated by male doctors when accompanied by a male chaperone and were threatened with public flogging and execution for violating the Taliban's laws. In the context of Iran, a strict application of Islamic law has been implemented since the revolution of 1979 by the morality police. In these and other examples, religious fundamentalists have used the state as an agent of moral and spiritual regeneration, changing the entire basis of the law towards religious jurisprudence. To critics of fundamentalist groups, such an approach results in a pernicious form of totalitarianism in which individual freedoms are violated. In the words of the English writer George Orwell *"a totalitarian state is in effect a theocracy"* – an observation with added salience in relation to the Taliban regime.

In a liberal democracy, the agents of the state are often **opposed** to religious fundamentalism. Whilst the freedom to practice and worship whatever religion we choose is upheld, the ability to impose those views upon others is heavily discouraged. Liberal democracy celebrates diversity and tolerance, whereas fundamentalism is - by definition - **intolerant** of other religions. There have been several cases where extremist groups have clashed with the agents of the state within a liberal democracy. Take the case of the 51-day siege at Waco, Texas in 1993 - when the Davidian group led by David Koresh was engaged in a shoot-out with the US government in which 76 people died. Students may be more familiar with examples relating to Islamic extremists engaged in terrorist activity including New York (2001), Bali (2002 & 2005), Turkey (2003), Madrid (2004), London (2005) and Mumbai (2008). Whilst such examples are hardly typical, they do illustrate the ideological tension between liberalism and religious fundamentalism. To people within fundamentalist groups, liberal democratic governments are very much part of the problem facing society. Countries based upon the concept of liberal democracy such as the UK and the US adopt social mores and values incompatible with the aims and objectives of religious fundamentalists. For example, radical Mullahs repeatedly put forward the argument that there is an incompatibility between Islamist teachings and the prevalent norms and mores of Western society. Obvious flashpoints include the role of women, the practise of homosexuality and the place of religion within the political process.

When the state is governed by the parameters of liberal democracy, the advance of fundamentalist beliefs is undoubtedly curtailed, yet to many religious fundamentalists it is the 'liberal' state that adopts a fundamentalist stance. Within a liberal democracy it is the state that upholds the right of a woman to abort a baby and thereby ignore the sanctity of human life. It is the state that protects the rights of a minority to conduct their sexually deviant activities, despite the fact that homosexuality is contrary to God's teachings. Moreover, it is the state that insists on separating religion from aspects of political life when society desperately needs a complete overhaul in regards to the place of religious teachings. From a completely objective standpoint, both religious fundamentalist groups and the state within a liberal democracy do perhaps adopt a 'fundamentalist' stance. Religious fundamentalism is an ideologically-driven movement through which adherents attempt to implement a religious-inspired conception of the world; whereas a liberal democratic state is also ideologically-driven and aims to protect and uphold a liberal-secular conception of the world.

Religious fundamentalism and equality

Religious fundamentalism rejects the concept of equality. Those who are devout in their beliefs and follow their sacred text in a literal sense are more 'worthy' than those who do not. Whilst this may or may not be specifically acknowledged by the ideology of religious fundamentalism, it is clearly implicit from its Weltanschauung. Liberal notions of universal human rights have no place within fundamentalist dogma. The 'rights' of non-believers do not need to be respected or tolerated; which can result in political violence and terrorism against non-believers or those who act contrary to the word of God.

One of the appeals of religious fundamentalism is that it provides a very real sense of superiority, often to those most alienated and discriminated against within that particular society. Those at the margins of society are presented with a vision of the world in which they are on God's side. Religious fundamentalism thereby provides hope to those who might otherwise be excluded from a society governed by the practise of liberal democracy.

Fundamentalism has often flourished amongst those minorities seeking an attachment to a wider collective, thereby providing a sense of belonging and a spiritual reward to God's chosen people. So whereas socialism offers the promise of genuine equality to the exploited masses, religious fundamentalism offers supremacy over all others regardless of their social and economic status. This is an important point to grasp because fundamentalist beliefs appeal to those who might otherwise have been won over by socialism, particularly within the Islamic world.

Religious fundamentalism is also **elitist** in its conception of a utopian society. Theocracies that have implemented a fundamentalist conception of the world are deeply hierarchal with religious figures near to (or at) the top. Some of those theocracies have been headed by a spiritual figure chosen by God – as in the case of the Ayatollah Khomeini. Such figures represent the word of God, and by subordinating to the laws and dictates derived from such figures, everyone in society will benefit. This system is morally superior to any other form of government – including liberal democracy. Hierarchical structures centred upon religious beliefs are the hallmark of fundamentalist ideology. There is no equality of respect in accordance with religious fundamentalism. Such thinking often reflects itself in the context of gender. From a Western-centric perspective, the attitude taken by fundamentalists (particularly Islamic fundamentalists) is at best patronising and at worst downright sexist. Such societies are deeply **patriarchal** with women often treated as inferior to men – in part a reflection of the fact that God is regularly portrayed as a figure we would commonly recognise as male or masculine.

The relationship between religious fundamentalism and liberal democracy

Viewed through the dominant paradigm of ideological discourse (liberalism), religious fundamentalism comes over in a negative light. Labels such as extremists, terrorists and fanatics are routinely employed to describe those who hold fundamentalist views centred upon religion. The underlying assumption at work here is that fundamentalists are irrational, unreasonable and potentially dangerous. To liberals, religious fundamentalism entails a closed mindset and a degree of intolerance. Liberals often perceive themselves as enlightened individuals, whereas fundamentalists are backward-looking and would – if given a hold on power – take us back to the Dark Ages. The entire discourse of liberalism often seems unsympathetic – even hostile – to religious fundamentalism. Unless that religion is part of a minority suffering from the tyranny of the majority, liberalism does not sit too well with religious fundamentalism. Liberalism has often been opposed to the spread of religious fundamentalism, a situation which continues to characterise modern-day politics. In order to explore these arguments further, it is necessary to analyse the true character of religious fundamentalism.

It is important for students to recognise that religious fundamentalism is a deeply illiberal ideology. One of the core elements of religious fundamentalism is a rejection of the liberal view that religion and politics are separate spheres. For religious fundamentalists ***"politics is religion – and religion is politics."*** Fundamentalists also reject the live and let live attitude of moral relativists, believing that tolerance leads to divergence from the word of God. Multiculturalism is also contrary to the objectives of religious fundamentalists. Liberal notions of universal human rights and free speech are also contrary to the teachings of fundamentalism. Other tensions between religious fundamentalism and the main tenants of liberal democracy are equally in evidence. Within a liberal democracy consumerism presents itself as a false God, and to an increasing extent our identity is shaped by conspicuous consumption. In contrast, religious fundamentalism represents a rejection of all superficial notions of identity in favour of a soulful search for that which is enduring and meaningful in life. Furthermore, there is a sharp epistemological tension between scientific reason and a literal interpretation of religious texts. As a branch of knowledge science does not sit comfortably with devout faith, an issue exacerbated within liberal democracies that champion rational thought and reasoning against theocracies which place faith above all else. Further points of contention include the place of women within society, the concept of morality and the attitude taken towards lifestyle issues. Consequently, religious fundamentalism has an antagonistic relationship with liberalism. Western powers may even justify intervention in the affairs of a theocracy in order to protect human rights – as in the case of Afghanistan.

One of the main elements of liberal democracy is the belief that a market of ideas exists within society, and from an open and reasoned debate amongst those competing views, the best available approach will emerge. The raison d'etre of liberal democracy could therefore be said to express the politics of compromise. Yet to religious fundamentalists, compromise simply cannot be facilitated. For fundamentalists, there is no *"market of ideas"* in the manner envisaged by liberals. So whereas liberal democracy is based firmly upon the Aristotle-view of politics as the search for compromise, the very nature of religious fundamentalism is implacably hostile to such a conception. The normal bargaining process amongst a plurality of groups within a liberal democracy is entirely inappropriate for the goals and objectives associated with fundamentalist groups. One of the damaging consequences of such intransigence is the **intractable** character of religious-based conflicts. The

Middle East is the most palpable illustration of this point, although a brief consideration of history would confirm several other examples.

The practicalities facing fundamentalist groups towards securing their aims within a liberal democracy is in part a reflection of how 'available' that system is to capture by such groups. For example, ultra-orthodox Zionist parties can exert considerable influence in the Israeli Knesset. Such parties can wield disproportionate influence via an electoral system based upon proportional representation. Ultra-Orthodox Jewish parties always take an intransigent stance on the issue of Jewish settlements in Gaza and the West Bank and can withdraw support from the main party in the government *if* Israel takes a conciliatory stance towards the Palestinians. However, several other fundamentalist groups totally reject the politics of compromise because they cannot satisfy their objectives within the conventional political process, especially within majoritarian electoral systems such as the United States and the United Kingdom. Take the case of the Islamic extremist parties that aim to turn Britain into an Islamic Republic governed by Sharia law. As these parties have absolutely no chance of fulfilling this fanciful aim via the conventional political process, they have largely rejected the conventions of liberal democracy on issues such as free speech and tolerance. Such parties may also feel that liberal democracy itself is an inappropriate political system for fundamentalists to associate with, a view often reciprocated by the laws which govern that particular liberal democracy. Some religious fundamentalists are considered so intolerant that they are effectively denied a platform to express their views and pursue their brand of politics within a liberal democracy.

On a less confrontational level, certain fundamentalist groups have concentrated their efforts upon single issues in order to advance their cause. This approach is more common amongst Christian fundamentalist groups in the United States – as in the case of a recent campaign in favour of preventing state funding going towards stem cell research. Their demands were supported by George Bush, a man widely known for his Christian beliefs. In the United Kingdom, Christian fundamentalists have found a much less receptive audience both from the decision-making elite and wider society. In order to fully understand the impact of fundamentalist beliefs it is often useful to consider the religiosity of that particular society.

Finally, there are a small number of groups who have combined a conventional attitude towards liberal democracy alongside the use of political violence. For example in Bangladesh, the Harkat-ul-Jihad-al Islami Bangladesh (HuJI-B) aims to establish Islamic *Hukumat* (rule) in that country by killing progressive intellectuals and waging war against liberal-secularism. Its slogan *"We will all become Taliban and we will turn Bangladesh into Afghanistan"* is a clear expression of their political outlook. Not surprisingly, its followers have engaged in political violence to further their cause. However, they have also worked within the democratic system and actually gained a share of power when the Bangladesh Nationalist Party formed a coalition in October 2005. In all such cases one might consider throughout the world, fundamentalists have acted like many other political movements and groups in striving to maximise influence and power when facing the parameters of a liberal democracy.

Individual and society

Whereas liberalism is deeply individualist, religious fundamentalism takes a **holistic view** of society in which each knows his / her place and the emphasis is firmly upon our duties as opposed to our rights. In this utopian society human beings are not the centre of their moral universe but merely a tiny part of a world created by a deity who moves in ways we cannot possibly understand. We should therefore show great humility in the presence of the Almighty and forgo arrogant assumptions about our place within the universe. Humans are very foolish to believe that they as individuals can decide what is right and what is wrong. Liberal assumptions about individualism and the need to separate politics from religion have absolutely no place within a theocracy, and neither do secularist assumptions about the non-existence of God.

According to religious fundamentalists, an emphasis upon individualism will bring out the worst in human nature. Within a liberal democracy individuals lead increasingly atomised lives and experience a deep sense of **disconnection** from spiritual matters. Religious fundamentalism rejects the individual-centred concepts of choice and free will in favour of submitting oneself to a more spiritual sense of purpose. One can see clear evidence of this in relation to a woman's right to terminate a pregnancy, or an individual's freedom to choose an alternative lifestyle. Allowing people to do whatever they want without a moral absolutist code will merely contribute to sinful behaviour. The problem with a liberal society is that people are allowed to bring about their own moral and spiritual downfall. Inevitably, this will impact in a negative manner upon social cohesion. The values that underpin society and hold its members together will be undermined, which may even result in the total breakdown of society. In order to counter this worrying trend within liberal societies, religious fundamentalist groups advocate a very different path for individuals to follow, one which recognises our true place within the greater scheme of things.

From the perspective of the individual, belief in religious fundamentalism does not come without a price. It demands self-sacrifice and consists of participating in a struggle between good and evil – therefore holding some similarities with fascism, particularly in terms of language and world-view. Followers are encouraged to reject material wants in favour a higher spiritual purpose. According to the Weltanschauung of the religious fundamentalist humans are placed upon this Earth to perform God's will. That – and that alone – is our one true purpose in life! Under a theocracy individual rights are subsumed *not* to the nation (as in nationalism), the state (as in fascism) or the creation of a classless utopian society (as in Marxism); but to a religious deity of some kind. In a practical sense, this may entail the suppression of individual rights to a spiritual figure within that society.

To fundamentalists, our duty is to **observe** and solemnly **uphold** the word of God. If the law of the land differs from that, then it is entirely justifiable to break the law. In short, it is the law which is wrong because the word of God is the unchallengeable and infallible source of truth. At its most extreme, this argument can be used to justify acts of political violence. These can range from suicide bombers to militant pro-life campaigners in the United States posting letter bombs to abortion clinics. Fundamentalists also believe that God's judgement is right and proper, unlike the judgements of humankind on this Earth which can be deeply flawed. That is why sacred texts must be interpreted literally as opposed to decision-makers attempting to take into account the permissive and tolerant attitudes of the day. According to fundamentalists, those who have misinterpreted the sacred word of God have fatally compromised his will to the liberal-secular characteristics of the modern word. This reaction or backlash to the modern world is particularly important within Islamic fundamentalism, where radicalised Muslim leaders wish to turn the clock back to a time when Islam was uncorrupted by the spread of Western crusaders.

Whatever the strand of religious fundamentalism we might consider; all are united in their opposition to **post-modernism** and **multiculturalism** (see Chapter 10); two of the main tenants in today's increasingly globalised world. In the case of the former, post-modernism challenges the notion that there is one correct way of seeing and doing things, or that there is any established purpose in human life. Thus if we desire a sense of purpose to our lives, we as individuals have to find it ourselves. Yet according to fundamentalists, the ponderous questioning that some of us are prone to over the meaning of life is completely flawed. Sacred texts have revealed the true meaning of life. Multiculturalism is also opposed for resulting in a deviation from the true path towards God. For fundamentalists, society should adopt a monoculture in order to save individuals from themselves and the consequences of their sinful actions. A theocracy is, by definition, the polar opposite of a multicultural society.

The religious fundamentalist stance on lifestyle issues

Religious fundamentalists are deeply concerned with lifestyle issues. There are five main areas to consider; the place of religion with society, abortion, homosexuality, the nuclear family and the issue of free speech. In each case, religious fundamentalism offers a lucid moral compass by which to lead our lives. Religious fundamentalism can therefore be said to be unique within the realm of political ideology. Whereas other ideologies prescribe certain parameters towards our behaviour, religious fundamentalism offers a forceful outline of exactly *how* we should conduct our lives in accordance with a higher being. Religious fundamentalism therefore reflects a passionate desire to implement and preserve the word of God. Furthermore, it is an ideology that offers a robust **critique** of the liberal-secular character of modern society.

Whereas the prevalent notion within Western society is to internalise religion and adopt a tolerant attitude to all lifestyle choices, religious fundamentalism seeks to externalise religious beliefs towards the totality of society and prescribes a righteous path towards the conduct of our lives. These are firmly opposing world-views with no realistic opportunity of reaching any meaningful compromise. There are several illustrations of this point. One of the most important areas of conflict in contemporary politics between liberal-secularism and religious fundamentalism relates to Turkey. A secular country reflecting the legacy bequeathed by Mustafa Kemal Ataturk, radical Islamists have gained greater influence in recent years, a trend that worries Western policy-makers. The country is almost exclusively Muslim and has a lengthy tradition of looking 'West' (with its prevalence of liberal democratic values) rather than 'East' (with its emphasis upon a close relationship between religion and politics). Turkey's position as a secular Muslim country holds wider significance within global politics. Whilst its Constitution prevents religious laws dominating society and upholds the separation of the state from religion, there are fears that the country might turn towards a militant form of Islam. If the fundamentalists implement their ideas, Turkey will forgo its secular basis.

Another country to consider is India. Since gaining independence from the British in 1947 India has been a secular country home to an eclectic range of religious (and non-religious) beliefs. Whilst the majority religion is Hindu, there are more Muslims within India than in neighbouring Pakistan. There is also a sizeable Sikh population. The world's largest democracy has witnessed a surge of support for Hindu fundamentalists. The aim of Hindu fundamentalists is to cleanse India from the corrupt influence of Western-based notions such as liberal democracy (with all that entails for cultural diversity and religious tolerance) and implement a form of Hindutva (the

Hindu way of life). India is also home to an increasingly militant form of Sikh fundamentalism who campaign for a separatist state.

In the United States, Christian fundamentalists have long been active within the political process. During the mid-1970s the support of the religious right went to the Democrat President Jimmy Carter. However since the 1980s, the religious right has consistently endorsed right-wing Republican candidates and mobilised followers to campaign against liberal pro-choice Democrats. One of the core objectives of groups such as the Moral Majority is to restore Christian values to the political realm and American society, and several policy initiatives have been implemented in order to strengthen the role played by religious values within American politics as a result of such groups. These issues have ranged from state funding for stem-cell research to limits placed on the ability of a woman to terminate her pregnancy. In all such cases, the aim of Christian fundamentalists is to rescue America from moral and spiritual decay. Christian fundamentalists have also been active in the desire to foster the teaching of creationism within schools. Creationism is the belief that humanity, life, the Earth and the universe were created in their original form by God. In the US, Christian fundamentalists have campaigned in favour of creationism being taught alongside evolutionism. There have also been efforts to teach flood geology, creation science and intelligent design in American schools. Once again, the desire amongst fundamentalists to 'politicise' the role of religion within society is in evidence.

Religious fundamentalism and what we might broadly define as the women's movement disagree over a number of lifestyle issues, the most important of which is undoubtedly abortion. According to religious fundamentalists the centrality of choice within feminism, particularly its modern third wave manifestation, is based on sinful depravity. The result is a society that champions the right of a woman to choose an abortion over the right to life of the unborn child. The foetus is part of God's ordained plan and should always be seen as a blessing. To abort a human life is fundamentally wrong because in the words of the Sixth Commandment *"thou shalt not kill."* Religious fundamentalists are also opposed to the freedom of women to wear 'provocative' clothes. One of the most obvious illustrations of this point concerns the controversy over the wearing of the veil amongst Muslim women. The Koran stipulates that women should *"dress modestly,"* yet fundamentalists interpret this religious command in a highly literal sense, thereby dictating what women should or should not wear within the public realm. The desire to implement an Islamic code of behaviour is entirely contrary to the prevalent attitude within Westernised societies where women have a considerable degree of freedom over their choice of clothing. Within countries with a majority Muslim community, the demands of Islamic fundamentalists take a more

The Definitive Guide to Political Ideologies

defensive tone, with signs of Westernised attitudes amongst women being perceived of as corrupting the true teachings of Islam. Within Christian fundamentalism, the line from Genesis 3: 16 contains an important blueprint for society to follow (*"Unto the woman He said ... thy desire shall be to thy husband, and he shall rule over thee"*).

Religious fundamentalists are also opposed to the generally tolerant attitude shown towards homosexuals and lesbians within liberal democratic societies. Men and women are biologically designed to procreate. Consequently, same-sex relationships have no place within God's divine plan. Such activity is therefore contrary to the moral absolutism offered by a fundamentalist viewpoint. In the United States, the Christian fundamentalist slogan ***"God created Adam and Eve, not Adam and Steve"*** represents a clear illustration of this point, as does the slogan *"AIDS is divine punishment for homosexuality."* According to fundamentalists, sodomy plays absolutely no part in God's plan, a view that can form the basis of a highly illiberal Weltanschauung. For example during the Dispatches documentary *Undercover Mosque* shown in 2007 extremist Muslim clerics repeatedly put forward homophobic comments – going as far to describe gay people as *"filthy dogs."* In a more recent example, fundamentalist groups in America daubed *"and went straight to hell"* over advertisements for Katy Perry's song '*I kissed a girl.*' Of more political substance, opposition to gay marriage has been a major component of electoral support for the Republican Party; along with the other two G's (God and guns). There are even some camps in America that strive to 'cure' homosexuals from their 'illness.' Fundamentalist groups have even argued that America is losing in Iraq because the authorities allow gays to join the military.

On the issue of homosexuality, it is perhaps worth reflecting on the point that religious fundamentalists do not reflect the views of many of their co-religionists. It is here that we can identify a particularly intolerant stance taken by fundamentalists on this issue. There are no such concerns about minority rights, the need for tolerance or the need to prevent the tyranny of the majority persecuting the lives of minorities. One of the most unusual illustrations of the link between fundamentalist beliefs and attitudes towards homosexuality can be found in Iran. In Iran homosexuality is illegal whereas transsexuality is categorised as an illness subject to a cure. Many gay people have actually undertaken a sex change since the revolution of 1979. During an international conference held in 2009 the Iranian leader 'boasted' that his country contained no homosexuals, although the rate of sex changes is ironically one of the highest in the world.

Amongst Christian fundamentalist groups there is a firm belief that the traditional nuclear family represents the best possible environment from the perspective of both the child and society as a whole. When a husband and wife make their wedding vows in a place of worship they do so in the presence of God; and it is both right and proper to maintain a marriage because both the husband and the wife have pledged to remain so *"until death do us part."* In addition, the ease by which a couple can get a divorce is considered detrimental to the child. Many social problems derive from a failure within the family to teach children the basic difference between **right and wrong**.

Whilst all fundamentalist groups offer a firm defence of the nuclear family, such groups also reflect the specific teachings of that particular religion. Islam for example enables a man to marry more than one wife on the condition that he deals justly with them. Islamic fundamentalist groups thereby advocate a family structure based around this approach. What is constant throughout *all* fundamentalist groups is a desire to champion the traditional family structure in order to resolve the various problems that plague modern society. Take the case of religious adherence within the family unit. *"The family that prays together stays together"* is a euphemism credited to Al Scalpone and was used as the slogan of the Roman Catholic Family Rosary Crusade by Father Patrick Peyton. It has since become synonymous with Christian fundamentalists in the United States, although it is an argument clearly applicable to other strands of fundamentalist thought. Sacred texts sanction the nuclear family above any possible alternative, and moral relativism on this (and other) issues is anathema to fundamentalist groups.

Another crucial lifestyle issue in relation to religious fundamentalism is the concept of **free speech**. According to the norms and values that govern a liberal democracy individuals are free to say whatever they like provided they are not harming the liberty of others. The 'offence' such words might cause is not sufficient warrant for the state to prevent us exercising our right to free speech. Moreover, there is no accepted universal truth within a liberal democracy. In the words of John Stuart Mill; *"Mankind are greater gainers by suffering each other to live as seems good to themselves than by compelling each to live as seems good to the rest."* The codes that govern free speech within a liberal society are therefore firmly based upon moral relativism. In stark contrast, religious fundamentalism prescribes a dogmatic code by which to conduct our lives. Inevitably, this has an impact upon the arena of what we can and cannot say. For liberals, free speech is an article of faith. For religious fundamentalists, freedom of speech is entirely contrary to the prescribed path outlined by God. There are certain areas of speech that lie outside the remit of what is acceptable. Causing offence to a deity in some manner is not permitted within fundamentalist teachings, and there are several examples we might consider.

After publication of the Satanic Verses in 1989 the author Salman Rushdie was forced into hiding when the Ayatollah Khomeini issued a fatwa against him. Rushdie's 'crime' was to portray the prophet Mohammed in a blasphemous manner. As the publication of the book occurred in a liberal democracy, Rushdie may have felt that his work was entirely in keeping with moral relativism. To this day, the Rushdie affair remains a celebrated case in the obvious tension between fundamentalist beliefs and the right of free speech within a liberal society. However, it is certainly not the only one. In February 2006 the Danish newspaper (Jyllands-Posten) published a cartoon that depicted the prophet Mohammed as a terrorist, causing outrage amongst Muslim groups. After the controversy generated by the affair the British government decided to prohibit publication of the cartoon. These and several other cases completely divide liberals from fundamentalists and expose an increasingly important fault-line within politics. Whereas a relativist approach stipulates that each case must be judged on its specific merits, **moral absolutism** takes a completely opposite path.

Change or the status quo

For many people, being devout in one's religious beliefs is a worthy and perhaps necessary endeavour, but it remains ostensively a private one. It is not right to force others to accept their religious faith, merely to abide by what their religion stipulates to be a good life. However, fundamentalists are very different to mainstream believers and advocate a deeply committed approach to religion itself. Religious fundamentalists believe that it is their mission to spread God's word. In doing so, they are doing what is right and saving others from the wrath of a higher being. Fundamentalists also believe it is their duty to implement the **literal word** of God. Anything less is contrary to the fundamentalist standpoint.

Despite such fervent commitment to the cause, religious fundamentalists have been divided on the basis of achieving their goals within the parameters of a liberal democracy, and the division between moderates and extremists reflects all other reformist-minded ideologies such as socialism and feminism. Amongst the more pragmatic elements of such groups, campaigns have been conducted on a **single-issue** basis. Candidates have also been supported (or targeted) depending upon their voting record on moral issues such as abortion and stem-cell research. This approach is more commonly associated with Christian fundamentalists in the United States. The more extreme elements of religious fundamentalism believe that political violence is both justified and necessary to overcome their oppressors. Such extremism is more closely associated with elements of Islamic fundamentalism, and is arguably the more relevant towards our understanding of international relations due to its potential impact on the relationship between the West and Islamic countries.

The relationship between political violence and religious fundamentalism has always been evident throughout history, and that remains the case within contemporary politics. Suicide bombers, assassinations, separatist movements, imperialistic conquest and terrorism characterise the extremist approach of certain fundamentalists from *all* strands of thought. This might appear inconsistent with the centrality of peaceful concerns within religious beliefs, although the counter-argument is that some truths are worth dying for. Furthermore, some aspects of fundamentalist thought have been more prepared than others to employ violent measures to further their cause, such as Islamic fundamentalism. Part of the reason is that Islamic fundamentalism differs to other strands of fundamentalism in that it reflects a backlash against Western colonialism. Radical Mullahs have argued that the spread of both Christianity and a secular-driven view of the world is a corruption that derives from the West, especially the United States. The supremacy of Islam and its values are therefore under threat from Westernisation in all its forms. In order to counter such a major threat, political violence has been justified. Islamic fundamentalism could therefore be depicted as an alternative - and direct challenge - to the hegemony of Western liberalism. This has implications for the end of ideology argument, a point we will consider in a later Chapter.

Whereas Islamic fundamentalism has a trans-national character, Hindu fundamentalism is largely contained within India. The aim of Hindu fundamentalism is to overturn the secular and multi-cultural character of Indian society. If such groups succeed, the world's largest democracy would become a fundamentalist state bordering a country (the Islamic Republic of Pakistan) engaged in an arms race with India. As such, the consequences of Hindu fundamentalism within India hold considerable importance for the rest of the world. There are two main Hindu fundamentalist groups - the SRS and the Shiv Sena. The SRS are a violent group of Hindu extremists who wish to end all forms of degenerate Western behaviour and thereby reform the entire basis of the Indian state. The Shiv Sena (which stands for *"army of Shivaji"*) has been part of several Maharashtra state governments, and was a coalition partner in the National Democratic Alliance that ruled India from 1998 to 2004. Both the SRS and the Shiv Sena claim to represent the ideology of Hindutva, a hard-line view of Hindu teachings which has been portrayed by opponents as threatening the Talibanisation of India and with it the end of the tolerance of other religions that characterises Hinduism. In the words of the celebrated Indian sociologist Ashis Nandy; *"Hindutva will be the end of Hinduism."*

The final point to consider is that fundamentalism can result in violent **objection** against the state itself. Although such activity is rare, it is not entirely unknown. This is most prevalent within Western societies governed by the parameters of liberal democracy, where religious extremists break the law in order to implement what they consider to be the word of God. Inevitably, this can entail terrorist activity. The basis of such activity can be traced back to the 13th century scholar Thomas Aquinas (1225-1274) who argued that God had provided humankind with reason and thereby permitted secular authority to act on his behalf. He also believed that the law should be based upon nature as interpreted by reason, and if the secular law was at odds with natural law, then the latter should always take precedence. The Law of God was therefore greater than the law of man. Amongst fundamentalists, the stance taken by Aquinas is taken to its logical conclusion. Individuals are justified in disobeying the law *if* that law is implemented by hostile powers (such as Western crusaders) and is contrary to the word of their God(s).

Religious fundamentalism in contemporary politics

Religious fundamentalism reaches those parts that other ideologies cannot reach. Religious fundamentalism fills a void in people's lives, and yet its impact upon politics remains constrained. In part, this derives from the opposition of liberal democratic states. However, it is also revealing to note that a great many people believe that fundamentalism itself represents a complete distortion of God's will because of its association with intolerance and acts of violence. Fundamentalists are therefore often opposed by their own co-religionists; which does to some degree limit their political impact.

On a wider international scale, the *"clash of civilisations"* (Huntingdon, 2002) between the liberal-secular West and a fundamentalist view of Islam is potentially more serious to the future of humankind than even the cold war, but as yet we have not seen anything comparable to the level of destruction that characterised the conflict between America and the Soviet Union. Whilst millions of people could potentially find themselves unwilling participants in an apocalyptic struggle between West and East, such an all-encompassing struggle seems a little far-fetched. What seems more likely is that liberalism will continue to spread its ideology throughout the world. There is considerable evidence to suggest that liberal democracy and capitalism hold far greater popularity and influence than fundamentalist beliefs. However, it is also true that certain parts of the world appear largely immune from the supposed attractions of liberalism. These regions of the world could remain hotbeds of radicalism and outposts of fundamentalism in an increasingly globalised world, thereby fuelling terrorist activity. And sadly, no country appears to be immune from the effects of terrorism – a point with major implications in the contemporary era.

How to deal with terrorist activity fuelled by religious fundamentalism presents a considerable dilemma for governments based upon the tenants of liberal democracy. Because that terrorist group is based on ideology rather than a nation it cannot be defeated in the conventional sense of the phrase. This has important implications within contemporary international relations. For instance, the United States stands unchallenged as the world's military superpower but it cannot possibly defeat an enemy such as al-Qaeda in a manner comparable to combating a *"rogue state."* Powerful nations have also found it difficult to deal effectively with suicide bombers and other acts of terrorism, particularly when the source of such actions derives from their own countrymen and women. Moreover, whatever nation is selected for military action, it is by definition the wrong target. For example, Iraq had no direct link to al-Qaeda and the terrorist attacks of September 11th 2001. In addition, targeting the wrong country merely strengthens the arguments put forward by religious fundamentalists who present America as hostile to Islam and committed to conducting a crusade against Muslims everywhere. Another issue to consider is to what extent should liberal democratic countries restrict civil liberties in order to defeat the threat of terrorism? In the words of Michael Ignatieff during his Gifford lectures in 2003 -*"How can democracies resort to* [violence] *without destroying the values for which they stand?"* This is an important question because the response from the West to the *"war on terror"* looks likely to define international relations in the contemporary era, and the wider clash between religious fundamentalism and liberalism is also likely to shape contemporary politics in the UK.

At its most visceral, religious fundamentalism provides meaning and a secure identity to those that are bereft of both. Whereas globalisation generates doubt, displacement and alienation; religious fundamentalism offers reassurance and belonging. Although fundamentalism is often stereotyped as limited in appeal towards the easily-impressionable and those alienated from society, its impact is actually much greater than that. Religious fundamentalism appeals to a group that perceives itself to be neglected within that liberal democracy. Crucially, this feeling may be more imagined than real. Fundamentalism also gives expression to those who feel completely alienated from the individualistic and secular character of life within a liberal democracy. In the context of Islamic fundamentalism, it is an ideology which represents a reaction against the threat from secularism and liberalism to traditional social mores. The rise of fundamentalist beliefs can be viewed as a backlash against the predominance of the West. Christian fundamentalism is also strong in the United States and shows no signs of dissipating.

The basic appeal of religion as the source of political identity is that it provides an unchangeable basis for group membership in a world of bewildering change. Religious fundamentalism therefore offers a collective sense of identity that transcends the individualism prevalent within liberal democracies. Religious fundamentalism also has the capacity to unite people towards a higher purpose. It tends to provide convincing answers to those questions that liberal democracy finds difficult to adequately answer (such as *"what is the purpose of life?"*). Fundamentalism also offers hope and salvation amongst disaffected and troubled souls. It articulates the insecurities of those with seemingly little to gain from the process of increasing interdependence throughout the world. Religious fundamentalism thereby fills an ideological vacuum that might have otherwise been met by other totalitarian ideologies such as fascism. For these and other reasons, religious fundamentalism looks highly unlike to disappear in the near future and may well present a powerful riposte to the prevalence of liberalism within contemporary politics.

Further quotes on religious fundamentalism

"What we've seen in Europe and the rest of the world is that freedom has a much stronger attraction than radical fundamentalism." Gijs de Vries
"When we blindly adopt a religion, a political system, a literary dogma, we become automatons. We cease to grow." Anais Nin
"As you look at the flow of Muslim fundamentalism, or fundamentalism in various areas and various religions, they all play on the people who have very little." James Wolfensohn
"Yes, we are reactionaries and you are enlightened intellectuals. You intellectuals do not want us to go back 1,400 years." Ayatollah Khomeini
"I want to take apart the entire political and philosophical structure of modernity and return Islam to its unpolluted origins." Sayyid Qutb
"We may have to fight the battle for the Enlightenment all over again." Salman Rushdie
"I regard Christian and Jewish fundamentalism, and all other forms of fundamentalism, as the enemies of God – and I hope you'll quote me on that." Arthur Hertzberg
"As a scientist, I am hostile to fundamentalist religion because it … teaches us not to change our minds." Richard Dawkins

"Typically, fundamentalists aim to cleanse 'false believers' from their midst, or to separate themselves from them. This is why fundamentalism sometimes leads to violence and usually leads to schism." Harriet Harris

"Fundamentalism isn't about religion, it's about power." Salman Rushdie

Recommended reading

Ali, T. (2003) *The Clash of Fundamentalism : Crusades, Jihads and Modernity.* Ali takes a critical look at the rise of fundamentalism within contemporary politics, believing that conflict between liberal modernity and fundamentalism is inevitable. A comparison with Huntingdon's work is very useful for students to consider.

Humphrys, J. (2007) *In God we doubt : Confessions of a failed atheist.* A sage reflection of how life experience has shaped Humphrys' own views on religion. Whilst he is not concerned with fundamentalism itself, he offers a great deal for students to ponder in terms of the relationship between religion and society.

Huntingdon, S. (2002) *The Clash of civilisations and the remaking of World Order.* Huntingdon takes an in-depth look at the importance of culture and Western civilisation towards the course of human history, leading towards the conclusion that fundamentalism and civilisations are in conflict with one another. Huntingdon's analysis was influential upon the mindset of the Bush administration and remains an influential work amongst neo-conservatives.

Husain, E. (2007) *The Islamist.* An inside account of how Islamic fundamentalism aims to convert people to its cause. Husain offers a revealing insight into why fundamentalism appeals to some people.

Satrapi, M. (2006) *Persepolis.* Marjane Satrapi's account of her own personal experiences is an entertaining account of how life under a totalitarian regime operates. Her search for identity and the contrasts between 'liberal' Austria and theocratic Iran is both compelling and entertaining. 'Persepolis' is also available as a cartoon film.

Ideas for further discussion

What are the core elements of religious fundamentalism?

What is the stance taken by religious fundamentalists upon human nature?

To what extent is it possible to identify various 'strands' of religious fundamentalism?

What is the role of the state within a theocracy?

What is the stance taken by religious fundamentalists upon the concept of equality?

What is the attitude taken by religious fundamentalists towards liberal democracy?

Why are religious fundamentalists opposed to individualism?

What common themes exist in terms of the stance taken by religious fundamentalists over lifestyle issues?

To what extent does religious fundamentalism justify the use of political violence?

To what extent does religious fundamentalism pose an alternative to liberalism?

Key terms

Asceticism A practise whereby hedonistic pleasure is denied for the enhancement of the spiritual self. The German sociologist Max Weber argued that asceticism within Protestant societies was an important element in the development of capitalism. In contemporary politics, asceticism holds relevance towards an understanding of religious fundamentalism and ecologism (see next Chapter).

Clash of civilisations A term associated with the American political scientist Samuel Huntington (2002). He argued that a Western secular ideology is incompatible with a more traditional Islamist view of society. The clash of civilisations holds major implications for British society and for the wider context of international relations. According to Huntington's argument issues such as the position of women within society, the relationship between the state and religion, the importance of free speech and attitudes towards homosexuality are essentially incompatible between an Islamist culture and Western culture. Future conflicts may be based on these distinct viewpoints.

Fundamentalism An ideological doctrine which demands complete obedience from its members. The term is usually applicable in the context of political / religious extremism and can even form the motivation for terrorist activity. Fundamentalism represents a rejection of liberal democratic norms and values. As with fascism, the spread of religious fundamentalism can be interpreted as the failure of liberalism to meet the needs of the population and win over hearts and minds.

Sectarianism Ignorance and prejudice based upon hostile attitudes towards a person's religion. There are many societies throughout the world in which sectarianism is a feature of everyday life. For example, Iraqi society is characterised by sectarian conflict between various strands of Islamic thought. In the context of mainland Britain, sectarianism is rare.

Secular society A term used to depict the lack of religious observance within a society. This term is commonly applied to British society, although the term could equally be applied to many Westernised countries – with the notable exception of the United States.

Secularisation The process by which religious practise, thinking and institutions lose their significance within society.

Sharia law A religious doctrine within the Muslim community based on a body of Islamic law. The word law is actually misleading, in that Sharia offers a set of guiding principles as opposed to a coherent legal framework. Sharia deals with many aspects of day-to-day life, and arouses deep controversy within British society for the desire amongst some Muslims to live by a different code of behaviour to that prescribed within British law and the wider values of British society.

Terrorism Defined under Section 1 of the Terrorism Act 2000 as *"the use or threat of action ... designed to influence the government or to intimidate the public ... and the use of or threats made for the purpose of advancing a political, religious or ideological cause."* Terrorism can be applied as a label to several political movements. In broad terms, it consists of the use of political violence to demand social change. As the name implies, terrorism aims to spread fear amongst the public in order to influence the stance taken by decision-makers. Terrorism has a lengthy history within political ideology.

Theocracy A regime based upon a strong adherence to religious beliefs, as in the case of Iran after the 1979 Revolution. The term is used to distinguish such a regime from a democracy or a dictatorship. In the words of the English writer George Orwell *"a totalitarian state is in effect a theocracy."* Theocracy is the least common form of dictatorship, but is also one of the most brutal.

CHAPTER 9
ECOLOGISM

The core elements of ecologism

Of all the ideologies we will consider, ecologism is the most thought-provoking and the most philosophical. Ecologism marks a concerted attempt to overhaul conventional wisdom and thereby transform the entire conduct of human behaviour, and just as anarchism significantly extends the kaleidoscope of ideological discourse, so too does ecologism. The Weltanschauung of ecologism and the solutions prescribed by it are profoundly different to anything we have yet encountered. Furthermore, ecologism considers deep philosophical questions such as *"Why are we here?" "What is our place within the natural order of things?"* and *"How can we live in harmony with nature?"* It is these questions, and the conclusions one might reach, that mark out ecologism from all other political ideologies.

Before we go any further, students have often told me that the distinction between ecologism and environmentalism is confusing. The picture is further complicated by the fact that the term environmentalism is far more widespread than ecologism; both within academia and the political process itself. Nonetheless, the distinction between the two is a straight-forward one. Whereas ecologism is a political ideology, environmentalism is a policy-based approach based upon an attempt to secure the aims and objectives of the green movement. To use a simple distinction, ecologism is the *theory* and environmentalism is the *practise*. For obvious reasons, the focus here is upon ecologism. However, the term environmentalism will be used to aide our understanding – principally in relation to the political activities associated with the green movement.

The term ecology derives from Ernst Haeckel in reference to the Greek words for *"household"* and *"study."* Ecology can therefore be said to mean the *"study of the household (of nature)."* Ecology consists of a scientific study of the distribution and abundance of living organisms and how they are affected by interactions with their environment. Ecology confirms the important scientific fact that *all* species exist within

Core elements
Prevent the destruction of the environment
Overturn conventional wisdom about economic growth and human behaviour

an ecosystem – the largest of which is the ecosphere. As such, we as human beings exist within an ecosystem. As ecosystems can only sustain themselves in a state of harmony, humans must act in a manner that recognises their responsibilities to the ecosystem. The core element of ecologism is that *everything* is interconnected. Ecologism adopts a holistic approach towards its understanding of the world, not just in relation to human beings but to the entire ecosystem itself. We need to adopt a **holistic** rather than reductionist approach. Human beings are part of a greater whole, and to ignore this basic point would be to misunderstand the nature of the problem that faces all of us. Our common home is planet Earth, and yet humankind lives well beyond its ecological limit. Human beings have depleted much of the world's resources and have polluted the planet. Just by the mere act of existing, humans and their dependant animals are responsible for more than 10 times the greenhouse gas emissions of all the airline travel in the world (Lovelock, 2009, p.4). The conclusions are both stark and shocking - humankind can *only* be preserved if it fundamentally changes its entire pattern of behaviour. Sadly, we already stand on the precipice of an environmental catastrophe of unimaginable proportions. Indeed for one of its most important figures – James Lovelock - we are already too late.

Ecologism is commonly associated with the left of the political spectrum, but it is not entirely *of* the left. It is certainly true to state that ecologism emerged as a reaction against the depersonalised and exploitative nature of industrialisation. Ecologism derived from the Industrial Revolution (although elements of such thinking can be traced back to Buddhism, Taoism and the Cathari sect of the 13th century) and offered a critique of an economic system based upon unbridled capitalism – a view widely associated with the left. Furthermore, ecologism was at the forefront of the New Left movement during the 1960s. Today, opposition within the green movement towards materialism and free market capitalism once again confirms the left-wing position widely attributed to ecologism, as does the demand for social justice and the desire to alter the entire course and direction of globalisation. Typical of this left-ish language are the words of Murray Bookchin - *"Owing to its inherently competitive nature, bourgeois society not only pits humans against each other, it also pits the mass of humanity against the natural world. Just as men are converted into commodities, so every aspect of nature is converted into a commodity, as resources to be manufactured and merchandised wantonly ... The plundering of the human spirit by the marketplace is paralleled by the plundering of the earth by capital."* Having said this, ecologism also accommodates those on the right of the political spectrum such as conservatives and even fascists. There is trait of romanticism within ecologist thought that lends itself to ideologies of the right. On the libertarian-authoritarian axis, ecologism belongs on the former. The emphasis within ecologism is on small-scale local action characterised by public participation in the local community, a view best summarised by the slogan *"think globally, act locally."*

Within political discourse that which cannot be proven in a scientific sense must be assumed, and all the ideologies considered thus far begin with certain assumptions. For example, liberalism is based upon the assumption that the individual is a rational actor; whereas anarchism assumes that individuals are reasoned and enlightened creatures whose innate goodness will come to the fore once we abolish the state. From these basic assumptions, all ideologies aim to provide a deeper understanding of the political world and offer solutions to particular problems. But whereas other ideologies are based primarily upon assumptions, ecologism is shaped to a considerable extent by **scientific study**. This makes its observations all the more compelling, and gives ecologism a certain degree of credence that no other ideology can possibly match. Students should also be aware that ecologism offers a highly challenging perspective towards what one might call conventional wisdom.

The ecologist perspective on human nature

There is no shared perspective on human nature within the ideology of ecologism. Some place their faith in human beings; whereas others see human beings in a negative light. Humans are therefore either part of the **solution** (or the **problem** itself) depending on one's point of view. This is reflected in the division between anthropocentricism and ecocentricism, a point we will consider in the next section. However, ecologists offer a critique of human behaviour within a consumerist society, and in that sense, there is at least one common trait to identity. Ecologists point out that humans have all too often asked the question *"can we"* when the more appropriate question is *"should we?"* Technological developments have fundamentally and irrevocably changed the ecosystem itself with devastating consequences for us all. Climate change is a man-made phenomenon, and human beings are to blame. The only significant debate to be had is the solution to that problem, a point which significantly divides the green movement and one we will now consider.

The main strands of ecologism

There are essentially **two** main strands of thought within ecologism – **anthropocentricism** and **ecocentricism**. The meaning of these rather convoluted words is actually quite straight-forward. *"Anthro"* simply means derived from man. This view stipulates that humans are at the centre of the Earth's biosphere. All the ideologies we have considered thus far are anthropocentric in their outlook. In terms of the green movement, an anthropocentric approach is associated with the former leader of Greenpeace Jonathon Porritt. He argues that human beings are custodians of the Earth's resources, and that we can work together to resolve the issue of climate change via reaching a balance between capitalist modernity and green thought. It is entirely possible to take an enlightened anthropocentric stance in order to resolve perhaps the most serious problem facing humankind.

Another significant contribution from the anthropocentric school of thought derives from Garrett Hardin's (1968) *"tragedy of the commons"* argument. Hardin was an American biologist who argued that a tension exists between the private good and the collective whole. He claimed that if land was owned in common we would access any land we liked. However, the collective consequences of this would be catastrophic for the environment. He based his argument on a simple parable to illustrate the dangers of unrestrained private behaviour and the various problems which face the environment (what he called the *"global commons"*). Hardin's argument is a good illustration of how the anthropocentric school of thought identifies the *problem* of climate change. The manner in which the anthropocentric perspective views climate change places hope in the ability of human beings to analyse the problem in hand and to act in a rational manner in order to solve it.

According to the anthropocentric perspective, the solution to the problem of climate change is much more practical than that offered by the ecocentric school of thought. Anthropocentricism takes a **reformist stance** to the issues presented by environmental damage. Engagement with the political process, even if it entails co-operation with the major political parties, is both desirable and necessary. Ultimately, the means by which human beings can protect the environment can be achieved within the parameters of liberal democracy.

	Anthropocentricism	Ecocentricism
View of humans	Term means derived from man. Humans are at the centre of the biosphere	Critical of human arrogance. We are merely part of a wider ecosystem
Core elements	Focus upon what is practical and achievable	Philosophical outlook with an emphasis upon the Gaia as a holistic entity
Approach towards change	Reformist	Radical
Attitude towards the political process	Constructive engagement	Rejection of the conventional political process
View of economic growth	Sustainable level of growth	Zero growth
Stance on capitalism	Supportive, albeit with some degree of state intervention	Largely opposed to capitalism due to its focus on the profit motive
Key figures	Porritt, Hardin	Naess, Lovelock
Shading	Light greens / bright greens	Dark greens

Most importantly, capitalism has the ability and the motive to meet consumer needs and public opinion; thereby facilitating the aims of the green movement. Furthermore, environmental pressure groups such as Friends of the Earth and Greenpeace can influence decision-makers in a variety of ways. For instance, the basis of taxation may be changed from its current focus upon income and expenditure towards preventing pollution and rewarding a firm's green credentials. Sustainable development is another method consistent with the anthropocentric school of thought, as is technological development to harness renewable resources. The anthropocentric view states that economic growth is desirable *provided* it is sustainable; and it is clearly in our interests to have sustainable economic development.

Ecocentricism is a belief-system based upon the **inter-relationship** between humans and the natural world. Unlike the anthropocentrist world-view, human beings are *not* at the centre of the Earth's biosphere and it is incredibly arrogant of us to think so – a point described by David Ehrenfeld (1978) as *"the arrogance of humanism."* Ecocentricism entails a complete rejection of anthropocentric assumptions and is associated with a variety of issues such as biocentric equality, diversity and de-centralisation. Biocentric diversity can be understood as a principle whereby all organisms in the ecosphere are of equal worth. In the words of the American ecologist Aldo Leopold (1968), we are merely *"plain citizens"* who have no more rights than any other member of the ecosystem. The implication of this standpoint is a firm support for biodiversity in terms of the benefits entailed for the ecosystem itself (e.g. it is often from rare plant species that we derive new medicines). Furthermore, there is a firm belief in the need for a decentralised approach to the issue of climate change. One of the core elements of ecocentricism is a substantial reaction against industrialisation and the mania amongst policy-makers for economic growth. A **zero rate of economic growth** is entirely consistent with ecocentricism.

The main implication of ecocentricism is that we must radically transform the way we think about the world in order to prevent the destruction of the environment. Our behavioural patterns and our entire way of life must be totally overhauled if we are to survive as a species on planet Earth. Humans must not override others within the ecosystem, but rather seek a balance and **harmony with nature**. Human beings must also recognise that they are merely part of a wider whole, and not the centre of the natural world. In the words of Peter Singer (1976), humans all too often adopt a form of speciesism – portraying themselves as superior to other species by denying other animals a moral significance. In order to prevent the destruction of the planet, humans must adopt a philosophical plane as opposed to conducting in the mindless pursuit of consumer wants.

One's stance on this important dividing line depends entirely upon one's faith (or lack of) in human beings. Are we the most destructive animal on Earth, or are we the only hope for the future of the planet? There is considerable evidence to back up either assertion. Humans have been (and continue to be) responsible for the manifold atrocities inflicted upon planet Earth. Similarly, humans have harnessed knowledge that has enhanced the natural environment, albeit primarily for the satisfaction of human wants and needs. Whatever perspective taken, it is certainly the case that human beings are both highly destructive *and* capable of noble deeds. We are also the *only* species capable of dramatically affecting our own ecosystem.

Now that we have considered the two main strands of thought, there are several sub-theories within the green movement to be aware of. In terms of understanding these various sub-theories it is increasingly common for scholars to use the terminology of shades. Whilst these shades are not *strands* of thought in the conventional sense, they can greatly assist our understanding of the green movement. There are three different shades to consider; light greens, bright greens and dark (or deep) green.

Light greens are closer to the centre of the political spectrum and are anthropocentric in their outlook. Light greens see the protection of the natural environment as our shared responsibility. They take a reformist stance within the political process, and advocate environmentalism as a choice of lifestyle. They are the closest to the centre of the political spectrum and can be described as adopting a moderate approach to change. Their slogan *"Green is the new black"* is a useful summary of the position taken by light greens. It is also worth noting that the term light green can be a negative one when used by those further away from the centre of the political spectrum. They accuse light greens of compromising the core values of the green movement. In reply, light greens claim to be offering practical solutions to win over hearts and minds.

Bright greens adopt a more uncompromising stance than light greens. They too are broadly anthropocentric in their outlook, but unlike light greens they are much more firmly committed to the necessity of radical change. They argue that fundamental and irrevocable change to the political and economic structure of society is needed in order to protect the environment. Bright greens perceive themselves as offering more effective solutions than either light greens or dark greens. In the words of Ross Robertson; *"Bright green environmentalism is less about the problems and limitations we need to overcome than the 'tools, models and ideas' that already exist for overcoming them. It forgoes the bleakness of protest and dissent for the energising confidence of constructive solutions."* It is a world-view which stipulates that we can neither shop our way to sustainability, nor can we protest our way to it. Only via reaching a compromise position and engaging in constructive action can we ever hope to save the planet. Of all the three terms in use, bright green is the most recent and the least common. Commentators and academics still tend to use either light green or dark green in the context of shades.

Dark greens are ecocentric in their political outlook. Of all the three shades within the green movement, dark greens are the most philosophical. For dark greens, all other political ideologies are industrialist and anthropocentric. This branch of thought uses the language of the left and the motto *"Green is the new red"* has been used to describe their mindset. Dark greens seek a seismic change in the political and economic structure of society. In short, they are the fundamentalists within the green movement. Another useful term for dark greens is deep ecologists, and the most influential contribution from this particular approach derives from the Gaia hypothesis of James Lovelock – an argument that deserves much closer attention. Gaia was the Ancient Greek Goddess of the Earth and Lovelock (1979, 2009) developed an argument which claimed that life on Earth can be understood as a single living organism. He also argued that Gaia will exterminate that which presents a threat to her. The implication of Lovelock's argument is both stark and frightening. Humankind is currently sowing the seeds of its own destruction with climate change representing **the revenge of Gaia** on humanity itself. Although Lovelock's arguments are not shared by all ecologists, he does present a very cogent explanation of why climate change is happening. Gaia is the *only* living planet in the solar system, and we have made it serve our needs with disastrous results. For Lovelock, the view that 'we' need to save the planet is also mistaken. He believes that *"the real Earth does not need saving. It can, will and always has saved itself and it is now starting to do so by changing to a state much less favourable for us and other animals."* Gaia will therefore always maintain an ecological balance despite major changes to the ecosystem. Moreover, Lovelock asserts that Gaia will *always* dictate the terms of how life is conducted (including that experienced by human beings). [21]

Dark greens such as Lovelock gain their name because they adopt a philosophical stance. They firmly reject anthropocentrism and fully embrace ecocentricism. In answer to the philosophical question *"why are we here?"* dark greens contend that our purpose in life is to live in harmony with nature. Light greens take the opposite view, believing that humans must use nature to serve our ends. Dark greens set a demanding ethic and have been criticised by light greens for adopting an irrational – even mystical – approach. According to light greens, those who adopt anthropocentric assumptions seem more interested in setting unrealistic goals than working towards achievable gains for the green movement. The division between light greens and dark greens was graphically illustrated in 2001 within the German Green party. The Realo faction of the party disagreed with the Fundi faction over the proper strategy of the party. Whereas the Realo faction was firmly committed to conventional

---

[21] A number of ecologists even reject the label 'ideology' because of the association between ideology and an *anthro*-centred world-view. However, to accept the logic of this argument would prevent our study of ecologism as an ideology. If an ideology can be understood as a means by which we view society through a particular perspective with a relatively consistent set of beliefs and attitudes that aim to conceptualise the political world and, in doing so, prescribe a means by which we might establish a better way of doing things; then ecologism clearly satisfies the criterion of an ideology.

parliamentary politics and the necessity of compromise in order to achieve change, the Fundis were rather more dogmatic and idealistic. The tensions between the two were laid bare when the German Green Party supported the government's decision to send troops to Afghanistan. Such a decision seems entirely at odds with the broader ethos of the green movement and would very much support the ecocentric view that an anthropocentric approach fundamentally compromises the objectives of the green movement. Similar tensions exist within the British Green party between so-called *"spikies"* (modernisers) and *"fluffies"* (idealists).

Whilst students need to be fully aware of the terminology of shades within the green movement, there are even more categories to consider within the ecocentric school of thought. All the following could be classified as dark greens, although to paraphrase George Orwell's classic 'Animal Farm' some are **darker than others**. To expand our knowledge we need to begin with the term **social ecology**. This term was developed by the celebrated figure Murray Bookchin during the 1960s and 70s. He argued that ecological problems are based upon ingrained social problems, namely the hierarchal nature of society and the political system. Such problems can only be resolved if we recognise that they are deep-seated and require a complete overhaul of society and the economy. Social ecology is therefore based on the notion that a natural harmony should exist between humankind and nature. What is widely conceived of as society operates according to ecological principles. Within the branch of social ecology, there are three perspectives to be aware of (eco-socialism, eco-anarchism and eco-feminism). Each ideological standpoint identifies the *source* of environmental destruction differently, as does their prescribed *solution* to the problem.

	Source of the problem	Solution	Key figures
Eco-socialism	Capitalism	Social justice	Gorz, Bahro
Eco-feminism	Patriarchy	Empower females	Biehl, Daly
Eco-anarchism	The State	Abolish the state	Bookchin

For **eco-socialists** such as André Gorz (1991) and Rudolph Bahro (1984), environmental problems are the product of capitalism. The never-ending desire for profit, the prevalence of consumerism and the prioritisation of economic growth over social justice means that environmental destruction and capitalism are axiomatic. Free-market capitalism is characterised by exploitation not just of the proletariat but also the environment. In an era of globalisation, multi-national companies wield enormous economic power and act in an entirely unaccountable manner. To exacerbate the problem governments are either unwilling or (in the case of less developed countries) powerless to ensure that MNCs abide by environmental laws. In terms of resolving the problem, eco-socialists argue that we must address the environmental crisis *before* the class struggle. In other words, 'green' issues must come before 'red' issues. However, by addressing environmental concerns we can at the same time advance the cause of social justice. For instance, Gorz favours a guaranteed wage funded by indirect taxation which would have no effect upon the balance of competitiveness between companies. Eco-socialists have been labeled *"watermelons"* because they are 'green' on the outside and 'red' on the inside.

For **eco-feminists** such as Janet Biehl (1991) and Mary Daly (1979), the source of the problem is patriarchy. The dominance of men over women has led to environmental destruction on a massive and life-threatening scale. Eco-feminists claim that the relationship between women and nature itself is of political importance, and the solution to the environmental damage being done by the patriarchal structure of society is to empower females. This broadly essentialist argument implies that women are closer to mother Earth and the rhythms of nature itself. Therefore, women are far more suitable to the task of protecting the environment than men. Eco-feminism has also taken on an anti-colonial character. For instance, the Indian writer Vandana Shiva argues that the exportation of Western notions of development to non-western countries is underpinned by the assumption that there is only one path towards modernity and progress. For Shiva, this is a modern-day reflection of colonialism. There is also a patriarchal connotation to such views, regulating the role of females to the margins. Female labour is therefore rendered invisible and dismissed as unprofitable in the global capitalist order, despite the fact that women are the primary food producers and processors in the global economy. Furthermore, the celebration of profit over life itself is a reflection of a male-dominated world.

For **eco-anarchists** such as Murray Bookchin (1975), the source of environmental problems is the state itself. Only via the abolition of the state can the planet be saved from total destruction. For them, there is an obvious symbiosis between the desire to rid ourselves of the state and the need to save the planet from environmental catastrophe. The solution to environmental problems is therefore communal living along the lines of a direct democracy. This entails a form of de-centralisation in which the state would disappear. Bookchin also claims that capitalism leads to the commodification of the environment. Furthermore, he is critical of the excessive faith placed in the hands of the proletariat amongst orthodox Marxists. Instead, Bookchin believes that those at the margins of society – such as students, artists, women, etc. – have the greatest potential to engage in a liberation movement. Any ideological movement concerned with the overhaul of society must therefore recognise that fact and move on from narrow class-based concerns. The eco-anarchist approach of Bookchin and others has been criticised by other strands of green thought for leading to a destabilised world in which environmental destruction would be exacerbated. Indeed, for many within the green movement state regulation is an absolute necessity in order to prevent environmental destruction.

Each of the three strands of social ecology offers something distinct, but there is of course one observation common to all. Each perspective believes that the root cause of the problem is a form of *domination* – either in terms of social class (eco-socialism), gender (eco-feminism) or the existence of the state (eco-anarchism). Of all the three strands of social ecology we have considered, it is eco-socialism that has contributed the most to the bourgeoning alter-globalisation movement in contemporary politics. In contrast, eco-conservatism is not a form of social ecology, and neither is eco-fascism. Both these strands of thought can be classed as romanticist in outlook, although beyond this observation they have little else in common. **Eco-conservatism** emerged as a reaction to industrialised notions of 'progress' and 'development.' Conservative concepts of tradition and continuity with the past find an obvious home within the green movement. Each generation holds the Earth in trust and cannot appropriate the environment without violating their duty to the next generation. We must therefore conserve the planet for others. The Burkean concept of society as a contract between the generations is easily applicable to concern for the environment (where society is a *"partnership not only between those who are living, but between those who are living, those who are dead, and those who are to be born. Each contract of each particular state is but a clause in the great primeval contract of eternal society"*).

Further to the authoritarian-right of the political spectrum, a form of fascist ecologism emerged from the work of Walter Darré. The 'back to the land' movement which centered upon a romanticised ideal of the rural way of life in Germany was a key component of the appeal of Nazism. Neither eco-conservatism nor **eco-fascism** could be said to be influential elements within the green movement. However, students do need to be aware of them to complete their knowledge of the multitude of strands within this particular ideology. So whilst ecologism is often associated with the left, it does have a degree of overlap with right-wing ideologies.

Amongst the various perspectives taken within ecologism, the terminology of shades is once again employed to describe a person's commitment (or lack of) to the principles of the green movement. The two terms used are **shallow**

ecologists and **deep ecologists**. However, the term shallow ecologist is widely used in a prerogative sense by deep ecologists. A more neutral description would be the term humanist ecologists. This is because they claim to employ the lessons of ecology for the benefit of humankind. Humanist ecologists therefore attempt to harness the lessons of ecology to satisfy the needs of humanity. This moderate strand of ecologism is associated with values such as conservation and sustainability. It is important to note that humanist ecologists therefore reach anthropocentric ends based upon the principles of ecologism. In contrast, deep ecologists take a much more fundamentalist approach. They argue that the moderate route employed by what they see as shallow ecologists ultimately undermines ecologism.

As one can see, the green movement offers by far the most numerous categories of any political ideology. However, one needs to recognise that the most important definition is that between anthropocentricism and ecocentricism. From this basic distinction, all other sub-theories can be ascertained. The terminology of shades can also assist our study, and students should be aware of how ecology overlaps with other well-established ideologies (such as socialism, feminism, anarchism, conservatism and fascism).

The role of the state

The division between anthropocentricism and ecocentricism is an illuminating one when considering the role of the state within the green movement. Consistent with anthropocentricism, the state has an important role to play in terms of protecting the environment and addressing the problem of climate change. It is also one of the main sources of environmental destruction, but crucially there is a belief that human beings are rational enough to change the direction of government policy and thereby prevent complete environmental meltdown. So-called light greens firmly believe that liberal democracy provides the best means by which to influence the role of the state and thereby secure the political objectives of the green movement. This is very much a **mainstream** position within the political process, and is probably the more effective for it.

Dark greens take a slightly different stance. Agents of the state act as a barrier towards the fulfilment of environmentalist objectives because it provides a means by which the most powerful agents within society, principally big business and governments, can exploit the environment. The consensus-minded approach of so-called light greens will do nothing to address the root cause of the problem. As such, deep ecologists do not place a high priority on the role of the state, believing that the answers lie in a more philosophical / empirical approach. For deep ecologists such as Lovelock and Naess, advocating a role for the state is a reflection of anthropocentric assumptions. Having said this, the various branches of social ecology all offer a critique of the state. Most obviously, eco-anarchism stipulates that the source of climate change is the state itself. Eco-feminists believe that the state perpetuates the patriarchal structure of society, and it is patriarchy that is the source of environmental problems. Eco-socialism stipulates that the state implements an agenda favourable to powerful capitalist forces. The role of the state under capitalism is both exploitative of the environment and the proletariat. Those resources on which we all depend should be distributed according to the collective needs of society. Importantly, the role of the state under a reordered society is very different according to which element of social ecology we might consider.

Eco-anarchism is firmly opposed to any notion of hierarchy and advocates the abolition of the state. This objective is consistent with all aspects of anarchist thought. Eco-feminists believe that the state can facilitate a world based upon the emancipation of women. Notions of women's liberation and sexual equality can be secured via mobilising the various agents of the state. For eco-socialists, the economic system needs to be overhauled from capitalism towards one based upon a planned economy. The state must regulate all those activities that in some way impact upon the ecosystem. The environment is inexorably linked to the issue of social justice, and in no sense should we leave these important issues solely to market forces. In order to achieve an eco-socialist scenario, a strong role for the state seems inevitable. The eco-socialist line of argument has been reinforced by the 2006 Stern report, which called climate change the *"biggest market failure of all."* The recommendations of the Stern report would, if implemented, represent a major expansion in the role of the state over environmental issues. The report claims that the state needs to regulate to an adequate and effective level in order to prevent the destruction of the environment.

Ecologism and equality

In terms of equality and ecologism one needs to consider the relationship between human beings and other animals. For those who take an anthropocentric position, the entire basis of their approach to environmental issues is grounded upon a **humanist** outlook. The anthropocentric approach strongly refutes the ecocentric claim that humans and other living things are equal. Humans are *not* equal to other living things. We are clearly unique within the animal kingdom and the natural world, and we alone have the power and capability to save the planet. Only from anthropocentric assumptions can we ever hope to deal with climate change.

Ecocentricism takes a more holistic and **philosophical** outlook. Human beings are wrong to believe that they lie at the centre of the universe. This flawed assumption has been a key part of the problem, and only by removing ourselves from such anthropocentric assumptions can we ever hope to reverse the destruction of the planet. The ecocentric position stipulates that all living things are interdependent within the ecosphere. This view is articulated by the Gaia hypothesis of James Lovelock (2009) and the web of life argument offered by Fritjof Capra (1997). The ecocentric position claims that the relationship between humans and other elements of the ecosphere should be based upon equality. Human beings are part of a wider ecosystem and are in no sense morally superior to any other element of the ecosphere.

This fundamental distinction between the anthropocentric and ecocentric position encapsulates the various sub-theories and perspectives within the green movement as a whole. Students should also be aware that equality does not play the same role within ecologism as it does within other reformist / revolutionary ideologies such as socialism or feminism. Although equality holds a certain level of importance within eco-socialism and eco-feminism; it does not play the same defining role it does within socialism and (to a lesser extent) feminism. Strands of ecologism that overlap with right-wing ideologies (such as eco-conservatism and eco-fascism) do not endorse the concept of equality.

The relationship between ecologism and liberal democracy

The method by which change can be achieved within a liberal democracy deeply divides the green movement. Those closer to the centre of the political spectrum believe that liberal democracy is sufficiently pluralist and open to influence that the objectives of the green movement *can* be met. **Constructive engagement** with the political process is the best means available to protect and preserve the environment. There is absolutely no contradiction between working the system *and* being committed to the principles of the green movement. This mainstream approach is exemplified by the Green party and environmental pressure groups with insider status. Placing practicality over philosophical concerns enables the green movement to change government policy, shape the political agenda and even modify the behaviour of firms and individuals. Most Green parties are located on the left of the political spectrum and have tended to form coalitions with centre-left parties, most notably in the case of Germany. In the UK, the Green party signed a policy agreement with the Scottish Nationalists back in 2007 to support the minority administration. The SNP is of course a nationalist party but it is also a centre-left party, which once again suggests that Green parties tend to be left-ish in their outlook. It is also the case that Green parties are part of the left-wing group within the European Parliament.

Insider pressure groups such as Friends of the Earth and Greenpeace exemplify the moderate approach within the green movement. They operate on the basis of mainstream politics and they are all the more successful because of that. In contrast, outsider pressure groups such as Earth First! and the Earth Liberation Front set out to force change upon what they see as an unaccountable capitalist elite intent on destroying the Earth. Some outsider pressure groups go further and claim that political violence is justified given the gravity of the situation and the lack of an adequate response from politicians and major companies. The undemocratic character of such extremist groups represents a complete rejection of the core tenants of liberal democracy. In their defence, outsider groups believe that powerful forces will *always* dominate the political process. Whilst liberal democracy 'may' be pluralist in character, all too often those with power manage to dominate decision-makers and effectively dictate policy. Furthermore, the opportunity for radical change is effectively closed off because of the influence of powerful forces; especially those of big business.

There are several illustrations of what might be called **eco-terrorism** amongst outsider groups where direct action is employed in order to advance their cause. Such behaviour invariably gains media attention, and yet it is a truism of politics that those who make the most noise have the least influence. In contrast, insider pressure groups tend to have an effective lobbying strategy. It would seem evident that the only real source of influence derives from being firmly on the inside of the political process. Industrial sabotage and monkey wrenching may gain media headlines, but such actions may actually lose public sympathy for the green movement as a whole.

For those in the green movement grounded upon ecocentric assumptions, the pluralist character of liberal democracy will always represent an Aristotle-based view of *"politics as the art of compromise."* Engagement with the conventional political process cannot deliver the fundamental objectives of the green movement. So-called **grey parties** will never implement the demands of ecologists because they profligate the false view that no limits should be placed upon economic growth. Indeed without economic growth, political parties could not deliver their manifesto pledges. Yet in contrast, ecologists believe that we must free ourselves from any concern over the level of economic growth. Zero growth is the way to go, advocacy of which seems highly improbable within a liberal democratic system.

For so-called dark greens, the problem with liberal democracy is that politicians and political parties can only gain power if they persuade enough people to vote for them. To achieve this, a variety of unpleasant facts of life may be hidden away or simply embellished with 'spin.' One must also consider the motivations of the electorate itself. When confronted by the secrecy and anonymity of the ballot box it is unlikely that enough people would be prepared to vote for a party proposing such a radical change to our way of life. Does the electorate have the appetite for massive changes in taxation, regulation, consumer behaviour and economics that dark greens wish to implement in order to prevent global catastrophe? Given the magnitude of the catastrophe facing the environment, liberal democracy is therefore seen as a wholly inappropriate means by which to save the planet. In order for a politician / political party to resolve the environmental crisis they would have to campaign on a very radical and probably unpopular manifesto, and that surely prevents them from ever gaining power? So whereas so-called light greens believe that the responsiveness of liberal democracy to people's wishes and concerns offers the means by which to secure the objectives of the green movement, dark greens believe that this 'responsiveness' to the electoral process is a fundamental barrier towards meaningful change.

Deep ecologism also offers a **critique of free-market capitalism**. Albeit not in the same context as socialism, ecologism states that the process of globalisation must be profoundly altered in order to avert the continued destruction of the environment. According to the Living Planet Report (2008) more than three-quarters of the world's population live in countries where consumption levels outstrip environmental renewal, and in terms of food, around a quarter of European and North American adults are obese and another third are overweight – with the majority of Westerners predicted to be overweight or obese in the next 20 years (Naish, 2008, p.54). On the basis of such evidence, the entire basis of our culture must change - particularly in relation to economic growth and how we use natural resources. First and foremost, the Earth's resources are finite and we all must recognise that. This view is encapsulated in the concept of *"Spaceship Earth."* Just as a Spaceship will eventually run out of resources, so too with planet Earth, and in the words of Marshall McLuhan *"there are no passengers on Spaceship Earth. We are all crew."*

Secondly, capitalism's reliance upon exploiting environmental resources is a source of military **conflict** throughout the world. To back up this point, it could be argued that many of the wars and conflicts within international relations are related to the acquisition of valuable resources such as oil. Take the case of the Middle East, an area of the world rich in oil *and* a hotbed of conflict. Whilst such conflicts may be understood on the lines of religious differences, the real reason could be the acquisition of oil fields. This line of argument was given further impetus by a report published in August 2006 predicting that the middle of the next decade could see widespread civil unrest over a shortage of clean water. Furthermore, the International Water Management Institute confirmed that global demand for water will double by the year 2025. If this line of thought proves accurate, future conflicts may be fuelled by control of fresh water supplies and access to fertile land. Following on from this argument, the influential biologist James Lovelock (2009) has warned that *"our gravest dangers are not from climate change itself, but indirectly from starvation* [and] *competition for scarce resources."*

Ecologists have also offered new ways of conceptualising capitalism (which is a core component of liberal democracy). As an academic discipline, Economics is based upon the assumption that humans are self-serving utility maximisers and our behaviour can therefore be understood on a rational basis. Ecologism however challenges this assumption. The most notable example of this point derives from the German ecologist Ernst Schumacher (1911-1977) and his best-selling book *Small is Beautiful : A study of Economics as if people mattered* (1973). Schumacher developed the principles of **Buddhist economics** in order to show that assumptions about rationality are anthropocentric and therefore flawed. Schumacher argued that human beings regard energy as income that can be topped-up periodically, as opposed to addressing the fact that energy is a finite resource that we must all live off. As a consequence, humankind has engaged in the wanton destruction of the planet. Schumacher also argued that the utilitarian notion that greater consumption equates to greater happiness is fundamentally wrong. From the eastern perspective he celebrates, the lifestyle of the affluent consumer is shallow and doomed, whereas Buddhist economics is based on the idea of *"right livelihood."* The contribution offered by the American biologist Garrett Hardin (1968) in his celebrated *"tragedy of the commons"* article also illustrates the ecologist argument that rational behaviour can have entirely **irrational outcomes**. Furthermore, the eco-socialist André Gorz (1991) criticises *"the domination of economic rationality embodied in capitalism* [and] *the domination of political thinking by economics."*

The ecologist stance on lifestyle issues

One of the main contributions to ideological debate from ecologism concerns the subject of lifestyle issues. Throughout the green movement there is a belief that we must all adopt a more **environmentally-conscious lifestyle**, although the extent to which we need to change our behaviour differs significantly. In order to assess the various standpoints within the green movement, it is useful to employ the terminology of shading. Light greens seek no more than a modest change in our lifestyles. They advocate a series of achievable and practical measures designed to protect and preserve the environment. Take the case of reducing our carbon footprint. This can be achieved via schemes such as carbon offsetting, recycling programmes, greater use of public transport and so on. Giving up meat is another example to consider. Indeed, it has often been argued that *"you cannot eat meat and call yourself an environmentalist."* Such changes are very much in keeping with their anthropocentric world-view.

Dark greens, however, advocate an entire reappraisal of what it means to be human and of our place within the ecosphere. They take a more spiritual and philosophical approach that inevitably derives from their ecocentric assumptions. First and foremost, ecologists believe that it is incredibly **arrogant** of humans to place themselves at the centre of the environment. It is equally arrogant to think that human beings can ever really understand the consequences of their actions, especially in the long-term. The effects of technological change and consumerist behaviour may not reveal themselves until generations later. We should therefore fundamentally alter the course of what is conventionally understood to be human 'progress.' We must overturn industrialisation, liberate ourselves from our reliance upon a consumerist lifestyle, reverse the entire basis of globalisation and re-order the focus of everyday life. Of all these points, the ecologist stance on consumerism is of most importance in relation to lifestyle issues.

The core of the ecologist argument is that materialism has proved itself **incapable** of providing for our needs and desires. Whilst market forces of supply and demand can satisfy many of our material wants, consumerist activity represents merely a small part of who we really are. In a *post*-material world the various issues surrounding our quality of life become ever more important, particularly as our income increases. Once our material needs have been satisfied people search for the acquisition of other goals, such as **spiritual enlightenment**. The proper response to this trajectory of progress is self-actualisation, the idea that personal fulfilment can be gained by the refinement of sensibilities. We must transcend the egoism and materialism of our consumerist society and thereby move *beyond* materialism. The influential Norwegian writer Arne Naess (1973) suggests that self-realisation can be reached via a philosophical attachment and identification with others. This mystical approach is most commonly identified with the Buddhist religion. Naess also claims that there is no *"I"* separate from the environment. To distance ourselves from the natural world is therefore to cut ourselves off from an integral part of who we are. From a similar line of thought, the psychologist

Eric Fromm (1900-1980) developed a form of holistic individualism in which we achieve a higher stage of enlightenment via the experience of being (1979, 1984). In doing so we derive satisfaction from experience and sharing, resulting in personal growth and spiritual awareness. The purpose of life is therefore *to be*, not *to have*! In contrast, a mindset centred upon consumerism and materialism cannot elevate the human spirit. The inevitable consequence of a consumerist society driven by material desires is resource depletion and the continued alienation of human beings from the ecosystem. Postmaterialism is a vital element of the ecologist stance on lifestyle issues. Often associated with the anti-capitalist message of the left, postmaterialism also reflects the eco-conservative notion that society needs to be held together by something more meaningful than simply the consumption of material goods and services.

On the vexed issue of how we live our lives, ecologism asks deep philosophical questions for us all to consider. Ecologism requires us to re-examine and radically alter the way we think about ourselves and our place within the natural world. The ecologist strategy would entail a fundamental and irreversible change to our entire way of life, which naturally raises vital questions. Will we recognise our failings and change our lifestyle? Will we give up economic growth? Will we reject the manifold conveniences of our consumerist lifestyle? These questions sit at the very core of the ecologist stance on lifestyle issues.

As one can clearly see, the manner in which we should lead our lives divides the green movement. Deep ecologists claim that so-called light greens are merely tinkering with a system on the precipice of a global catastrophe which threatens every living thing within the ecosphere. Those human activities that foster materialism, industrialisation and state activity have contaminated Gaia. We should therefore reject anthropocentric-based issues such as the achievement of economic growth in order to acquire a more spiritual and philosophical plane. Self-actualisation, rather than the acquisition of material goods, should be our guiding principle. The emphasis of human activity should focus upon the sustainability of the planet. Anything less will inevitably exacerbate the deforestation and desertification of the planet. In doing so, we should transform our own consciousness in order to live in harmony with the planet. This philosophical approach to lifestyle issues completely rejects the anthropocentric assumptions of so-called light greens and for that matter all other ideologies considered thus far. In essence, the dark green approach to lifestyle issues is more of **a state of mind** than a branch of political ideology. From the perspective of light greens, the ecologist approach has been criticised because it will prove incredibly difficult for people to simply give up their comfortable lifestyles. The overwhelming majority become used to the convenience and ease of modern life, and it is unlikely that such an ingrained way of life will disappear overnight. The green movement should therefore concentrate upon more achievable and practical measures.

Change or the status quo

As with all ideologies implacably committed to a complete overhaul of the existing order, it is far easier to state what ecologism is opposed to than to generalise as to how it proposes to change the existing system. All of those within the green movement believe that we must change our ways in order to prevent the destruction of the planet. On that point, there is unanimity. Predictably, divisions emerge over *how* to achieve change, and as with other ideologies that aim to overhaul the status quo (such as socialism, anarchism and feminism), these internal divisions provide much of the ideological ferment derived from the green movement. However, it is also important for students to recognise that certain questions relevant to the issue of change do not fall neatly into the categorisation of ecocentricism and anthropocentricism. **Nuclear energy** is a good illustration of this point. Despite being the one of most prominent theorists amongst deep ecologists, James Lovelock describes nuclear energy as the cost-effective way to reduce the emission of carbon dioxide. He also dismisses opposition to nuclear energy as *"irrational."* Lovelock's views on nuclear energy are very much outside the mainstream of deep ecology.

In order to provide a more accurate picture of the divisions between the two main branches of green thought it is appropriate to employ the distinction between **gradual reform** and **radical change**. The more moderate stance is exemplified by the anthropocentric branch of green thought. What lies at the core of this approach is the assumption that the self-interest of human beings and the protection of the environment are mutually reinforcing. Protecting the environment is to our benefit, and human beings are rational enough to recognise this and act accordingly. There is considerable evidence to back up this assumption due to an increasing awareness of green issues, particularly amongst the younger generation.

This gradualist approach holds faith in a form of *"green capitalism"* – a point also endorsed by eco-conservatives. As the most responsive economic system available, capitalism will always reflect the wants and needs of consumers. Firms therefore have a rational interest in meeting consumer demands, and with the rise in ethical shopping, many businesses have already adapted to such concerns. Even supermarkets now sell reusable bags and fair trade products. The increasing number of recycling schemes is another case in point, as too is the emergence of corporate social responsibility, with firms striving to demonstrate their 'green' credentials. Furthermore the widespread availability of information on such matters facilitates a more informed consumer and a more responsive approach from companies. Schemes ranging from carbon offsetting, energy-conservation programmes and alliances formed with environmental pressure groups demonstrate the ability of capitalism to facilitate the core objectives of the green movement. To further support this argument one only has to contrast the environmental disasters of planned economies; all of whom were denied the signalling nature of the price mechanism. [22]

According to the reformist strand of green thinking, effective change can only be achieved via engagement with the conventional political process. The pluralist character of liberal democracy provides the best opportunity for the green movement to secure its aims. Typical of this viewpoint is the argument put forward by the former leader of the Green party Jonathon Porritt (2007), who claims that liberal democracy is sufficiently responsive to consumer demand to address the manifest problems which face the environment. He is also supportive of state intervention because he believes that governments can and will respond to public concern over environmental damage and will therefore change policy accordingly. This may occur via more stringent controls on pollution, reordering the basis of taxation away from income and expenditure towards the impact upon the environment and long-term investment in the development of renewable energy resources. Porritt's argument is a clear illustration of how the green movement can work within the existing political and economic structure in order to preserve the environment. Jonathon Porritt also argues that there are simply too many of us for the Earth to sustain human life, and as such the maximum size for families should be set at two in order to limit our carbon footprint. However, it is difficult to see *how* such a policy could be enforced without a form of **green authoritarianism**. Brutal dictators such as Adolf Hitler and Chairman Mao have tried to manipulate population levels, and Porritt's recommendations may instigate something of a public backlash against green extremism (despite the fact that Porritt is a moderate within the green movement).

Light greens also believe that international co-operation amongst states and organisations can facilitate the goals of the green movement. A clear illustration of this point is the European Union, which has over time proved a beneficial forum for tackling environmental problems. The reliance upon

---

[22] To dark greens, such optimism in the ability of business to serve the interests of the environment is deeply flawed. The profit motive has bought widespread destruction to the planet's resources, and our continued reliance upon economic growth has been a major source of the problem.

supranational institutions has facilitated a much more 'green' approach to such matters than might otherwise have been the case; particularly in the United Kingdom. As environmental problems do not respect national borders, member states undoubtedly share a common interest in pooling sovereignty to tackle cross-border issues. The EU's environment policy dates back to 1972 and has established itself as one of the most active arenas of European integration. The EU is required to incorporate *"the protection of the environment"* and the principle of *"sustainable development"* into all relevant legislation. Member states must also meet environmental targets set by the Commission and implement decisions made by the EP. If they fail to do so, they may be prosecuted by the European Court of Justice. To light greens, the EU's role over the environment transcends the sovereignty of the nation-state and is consistent with the aims and values of the green movement. Having said this, the Green party of the UK is opposed to further European integration. The Green party favours the abolition of the Common Agricultural Policy (CAP) and other protectionist measures that work against fair trade. Furthermore, the CAP is wasteful in terms of agricultural resources – a point that has a welcome audience within British politics.

For deep ecologists, effective change requires a complete transformation in **human consciousness**. The task for human beings is to liberate ourselves from a debilitating dependency on the ease of consumer life and thereby exist in harmony with the natural environment. We should return to a more primitive / natural way of life; one that existed *before* the onset of industrialism. Within such a world the pace of life would be considerably slower, a form of localised barter would operate and people would be closer to nature. Perhaps the best illustration of this point would be the lifestyle adopted by the indigenous cultures of the Maoris, Aborigines and Navaho Indians. Most importantly of all, philosophical issues would replace consumerist concerns. On the inter-related subject of economic growth, dark greens believe the solution to climate change is zero growth. Dark greens represent a romanticist trait within the green movement derived from a holistic view of the ecosphere. Ecologists firmly believe that human nature can only be understood by fully recognising our place within the ecosphere and changing our behaviour via a philosophical attitude. Our quality of life can *only* be improved by consuming less and approaching life from the ecological perspective, thereby refining our perceived needs and desires in response to thoughtful reflection.

Within the main elements of social ecology, eco-anarchism offers the most radical and far-reaching solution to the problem of climate change. The guiding principle of eco-anarchism is absolute individualism. Not surprisingly, this approach is rejected by others within the green movement who view the abolition of the state as undesirable. Further to the left of the political spectrum, eco-socialists advocate the virtues of common ownership and accept the need to regulate that activity which impacts upon the natural environment. However, the significant damage wrought upon the environment by the planned economies of the Communist bloc does tend to undermine the eco-socialist argument. Denied the benefits of either a price mechanism or the political elements of a liberal democracy, Communist regimes contributed significantly to environmental damage. Finally, eco-feminists have been criticised by other strands of social ecology for ignoring the true cause of the problem (be it capitalism *or* the existence of the state).

Following on from the previous point, both the anthropocentric and ecocentric positions have been subject to widespread criticism. Within an ideological movement so deeply concerned with changing the status quo, this is perhaps to be expected. The 'light green' assumption that mainstream politics provides an opportunity for the green movement to secure its objectives could be viewed as somewhat naïve. It is already the case that green issues are increasingly subject to opportunism from mainstream politicians striving to rebrand their party's image. All too often, the 'green' policies offered by the main parties and mainstream politicians are subject to political expediency. There is also a staggering degree of hypocrisy amongst many of those politicians who profess their green credentials. In an age of videoconferencing it is somewhat revealing that politicians such as Al Gore (2006) fly thousands and thousands of miles (thereby emitting considerable levels of carbon dioxide into the atmosphere) in order to secure that all-important photo opportunity. The light green approach has also been criticised by those on the left of the political spectrum due to its bias towards affluent consumers whose material needs have been largely met. In doing so, light greens have sidelined those who cannot afford to shop ethically or concern themselves with green issues. They ignore the fact that many people throughout the world are simply *"too poor to be green."*

It is also unclear exactly *how* the public's concern for the environment might be translated into effective action from governments throughout the world. Those governments would have to place heavy restrictions upon our present lifestyle, a feat extremely difficult to achieve within the parameters of a liberal democracy. Surely it is naïve to think that politicians and political parties will place long-term interests ahead of short-term electoral considerations? Moreover, it will require international action on a scale never attempted before. Concepts such as national sovereignty would have to be pushed aside for the greater good, which again looks highly improbable. Another difficulty posed by conventional engagement with the political process is how to implement international agreements. This issue is further exacerbated by the desperate need for international co-ordination in order to deal with a problem that is trans-national in character and content. In addition, there are perhaps deeper problems to consider in terms of relationship between the developed world and the emerging economies. It is somewhat hypocritical of the West to tell India and China that they must change their behaviour when it is the West that has done so much to pollute the planet. These are serious issues to be addressed by those who take a reformist stance within the green movement.

The dark green perspective has also been subject to criticism. Leading ecologists such as Lovelock, Capra, Fromm and Naess all set a highly demanding ethic, a point not lost upon light greens. They claim that people simply do not wish to regress back to a pre-industrialised world. Practical action is the only effective route to take for the green movement. The pragmatic approach of the light greens enables a sustainable level of growth in which we all become wealthier, albeit at a slower pace to that which we are used to, without regressing back to a primitive state of being. Ultimately the more militant and extreme approach of the dark greens will prevent the progress of the green movement, whereas constructive engagement provides a practical and effective route for the green movement to secure its objectives. On this basis, light greens adopt an issues-based approach to change, which once again lies in stark contrast to the philosophical approach of the deep ecologists. As the Green party leader Caroline Lucas once argued; *"We've got to get better at painting a positive vision of a post-carbon word. This is not about sitting around a candle in a cave."*

Ecologism in contemporary politics

Few other ideologies have changed people's behaviour as much as the green movement; which is undoubtedly a reflection of its importance within contemporary politics. Ideas considered on the fringe of political debate merely a generation ago are now firmly established as part of the mainstream. Green issues also hold a high degree of salience within the alter-globalisation movement. Yet revealingly, the measure of the green movement's influence is in no sense reflected in the conventional political process. The Green party has no MPs, no peers in the Lords and only a small number of councillors. Nonetheless, the influence of environmental pressure groups is obvious. In the contemporary era, many of the most effective lobbyists derive from environmental pressure groups. The green lobby has successfully shaped the political agenda and influenced the decision-making process for many years. The idealism and amateurism of the 1960s and 1970s has given way to a more hard-headed and strategic approach to the political process since the 1980s with obvious political dividends. Today, no politician or political party within UK politics can afford to ignore the green lobby or green issues.

The second point to consider is that protecting the environment is very much an idea whose time has come. There is a momentum behind green issues like never before. The Chernobyl disaster of 1986, the Exxon oil-spill of 1989, the stifling European summer of 2003, the Asian Tsunami of 2005 and the 2009 droughts in Australia all illustrate the need for effective action in terms of protecting the natural environment. Not surprisingly, there has in recent years been a seismic change in people's attitudes. Whilst anthropocentric assumptions remain predominant, a growing number of people have adopted a more ecocentric position and modified their lifestyle. Environmental issues can also mobilise people into political action like few others. A combination of NIMBY-ism (Not In My Back Yard) and genuine concern for the environment is a powerful one. It even has an apolitical quality, which once again strengthens its impact within society. Politicians and political parties are also keen to court the green vote, and several government-backed schemes have successfully encouraged us to do more to protect and preserve the environment.

However, not everything is going in a green direction. Most of the opposition encountered by the green movement tends to derive from the right of the political spectrum (Lawson, 2008). More importantly, there is a significant fragmentation of thought within the green movement. Inevitably, such divergence debilitates the impact of the green movement. Moreover the trend within the green movement has been towards one of fragmentation as opposed to convergence, and at the time of writing, it seems improbable that a **common strategy** will forge together such a disparate movement. Another point to consider is the global financial crisis. It is debateable whether or not green issues will survive the credit crunch. Powerful politicians have much more pressing economic issues to consider, and yet there is an undoubted link between environmental issues and economic ones. Furthermore, a backlash against the alarmist language of ecologism cannot be ruled out, particularly if deep greens become tarnished in the public's eye with unrealistic and impractical solutions.

In summary, ecologism challenges the entire basis of conventional wisdom and thereby presents us with perhaps the most radical prescription of all. More than any other ideology, ecologism holds the promise of a **far-reaching paradigm shift** in the behaviour of human beings. It is a big ask, but the moment to act becomes ever more pressing. Most of us *are* prepared to do something, but how far will we go? More than any other ideology, the position of the green movement within contemporary politics is very much in *our* hands. We may be the first generation to experience the irreversible destruction of our planet. We may also be the generation that 'does something' about it …

Further quotes on ecologism

"The fruits of the earth belong to us all, and the earth itself belongs to nobody." Jean-Jacques Rousseau

"The word Greenpeace had a ring to it – it conjured images of Eden; it said ecology and antiwar in two syllabus; it fits easily into even a one-column headline." Robert Hunter

"The white race is the cancer of human history … which has upset the ecological balance of the planet, which now threatens the very existence of life itself." Susan Sontag

"We shall never achieve harmony with land, any more than we shall achieve absolute justice or liberty for people. In these higher aspirations, the important thing is not to achieve but to strive." Aldo Leopold

"The sun, the moon and the stars would have disappeared long ago … had they happened to be within the reach of predatory human hands." Havelock Ellis

"We abuse land because we regard it as a commodity belonging to us. When we see land as a community to which we belong, we may begin to use it with love and respect." Aldo Leopold

"Because we don't think about future generations, they will never forget us." Henrik Tikkanen

"Nature provides a free lunch, but only if we control our appetites." William Ruckelshaus

"Currently mankind is not at one with the harmonious flowings of life throughout the world and this is proving detrimental to all life on earth … Humans must realise that their species is not superior, we are all … dependent on each other for our survival and continued well being." Richard Milburn

"Modern technology … owes ecology … and apology." Alan Eddison

Recommended reading

Baxter, B. (2000) *Ecologism : An Introduction.* A solid introduction to the essential elements of ecologism.

Biehl, J. (1991) *Rethinking Ecofeminist politics.* An important contribution towards the theory of eco-feminism. Students should be aware that Biehl is more accessible that Daly (see next page).

Bookchin, M. (1975) *Our Synthetic environment.* A superb account of the need for a greener approach to the way we conduct our lives, Bookchin is an important figure within the green movement. He is widely regarded as the founder of social ecology and began his political life as a member of the Communist youth movement, but in his later work targeted much of his fire against left-wing groups.

Capra, F. (1997) *The Web of Life : A new synthesis of mind and matter.* Capra outlines his web of life argument to advocate an ecological path for human behaviour.

Daly, M. (1979) *Gyn/Ecology : The Meta-Ethics of Radical Feminism.* Daly offers a synergy of feminism and ecologism. Existing at the margins of ideological debate, Daly remains relevant towards an understanding of two separate ideologies.

Ehrenfeld, D. (1978) *The arrogance of Humanism.* Ehrenfeld sets out to destroy the arrogant assumptions of anthropocentric thought and, in doing so, restructure the debate around ecocentric principles.

Fromm, E. (1979) *To Have or To Be.* One of the clearest accounts of deep ecology, Fromm argues that we should concentrate upon the process of 'being' as opposed to defining our lives by what we do and what we purchase.

Gore, A. (2006) *An inconvenient truth.* A succinct introduction to the light green perspective. Gore is perhaps the best-known example of a contemporary politician who constructively engages with the political process to advance the cause of the green movement.

Gorz, A (1991) *Capitalism, socialism and ecology.* A left-wing critique of how capitalism destroys the environment.

Hardin, G. (1968) *"The Tragedy of the Commons"* in Science (Volume 162 p.1243-1248). A seminal work within the green movement, Hardin claims that a relationship exists between sharing collective resources and environmental destruction.

Lawson, N. (2008) *An appeal to reason : A cool look at global warming.* A critique of how environmentalists have put forward their message. Lawson takes a right-wing stance upon the issue of global warming and offers a firm rebuttal to the wilder claims of radical environmentalists.

Lovelock, J. (1979) *Gaia : A new look at life on Earth.* James Lovelock outlines his Gaia hypothesis. Lovelock is a key figure within the green movement and his main contribution remains his work on Gaia.

Lovelock, J. (2009) *The Vanishing face of Gaia.* A dire warning from Lovelock as to the revenge Gaia will unleash upon human beings. Lovelock believes that we are already too late and that Gaia is currently destroying that which presents a threat to her.

Milburn, R. (2008) *Savannah Memories.* A poignant account of how every living thing is connected together within the ecosphere and the need for harmony within it. I have the pleasure of saying that I taught Richard for three years.

Porritt, J. (2007) *Capitalism: As if the World Matters.* The clearest account of how a form of green capitalism facilitates the aims of environmentalists. Porritt is the principal exponent of the light green school of thought within British politics and his book is underpinned by an impassioned belief in the rationality of human behaviour.

Schumacher, E. (1973) *Small is Beautiful : A study of Economics as if people mattered.* An attempt to link spiritual concerns to real-life Economics. Schumacher's book is an excellent and succinct introduction to environmentalism.

Ideas for further discussion

To what extent does ecologism differ to all other political ideologies?
What is the ecologist stance on human nature?
What are the main strands of thought within the green movement?
What is the stance taken by ecologists over the role of the state?
In what sense do ecologists support equality?
What is the stance taken by ecologists over liberal democracy?
To what extent do ecologists advocate changes to our consumerist lifestyle?
To what extent do ecologists believe that the goals of the green movement can be achieved within the parameters of a liberal democracy?
How important is ecologism within contemporary politics?

Key terms

Anthropocentrism A world-view that places human beings at the centre of the Earth's biosphere. This view is associated with light greens who believe that human beings are custodians of the Earth's resources. Anthropocentrism is rejected by so-called dark greens, who take an ecocentric stance. It should be added that the Swiss geographer Edward Suess coined the term biosphere in 1875 for the geographical region of the Earth where life is found.

Ecocentricism A belief-system associated with the environmental movement that advocates an equal relationship between human beings and the environment. According to this view, humans are part of a wider whole with no particular elevated status amongst animals. Indeed, we have been the most destructive of all the animals on the planet. The savagery of humankind is truly staggering either in terms of war, pollution or the massively uneven distribution of resources that sees people die through lack of clean water whilst others live a life of unbridled material luxury. Such a misguided belief should be replaced by ecocentricism; where human beings recognise that they are merely part of a wider whole and not the centre of the natural world. The alternative to this perspective is called anthropocentricism.

Gaia hypothesis A view associated with the ecologists James Lovelock and Lynn Margulis, who claimed that life on Earth could be understood as a single living organism. This is an important element of deep green thought, although it is not shared by all environmentalists. Gaia was the Ancient Greek Goddess of the Earth. The hypothesis dates from the early 1970s and was at the time contrary to conventional wisdom.

Gaia theory A view of the Earth developed during the 1980s that sees it as a self-regulating system with one goal – the regulation of surface conditions so as always to be favourable for living organisms.

Spaceship Earth A concept associated with the ecologist movement. Just as a spaceship will eventually run out of fuel and other resources, so too will Planet Earth. We must therefore take greater care over how we use national resources, and amend our ways accordingly.

Sustainable development That level of development which does not exhaust the world's natural resources, or that country's own natural resources. The term has increased in salience due to widespread concerns over climate change.

CHAPTER 10
MULTICULTURALISM

Why multiculturalism?

It is in the nature of political discourse that a myriad of terms are contested in some manner, and in the context of multiculturalism contestability reaches new depths (or heights, depending on your perspective). There is considerable controversy over the applicability or otherwise of the term itself and of its subsequent position within the field of political ideology. To some, multiculturalism is a legitimate arena for ideological debate (Heywood, 2007, p.310), but this assessment is by no means shared by all. Indeed, some commentators within the field of political ideology do not devote a section of their work to multiculturalism (McNaughton, 2005; Adams, 2001). For the purposes of this book, multiculturalism will be treated as an area of interest to our enquiry. There are several reasons for this.

First and foremost, multiculturalism is an **increasingly important** feature of all our lives and is therefore worthy of closer examination. The process of **globalisation** has done more than any other related phenomenon to change the contours of ideological discourse and the context of contemporary politics. Love it or loathe it, globalisation is shaping the world like nothing else. It truly defines the zeitgeist of our times, and this trend looks set to increase rather than dissipate. More and more of us are shaped by globalisation in ways unimaginable just a few years ago. Increasingly, the ideological fault-line is no longer about traditional left-right divisions (such as equality) or libertarian v. authoritarian (such as the role of the state) but is increasingly focused upon the issue of globalisation. It is possible to identify **four** main categories here. There are those who are entirely supportive of globalisation (mostly liberals), those who support it but wish to ensure that the process is counterbalanced by the need for social order (conservatives), those who recognise its inevitability but wish to alter globalisation in some manner (those on the left of the political spectrum) and those who oppose globalisation outright (such as fascists and religious fundamentalists). As we have already considered, all other ideologies are affected to a greater or lesser degree by globalisation. In the context of multiculturalism, the influence of globalisation is of immense significance.

Globalisation and multiculturalism are **axiomatic**. We live in a global village inter-connected to an increasingly significant extent. The process of globalisation has made the world smaller, both in the speed of travel and in people's minds; and some academics have even speculated that we will reach the *"death of distance."* The inevitable product of an increasingly globalised world is the speed and extent to which ideas, capital and people - especially labour – are transported throughout the globe. In light of this, multiculturalism is a key element of political ideology within the contemporary era. What happens in one country increasingly impacts upon others, and contemporary political issues tend to be trans-national in character. Our identity is also being shaped by the process of globalisation, a development that multiculturalism aims to conceptualise and offer prescriptive remedies to. Furthermore, the needs of global capital are increasingly met by a flexible labour force prepared to move major distances in order to fill job vacancies or simply gain a higher wage.

Although the history of multiculturalism is lengthy, the term itself is a relatively recent addition to the political lexicon. Whereas Ancient Babylon was an early illustration of enforced multiculturalism, the term itself was first used in Canada to describe a distinctive approach to addressing the issue of cultural diversity. Today, most societies have adapted multiculturalism in both its prescriptive and descriptive sense. As an obvious consequence, the very term multiculturalism is used increasingly within political discourse and is shaping the context and character of how we understand politics and society itself. Having said this, it is important to note from the outset that multiculturalism is in part a reflection of the **predominance of liberal values within the political process**. It is also bound up with the process of globalisation. The salience of multiculturalism should therefore be placed alongside the wider debate over globalisation and the 'victory' of liberalism over rival ideologies – a point we will consider in the next Chapter on the *"end of ideology"* thesis (Fukayama, 1992). But for now, there is a need to define exactly what the term multiculturalism actually means.

What exactly is multiculturalism?

The term multiculturalism escapes a simple definition. Even Tony Blair admitted that he did not really understand what the term actually means. Nonetheless, there are a few initial steps we can take to identify the true meaning of the term. To begin with, multiculturalism can be used in both a **descriptive** sense and a **prescriptive** sense. In terms of the former, multiculturalism describes the growing diversity and multiple identities that have come to characterise the era in which we live. Multiculturalism is therefore used to identify those societies that encourage and foster a positive view of the concept itself. The context of that benefit ranges from purely economics to the more contested notion of cultural diversity, but what remains constant is the promotion of multiculturalism itself. A vibrant society is one characterised by an active celebration of many diverse cultures. The homogeneity of a monoculture is rejected in favour of diversity. Embedded within this positive endorsement of multiculturalism are various liberal concepts such as tolerance, pluralism and the protection of minority rights from the tyranny of the majority. The normative element of multiculturalism can be understood as one at ease with the rich tapestry of human life and the desire amongst people to express their own identity in the manner they see fit.

The prescriptive sense of the term relates to those political parties and movements who wish to **advance** what they perceive to be the merits of multiculturalism. Such parties and movements tend to be essentially liberal in character with a desire to champion diversity within society. There is a sharp contrast to be made here between such parties / movements and those who take a very different perspective. As we will consider later, opposition tends to derive from the right of the political spectrum – especially far right parties that campaign on an anti-immigration and anti-globalisation platform. [23]

The main strands of multiculturalism

Within multiculturalism itself, there are **three** strands that students need to be aware of. The most dominant of those strands is **liberal multiculturalism**. We live in an era that firmly reflects liberal values, and it should hardly surprise the reader to discover that liberal multiculturalism is the predominant

---

[23]   Within everyday political discourse, it can be difficult to properly identify one from another. Nonetheless, it is useful to keep in mind that many political concepts and ideas are used in both a descriptive and prescriptive context (e.g. liberal, left-wing, feminist, etc.). It is also revealing to note that the prescriptive sense of the term is less in evidence than the descriptive meaning of the term.

	Liberal multiculturalism	Pluralist multiculturalism	Cosmopolitan multiculturalism
Core elements	Cannot tolerate illiberal actions, moral neutrality and hyphenated nationality	Toleration of all cultures, all cultures have equal worth and a live and let live attitude to multiculturalism	Pick and mix approach in which we have multiple identities. Recognition of a global consciousness and a melting pot
Issue of diversity	Diversity should have a private face	Diversity should have a public face	Deep commitment to diversity
Prescriptive view of citizenship	Universal citizenship	Differentiated citizenship	Global citizenship

strand of multiculturalism. This is of course an observation equally applicable to the liberal strands of feminism and nationalism. None of the other strands (pluralist multiculturalism and cosmopolitan multiculturalism) come close to challenging the pre-eminence of liberal multiculturalism. What divides the three strands is less to do with core elements and more to do with their attitude towards diversity. Furthermore, each offers a different conception of civic cohesion and thereby their prescribed view of citizenship. Whereas liberal multiculturalists argue in favour of universal citizenship, pluralist multiculturalists prefer a type of differentiated citizenship. In contrast, cosmopolitan multiculturalists stipulate a form of global citizenship.

As with all things liberal, liberal multiculturalism is based upon a firm belief in **toleration and diversity**. As a consequence, adherents claim that we should adopt a degree of moral neutrality in a prescriptive sense. It is not the job of 'society' or any other group (including decision-makers) to restrict those rights and activities associated with various cultural / ethnic groups. We must therefore facilitate a wide remit of liberty, even if this includes activities that run counter to the wider norms of society. Having said this, it is important for students to recognise that toleration is only applied to those cultures and groups that are themselves tolerant of others. Liberal multiculturalism therefore sets a crucial boundary upon toleration within society. Such distinctions are important in both a political and legal sense. The issue of society is another important aspect of liberal multiculturalism. In striving to avoid social disintegration, liberal multiculturalists seek to divorce the private realm from the public. The natural consequence of this stance is a form of **hyphenated nationality** (e.g. Afro-Caribbean, Irish American, British Asian, etc.). One of the leading exponents of this approach to multiculturalism has been the United States, although the United Kingdom has in recent years also followed this trend. Moreover, the increased salience of hyphenated nationality amongst social scientists also suggests a growing acceptance of liberal multiculturalism within academia.

On the crucial issue of citizenship, liberal multiculturalists claim that diversity should be in the personal or private realm whereas a shared degree of uniformity should characterise the public realm. Liberal multiculturalists therefore aim to reach a balance between private diversity and public unity. In doing so, society gains the full benefits of multiculturalism. This approach is consistent with **universal citizenship**. Furthermore, the endorsement of liberal democracy amongst liberal multiculturalists as the only legitimate means of political organisation holds important political implications. For example, the establishment of Sharia law is opposed by liberal multiculturalists due to its illiberal and anti-democratic connotations. For liberal multiculturalists, the norms and mores that characterise Sharia law are incompatible with their particular view of multiculturalism. The issue of Sharia law marks an intriguing point of contestability with the next strand of multiculturalism we will consider - that of pluralist multiculturalism.

Pluralist multiculturalism is based on the assumption that all cultures are **equal**. In order to avoid the problem of cultural imperialism it is important that society adopts a pluralist stance. The preference for liberal values within a society based upon liberal democracy must be abandoned in favour of a more egalitarian stance on the issue of cultures. As a consequence, values that are incompatible with one another (such as laws on bigamy against those cultures which facilitate marriage to more than one partner) should be treated as equally legitimate, even if those cultures are illiberal. One clear example of this stance concerns Sharia law, which for pluralist multiculturalists should be adopted within British society if there is sufficient support for it amongst the Muslim community. On the vexed issue of citizenship, pluralist multiculturalists argue in favour of **differentiated citizenship**.

For pluralist multiculturalists diversity should have a public face, not just a private realm as advocated by liberal multiculturalists. It is an approach which draws heavily upon Isaiah Berlin's work on ethical / moral pluralism and from the theory and practise of identity politics. The commitment to pluralism within this particular strand of multiculturalism enables it to tolerate that which many members of society might perceive of as *in*tolerant.

The implacable stance taken by pluralist multiculturalists bears important implications for lifestyle issues and the relationship between the state and the individual. Moreover, pluralist multiculturalism can be characterised as adopting a form of *"live and let live multiculturalism"* that reflects the politics of indifference. For pluralist multiculturalists, it is simply impossible for one value system or set of moral beliefs to prove itself superior to any other. However, this stance has been criticised as it undermines the legitimacy of certain institutions. For example, John Gray (1995) argues that pluralism takes us towards a post-liberal era in which liberal democracy and other elements of liberalism no longer hold a monopoly on legitimacy.

Cosmopolitan multiculturalism is based upon the assumption that we have multiple identities and should therefore adopt an appreciation of different cultures. More urbane than either liberal multiculturalism or pluralist multiculturalism, this particular perspective can be characterised as adopting a *"pick and mix approach to multiculturalism."* Supporters claim that there is an inherent value in a hybrid of different cultures, and that recognition of multiple identities more accurately reflects the realities of the post-modern world. On the issue of citizenship, cosmopolitan multiculturalists favour a form of **global citizenship**.

Cosmopolitan multiculturalists endorse cultural diversity and identity politics provided they are underpinned by the development of a **global consciousness**. The cosmopolitan strand of multiculturalism is most in evidence amongst the young for whom national boundaries and cultural identity are essentially fluid. Unlike other strands, cosmopolitan multiculturalism states that we widen the scope of our self-development by facilitating the exchange of cultures. This so-called *"melting pot"* embraces cultural **hybridity** that reflects our multiple identities. To its supporters, this approach enables the emergence of a one world perspective and thereby facilitates global peace. To its critics, this approach entails the demise of national identities and the spread of potentially undemocratic organisations and institutions such as the supranational bodies of the European Union.

Multiculturalism and social advancement

Multiculturalism holds both a descriptive and prescriptive element, and in the context of the latter the issue to consider is social advancement. It is possible to trace **three** distinct and coherent approaches to social advancement; republicanism, social reformism and orthodox multiculturalism. Each of these three approaches provides a means by which those groups marginalised within society may secure their full rights and achieve equality of opportunity. This is a major element of multiculturalism in the context of change and the status quo. Once again, it will become clear that liberal values and liberal ideology shape a great deal of our understanding here. For obvious reasons, we are primarily concerned with the multiculturalist approach to social advancement.

	Republicanism	Social reformist	Multiculturalism
Approach to social advancement	Legal egalitarianism	Social egalitarianism	Celebrate cultural differences
Key element	The politics of indifference	The politics of difference	The politics of cultural self-assertion

Republicanism is based squarely upon universal citizenship. According to this school of thought the damaging effects of legal and political exclusion should be dealt with on the basis of a legal egalitarian methodology. In doing so, republicanism aims to strike a balance between equality of cultures and cultural diversity. This approach is – as the term readily implies – associated with republican systems such as France. However, there is no obvious impediment to applying its core beliefs towards a monarchical system such as the UK. Republicanism can be said to practise the politics of indifference.

The **social reformist** method emerged due to the shortcomings of legal egalitarianism. As the French system graphically illustrates, an emphasis upon treating everyone as a *citoyen* or *citoyenne* regardless of ethnicity fails to address the root cause of problems within society. Persistently high levels of unemployment amongst ethnic minorities, a woefully low rate of ethnic minorities within the political process and a deep sense of resentment at the unfair treatment by the police towards certain ethnic groups characterise the French malaise in terms of ethnic identity and social integration. According to the social reformist perspective, we should both recognise cultural differences and try to **eradicate** those differences. In doing so, the guiding principle should be to deal with social disadvantage. In other words, a form of social egalitarianism should be practised. By implication, the government plays a greater role than it would under a republican approach. Whereas republicanism reflects the politics of indifference, social reformism practises the politics of difference.

The third distinct approach relating to the issue of social advancement is orthodox multiculturalism. The most important aspect of multiculturalism as

The Definitive Guide to Political Ideologies

a means to achieving social advancement derives from its stance upon cultural differences. Whereas republicanism largely ignores cultural differences multiculturalism is fully aware of such differences. Yet unlike social reformism, the multiculturalist stance **celebrates cultural differences**. Rather than trying to eradicate cultural differences, we should fully embrace that which makes us different and that which forms a key aspect of our identity.

The implications of a multiculturalist approach can be seen most clearly in terms of identity politics. How others perceive us and our cultural / ethnic group, and how we perceive ourselves and our cultural / ethnic group, is of central concern to multiculturalists from all the various strands of thought. Whereas the republican approach downplays such differences, and the social reformist approach aims to eradicate such differences; the multicultural approach centres firmly upon cultural differences and its importance in terms of identity. Not surprisingly, multiculturalists argue that we must counter negative stereotypes about ethnic and cultural groups. Only by addressing such negative stereotypes can those ethnic and cultural groups traditionally at the margins of society achieve a sense of empowerment over their lives. The need to counter these stereotypes is particularly acute amongst those groups who have - in historical terms – regularly been portrayed as scapegoats for wider issues within that society (an observation that holds an obvious racial content). In order to address those negative stereotypes, a degree of group self-assertion is deemed necessary. Perhaps the clearest illustration of this approach can be found amongst indigenous populations, who have formed a notable element of the anti-globalisation movement and have reclaimed negative images about their culture in order to counter hostile attitudes. Revealingly, this has occurred within those cultures marginalised by dominant imperialist groups (or the descendants of those groups). As such, multiculturalism can be said to practise **the politics of cultural self-assertion** – a point which leads neatly onto the next section.

Communitarianism and identity politics

Following on from the previous point, there are **two** aspects of cultural self-assertion to consider within the arena of multiculturalism. The first relates to communitarianism and belongs on the left of the political spectrum. The second approach relates to identity politics. These two elements are also important in terms of the prescriptive character of multiculturalism. Moreover, both represent a critique of the universal character and tone of liberalism – albeit from a different basis.

Communitarianism offers a **philosophical critique** of liberal universalism as they believe the former is based upon the false premise that we all have a unique identity. In reality, communitarianism is based on the premise that our identity is shaped by the social groups to which we belong. Our identity is therefore **embedded in a social context**. In other words, there is no 'I' outside the social context (which often holds a distinct cultural or ethnic quality). Without a social context to our identity we would suffer from a sense of what the celebrated sociologist Emile Durkheim (1912) described as anomie. The communitarian approach to cultural self-assertion has been categorised as the *"politics of cultural recognition"* (Taylor, 1994). In contrast, liberal universalism tends to oversimplify the concept of identity.

Identity politics offers a **political critique** of liberal universalism. Those who adhere to identity politics claim that liberal universalism is a form of cultural imperialism based upon the vested interests of dominant groups within society. Under liberalism, the dominant culture within society effectively disempowers those cultural groups that exist outside the mainstream. For example, the liberal emphasis upon individualism reflects the dominance of white, middle-class, heterosexual wealthy men. Those values and assumptions generated by liberalism ultimately serve the vested interests of those who dominate the political realm and society itself. Only by challenging this cultural imperialism can marginalised cultures assert their real identity. Liberation is thereby sought on the basis of re-defining identity, such as via raising consciousness. Evident illustrations of this point include gay pride, black nationalism and women's liberation.

Post-colonialism

There are **four** core elements of multiculturalism; post-colonialism, identity and culture, the rights of minority groups and cultural diversity. Of these, post-colonialism is arguably the most important whereas the issue of identity and culture generates the most controversy and debate.

Core elements
Post-colonialism
Identity and culture
Rights of minority groups
Cultural diversity

The political importance of **post-colonialism** is that it seeks to overturn the cultural dimensions of imperial rule by establishing the legitimacy of non-western (and on occasions anti-western) political ideas and traditions. Post-colonialism can therefore be understood as a reaction to Western dominance of the political, social and economic sphere. In terms of comparison to previous ideologies

The Definitive Guide to Political Ideologies

we have considered, the post-colonial character of multiculturalism bears some relationship to liberal nationalism. The core beliefs amongst liberal nationalists consist of support for the right to self-determination and an implacable opposition to imperialism. It should be relatively clear that both these elements of liberal nationalism have an obvious applicability towards post-colonialism.

An understanding of post-colonialism is bound up with the issue of political violence. Whereas some independence movements are conspicuous by their refusal to engage in violent means, they are very much the exception within the context of world history. The stand-out example of peaceful change remains the movement for Indian independence led by the charismatic figure Mahatma Gandhi (1869-1948) and his belief in *Satyagraha* (a soul force based upon moral strength). However, the majority of independence movements have been shaped by the view that political violence is both justified and appropriate in terms of overthrowing their colonial oppressors. One of the most important intellectual contributions to this position was offered by Frantz Fanon (1961). He analysed the psychological dimension of colonial role and claimed that a new type of citizen is deliberately created by the imperial power. Based on his analysis, Fanon argued that violence was the only means available to regenerate the nation and thereby end colonial rule. Yet perhaps the most seminal text within post-colonialism derives from the Palestinian writer Edward Said who offered a persuasive critique of the Eurocentric Weltanschauung that dominates global politics. He believed that values and ideas that are distinctly European in origin (e.g. democracy) have emerged as the dominant values within international relations, thereby shutting out other alternatives via hostile stereotypes and even ridicule from colonial powers. In his book *'Orientalism'* (2003) Said identified the methods by which the Western powers undermine oriental countries in order to maintain their hegemony.

The contribution made by post-colonialism to ideological discourse has been **two-fold**. Firstly, post-colonialism challenges the prevalence of Eurocentricism within political discourse and international relations. In doing so, it provides the non-Western world with a distinctive dialogue entirely removed from western-based ideological assumptions. As a result, non-western ideas and religions are now given much more serious attention than in previous generations, and ideas previously marginalised due to imperialist and even quasi-racist attitudes are now widely seen as legitimate and deserving of serious attention. Secondly, post-colonialism has served to emphasise the political importance of culture, principally in terms of cultural hegemony and cultural imperialism. This has enabled minority cultures to experience a form of collective emancipation via a discovery of their own native culture as opposed to meekly accepting the view presented by the imposing culture which – by definition – seeks to undermine them. For example, native Americans have developed a much more rewarding sense of identity than that fostered upon them by the dominant white culture which routinely presented them as savage Red Indians (!) always losing out to all-conquering white folk in Cowboy hats. A cursory glance at old black and white Western movies would confirm this assumption, as would research into the contemporary position of Navaho Indians within American society.

Identity and culture

The second element of multiculturalism concerns **identity and culture** and is of major significance towards our understanding of political ideology. Political movements who aim to advance the cause of their particular cultural group do so via raising awareness of their collective sense of identity and shared historical experience. Invariably, this is an experience shaped by oppression and injustice which thereby impacts greatly upon their sense of identity. For instance, the Republican movement within the north of Ireland fosters a sense of Irish cultural identity based on the oppression of Irish Catholics at the hands of both Protestants and the British state. Identity is therefore embedded within a wider grouping. This particular element of multiculturalism reflects communitarian thinking as expressed by theorists such as Alistair MacIntyre (1981) and Michael Sandel (1982). Communitarianism puts forward the view that the individual is embedded within the wider community. In other words, our sense of individual identity ultimately derives from the community to which we belong. According to the assumptions to which communitarianism is based upon, we seek the recognition of others in order to express our identity. Befitting a perspective of the left, communitarian thinking is highly critical of liberalism's obsession with the individual and its association with a rootless atomised society.

At a basic level, culture reflects the norms and values of society / a social group and is an important aspect of our socialisation. Culture is also important in that it shapes the values and assumptions through which our identity is created. Culture thereby gives meaning to everyday experience and enables individuals to feel a sense of connection to others. It stipulates that we are all part of something greater and more meaningful than simply ourselves, and that we therefore gain a sense of belonging via the acquisition of culture. Following on from this, culture enables multiculturalists to emphasise ethnicity, religion and / or language as a means of uniting a cultural group together. Moreover, recognition of cultural identity ensures social cohesion because it enables different cultural groups to live harmoniously with one another. Culture has an obvious resonance within contemporary British politics due to the impact of nationalism, an observation heightened by the process of devolution since the late-1990s. To Scottish and Welsh nationalists, devolution has provided a welcome channel by which to advance their distinct cultural identities against the dominant culture of the English nation. In the context of Northern Ireland, culture and identity have always played a hugely significant role, even within the context of the peace process.

Minority rights

According to Will Kymlicka (1995) there are **three** different types of minority rights; self-government rights, polyethnic rights and representation rights. This typology has become widely accepted within the discourse of multiculturalism and offers further clarity for any student of political ideology. Before we consider each in turn, we need to distinguish between minority rights and liberal rights. Whereas the latter applies rights on a universal basis towards individuals, minority rights are specifically attached to a particular group. The multicultural approach is therefore collectivist as opposed to individualist. Such rights are specific to the group in question and therefore recognise the differing needs of various groups. For example, those needs may be based upon religion or a shared historical experience. Furthermore, minority rights are sometimes designed to give an advantage to a particular group in order to deal with social and economic barriers such as racism, prejudice and / or a perceived injustice of some kind. In the UK, attempts by the Police Service of Northern Ireland (PSNI) to recruit more Catholics could be viewed as an illustration of this point. The PSNI replaced the Royal Ulster Constabulary (RUC) after repeated claims during 'the troubles' that the police had discriminated against Catholics; even to the extent of collusion with Protestant paramilitary groups. The PSNI thereby recognises the rights of Catholics and is at present making a concerted attempt to rectify past injustices.

In the context of **self-government rights**, Kymlicka claims that such rights belong to national minorities who are territorially concentrated and in possession of a shared language (e.g. the Maoris of New Zealand and the Aborigines of Australia). Recognition of self-government rights entails the devolution of power to a political unit dominated by that particular

Typology of minority rights
Self-government rights
Polyethnic rights
Representation rights

minority. In certain cases, this may lead to greater autonomy or even full-scale independence. In the case of Aboriginals in Australia, the issue of land rights bears obvious resonance in the context of minority rights, and after considerable pressure exerted by political campaigners the Federal government in Canberra has recently acquiesced upon certain land issues and restored rightful ownership to the Aboriginal people. In a related move, the Australian Prime Minister Kevin Rudd offered an apology in 2008 to the stolen generation of Aboriginal people for past injustices. This marked a historical moment in Australian politics and one that holds important implications for multiculturalism itself; particularly in the realm of self-government rights.

Polyethnic rights are of a slightly different character to self-government rights. Kymlicka suggests that polyethnic rights are those rights which facilitate the expression of cultural distinctiveness via the political process and the legal system. For instance, Sikh members of the police force are allowed to wear the turban whilst performing their job, and in the field of education, special disposition is usually given towards Muslim girls in terms of dress code. There is an intriguing contrast to be made here between the British approach to multiculturalism and the French approach. Whilst Britain has tried to facilitate polyethnic rights and cultural distinctiveness, particularly in the field of employment and education, the French have adopted a more dirigisme attitude towards minorities. In France, the legal emphasis has been upon upholding a sense of Frenchness regardless of ethnicity, whereas in Britain, the authorities have adopted a more culturally sensitive position.

Representation rights are solely concerned with the problem of under-representation amongst ethnic minorities. This entails the use of positive discrimination (or affirmative action) in order to redress the ethnic imbalance. Supporters claim that the use of positive discrimination enables the legal system, the political process and the realm of employment to reflect the true diversity of the people. A more equitable system is therefore seen as a fairer system.

The controversy generated by the whole issue of minority rights is an increasingly salient feature of contemporary politics, and it is possible to identify **four** main criticisms. The first is that minority rights have **prevented the full-scale integration of ethnic minorities into wider society**. Whilst the intention of minority rights is entirely understandable and even admirable, the consequences have been the exact reverse of what was intended. For instance, a multicultural society may have extended toleration towards cultural attitudes and activities that are themselves undesirable on some levels. This is most noticeable in the context of females. Certain cultures take the view that females should be confined to the private sphere, even in the context of married women. Such views have thereby prevented females from full assimilation within society, which has been both to the detriment of the women concerned and society as a whole. This has been particularly difficult for women who are part of a minority group, exactly the type of people multiculturalists are trying to help!

Secondly, the policy of positive discrimination as used in the pursuit of a multiculturalist society can be seen as **unfair to the ethnic majority**. Positive discrimination may therefore lead to a backlash against misguided attempts at social engineering influenced by the prescriptive character of multiculturalism. Criticism of positive discrimination is at its most visceral on the right of the political spectrum. This is particularly noticeable within America, where the entire issue of affirmative action takes on an unmistakably racial tone. The election of Barack Obama in 2008 is an interesting development to consider here. The undeniable fact that a black man has broken through the biggest glass ceiling of all and got himself elected to the highest office in the land will have major repercussions for racial relations within the United States. Whilst it is far too early to predict the long-term impact of Obama's victory, his election to the White House may lead to white people claiming that black people are using racism as an excuse for not gaining a job / promotion. To black people, the election of Obama may be a cause for celebration but ultimately it does little to address the profound inequities of life within American society.

Thirdly, it could be argued that positive discrimination is **patronising to ethnic minorities** themselves. To its many critics, the practise of positive discrimination implies that the *only* way a person from an ethnic minority can gain a job / promotion is via this particular form of intervention. As a consequence, positive discrimination may itself be entirely counter-productive. It may also be seen as a form of tokenism which does nothing to address the deeper problems facing society. Indeed, it may simply be a form of window dressing that covers the cracks over a far greater problem.

The final criticism of minority rights we need to consider is the **clash with individual rights**. Inevitably, there is a tension between our rights as an individual and the wider notion of rights in regards to our perceived cultural grouping. Whereas liberals go for the former, multiculturalists emphasise the latter. In practical terms, the clash between individual rights and minority rights presents us with something of a dichotomy. Society may ultimately champion one or the other, but it is very difficult to reconcile liberal individualism with minority rights. This particular issue may hold huge implications for say an Asian woman raised in a traditional manner facing pressure from wider society to adapt to a very different set of norms and values. This clash also holds implications for the issue of offence, perhaps one of the most widely used (and some might say *mis*used) terms within everyday politics. Claiming 'offence' empowers various groups to promote the politics of victimhood against the dominant ethnicity / culture. In an attempt to deal with the problems presented by offence it may be necessary to restrict traditional liberal freedoms. However, this is contrary to the prevalent norms and values within Western societies and may in turn foster something of a backlash against what is seen as preferential and unfair treatment of minorities that are often hostile to liberal democracy itself. Furthermore, there is a ratchet effect to consider. When one minority group claims it is an offence to insult their beliefs, the temptation for other comparable groups to do the same is magnified. Furthermore, enabling certain groups to claim offence (such as those of the Muslim faith) whilst denying it to others may lead to double standards, especially when placed in contrast to majority groups (such as those of the Christian faith in Western countries who often feel that their beliefs are fair game for ridicule and hostility).

Diversity

The final aspect of multiculturalism is **diversity**. The core multiculturalist argument is that diversity is in no sense incompatible with social cohesion. Multiculturalism takes a contrary path to those ideologies on the right of the political spectrum such as conservatism, fascism and religious fundamentalism. For multiculturalists, there is absolutely no tension between a celebration of cultural diversity and the wider objective of social cohesion. Crucially, stability within society does not require cultural homogeneity or ethnic purity. This is an intriguing contribution from multiculturalism towards ideological discourse and one that warrants further exploration.

The multiculturalist argument is based upon the premise that individuals hold multiple identities and multiple loyalties. For multiculturalists, that is the undeniable reality of the post-modern world we inhabit, and any ideology or political movement that fails to recognise this phenomenon is bound to exacerbate divisions within society. Take the case of conservatism. Applying the so-called *"cricket test"* (a term used by the then Conservative Cabinet Minister Norman Tebbit during the 1980s as a sign / test of loyalty to England amongst members of ethnic minorities) is entirely the wrong method to employ. This form of enforced cultural repression only fuels hatred and political extremism, an issue of growing relevance amongst disaffected Muslims within British (and Western) society. Multiculturalists contend that individuals are much more willing to co-operate and participate within society *if* they are allowed to hold a firm sense of identity rooted in their *own* culture. A society based upon multiculturalism therefore facilitates cultural diversity and multiple identities in order to maintain stability.

Secondly, multiculturalists support cultural diversity because it holds significant benefits for everyone within that particular society. A diverse society is one characterised by vibrancy and tolerance, whereas a monocultural society is plagued by inertia and stifling conformity. In blunt terms, we *all* gain from experiencing a full melting pot of ideas, cultures and lifestyles that the rich tapestry of life offers. By celebrating such differences, we gain a healthy respect for cultures other than our own. Ignorance and prejudice is therefore replaced by a shared sense of understanding. In such a welcoming climate, the full spectrum of human life is facilitated and we all benefit from that.

As with all other aspects of multiculturalism the issue of cultural diversity has been criticised, particularly from those on the right of the political spectrum. By championing diversity the contours of our own culture become somewhat blurred. This may ultimately weaken societal bonds and provoke a sense of insecurity amongst people that extremists can manipulate to generate hatred. The major problem to consider here is that extremists exacerbate social division and conflict. Multiculturalism has also been criticised for ignoring the obvious conflict between the rights of certain groups and the wider norms and values of society as a whole. The experience of Britain and other societies based to a greater or lesser extent upon multiculturalism confirms that certain groups and their activities / attitudes do not mix well within a cultural melting-pot (such as the example of arranged / forced marriages).

Relationship between multiculturalism and other ideologies

Multiculturalism holds both a descriptive and prescriptive character, and in the context of other ideologies, it is the latter that has generated the most debate and is of most relevance. A world shaped by multiculturalism tends to find a degree of support amongst what might broadly be classed as liberals. The prevalent norms, values and assumptions which underpin multiculturalism bear the closest resemblance to **liberalism**. Having said this, there are certain points of departure between liberals and multiculturalists that students should be aware of.

The main distinction between a liberal and a multiculturalist concerns individual rights. To liberals, the problem with multiculturalism is that it endangers our rights as individuals. Placing the rights of a minority group above those of the individual is contrary to the objectives and assumptions that drive liberalism. Thus for liberals, multiculturalism presents a threat to their cherish values of individualism and liberty. Unlike multiculturalists, liberals firmly believe that our rights as individuals must always come before cultural rights – otherwise the result might entail the *"tyranny of the majority."* So whereas multiculturalists believe that our identity is embedded within a collective group, liberals believe that our identity is based upon our inherent individualism. Furthermore, liberals claim that pluralist multiculturalism endorses both anti-democratic and illiberal beliefs. This is a particularly relevant argument in the context of what Huntingdon (2002) described as the *"the clash of civilisations"* – a phenomenon that occurs not just between societies but increasingly within societies.

The liberal critique of multiculturalism ultimately rests upon the view that a multicultural society ends up tolerating behaviour that is profoundly illiberal and possibly immoral. One example is the practise of honour killings, where wives and daughters have been murdered for bringing shame on their families by conducting in sexual relations with men outside of their ethnicity. In addition, the manner in which multiculturalism is imposed upon society generates some level of opposition amongst liberals. For genuine liberals, there should be no lessons in citizenship or oaths of allegiance enforced by the official authorities. The majority should never force its viewpoint upon the minority. If a member of an ethnic minority wishes to retain an emotional attachment to their (or their family members) country of origin, then that is their right. As such, the practise of multiculturalism is to some extent entirely contrary to individual liberty.

Left-wing ideologies such as socialism and feminism find **little common cause** with multiculturalism. The emphasis upon economic determinism and a class-based analysis of society provides little opportunity to mesh together socialism with multiculturalism. Furthermore, the core left-wing objectives of equality and social justice are hampered by the emphasis within multiculturalism upon minority rights and cultural assertiveness. In doing so, the root cause of conflict within society (the exploitation of the proletariat by the bourgeoisie) is left unaffected. As such, the critique of capitalism that is of absolutely central importance to socialism bears no link to multiculturalism. Similarly, the critique of patriarchy and the gender-based analysis of society put forward by feminism holds no obvious connection to multiculturalism. Whilst the emphasis of liberal feminism upon diversity does to some extent overlap with one of the core tenants of multiculturalism, the whole issue of patriarchy within society is ultimately ignored within multiculturalism. As for anarchism, the acceptance within multiculturalism that a state must be maintained is fundamentally at odds with the anarchist desire for a stateless utopia.

The Definitive Guide to Political Ideologies

Right-wing ideologies are **opposed to multiculturalism** on every level. Conservatives have offered a firm critique of multiculturalism based on the latter's entrenched position upon moral relativism, its emphasis upon multiple and cross-cutting identities / loyalties, its idealistic celebration of diversity and its desire to champion the virtues of diversity over social homogeneity. For conservatives, the whole ethos of multiculturalism is incompatible with their cherished goal of a stable and orderly society. Conservatives claim that societal bonds are ultimately weakened by the prescriptive character of multiculturalism. The same arguments apply to other right-wing ideologies such as fascism and religious fundamentalism, although the emphasis placed upon those arguments differs. For fascists, multiculturalism undermines the unity of the nation and is symptomatic of the wider malaise within all aspects of liberal theory. Multiculturalism also generates high levels of immigration which, to fascists, is both undesirable and potentially dangerous to the survival and moral health of the nation. Furthermore, multiculturalism is welded to the concept of liberal democracy – which for fascists is merely a recipe for weak government and corrupt politicians.

Opposition to multiculturalism from religious fundamentalists centres solely upon the issue of **morality**. The post-modern context of multiculturalism is in no sense congruent with fundamentalist beliefs. For some fundamentalist groups, the mindset of multiculturalism is bound up with a neutral stance upon various religious beliefs and practises. In doing so, a multicultural society therefore deviates from the prescribed path to God as outlined in sacred / holy texts. For religious fundamentalists, there is only *one* source of truth – whereas for multiculturalists there are many competing versions of the truth and that our *perception* of truth is somewhat fluid and changeable. The conflict of ideas between multiculturalists and religious fundamentalists is most evident within the United States and India, but is far less prominent in the UK because of our largely secular society and the failure of fundamentalist beliefs to win over hearts and minds.

Multiculturalism has a **problematic relationship** with nationalism which in part reflects the ideological shapelessness of nationalism itself. Although conventionally thought of as an ideology of the right, nationalism has been adopted by virtually all other ideologies. As such, it is possible to readily identity several strands of thought such as liberal nationalism, conservative nationalism, socialist nationalism and exclusive nationalism. This typology enables us to offer a more meaningful comparison between nationalism and multiculturalism. For instance, liberal nationalism bears some relationship to multiculturalism, whereas conservative nationalism does not. Whilst both these strands of nationalism are inclusive in character, the similarity ends there. For liberal nationalists, the progressive and pluralist nature of multiculturalism offers an appropriate means by which to maximise liberty whilst enabling society to hold together. For conservative nationalists, the multiculturalist argument that diversity facilitates social cohesion is based upon an abstract and utopian premise. As with all forms of conservative thought it is considered foolish to ignore the accumulated wisdom of previous generations in attempting to create an idealised world in which everyone expresses their own cultural identity regardless of the consequences for social order. For conservative nationalists, an entrenched policy of multiculturalism fostered upon the populace by an out-of-touch liberal elite has led to a fractured and increasingly divided society. Finally, socialist nationalism is little more than a marriage of convenience rather than substance. As such, it lacks the ideological coherence to offer much in the way of a riposte to multiculturalism. Nonetheless, the requirement of national unity and sense of purpose that is so important to the advancement of social justice and equality stands in stark contrast to the whole philosophy of multiculturalism.

Exclusive nationalism is the polar opposite of multiculturalism. This particular strand of nationalism reflects and expresses the fear held amongst certain members of the ethnic *majority* about the inexorable tide of multiculturalism and the threat of immigration to the predominant culture. The extremist character of exclusive nationalism can therefore be understood as a reaction to the phenomenon of multiculturalism. In the UK, the BNP have been able to exploit such fears amongst white people in order to bolster electoral support. Their implacable opposition to multiculturalism finds some level of support amongst disaffected whites who feel under threat from immigrants in terms of jobs and social housing. However, the First Past the Post electoral system combined with the reluctance of voters to endorse extremist parties places a significant handicap upon the progress of the BNP. Within continental Europe exclusive nationalism has gained rather more prominence, with several countries having witnessed a considerable increase in support for far-right anti-immigrant parties. Take the case of the Netherlands. Until Pim Fortuyn's party came second in the 2002 Dutch elections the Netherlands had been widely admired as a good illustration of a harmonious, multicultural society. Campaigning on the slogan *"Holland is full"* his views aroused deep controversy, and he was later murdered. The filmmaker Theo Van Gogh was also killed by an Islamic extremist after one of his films criticised the treatment of Muslim women within Islamic societies. As a reaction to such events many Dutch people feel that Islamic fundamentalism is incompatible with Holland's traditional association with liberal values. Other populist parties in Belgium, Austria, Denmark and Switzerland have all gained seats on the basis of a right-wing backlash against multiculturalism. The more proportional electoral system is of course one factor to consider here, but the manner in which multiculturalism has been implemented within such countries may also explain why certain sections of the electorate have been attracted by exclusive nationalism.

The final ideology we need to consider is ecologism. The objectives of the green movement are entirely compatible with cosmopolitan multiculturalism and its emphasis upon a form of global citizenship. By thinking in a global sense we become more aware of the environmental damage caused by our actions. Having said this, the morally neutral position taken by liberal multiculturalists does not sit easily with ecologism. Some actions and cultures are, by their very nature, less sympathetic to the objectives of the green movement than others. Liberal multiculturalism is therefore contrary to the green movement, as too is the egalitarian nature of pluralist multiculturalism.

Before we leave this section, it is worth reflecting upon the relationship between multiculturalism and post-modernism. As a conceptual framework, post-modernism stipulates that political ideas are not based upon any essential quality of humankind or society, but are **the product of individual perceptions and images** relative to a particular situation. Thus in order to understand a situation one has to place it into its relevant context. There is no right and wrong, merely a perception of what is right or wrong. Thus in a post-modern world there is no single correct path as to how we should lead our lives. Issues of an essentially moral and political character do not have one definitive answer. Thus unlike fascism or religious fundamentalism, post-modernism firmly rejects a monistic stance. Post-modernism is therefore interwoven with moral relativism. According to this argument it is entirely wrong for society to impose one view of the truth because that would be contrary to the core elements of multiculturalism. Indeed, that which might be considered right or wrong is often a reflection of cultural hegemony and thereby contrary to multiculturalism. For instance, the notion that democracy is the *only* appropriate political system available reflects a firmly Eurocentric / Westernised world-view. Recent experience in regards to American foreign policy suggests that the neo-conservative outlook has been hostile to cultural values that are anti-democratic. Indeed in the specific context of the Middle East, the US has been accused of cultural imperialism, particularly under the Bush administration.

Multiculturalism in contemporary politics

Globalisation looks likely to remain the **dominant** feature of global politics, and whilst certain ideologies and political movements wish to alter the direction of globalisation, no-one can realistically turn back the clock.

Globalisation has made a considerable impact on all the ideologies we have considered thus far, yet few are as intimately bound up with globalisation as multiculturalism. Thus in order to assess the status and influence of multiculturalism in contemporary politics, we need to locate our understanding within the context of globalisation.

There are some who speculate that multiculturalism will become **the dominant ideology of the 21st century** (Heywood, 2007, p.329), and there are persuasive arguments to back up this point. In the descriptive sense of the term, multiculturalism is an increasingly salient perspective within contemporary politics. The prescriptive sense of the term is, however, more controversial and less prevalent. Multiculturalism in a prescriptive sense faces significant resistance from powerful ideological forces. The most obvious illustration of this point is religious fundamentalism. The post-modern character of multiculturalism (with its emphasis upon moral relativism, cultural diversity and a profound rejection of the view that one absolute and unchallengeable source of truth exists) is entirely at odds with religious fundamentalism; and the conflict between these two opposing world-views shapes several political conflicts throughout the world. This observation gains even greater significance when one considers that fundamentalist ideas are a growing feature of contemporary international relations. Multiculturalism is also opposed by conservatives. As conservatism is one of the most influential of all ideologies, such resistance suggests that the impact of multiculturalism will be limited.

When assessing this question it is worth considering briefly what an **alternative to multiculturalism** would look like. In a prescriptive sense, the alternative to a multicultural society is that where only one culture exists. Whilst foreigners may be tolerated they would be compelled to conform to the norms and values of that society. This approach tends to be associated with those on the right of the political spectrum, although there are significant differences between a conservative stance and a fascist stance in terms of how to ensure this objective. Similarly, there is a considerable distinction to be made between a centre-right political party striving to achieve such an objective within the parameters of a democracy, and a religious fundamentalist regime aiming for the same goal within a theocracy. Nonetheless, what remains clear is that an alternative does exist to multiculturalism.

Liberalism is the most influential ideology of our time and liberal ideas are highly significant within the contemporary era. Globalisation is one of the more obvious illustrations of this trend, and multiculturalism itself is bound up with the fate of globalisation. Whilst it would be tempting to offer sweeping generalisations, it is fair to say that we increasingly perceive ourselves as citizens of a global world. Mobility is one of the defining qualities of the modern world, and it seems safe to claim that the numbers of people who wish to sample the benefits of increased interdependence will continue to grow. It would therefore appear that multiculturalism is simply a phenomenon that most countries have accepted, and any attempt to shut oneself off from the rising tide of globalisation (as in the case of North Korea) appears both futile and foolish. In retrospect, Mahatma Gandhi's observation that *"no culture can live if it attempts to be exclusive"* was way ahead of its time.

Perhaps more than any other ideology we have considered; the fate of multiculturalism is open to the greatest degree of fluctuation. In a purely descriptive sense, multiculturalism is crucial towards an understanding of contemporary politics. We are all inter-connected in a manner scarcely imaginable in previous generations. This brings with it both challenges and problems. If handled correctly, the prescriptive aspect of multiculturalism holds the promise of social stability alongside mutual tolerance of human diversity. If handled incorrectly, multiculturalism has the ability to divide like few other issues. Moreover, if multiculturalism fails in some way then alternatives derived from the right of the political spectrum will probably fill the vacuum. An increase in electoral support for quasi-nationalist movements and even fascist politicians cannot be ruled out if multiculturalism fails to win over hearts and minds. Both nationalism (principally its exclusive strand) and fascism offer simplistic and often persuasive remedies to those who feel a deep sense of dissatisfaction with multiculturalism and the process of globalisation.

Further quotes on multiculturalism

"If there were only one religion in England there would be a danger of despotism, if there were two, they would cut each other's throats, but if there are thirty they live in peace and happiness."
Voltaire
"The 7/7 bombers were the children of Britain's own multicultural society."
  Gilles Kepel
"What multiculturalism boils down to is that you can praise any culture in the world except Western culture – and you cannot blame any culture in the world except Western culture." Thomas Sowell
"Culture is the widening of the mind and of the spirit." Jawaharlal Nehru
"As the soil, however rich it may be, cannot be productive without cultivation, so the mind without culture can never produce good fruit." Seneca
"We live in a global village." Marshall McLuhan
"A culture is made – or destroyed – by its articulate voices." Ayn Rand

"I do not want my House to be walled in on all sides and my windows to be stuffed. I want the cultures of all the lands to be blown about my House as freely as possible. But I refuse to be blown off my feet by any." Gandhi

"Culture is roughly anything we do and the monkeys don't." Lord Raglan

"If we are to achieve a richer culture, rich in contrasting values, we must recognise the whole gamut of human potentialities, and so weave a less arbitrary social fabric, one in which each diverse gift will find a fitting place." Margaret Mead

Recommended reading

A-Brown, Y. (1999) *True Colours Public Attitudes to Multiculturalism and the Role of the Government.* An account of how the public perceives the issue of multiculturalism, revealing for the extent to which people misunderstand the concept and for their conflicting attitudes towards it.

Kymlicka, W. (1995) *Multicultural citizenship.* Kymlicka offers a useful typology of minority rights that gets to the heart of multiculturalism. His typology remains an essential aspect of any student's comprehension of multiculturalism.

Ouseley, H. (2001) *Community Pride, Not Prejudice : Making Diversity Work in Bradford.* A report instigated by that summer's race riots, the Ouseley report identified the problem of parallel lives in the context of modern-day Britain. The Ouseley report remains a template of how to approach the problems posed by a lack of meaningful interaction between ethnic groups.

Parekh, Lord B. (2000) *The Future of Multi-Ethnic Britain : report of the Commission on the Future of Multi-Ethnic Britain.* Parekh identifies three distinct approaches to the issue of multiculturalism; liberal, conservative and a hybrid of the two. The Parekh report was largely ignored by the government, yet it remains a useful report for students to consider in the context of multiculturalism.

Phillips, M. (2006) *Londonistan.* A right-wing perspective upon the problems building up for a society that is failing to integrate effectively, and for a government that is failing to implement an effective immigration policy.

Said, E. (2003) *Orientalism.* An excellent account of anti-imperialism from the foremost contemporary author on the subject.

Taylor, C. (1994) *Multiculturalism and 'the Politics of Recognition.'*
Taylor's work considers cultural recognition within a multicultural society and the issues presented by it.

Issues for further discussion

In what sense is multiculturalism a political ideology in its own right?
What is the relationship between globalisation and multiculturalism?
In what sense is multiculturalism a reflection of liberal hegemony within political discourse?
How important is the concept of post-colonialism within contemporary international relations?
What is the relationship between communitarianism and multiculturalism?
What are the main strands of multiculturalism?

Key terms

Ethnic identity An individual's identity based upon their ethnic group. Members of an ethnic minority may feel different to the majority, and may also be treated differently on the basis of their ethnicity, perhaps due to prejudicial attitudes within society. We therefore need to grasp the significance of ethnic identity in order to further develop our understanding of how society operates. Despite the somewhat vague and nebulous nature of the subject, ethnicity forms a key element of many people's identity and provides them with a sense of belonging.

Integration In the context of a multicultural society, integration consists of immigrants modifying their particular cultural norms and values to assimilate into a wider British culture. The conservative perspective upon multiculturalism is in favour of immigrants fully integrating into British society. Supporters of this stance claim that an emphasis upon integration generates a greater degree of social cohesion.

Multiculturalism A confusing concept that means different things to different people. In everyday usage, the term is often linked with the liberal perspective on multiculturalism; which places an emphasis on tolerance and respect for all faiths and beliefs, and states that all views should be accepted unless they endanger the freedom of others. In recent years, the term has grown in ideological significance.

Multi-ethnicity The existence of more than one ethnic group within a society. Multi-ethnicity is often confused with multiculturalism, yet the terms are very different.

Post-modernism A contemporary theoretical perspective that rejects traditional theories of modernity (such as Marxism) based on a belief that society has reached a new stage of development characterised by a proliferation of choice over lifestyles, identity, etc. In order to better understand this form of society we need to change the scope of our academic inquiry. In doing so, we can build up our understanding of human society. For example, post-modernism has increased the number of social identities which people can adopt, and facilitated a wider degree of choice over one's identity. This has contributed to a more unstable and fragile sense of identity within contemporary society, where terms such as the proletariat and the middle-class have become increasingly obsolete. Post-modernism has been criticised for its apparent lack of consistency and for its relativism.

Westernisation A term used by critics of globalisation to emphasise the extent to which Western governments and Western-based companies dominate the global economy and export their own particular values to other countries. Westernisation is associated with a number of issues facing global society – such as the Bush administration exporting democracy to Iraq and the loss of cultural diversity within the global economy to major Western brands such as Coca-Cola, McDonalds and Starbucks.

Postscript - Have we reached the "end of ideology"?

Any consideration of political ideology must inevitably address the aforementioned question, and to do so, one needs to begin with perhaps the most widely-discussed contribution to the study of political ideology of modern times. At the end of the 1980s Francis Fukayama published an essay entitled "The End of History?" in which he declared that we had reached the end of ideological conflict. A synergy of liberalism, capitalism and democracy had triumphed over all other alternatives - and with that victory the battles that had long characterised political ideology had come to an end. His Hegelian analysis claimed that history itself had come to an end, and that the battle of ideas was now over. To many people, Fukayama appeared to be offering something entirely new. In fact, his bold claim instigated debate over what was – in essence – a rather old issue. During the 1940s the political theorist James Burnham claimed that ideological contests were being replaced by a form of **managerialism** in which the main political parties were competing on the basis of who could manage society in the most successful manner. By the 1960s the American sociologist Daniel Bell (1960) famously argued that class conflict had come to an end and - as ideologies were based upon such conflict - ideology itself had come to an end. Yet whereas Burnham and Bell's analysis centred principally upon Western societies, Fukayama strived for a wider perspective.

Fukayama claimed that a combination of liberal democracy and capitalism had 'won' because of the enormous weaknesses within dictatorial regimes. Democracy had convincingly demonstrated that it was by far the best political system available. Similarly, capitalism had shown itself to be far more efficient and better able to generate high levels of economic growth than any other alternative economic system. Moreover, liberal concepts such as individualism, universal human rights and pluralism had established their superiority over the various concepts associated with illiberal regimes. Liberal democracy was therefore the only coherent political aspiration across different regions and disparate cultures throughout the world, and capitalism was the only workable economic system. The end of the cold war represented the last major ideological conflict and *"at the end of history, there are no serious ideological competitors left to liberal democracy"* (1992, p.211).

Fukayama's work in the late-1980s and early-1990s undoubtedly reflected the spirit and élan of the time. The 'West' was in a buoyant and optimistic mood after its victory over Communism. Liberalism had triumphed over its cold war rival (Marxism) in the same manner as it had triumphed over its mid-20th century rival (Fascism). There was real hope that the bloodiest century in history had bought with it the victory of liberalism itself. There was even talk of a 'peace dividend' for a short time. Today, such optimism appears very dated. Liberal democracy now faces a clear political challenge from religious fundamentalism, a point that Fukayama himself recognised in later work.

The impact of religious fundamentalism

Liberalism and religious fundamentalism are divided over many of the most fundamental aspects of political ideology. Take human nature, widely regarded as one of the most important elements of ideological discourse. Neither Christian fundamentalists nor Islamo-fascists share liberalism's innate optimism about human nature. Similarly, liberalism's perception of the individual as a rational actor is firmly rejected by religious fundamentalists, and liberalism's celebration of pluralism is dismissed by religious fundamentalists who claim that a higher and more spiritual purpose to life should govern both human behaviour and wider society. The separation of political activity from religious worship championed by liberals is anathema to religious fundamentalists. The role of the state is another divergence between the two ideologies. Under liberalism the role of the state is to maximise the concept of personal freedom, whereas religious fundamentalists contend that such an approach leads to moral pollution, decadent behaviour and social breakdown.

The impact of religious fundamentalism has grown substantially in recent years, providing something of a backlash against the norms and mores associated with liberal societies. Its appeal to the disaffected (mostly young) populace, and its ability to address resentment at liberal Western values, poses a challenge to the continued supremacy of liberalism. Yet whilst the *"clash of civilisations"* (Huntingdon, 2002) is very real, it is in no sense comparable to the titanic contest between Marxism and liberal democracy that characterised the cold war. Indeed, governments within liberal democratic countries such as the United States and the United Kingdom have a tendency to exaggerate the threat posed by fundamentalists. The motives behind such tactics are of course open to debate, but it is clearly the case that terrorism influenced by fundamentalist beliefs does not present the same kind of danger to the very existence of liberal democracy as that of Marxism. Moreover in terms of winning over hearts and minds liberalism is far ahead of religious fundamentalism, whereas at certain times during the cold war more people lived under Communist regimes than liberal democratic regimes. It seems highly unlikely that the number of people living under theocracies will come anywhere close to those living under a form of liberal democracy.

Within the international realm, Fukayama argued that the spread of liberal democratic values would prevent the outbreak of war. He was confident that the spread of liberal democratic values would create ***"zones of peace"*** throughout the world. Fukayama also claimed that the only appropriate solution to zones of turmoil (usually post-colonial struggles) was the spread of liberalism. Fukayama's argument can be traced back to prominent liberals of the 18th and 19th century such as Immanuel Kant, Baron de Montesquieu and Richard Cobden. It is based on the view that a habit of co-operation generated amongst liberal democracies gravitates towards inter-state diplomacy rather than war. Furthermore, liberal democracies are much more responsive to the wishes of the public than autocratic regimes and the electorate itself rarely has an appetite for war. According to Fukayama's liberal argument, one of the key benefits of globalisation is that we are all tied into it, thereby making the outbreak of war far less likely in the modern era. Rational individuals ultimately have a stake in the maintenance of peace and the spread of liberal values.

There are of course at least two sides to any issue that is political in nature, and the *"end of ideology"* thesis is no exception. In 2008 the American historian Robert Kagan offered a convincing refute to Fukayama's argument. In his opening line Kagan argues that *"the world has become normal again"* (2008, p.3), claiming that international relations is no longer characterised by the march to liberal modernity. Autocratic regimes such as China and Russia reject liberal democracy in favour of their own distinct version of nationalism. Greater levels of trade between liberal and autocratic regimes have *not* bought with it the bonds of eternal peace. According to Kagan, the liberal democratic world desperately wanted to believe that international relations had been transformed along liberal values. This has evidently not transpired. The old competition between liberalism and autocracy has re-emerged, violent conflict has erupted between radical Islamists and secular cultures, and struggles between the major powers are once again a central feature of international relations. Thus in Kagan's words, *"we have entered an age of divergence"* (2008, p.4).

Aside from Kagan's analysis, other threats to the continued primacy of liberalism include the clash of civilisations and the growing influence of so-called Asian values. These are the fault-lines of contemporary ideological discourse and the battle of ideas between liberalism and its rivals is certainly not over. Ecologism could also be said to present a major challenge to the continuation of liberalism, principally in terms of its ecocentric world-view and the issues arising from that. This point was developed further by the Italian political scientist Noberto Bobbio (1996) who claims that ideologies have not disappeared in the contemporary era. He claims that political ideology is very much with us because old ideologies are being replaced by new ones. He is also entirely correct to point out that *"there is nothing more ideological than declaring the demise of ideologies."*

Although the question *"have we reached the end of ideology"* is a mandatory one when studying the subject of political ideology, it is arguably much too soon to tell whether or not Fukayama was right. Perhaps we will never be able to say that ideology is at an end? A brief look back at historical analysis certainly supports this line of argument. Both Friedrich Hegel and Karl Marx claimed that the evolution of human societies would end when mankind achieved a form of society that satisfied its deepest and most fundamental longings. Both Hegel and Marx therefore believed that the *"end of ideology"* would eventually occur, albeit on the basis of different conclusions. For Hegel it would be a liberal state, whereas for Marx it would be a communist society. It was Hegel's analysis that influenced Fukayama's argument back in the late-1980s, yet there is much one can offer to refute his claim. Furthermore, Fukayama is not the first (nor will he be the last!) to claim that we have reached the end of ideology. There have been - and always will be – times when one ideology appears to be dominant; but none has at yet ever succeeded in *"ending history"* in the Hegelian sense of the phrase.

At the time of writing it seems safe to assume that ideological conflict will surely continue, and whilst liberalism is the most important ideology within global politics, it is clearly not entirely dominant. Perhaps the answer to this question lies in a historical consideration. Throughout history ideologies have always battled it out, and there are enough alternatives to liberalism to thwart the possible end of ideology and with it the end of history. Indeed, one of the common threads throughout this book is that political ideas are always being generated to offer an explanation of the world that surrounds us. Ideologies also undergo periods of renewal and change in order to avoid becoming fossilised. It is therefore in the nature of ideologies that they both respond to and transform the world around them. The battle of ideas continues - and such ideas will doubtless outlive us all …

Recommended reading

Bell, D. (1960) *The End of Ideology.* This early account of the end of ideology thesis provides a fascinating comparison with Fukayama.

Fukayama, F. (1992) *The End of History and the Last Man.* Fukayama's end of ideology argument remains the most important contemporary contribution for students to consider. Whilst certain elements of Fukayama's analysis have been overtaken by subsequent events, his argument remains both relevant and persuasive. A contrast with Kagan offers an informative insight into the whole debate surrounding the end of ideology thesis.

Kagan, R. (2008) *The Return of History and the End of Dreams.* Kagan's rebuttal of Fukayama's argument is both perceptive and highly persuasive. His argument that we are experiencing the return of history in the contemporary era is a compelling one.

Lucas, E. (2008) *The New Cold War: How the Kremlin Menaces Both Russia and the West.* A book that concurs with Kagan's argument and one that reminds us that not everyone thinks in the same way as the liberal democratic 'West.'

Key terms

End of ideology thesis A view which states that ideological conflict is no longer relevant within political discourse due to the victory of one particular ideology. The American political scientist Francis Fukayama claims that we are now living in a stage of human history characterised by the victory of liberal democracy and capitalism. The end of ideology argument was also prevalent during the 1950s and 1960s from academics such as Daniel Bell, Raymond Aron and Edward Shils.

Washington consensus A term associated with the contemporary economist John Williamson to describe a specific set of economic policy prescriptions for countries facing an economic crisis. The relevance of the term Washington is in terms of the location of both the International Monetary Fund and the World Bank. Reforms instigated in those countries invariably took the form of privatisation, de-regulation and the implementation of neo-liberal economics. The Washington consensus is a key element of globalisation and a major source of contention for the alter-globalisation movement. In April 2009 Gordon Brown declared that *"the Washington consensus is now over."*

Some further quotes on Politics to end with …

"Political language … is designed to makes lies sound truthful and murder respectable, and to give an appearance of solidity to pure wind." George Orwell

"Elections are won by men and women chiefly because most people vote against somebody rather than for somebody." Franklin Adams

"The best causes tend to attract to their support the worst arguments." R.A. Fisher

"Those who have greatness within them do not go in for politics." Albert Camus

"Politics is war without bloodshed while war is politics with bloodshed." Chairman Mao

"Diplomacy is to do and say the nastiest thing in the nicest way." Isaac Goldberg

"If voting changed anything, they'd abolish it." Ken Livingstone

"Better to be Socrates dissatisfied than a fool satisfied." John Stuart Mill

"It is not the man who has too little, but the man who craves more, that is poor." Seneca

"Politics is a choice between the impossible and the improbable." J.K. Galbraith

"He who knows he has enough is rich." Tao Te Ching

"The unexamined life is not worth living." Socrates

"Cogito, ergo sum." Descartes

"There can be only one true progress; the sum total of the spiritual progress of individuals. Self-limitation is the fundamental and wisest step of a man who has obtained freedom. It is also the surest path towards its attainment." Alexander Solzhenitsyn

"Laws can be free of a defect without society being free of that defect." Jonathon Wolff

"In politics, what begins in fear usually ends in folly." Samuel Taylor Coleridge

"Bernard, the Official Secrets Act is not to protect secrets it is to protect officials." Sir Humphrey Appleby in 'Yes, Minister'

"*Despotism is a legitimate mode of government in dealing with barbarians, provided the end by their improvement, and the means justified by actually affecting that end.*" John Stuart Mill

"*Philosophers have only interpreted the world in various ways, the real point is to change it.*" Karl Marx

"*Take sides. Neutrality helps the oppressor, never the victim. Silence encourages the tormentor, never the tormented.*" Elie Wiesel

"*You are either part of the solution or you are part of the problem.*" Eldridge Cleaver

Have we reached the "end of ideology"?

BIBLIOGRAPHY

A-Brown, Y. (1999) *True Colours Public Attitudes to Multiculturalism and the Role of the Government* (IPPR).

Acton, Lord (1956) Essays on Freedom and Power (Meridian).

Adams, I. (2001) *Political Ideology today* (2nd Edition, Manchester University press).

Alesina, A. & Giavazzi, F. (2006) *The Future of Europe : Reform or Decline* (MIT Press).

Ali, T. (2003) The Clash of Fundamentalism : Crusades, Jihads and Modernity (Verso).

Almond, G.A. & Verba, S. (1963) *The Civic Culture : Political Attitudes and democracy in five nations* (Princeton University Press).

Anderson, B. (1983) *Imagined communities : Reflections on the origins and spread of Nationalism* (Verso).

Arendt, H. (1999) *The Human Condition* (2nd Revised Edition, University of Chicago Press).

Atkins, C. (2007) *Taking liberties since 1997* (Revolver books).

Bahro, R. (1984) From Red to Green (Verso / New Left books).

Bartholomew, J. (2004) *The Welfare State we're in* (Politico's).

Basham, M. (2008) *Beside Every Successful Man : A Woman's Guide to Having it all* (Crown Forum).

Baxter, B. (2000) *Ecologism : An Introduction* (Georgetown University press).

Becker, H.S. (1963) *Outsiders : Studies in the sociology of deviance* (Free Press).

Bell, D. (1960) *The End of Ideology* (Collier).

Benn, T. (1980) *Arguments for socialism* (Harmondsworth).

Bennetts, L. (2007) *The Feminine Mistake : Are we giving up too much?* (Hyperion books).

Bergman, P.M. & Powell, W. (2002) *The Anarchist cookbook* (Ozark press).

Berman, P. (2003) *Terror and Liberalism* (W.W. Norton & Company).

Bernstein, E. (1961) *Evolutionary socialism* (Schocken Books).

Beveridge, W. (1942) *The Beveridge report* (HMSO).

Biehl, J. (1991) *Rethinking Ecofeminist politics* (South End press).

Bloor, K. (2008) *A Level Politics Made Easy* (2nd Edition, Book Guild).

Bookchin, M. (1975) *Our Synthetic environment* (Harper & Row).

Booker, C. & North, R. (2003) *The Great Deception the secret history of the European Union* (Continuum).

Bourdieu, P. (1977) *Outline of a Theory of Practice* (Cambridge University press).

Bourne, R. (1977) *"War is the Health of the state"* in Woodcock, G. (ed.) *The Anarchist Reader* (Fontana).

British National Party manifesto (2005).

Brown, S. (2002) *The Politics of individualism : Liberalism, Liberal feminism and anarchism* (Black Rose).

Brownmiller, S. (1975) *Against Our Will : Men, Women and Rape* (Simon & Schuster).

Burke, E. (1790) *Reflections on the Revolution in France* (P.F. Collier & Son Company).

Burleigh, M. (2001) The Third Reich : A new history (Macmillan).

Capra, F. (1975) *The Tao of Physics* (Fontana).

Capra, F. (1997) *The Web of Life : A new synthesis of mind and matter* (Flamingo).

Carsons, R. (1961) *The Silent Spring* (Houghton Mifflin).

Cecil, R. (1993) *"The Marching Season in Northern Ireland"* in MacDonald, S. *Inside European identities* (Berg).

Chomsky, N. & Herman, E.S. (1988) *Manufacturing Consent : The Political Economy of the Mass Media* (Pantheon books).

Clark, R. (2007) *The Road to Southend Pier : One man's struggle against the surveillance society* (Harriman House).

Cohen, N. (2007) *What's Left* (Harper Perennial).

Conservative Party manifesto (2005).

Crosland, A. (1956) *The Future of Socialism* (Jonathan Cape).

Daily Mail, 1/11/08.

Daily Telegraph, 19/1/08.

Dale, I. (2007) *500 of the most witty, acerbic and erudite things ever said about politics* (Harriman House).

Daly, M. (1979) Gyn/Ecology : The Meta-Ethics of Radical Feminism (Beacon Press).

Darwin, C. (1972) On the Origin of the Species (Dent).

de Beauvoir, S. (1949) *Le deuxième sexe* (Gallimard).

de Botton, A. (2004) *Status anxiety* (Hamish Hamilton).

Dorff, E.N. & Rosett, A. (1988) *A Living tree : The roots and growth of Jewish Law* (SUNY press).

Dowds, L. & Young, K. (1996) *"National Identity"* in British Social Attitudes (13th report, Dartmouth Publishing Company).

Driver, S. & Martell, L. (2002) *Blair's Britain* (Polity).

Durkheim, E. (1912) *The Elementary Forms of Religious Life* (Allen & Unwin).

Dworkin, A. (1987) *Ice and Fire* (Weidenfeld & Nicholson).

Dworkin, A. (1991) *Pornography : Men possessing Women* (Plume).

Ebenstein, A.O. (2003) *Friedrich Hayek: A Biography* (University of Chicago Press).

Economist, 21/6/07.

Ehrenfeld, D. (1978) The arrogance of Humanism (Oxford University press).

Etzioni, A. (1995) *The Spirit of Community : Rights, Responsibilities and the communitarian agenda* (Fontana).

Fanon, F. (1961) *The Wretched of the Earth* (Grove Weidenfeld).

Festenstein, M. & Kenny, M. (2005) *Political ideologies* (Oxford University press).

Fielding, S. (2003) *The Labour party continuity and change in the making of 'new' Labour* (Palgrave Macmillan).

Firestone, S. (1972) *The Dialectic of Sex* (Basic Books).

Foster, S. (2006) *The judiciary, civil liberties and human rights* (Edinburgh University press).

Foucault, M. (1975) *Discipline and punish : The birth of the prison* (Tavistock).

Friedan, B. (1963) *The Feminine Mystique* (Norton & Company).

Friedan, B. (1983) *The Second Stage* (Abacus).

Friedman, M. (1980) *Free to Choose: A Personal Statement* (Thomson Learning).

Friedman, T. (2005) *The World is Flat – A brief history of the twentieth century* (Farrar, Strauss & Giroux).

Friedman, T. (2008) Hot, Flat and crowded (Allen Lane).

Fromm, E. (1979) *To Have or To Be* (Abacus).

Fromm, E. (1984) *The Fear of Freedom* (Ark).

Fukayama, F. (1992) *The End of History and the Last Man* (Free Press).

Galbraith, J.K. (1967) *The New Industrial State* (Hamish Hamilton).

Gamble, A. (1994) *The Free Economy and the Strong State* (2nd Edition, Palgrave Macmillan).

Garner, R. (2009) *"Anarchism, socialism and utopia"* (p.27 – 29) in Politics Review, Vol. 18 No. 3.

Giddens, A. (1998) *The Third Way : the Renewal of Social Democracy* (Polity press).

Giddens, A. (2007) *Over to you, Mr Brown* (Polity press).

Ginsborg, P. (2008) *Democracy Crisis and Renewal* (Profile books).

Godwin, W. (1793) *Enquiry concerning political justice* (Woodstock books).

Goffman, E. (1959) *The Presentation of Self in Everyday Life* (Doubleday Anchor).

Goldberg, J. (2008) *Liberal Fascism* (Doubleday).

Goldman, E. (1969) *Anarchism and other essays* (Dover).

Gore, A. (2006) An inconvenient truth (Bloomsbury publishing).

Gorz, A (1991) Capitalism, socialism and ecology (Verso).

Grant, M. (2005) *"Is the Labour Party still a socialist party?"* (p.24 – 27) in Politics Review, Vol. 15 No. 1.

Gray, J. (1995) *Liberalism* (2nd Edition, Open University press).

Gray, J. (2000) *Two faces of liberalism* (Polity press).

Greer, G. (1970) *The Female Eunuch* (Harper Collins).

Greer, G. (1985) *Sex and Destiny* (Harper & Row).

Griffin, R. (1993) *The nature of fascism* (Routledge).

Griffith, S. *Ed.* (1999) *Predictions : 30 great minds on the future* (Oxford University press).

Gutman, A. (1995) *Multiculturalism : Examining the politics of Recognition* (Princeton University press).

Hardin, G. (1968) *"The Tragedy of the Commons"* (p.1243 – 1248) in Science Vol. 162.

Hayek, F. (1944) *The Road to Serfdom* (Routledge and Sons Ltd.).

Heywood, A. (2007) *Political ideologies : An introduction* (4th Edition, Palgrave Macmillan).

Himmelfarb, G. (2004) *The roads to modernity : The British, French and American Enlightenments* (Vintage books).

Hitchens, P. (2003) *The Abolition of Liberty : The Decline of Order and Justice in England* (Atlantic Books).

Hitler, A. (1998) *Mein Kampf* (Mariner Books).

Hobbes, T. (1651) *Leviathan* (Penguin).

Hobhouse, L. T. (1911) *Liberalism* (Thornton Butterworth).

Hobsbawm, E. (1983) *The invention of Tradition* (Cambridge University press).

Hobsbawm, E. (1994) *Age of Extremes : The Short Twentieth Century* (Michael Joseph).

Hoffman, S. (1995) *Beyond the State* (Polity press).

Humphrys, J. (2007) *In God we doubt : Confessions of a failed atheist* (Hodder & Stoughton).

Huntingdon, S. (2002) *The Clash of civilisations and the remaking of World Order* (Free Press).

Husain, E. (2007) The Islamist (Penguin).

Hutton, W. (1995) *The State We're In* (Jonathon Cape).

Hutton, W. (2002) *The World We're In* (Little Brown).

Jaeger, M. (1943) *Liberty verses Equality* (Thomas Nelson & Sons).

James, O. (2007) *Affluenza* (Vermillion).

Jenkins, S. (2007) *Thatcher and Sons : A Revolution in three acts* (Penguin).

Jones, B. et al. (1991) *Politics UK* (Philip Allan).

Kagan, R. (2008) *The Return of History and the End of Dreams* (Atlantic books).

Kautsky, K. (1902) *The Social Revolution* (Kerr).

Keynes, J.M. (1973) *The General Theory of Employment, Interest and Money* (MacMillan).

Kieran, D. (2007) *I fought the Law* (Bantam books).

Klein, N. (2000) *No Logo* (Harper Collins).

Klein, N. (2007) *The Shock Doctrine : The rise of Disaster capitalism* (Knopf Canada).

Kropotkin, P. (1914) *Mutual Aid* (Porter Sargent).

Kuhn, T. (1970) *The Structure of Scientific Revolutions* (2nd Edition, Chicago University Press).

Kymlicka, W. (1995) Multicultural citizenship (Oxford University press).

Labour Party manifesto (2005).

Lawson, N. (2008) *An appeal to reason : A cool look at global warming* (Gerald Duckworth & Co.).

Legrain, P. (2007) *Immigrants : Your country needs them* (Little Brown).

Leopold, A. (1968) *Sand County Almanac* (Oxford University press).

Levine, J. (2006) *Not buying it : My Year without shopping* (Simon & Schuster).

Liberal Democrat manifesto (2005).

Locke, J. (1690) *Two Treatises on government* (Digireads).

Lovelock, J. (1979) *Gaia : A new look at life on Earth* (Oxford University press).

Lovelock, J. (2009) *The Vanishing face of Gaia* (Allen Lane).

Lucas, E. (2008) *The New Cold War: How the Kremlin Menaces Both Russia and the West* (Bloomsbury publishing).

Ludlam, S. & Smith, M.J. (2004) *Governing as New Labour* (Palgrave Macmillan).

MacIntyre, A. (1981) *After Virtue* (Duckworth).

MacMillan, H. (1966) *The Middle Way* (Macmillan).

Marcuse, H. (1964) *One Dimensional Man : Studies in the Ideology of Advanced Industrial Society* (Beacon).

Marmot, M. (2008) *"Reducing inequalities in health : a policy choice"* (p.19 – 23) in Fabian Review Spring Edition.

Marx, K. & Engels, F. (1848) *Manifesto of the Communist Party* (Progress publishers).

McNaughton, N. (2005) *Political Ideologies* (Philip Allan).

Mead, M. (1949) *Male and Female* (William Morrow).

Michels, R. (1958) *Political Parties* (Free press).

Milburn, R. (2008) Savannah Memories (Vanguard press).

Miliband, R. (1973) *The state in capitalist society* (Quartet books).

Mill, J.S. (1859) *On Liberty* (Penguin).

Millett, K. (1970) *Sexual Politics* (Doubleday).

Mitchell, J. (1975) *Psychoanalysis and Feminism* (Penguin).

Molloy, P. (2009) *The lost world of Communism* (BBC Books).

Monbiot, G. (2000) *Captive State : The corporate takeover of Britain* (Macmillan).

Mosca, G. (1896) *The Ruling Class* (McGraw-Hill).

Mote, A. (2001) *Vigilance : A defence of British liberty* (Tanner publishing).

Murray, C. & Herrnstein, R. (1995) *The Bell Curve* (Free press).

Mussolini, B. (2006) *The Doctrine of Fascism* (Howard Fertig).

Naess, A. (1973) *"The shallow and the deep, long-range ecology movement : a summary"* in Inquiry volume 16.

Naish, J. (2008) *Enough : Breaking free from the world of excess* (Hodder & Stoughton).

Naughtie, J. (2003) *The Rivals Blair and Brown – The Intimate Story of a Political Marriage* (Fourth Estate).

Nietzsche, F. (1887) The Genealogy of Morals (Cambridge University press).

Nozick, R. (1974) *Anarchy, State and Utopia* (Blackwell).

Oakley, A. (1972) *Sex, gender and society* (Temple Smith).

Oakley, A. (1974) *The sociology of housework* (Martin Robertson).

Orwell, G. (1949) *Nineteen-Eighty Four* (Secker & Warburg).

Ouseley, H. (2001) *Community Pride, Not Prejudice : Making Diversity Work in Bradford* (Bradford Vision).

Paglia, C. (1990) *Sex, Art and American Culture* (Yale University).

Paine, T. (1791) *Rights of Man* (Penguin Group).

Parekh, Lord B. (2000) *The Future of Multi-Ethnic Britain : report of the Commission on the Future of Multi-Ethnic Britain* (Profile Books).

Passmore, K. (2002) Fascism : A very short introduction (Oxford University press).

Peston, R. (2008) *Who runs Britain?* (Hodder & Stoughton).

Phillips, M. (2006) Londonistan (Encounter books).

Plaid Cymru manifesto (2005).

Popper, K. (1962) *The Open Society and its Enemies Volume 2 Hegel and Marx* (Routledge & Kegan Paul).

Porritt, J. (2007) Capitalism : As if the World Matters (Earthscan publications).

Powell, D. (2001) *Tony Benn : A political life* (Continuum).

Putnam, R. (1995) *Bowling Alone : America's Declining Social Capital* (Simon & Schuster)

Raab, D. (2009) *The Assault on Liberty : What went wrong with rights* (Fourth Estate).

Rand, A. (1957) Atlas shrugged (Penguin).

Rawls, J. (1971) *A Theory of Justice* (Oxford University press).

Romer, S. (2008) *"Why did we end up between northern rock and a hard place?"* (p.32 – 35) in Economics Today Vol. 16 No. 1.

Rothbard, M. (1978) *For a New Liberty* (Macmillan).

Rousseau, J-J. (1762) *The Social Contract* (JM Dent & Sons).

Said, E. (2003) *Orientalism* (Penguin).

Sampson, A. (2004) *Who runs this place? The Anatomy of Britain in the 21*st *Century* (John Murray).

Sandel, M. (1982) *Liberalism and the limits of justice* (Cambridge University press).

Sardar, Z. & Davies, W. (2004) *American Dream Global Nightmare* (Icon Books).

Satrapi, M. (2006) Persepolis (Vintage).

Schumacher, E. (1973) *Small is Beautiful : A study of Economics as if people mattered* (Blond & Briggs).

Scottish National Party manifesto (2005).

Seldon, A. & Kavanagh, D. (2005) *The Blair effect 2001 – 5* (University press).

Seldon, A. (1997) *Major : A political life* (Weidenfield).

Sen, A. (2006) *Identity and violence* (Penguin).

Singer, P. (1976) *Animal Liberation* (Jonathon Cape).

Sinn Fein manifesto (2005).

Smith, A. (1776) *The Wealth of Nations* (W. Strahan & T. Cadell).

Solzhenitsyn, A. (1963) *One Day in the Life of Ivan Denisovich* (Penguin).

Sommers, C.H. (1994) *Who stole feminism? How women have betrayed women* (Touchstone).

Sorel, G. (1950) *Reflection on violence* (Macmillan).

Soros, G. (2008) *The New paradigm for financial markets : The credit crisis of 2008 and what it means* (Public Affairs Ltd).

Spender, D. (1980) *Man Made Language* (Routledge).

Stephens, P. (2004) *Tony Blair The price of leadership* (Politicos).

Stewart, M. (1972) *Keynes and After* (2nd Edition, Penguin).

Stiglitz, J. (2002) *Globalisation and its discontents* (The Penguin press).

Stirner, M. (1843) *The Ego and His Own* (Rebel press).

Stourton, E. (2008) *It's a PC World What it Means to Live in a Land Gone Politically Correct* (Hodder & Stoughton).

Swingewood, A. (1984) *A short history of sociological thought* (Macmillan).

Tawney, R.H. (1921) *The acquisitive society* (Bell).

Tawney, R.H. (1969) *Equality* (Allen & Unwin).

Taylor, C. (1994) *Multiculturalism and 'the Politics of Recognition'* (Princeton University Press).

Thompson, M. (2008) *Teach yourself Political Philosophy* (Hodder Education).

Thoreau, H.D. (1854) *Walden and civil disobedience* (Penguin).

Toynbee, P. & Walker, D. (2005) *Better or worse? Has Labour delivered?* (Bloomsbury).

Toynbee, P. & Walker, D. (2008) *Unjust rewards* (Granta).

Warren, J. (1852) *Equitable Commerce* (Burt Franklin).

Watkins, S.A., Rueda, M. & Rodriguez, M. (1999) *Introducing feminism* (Icon books).

Wolf, N. (1991) *The Beauty Myth* (William Morrow).

Wolf, N. (1997) *Promiscuities* (Balantine Publishing Group).

Wolf, N. (2008) *The End of America* (Chelsea Green publishing).

Wolff, J. (2006) *An introduction to political philosophy* (Oxford University press).

Wollstonecraft, M. (1792) *Vindication of the Rights of Woman* (Penguin).

Wright, A. (1995) *Socialisms* (Routledge).

Young, H. (1991) *One of Us* (Macmillan).

INDEX

The Definitive Guide to Political Ideologies